A New Conversation

Essays on the Future of Theology and the Episcopal Church

A New Conversation

Essays on the Future of Theology and the Episcopal Church

Edited by
Robert Boak Slocum

CHURCH
Church Publishing Incorporated, New York

Library of Congress Cataloging-in-Publication Data

A new conversation : essays on the future of theology and the
Episcopal Church / edited by Robert Boak Slocum.
p. cm.
Includes bibliographical references.
ISBN 0-89869-306-3 (pbk.)
1. Episcopal Church. 2. Twenty-first century Forecasting.
I. Slocum, Robert Boak, 1952-
BX5930.2.N43 1999 99-32379
283—DC21 CIP

Church Publishing Incorporated
445 Fifth Avenue
New York, NY 10016

5 4 3 2 1

Contents

II. Ministries for the Future of Theology and the Episcopal Church

Acknowledgments

I want to offer special thanks to the many contributors for this volume. They have been most cooperative, despite busy schedules, in meeting deadlines and making revisions. In many cases, the authors have done much to draw out the meaning of their own lives and ministries relative to their particular topics. For me, each manuscript arrived like a gift that I was delighted to open.

Outstanding technical coordination was provided for this project by Jacqueline B. Winter, assisted by Andrea Pedisich. Their competence, thoroughness, and clarity contributed greatly to this work. I want to thank Frank Hemlin and Frank Tedeschi at Church Publishing Incorporated. They were most supportive and encouraging from the time of my earliest proposal for this book on the future of theology and the Episcopal Church. I also appreciate Johnny Ross's capable editorial work on this book at Church Publishing.

I am dedicating this work to my father, James Robert Slocum (1911–1997), who died while the preparation of this book was underway. I certainly learned from him about the value of experience and the wonderful possibilities for sharing life through narrative stories. I am also dedicating this work to Louis Weil, who taught his students—emphatically—to *make connections.*

R.B.S.

Preface

This project began with a frustrating conversation. My friend was insisting on the importance of categories and labels for scholarly identity. He wanted to be very clear about "where people sit" in terms of their academic specializations and language. Of course, I agreed, we need specialized training and vocabularies. But it can go too far. In the Episcopal Church, it seems to me, we have become accomplished at losing touch with one another. We find it easy not to hear or value what others are saying, especially if their perspective or the way they express it differs from our own.

We have tended to let our pastoral experience and theological reflection become disconnected—to their mutual detriment. We haven't done enough to draw out the implications of faith for understanding or the implications of understanding for faith. Strange things can happen in the church without that integration. Pastoral life and decisions (including resolutions of conventions and conferences) can become shallow; academic theology can become unreal.

As William Porcher DuBose was fond of pointing out, we need each other and our various perspectives for our mutual completion. This is not just about being open-minded or inclusive for its own sake, good as that may be. Ultimately, it is a matter of life or death—that is, we share God's life and inspiration most fully as we listen and receive together. Our connectedness with each other in the church has everything to do with how we receive God's life.

How can we hear each other more fully as we draw together our experiences and understandings of faith? The essays in this book offer a wide range of answers to the questions of this project. The contributors have engaged the topic in light of their experiences, their faith, their work, their reading, and—perhaps most importantly—their hopes for what the Episcopal Church can be. Of course, the authors' opinions are their own.

We may discover how we can reach across disciplines, specializations, and jargon to share with and learn from all kinds of people. We may be amazed to see how much our faith and understanding can be brought to dynamic, fertile life. Our ability to do that can shape the future of theology and the Episcopal Church. It is my hope that the essays in this book will encourage a new kind of conversation for us all.

Robert Boak Slocum
Lake Geneva, Wisconsin
November, 1998

I.

Starting Points for the Future of Theology and the Episcopal Church

By Schisms Rent Asunder? American Anglicanism on the Eve of the Millennium

Harold T. Lewis

Our Anglican Roots: Bane and Blessing

The three "branches" of the Episcopal Church were once labeled as "low and lazy," "broad and hazy," and "high and crazy." They described, respectively, those who were ceremonial minimalists, and who, characteristically, expressed a decided preference for morning prayer; those who were middle-of-the-road folk, neither Spartan nor elaborate in their worship; and finally, the Anglo-Catholics, fond of "bells and smells." Although referring to their liturgical styles, the monikers nonetheless bespoke theological differences among the groups. The Low Churchmen were more likely to see life through scriptural prisms; the High Churchmen's bent was decidedly more sacramental. The Low Church party opined that forgiveness is obtained by the penitent's direct access to the throne of heavenly grace; those in the catholic wing of the church would be more likely to extol the virtues of auricular confession. The celebration of the eucharist was relatively infrequent among those closest to the Protestant shore of this church often likened to a bridge between Reformed and Catholic traditions—and when there was Holy Communion, it was a commemorative meal, the Lord's Supper. In Anglo-Catholic parishes, the celebrant would offer up "the holy sacrifice of the mass."

Despite such disparities, members of the Episcopal Church lived in a spirit of mutual respect and forbearance. Modes of worship and the theologies they represented were somehow not deemed sufficient to upset the ecclesiastical apple cart. This is because it is precisely such a tension that has traditionally characterized Anglicanism. Otherwise put, Anglicanism has been an umbrella under which adherents of widely divergent views have been able to find a happy home. There are two explanations for this phenomenon.

One is that Anglicans have purportedly always agreed on the fundamentals of the faith (although those who espouse such a view do not always agree on what they are). An Anglican archbishop, speaking at the 1968 Lambeth Conference, put it this way: "Comprehensiveness demands agreement on fundamentals, while tolerating disagreement on matters in which Christians may differ without feeling the necessity of breaking communion."[1]

Others would suggest that such fundamentals are found in the Lambeth Quadrilateral, in which Scripture, the historic creeds, the sacraments of baptism and communion and the episcopate are held up as the *sine qua non* of Anglicanism. Still others point to the (now rickety) three-legged stool of Richard Hooker: Scripture, tradition, and reason. And many would agree that the Book of Common Prayer itself has "established the fundamental outline and spirit of Anglican theology and practice."[2]

But a second view is that the reason that such coexistence has been possible among Anglicans is that there has never really been a distinctive Anglican theology. Anglicanism is bereft of a counterpart to a Luther or a Calvin on the one hand, or a Roman magisterium on the other, which would give it a peculiar stamp. Henry McAdoo states that "Anglicanism is not a theological system and there is no writer whose work is an essential part of it, either in respect to content or with regard to the form of its self-expression."[3] Or, as Bishop Stephen Neill expressed it, "There are no specific Anglican doctrines, there is no particular Anglican theology, . . . there is, therefore, no particular Anglican faith."[4] By making such statements, Neill and others are not suggesting that Anglicanism is deficient. On the contrary, they contend that the absence of a distinct Anglican theology proves that Anglicanism is not a sect, but an integral part of historic Christianity; there is nothing new in Anglicanism because the Anglican reformers strove to ensure that their branch of Christendom would forever bear the marks of catholicity.

This is both the bane and the blessing, the flaw and the genius, of Anglicanism. Because Anglicanism lacks an identity forged in protest and identified with a charismatic leader, or because *fides anglicana* is not articulated periodically for us through such instruments as papal bulls and encyclicals, it runs the risk of becoming a theological catchall. The views held by those seeking refuge under the Anglican umbrella are becoming so divergent that some adherents are now claiming that only certain believers have a right to its protection, and deem that others must fend for themselves in the rain. The rain-soaked adherents have, in turn, either found shelter under newer, smaller umbrellas, declaring that those under the larger one are no longer true believers; or they have claimed new turf under the old umbrella, demanding that others subject themselves to the elements. So at the end of the twentieth century, Episcopalians are rescuing from obscurity such epithets as "fundamentalist," "literalist," "revisionist," "apostate," and "heretic," and are hurling them at each other with what we used to call gay abandon. The words that Samuel John Stone wrote more than one hundred years ago seem prophetic: "Though with a scornful wonder men see her sore oppressed, / By schisms rent asunder, by heresies distressed."[5]

It has been said, only partly in jest, that our nation's founding fathers, having drawn up the Constitution, went across the street to found the Episcopal Church. As I pointed out elsewhere, in a discussion of the civil rights movement,[6] the adage "As the nation goes so goes the church" is an especially fitting description of the *modus operandi* of the Episcopal Church in every age. It has been a non-prophet organization, that is, a body that has not, historically, set a moral example for the nation to follow, but rather has taken its lead from the mores of the nation with which it has had a unique, symbiotic relationship, since they both came into existence, almost simultaneously, at the end of the eighteenth century. Because of that unique relationship, the Episcopal Church, numbering among its faithful the "carriage trade" and the movers and shakers of American society, has traditionally served as a chaplain to the status quo, not as a champion of the oppressed. Although slow to take the lead in any particular social issue, it has, nevertheless, demonstrated throughout its history a chameleon-like quality "to become the champion of new relationships for the purpose of creating a new order."[7] Believing, indeed, that "new occasions teach new duties, time makes ancient good uncouth,"[8] the Episcopal Church has shown a remarkable propensity for developing theological positions in response to changes in the societal landscape.

We believe that this historical tendency in the Episcopal Church speaks to the fact that Anglican theology, or what passes for it, has appended, as it were, a fourth leg to Hooker's stool as an equally important source of its development, and that is culture. It is precisely because we do not claim the party line of a Calvin or a Luther, or a central authority whose dicta are not to be gainsaid, that we have sought to respond contextually, developing theologies for situations which could not have been foreseen either by the ante-Nicene fathers or the founding fathers of the Episcopal Church. This theological method was aptly described by the compilers of the first American Book of Common Prayer. Their approach to the worship of the church, as reflected in its theology (and, it can be said, their approach to its theology, as reflected in its worship) is succinctly stated in the preface:

> It is but reasonable that upon weighty and important considerations, according to the various exigency of times and occasions, such changes and alterations should be made therein, as to those that are in place of Authority should, from time to time, seem either necessary or expedient . . . yet so as that the main body and essential parts of the same . . . have still been continued firm and unshaken.[9]

Cultural Influences on the Church's Theology from Without

A few examples will illustrate this leitmotif. The Episcopal Church condoned slavery up until the time of the Civil War (at a time when other denominations split over the issue), and then, one hundred years later, according to John Kater,[10] acquiesced in and tacitly approved a *de facto* segregated church in a segregated society, as long as a relative calm blanketed black/white relationships in the United States. Indeed, the Episcopal Church, in whose congregations, institutions, and diocesan conventions segregation had long been *de rigueur*, gradually began to adopt an integrationist policy only after the U. S. Supreme Court's historic *Brown vs. Board of Education* decision in 1954. The 1955 General Convention urged Episcopalians to "accept and support the ruling of the Supreme Court," and, making no attempt to mask the fact that its thinking had been influenced by the Court, added: "In the work of the Church we should welcome people of any race at any service conducted by a priest or layman of any ethnic origin, and bring them into the full fellowship of the congregation and its organizations."[11]

The civil rights movement, during which, as John Booty reminds us, "Episcopalians were jolted out of their complacency,"[12] made new and more stringent demands upon the church. As a result, diocesan commissions on racism were established and began to address racist practices within church institutions. Presiding Bishop Arthur Lichtenberger proclaimed that "discrimination within the Body of the Church itself is an intolerable scandal."[13] The Episcopal Society for Cultural and Racial Unity (ESCRU) came into being, proclaiming that "racial relations is the number one social problem of our day and . . . the number one challenge before the Christian Church."[14]

It must be remembered that the civil rights movement, in turn, gave rise to movements of other groups in society who saw themselves as oppressed. The women's movement piggybacked on the agenda of the black civil rights movement, and the Episcopal Church, in much the same way as it addressed its own shortcomings on the racial issue, examined itself on issues of gender. The struggle for women's rights in secular society served to encourage many Episcopalians, men as well as women, to make similar demands of the church. Accordingly, the Episcopal Women's Caucus was formed in 1970, "a lobby which encouraged the expansion of opportunities for women in the Church with special focus on the priesthood."[15] Largely due to the consciousness-raising achieved by this group, women's ordination to the priesthood was approved at the General Convention of 1976.[16]

Persons of homosexual orientation were the next group to seek redress for having been the victims of discrimination. Integrity, a caucus of gay Episcopalians and their supporters, was formed in 1974. Emboldened by the attention given to homosexuals in society at large and their success in removing some of the barriers that had been erected in such arenas as employment and housing, it made demands on the church for full recognition. Thus, homosexual persons—whose mode of sexual expression, according to Oscar Wilde, was "the love that dare not speak its name"—became a vocal and strident force in the life of the church, much to the discomfort of many Episcopalians. Integrity elicited concern among many Episcopalians because it sought *open* acceptance of homosexual orientation. Episcopalians had long recognized the presence of homosexuals in the church, both lay and ordained, but there was a tacit expectation that such persons take a "vow of silence." The church, taken aback as it was, did not move as quickly on this issue as it had done when faced with challenges from blacks and women, and yet each concession was taken as encouragement by the movement. More and more demands were made, so that today, General Convention is faced with resolutions which would have been unimaginable a generation ago: whether avowed and practicing homosexuals should be ordained, and whether the church should sanction same-sex unions and authorize a liturgical rite for them.[17]

Cultural Influences on the Church's Theology from Within

Prayer Book revision, with its trial uses and "Zebra book" in the 1960s and 1970s, was not simply a matter of modernizing and updating the language, of changing "thee" and "thou" to "you," which to many Episcopalians was upsetting enough. The 1979 American Prayer Book embodied and promulgated new theological concepts (although admittedly, most were old concepts reintroduced). It should be pointed out that, in a church without a distinctive theology, the worship manual of the church becomes its principal theological document. In many cases, these theological changes brought, not peace, but the sword. By declaring the eucharist to be "the principal act of Christian worship on the Lord's Day,"[18] the Prayer Book threatened to relegate to second-class citizenship those for whom matins was still standard fare at eleven o'clock. Through the wording of the ordinal, the Prayer Book made it clear that ordination was open to both sexes, an affront to those who were given permission not to accept the General Convention's approval of women's ordination.[19] The rites for the administration of all the sacraments reflected theologies which in many cases were a departure from those of the 1928 Prayer Book.[20]

But perhaps one of the most radical changes took place in the catechism. The answer to the question, "Who are the ministers of the Church?" is "The ministers of the Church are lay persons, bishops, priests, and deacons."[21] The good news here is that, by including the laity among the ministers of the church, the Prayer Book returns to a more biblical understanding of ministry as *diakonia*, and potentially frees the church of a medieval, hierarchical, and therefore patriarchal view of ministry. The bad news is that it has served to blur lines. The recognition of lay chalice bearers is but one example. The privilege of administering the chalice was granted to the laity with the understanding that they would so function when a sufficient number of ordained ministers was not available. But what began as a privilege has in many places become a right, so that it is not an uncommon occurrence for chalice bearers to administer the cup while clergy, *parati*, are seated in the sanctuary. "Ministry" is now used to describe virtually every act done in or on behalf of the church; parishioners may sign up for the newcomer ministry or the handbell ministry.

Moreover, the expansion of lay ministries has in large measure accounted for the increase of vocations to the *ordained* ministry. It would appear that a goodly number of seminarians are no longer those whose vocations have been nurtured in the bosom of the church, but those who have been nominal Christians or even unchurched persons, whose first religious experience may have been at a weekend retreat. It is at such retreats that they learn that they have gifts for ministry, as yet untapped. But since the church has not yet designed a way to recognize and affir m such ministries in any systematic way, they seek ordination almost by default. One of the effects of such a development is that many of the church's ordained leaders today are those who have had virtually no experience in the rank and file of church life.

The most serious effect of our new theology of ministry and ministries is that it has removed any vestige of distinction between clergy and lay people. While the 1979 ordinal places less emphasis than does the 1928 ordinal[22] on what might be called a "theology of a higher standard," it does nevertheless include these words:

> *Bishop*: Will you do your best to pattern your life . . . in accordance with the teachings of Christ, so that you may be a wholesome example to your people?
> *Answer*: I will.[23]

But neologisms such as "shared ministry," "total ministry," and "mutual ministry" tend to minimize differences in either the execution of the office or in behavioral expectations of any of the ministers. As is so often the case, the Episcopal Church establishes a policy without considering its ramifications.[24] This new theology of ministry is a case in point. It is worthy of note that this egalitarian view of ministry is totally abandoned when it comes to the issue of sexual misconduct involving clergy and laypersons. In new canons enacted by the General Convention,[25] the clergyperson virtually gives up his or her rights when accused of any sexual wrongdoing. What is more, the assumption of bishops, standing committees, ecclesiastical courts, and others involved in the investigation of the allegations is that the clergyperson misused the power of his or her office, a power that is nowhere recognized and certainly not mentioned in any reference to the new theology of ministry. It is further assumed that the other person, even if an affair is of many years' duration, has been under the clergyperson's thrall.

There is yet another perhaps more complex impact which the Episcopal Church's new theology of ministry has had on the life of the church. Having placed all ministries on, as it were, the same level, and having eschewed any hint of a "double standard," the church cannot now logically and consistently maintain that certain ministries are closed to certain classes of people. It should not be surprising, for example, that the question should arise of whether avowed homosexuals should be admitted to holy orders. The right to ask the question was granted when the 1976 General Convention passed a resolution declaring that "homosexual persons are children of God who have *a full and equal claim with all other persons* upon the love and acceptance and pastoral concern of the Church."[26] Can we say to the homosexual that he or she may sing in the choir, work on the altar guild, or swing a thurible, but tell that person that another ministry, namely the ordained ministry, is not open to him or her? While many would assert that there are theological, moral, or even practical reasons to deny ordination to homosexual persons, the fact remains that it is inconsistent for the church to do so given its own newly articulated theology of ministry.

ECUSA's Theology: *Quo Vadis*

The Episcopal Urban Caucus (EUC), a group started in the 1960s with the agenda of striving for racial and economic justice, especially in our nation's cities, is affectionately referred to today as "what's left of the left." While the EUC clearly is not the only organization with liberal credentials remaining in the church, the point is well taken. Mirroring the pendulum swing in national politics, the theology of the Episcopal Church has taken a decided turn to the right. The church—which was at the forefront of civil rights struggles; which established the General Convention Special Program to empower the powerless in our society; which championed women's ordination; which developed a slogan called "Our Church Has AIDS"; which has established special ministries for homosexual persons—has rediscovered its conservative roots. Or perhaps it would be more accurate to say that the church had never been severed from those roots.

While the church officially embraced integration, Prayer Book revision, women's ordination, and recognition at some level of homosexual persons, these and other "liberal" causes, constituting as they did a theological, attitudinal, and social sea change in the space of a few decades, have consistently met with the consternation and disapproval of many persons.[27] As William Sachs observes:

> Revision of the Church's Prayer Book, and the ordination of women and the surfacing of homosexual aspirations were unrelated issues which arose contemporaneously. . . . To those who pressed the Church for change, its leadership seemed stodgy; other Episcopalians, however, were distraught by the changes which had occurred in the Church's life and concluded . . . that Episcopalians had abandoned their historic faith to embrace the trendy social activism of the moment.[28]

Factions in the church are engaged in pitched battles. Examples abound. Groups (none of which reflect the racial and ethnic diversity of the Episcopal Church) like the American Anglican Council and "The First Promise" are rallying under the banner of "orthodoxy" and have made it abundantly clear that they owe no allegiance to the Presiding Bishop. Robert Duncan, the Bishop of Pittsburgh, has labeled John Spong, the Bishop of Newark, as "apostate" because of his writings, especially his much-touted "Twelve Theses."[29] A group of bishops, many of whom were affiliated with the Episcopal Synod of America, wrote to their colleagues in the Diocese of Pennsylvania, accusing them of departing from "the clear Biblical teaching of the Church" on the matter of human sexuality. As talk of "porous" boundaries of dioceses is bruited about, several dioceses are withholding their support of the national church, and at least one congregation within the boundaries of the Diocese of Arkansas has sought and received permission from the Archbishop of Rwanda to be a parish in his province. Another congregation, itself a community formed when it broke away from an Episcopal parish over a question of clerical leadership, has become, *mirabile dictu*, a parish under the protection of a bishop in Uganda.

The resolution passed at the 1998 Lambeth XIII Conference declaring homosexual practice to be "incompatible with the Gospel" made it abundantly clear that this theological shift is not merely an American phenomenon. While many will disagree with Bishop Spong that the conference presaged "the sunset of the Anglican Communion,"[30] it is clear now that the growing conservative forces in ECUSA have forged alliances with Anglican churches in Africa and Asia (who now constitute the overwhelming majority among Anglicans)[31] owing in part to shared theological views of biblical orthodoxy. Anglicanism is perhaps at last trying to carve out for itself a distinct theology, but it is taking a course that few would have expected, even as recently as Lambeth XII (1988).

New Paradigm, New Voices

What has happened? We seem no longer a church likened to Richard Hooker's three-legged stool of Scripture, tradition, and reason. The legs have now been wrested from the seat and are being used as weapons. Some shake the Scripture stick, pointing to the inerrancy of the Bible as our only standard; others, for whom, perhaps, revelation is a sudden and not a gradual, ongoing process, brandish the tradition stick, mouthing the seven deadly words of the Episcopal Church: "We have always done it that way"; those left with the stick of reason find themselves with an ineffective weapon. Since reason's purpose was to temper the effect of the other two legs, it is rendered useless without its two counterparts. In a former age, the three legs acted together to provide some balance for *Ecclesia Anglicana*.

John Pobee, a Ghanaian theologian, offers a fresh look. The use of Scripture, he maintains,

> is not a one-way street. It speaks to us. But also we question Scripture even in its message of salvation. . . . Tradition is not some solid rock from the dead past. Tradition is understanding the complexity of the past so as to secure the future. . . . The Johannine affirmation that "the Word (Reason) became flesh" commits us to rationality. For this reason I am unhappy with the fundamentalist reading of Scripture.[32]

As we prepare to enter the third millennium, we do indeed seem to be a church "by schisms rent asunder, by heresies distressed." Anglicans in general and Episcopalians in particular must learn to follow the advice of the prophet Isaiah and come and reason together. We must rediscover the *via media*, a concept traditionally at the heart of the ethos of Anglicanism, and seek some common ground on which we can build and perhaps even reconstruct Hooker's three-legged stool. Again, the genius of the compilers of the 1789 Book of Common Prayer is instructive: they sought "to keep the happy mean between too much stiffness in refusing, and too much easiness in admitting variations in things once advisedly established." This means that opposing groups must be willing to eschew, on the one hand, a "stiffness" in which tradition becomes, to use Pobee's phrase, "a solid rock from the dead past;" and avoid, on the other hand, an "easiness" in which Episcopalians are "tossed to and fro by every vain blast of doctrine."

To achieve such a new *via media*, the church must first recognize that Anglicanism is undergoing a major paradigm shift. While we have agreed that the Anglican church "possesses a Catholic nature, an English heritage, and an inclination to absorb modern social and intellectual currents," we have nonetheless "lacked the means to resolve differing perception of these ideals."[33] In order for our theology to be reflective of our claims of inclusiveness and catholicity, we must be open to new voices, new participants on the theological playing field. We must be honest enough to admit that theology, as the church has historically understood it, has been God-talk from the perspective of a particular group, namely white males from Europe and the British Isles. It should not be surprising, therefore, that many of the "new voices" belong to women and people of color.

While we are quick to tout the southward expansion of Anglicanism as evidence of the catholicity of Anglicanism, we cannot reasonably expect that Africans and Asians will march in lock step with traditional Western theology. In this connection, attention must be paid to those in the Afro-Anglican movement. The first conference on Afro-Anglicanism, held in 1985 at Codrington College, Barbados, the oldest Anglican seminary in the Western hemisphere, was entitled "Present Issues, Future Tasks."[34] It brought together 200 theologians, bishops, and others who believed that Anglican theology did not come to a grinding halt when Hooker's pen ran out of ink! Participants from Africa, the West Indies, North America, and elsewhere had in common that they and their ancestors had been brought the gospel by English missionary societies. They felt it was time for the "daughter churches," having come of age, to add to the corpus of Anglican theology from their peculiar vantage point. The second conference, held in Cape Town, South Africa, in 1995, was entitled "Identity, Integrity and Impact in the Decade of Evangelism."[35] At that Conference, Sehon Goodridge set the stage for dialogue when he stated that "Ecclesia Anglicana" does not mean what it used to mean. No longer referring to "that branch of Christianity established by St. Augustine over thirteen centuries ago," it now bears reference to "Christians of all ethnic origins and national identities [who] have attempted to come to grips with the implications of appropriating it to themselves."[36]

John Pobee, Director of the Programme for Ecumenical Theological Education at the World Conference of Churches, remarked that he saw the mission of Afro-Anglicanism as nothing less than a "prophetic movement within Anglicanism, dedicated to kingdom values and committed to calling the rest of the Church and society to those values."[37] In my opening address at that conference, I struck a similar chord, when I remarked that the words "They call them to deliver their land from error's chain" from Bishop Heber's famous missionary hymn, "From Greenland's icy mountains,"[38] today refers to those countries in Africa and the African diaspora who are being called to deliver from error's chain—of racism and oppression—those lands which sent forth missionaries to them in the first place.[39] In this connection, Afro-Anglicans are painfully aware of the truth of Kortright Davis's statement that blacks have been "a particular type of people who have had the distinction of being the only ones in history whose claims of being human have been systematically called into question."[40] Cyril Okorocha, then evangelism officer for the Anglican Communion, observed: "To the African peoples, Yahweh is always a God of the oppressed, the Saviour of the poor, and the Judge of the oppressor."[41] In citing this contribution of Afro-Anglicanism, which may be described as an Anglican version of liberation theology, theological thought originates not with the privileged classes, as did most of Western theology, but begins from the perspective of the have-nots.

Of course, no discussion of the influence of African Anglicans is complete without mention of Desmond Tutu, former Archbishop of Cape Town, who most recently headed the Truth and Reconciliation Commission in South Africa. He wielded considerable influence on the whole of the Anglican Communion. Virtually single-handedly, he theologized the struggle against apartheid, named it as sin, and encouraged an international boycott to help to dismantle it. In his sermon at the closing eucharist in St. George's Cathedral, in Cape Town, the Archbishop said:

> "Ubuntu" is the essence of being human . . . "a person is a person through other persons." Ubuntu speaks about an inclusive kind of community. Apartheid depended on being exclusive, on separating, on alienation. I want to suggest that whatever is peculiar to your own local situation, how about all Afro-Anglicans saying that we will work for a society that is more inclusive, a society that says we stand up against sexism, against ageism, against excluding people on the grounds of sexual orientation, or physical or other disabilities.[42]

It is easy to see how his words are applicable to all communities that suffer from alienation of any sort. Indeed, it is this very theme, central to Tutu's ethics, that Michael Battle, a young African American professor at Duke University, explores in his recent book.[43] African Americans, too, bring not only their "brand" of black theology, but "womanist" thought as well, which provides a corrective, from the black female perspective, of "feminist" theology. Clearly the most distinguished Anglican theologian espousing a feminist theology is Kelly Brown Douglas, whose *Black Christ*[44] challenges the church to rethink its traditional Christology. She will soon publish a long-awaited volume on sexuality and the black community.

The reader may well ask: How can these voices, which do not represent the majority of Episcopalians, and most of whom are from other continents and cultures, speak to the whole church, and indeed presage a new wave of theological enterprise in the next millennium? The first answer concerns a lesson that American bishops learned at Lambeth XIII. The Western churches within Anglicanism can no longer take for granted their cultural, theological—and indeed numerical—domination of the Communion. We can hardly expect to applaud the growth of Anglicanism "o'er every continent and island" and expect it to remain the same, with world headquarters on the banks of the Thames and smaller outposts, different more in degree than in kind, dotting a globe which was virtually synonymous with the Empire on which the sun never set. Secondly, it is precisely because these voices have been silent—or more correctly, silenced, that their message is fresh and welcome. White Episcopalians, hardly immune to the vicissitudes of Wall Street, downsizings, and other factors that have affected their lives and lifestyles, have learned that they can identify at some level with those who historically have suffered and been marginalized. It is no coincidence that there is a great resurgence of interest in spirituality these days, as well as a rediscovery of the songs called spirituals, sung by those under the yoke of slavery.

Perhaps the new *via media* will be one whose identity takes shape somewhere between the Anglican theology promulgated by the missionaries on the one hand, and an Anglican theology forged in the crucible of suffering and embraced by those who have been missionized, on the other. In facing the task of developing such a new *via media*, Mr. Stone does not leave us comfortless:

Yet saints their watch are keeping, their cry goes up: "How long?"
And soon the night of weeping shall be the morn of song.

Notes

1. Archbishop Henry McAdoo, Lambeth Conference 1968 (London, 1968), 140.

2. W. Taylor Stevenson, "Lex Orandi, Lex Credendi," in Stephen Sykes and John Booty, *The Study of Anglicanism* (Philadelphia: SPCK/Fortress Press, 1988), 175.

3. Henry McAdoo, *The Spirit of Anglicanism* (New York: Charles Scribner's Sons, 1965), 49.

4. Stephen Neill, *Anglicanism*, 3rd ed. (Baltimore: Penguin Books, 1965), 417–418.

5. "The Church's one foundation," *The Hymnal 1982* (New York: The Church Pension Fund), Hymn 525.

6. Harold T. Lewis, *Yet With a Steady Beat: The African American Struggle for Recognition in the Episcopal Church* (Valley Forge, Pa.: Trinity Press International, 1996), 147ff.

7. John Kater, "Experiment in Freedom: The Episcopal Church and the Black Power Movement," *Historical Magazine of the Episcopal Church* (March 1979): 67–81, especially 68.

8. "Once to ev'ry man and nation," *The Hymnal 1940* (New York: The Church Pension Fund, 1940), Hymn 519.

9. "Preface," The Book of Common Prayer (New York: The Church Hymnal Corporation, 1979), 9–10.

10. Kater, "Experiment in Freedom: The Episcopal Church and the Black Power Movement," 68.

11. *Journal of the General Convention*, 1955.

12. John Booty, *The Episcopal Church in Crisis* (Cambridge, Mass.: Cowley, 1988), 5.

13. Arthur Lichtenberger, "Whitsuntide Message, 1963," Records of the Presiding Bishop, 1958–1964: Lichtenberger, Archives of the Episcopal Church, Austin, Tex.

14. Joseph A. Pelham, 1st V.P. of ESCRU and Director of Christian Social Relations of the Diocese of Michigan, 7 December 1959.

15. William L. Sachs, *The Transformation of Anglicanism* (Cambridge: Cambridge University Press, 1993), 330.

16. Women's ordination to the diaconate was approved at the General Convention of 1970, the same year, interestingly enough, in which women deputies were allowed to sit in the House of Deputies. It should also be

pointed out that in 1974, the year following the General Convention at which the resolution to approve women's ordination was defeated, an illegal ordination of women was held in the Church of the Advocate in Philadelphia. The House of Bishops, meeting soon after the event, declared the ordinations "valid but irregular." After the 1976 vote, the ordinations were "regularized."

17. The ordination of avowed homosexuals is not new to the church. Bishop Paul Moore of New York ordained Ellen Barrett in 1975, which earned him the censure of the House of Bishops. More recently, Bishop Walter Righter, assistant bishop in the Diocese of Newark, was brought to trial for the ordination of a gay man to the diaconate. But the ecclesiastical court found that the Episcopal Church had no "core doctrine" prohibiting such ordination.

18. "Concerning the Service of the Church," The Book of Common Prayer, 13.

19. In 1977, the year following the General Convention's decision to allow the ordination of women to the priesthood and episcopate, the House of Bishops, meeting in Port St. Lucie, Florida, passed a resolution, later known as the "conscience clause," which provided canonical protection for those bishops, clergy, and laypersons who, because of their theological convictions, were unable to accept the ordination of women. This was a stopgap measure designed to keep Episcopalians of differing persuasions within the fold. The resolution did not, however, consider its long-term ramifications, namely, that it gave bishops who refuse to ordain women the right to disregard the canons of the church, which specifically provide for the admission of women to all the orders of the church. At the 1997 General Convention, predictably, a canon was passed to make women's ordination mandatory, giving dissenting bishops three years to comply with the decision.

20. Notable among these are new teachings regarding confirmation, which is no longer a prerequisite to receiving communion; and the explicit provision for auricular confession.

21. The Book of Common Prayer, 855.

22. The Bishop's Charge in the ordination of priests contained such phrases as "Remember that they are the sheep of Christ, bought with Christ's own Blood," and admonished that doing "aught" against them would ensure that a great punishment would ensue. The bishop also reminded the ordinand, who had "pondered these things in his heart long before now," that "there be no room in you either for error in religion or for viciousness in life."

23. The Book of Common Prayer, 532.

24. See, e.g., above, note 16.

25. The new procedures—including clergy questionnaires from Church Insurance Company, which are intrusive in the opinion of many—place the clergy at greater risk.

26. *Journal of the General Convention*, 1976 (emphasis added).

27. Several "splinter groups" were formed over the years, protesting an alleged departure from orthodoxy on the part of the Episcopal Church. Among these were the Southern Episcopal Church, the Anglican Orthodox Church, the American Episcopal Church. Organizations such as the Fellowship of Concerned Churchmen and the Society for the Preservation of the Book of Common Prayer were also formed.

28. Sachs, *The Transformation of Anglicanism*, 323–324.

29. John Shelby Spong, "Twelve Theses," The Living Church (17 May, 1998).

30. John Shelby Spong, "Anglicans Get Liberal," *New York Times*, 13 August 1998.

31. At Lambeth XIII, African bishops numbered 224, surpassing every other continental group. There were 180 bishops from North America, and 140 from the United Kingdom. African Anglicans now number approximately 27 million, compared to 2.4 million in the Episcopal Church (Lambeth Conference Communications Office, 20 July 1998).

32. John S. Pobee, "An African Anglican's View of Salvation," in ed., Andrew Wingate et al., *Anglicanism: A Global Communion* (London: Mowbrays, 1998), 81–82.

33. Sachs, *The Transformation of Anglicanism*, 336.

34. The proceedings of the Conference were published in *The Journal of Religious Thought* 44, no. 1 (1987).

35. The proceedings of the second Conference were published in the *Anglican Theological Review* 77, no. 4 (1995).

36. Sehon Goodridge, Bishop of the Windward Islands, "The Integrity of Anglicanism: Myth or Mission," Ibid.: 472–473.

37. John Pobee, "Afro-Anglicanism: *Quo Vadimus?*" Ibid.: 502ff.

38. See Hymn 254, "From Greenland's icy mountains," in *The Hymnal 1940* (New York: The Church Pension Fund, 1940).

39. Harold Lewis, "They Call us to deliver their land from error's chain," *Anglican Theological Review* 77, no. 4 (1995): 455–461, especially 459.

40. Kortright Davis, *Emancipation Still Comin', Exploration in Caribbean Emancipatory Theology* (Maryknoll, N.Y.: Orbis, 1990), 118.

41. Cyril Okorocha, "African Social History and the Christian Mission in Africa: Implications and Challenges for the Afro-Anglican Movement," *Anglican Theological Review* 77, no. 4 (1995): 481.

42. Desmond Mpilo Tutu, Archbishop of Capetown, sermon at the closing eucharist of the second Conference on Afro-Anglicanism in St. George's Cathedral, Cape Town, January 1995, in *Anglican Theological Review* 77, no. 4 (1995): 522–23. It should be noted that Archbishop Tutu specifically mentions discrimination against people because of sexual orientation. At Lambeth XIII, the churches in South and Central Africa were among the few on the continent of Africa that did not support the resolution declaring homosexual behavior to be contrary to Scripture.

43. Michael J. Battle, *Reconciliation: The Ubuntu Theology of Desmond Tutu* (Cleveland: Pilgrim Press, 1997).

44. Kelly Brown Douglas, *Black Christ* (Maryknoll, N.Y.: Orbis, 1994).

A Story to Tell: Personal Narrative in the Synthesis of Pastoral Experience and Theological Reflection

Robert Boak Slocum

For too long, the lived experience of the church and parishioners has been distant from the work of theological reflection. The pastoral life shared by lay people and pastors has been remote from many who are involved in theological writing and education. Clergy and parishioners may doubt that they have anything of substance to add to the writing and teaching of theology, and they may wonder whether they can gain anything of value for their lives and parishes from theologians. Similarly, theologians may feel that the needs, demands, and crises of parish life are a world apart from the academic discipline of theology. Pastoral life and theological reflection can seem to be distant cousins at best—mutually supportive in a remote sort of way, but rather clearly separated by what they do, and how they talk, and what they value. When these distant cousins have been brought together for the occasional "family gathering," they may breathe a sigh of relief when the awkward conglomeration is over, and they can return to their own proper places and ways.

This distancing of pastoral life and academic theology reflects the wrong kind of specialization. It leads to a narrowness of vision that is harmful to the individuals involved, and the value of their work, and the church as a whole. If pastoral life becomes disconnected from substantive theological reflection, the church may come to be characterized by a superficiality that is prone to trends, fads, and over-reactions. Without a theological base, the church can be buffeted by all kinds of peculiarities and agendas. And if the world of theological reflection is distanced from the life and experience of the church, theology may become abstract, unreal, and a mere "field of study." The meaning in faith of theology can be lost in the very process of analysis and categorization.

The truth of Christ in the parish is the same truth of Christ that theologians seek to analyze and describe. Greater depth and vibrancy of life can be known in both the pastoral and theological areas if the Christians who populate those "worlds" would share more effectively with one another. In this regard, the need for a common language may be a significant problem. This situation suggests the problem of different computer programs that will not "talk" to each other, even though they both process the same kind of data. A point of intersection is needed for sharing.

In parish life and in theological education, we may at times circumscribe the boundaries of our interests by the language we use. We can encapsulate ourselves with terms, jargon, and "buzz words," even when the same meaning could be expressed in ways that would reach a much wider audience without compromising the integrity of our ideas. We may need to resist the trend to let a "hot" speaker or movement so dominate a topic that only one perspective is allowed. The disciples of a guru or the initiates in the latest program can be the only ones who will be heard. Even if a new program or speaker is captivating, there may be other approaches to be considered and valued. We can listen to all kinds of people and draw from a variety of sources as we seek the truth of Christ in our parish, our work, our lives.

Each area of specialization may have its own contribution to make, and its own favored way of sharing the insights it has to offer. We need to be open to the contributions that may come from those who are not our usual conversation partners, and from those whose formative experiences have been much different from our own. We need a point of synthesis and a common language to draw together the pastoral life and the theological reflection of the church.

Personal narrative can be a significant point of synthesis for the life and theology of the church. In recent years there has been increasing emphasis on the role of story in evangelism and Christian formation. We can situate the story of our individual lives and the story of our parish in the larger sweep of salvation history. We may claim the gospel story as our own, and tell why faith makes a difference for us. We can explain how God has been actively present in the moments of our lives. Personal narrative, "telling our story" of faith and love in Christ, can be effective because it is based in real life and speaks to human need. It can reach the heart of the listener because it is drawn from the heart of the speaker or writer. Experience speaks to experience, allowing the realities of divine love and faith to be shared most effectively.

Personal narrative can also be the basis and context for serious theological reflection. We can consider the meaning of faith relative to the story of another's life, or our own story. Personal narrative can make it possible for us to encounter or share the reality of salvation in Christ. In this regard, personal narrative can be understood to include both biographical and autobiographical writings. The Christian tradition is filled with such works. It includes autobiographical writings from a variety of sources, such as Augustine, Theresa of Avila, Ignatius of Loyola, Thérèse of Lisieux, Devereux Jarratt, John Henry Newman, Phoebe Palmer, C. S. Lewis, Thomas Merton, and Rachel Hosmer.[1] The tradition also includes biographical works as varied as Athanasius's *The Life and Affairs of our Holy Father Antony*, Bonaventure's *The Life of St. Francis*, Anne Ayres's *The Life and Work of William Augustus Muhlenberg*, and Vida Dutton Scudder's *Father Huntington, Founder of the Order of the Holy Cross*.[2]

Of course, not every work of autobiography or biography can be studied as a work of theology. Sometimes a story is just a story—except in the broadest sense that all life and all history have theological significance. The connections must be made between lived experience and theological reflection. Nevertheless, personal narrative *can* provide a significant point of synthesis for pastoral experience with theological reflection.[3] In this essay I will consider personal narrative as a point of synthesis for experience and theology relative to the narratives and theological works of William Porcher DuBose (1836–1918) and William Stringfellow (1928–1985).

The Experience and Theology of William Porcher DuBose

There is an interesting disagreement about how many books of theology were published by the noted Episcopal theologian William Porcher DuBose.[4] In addition to six other books, DuBose published a work of spiritual and theological autobiography that is the basis of the disagreement.[5] He read autobiographical papers to a reunion of his former students at the University of the South on the fortieth anniversary of his coming to Sewanee. These autobiographical papers and other materials were subsequently published as his *Turning Points in My Life.*[6] DuBose told the story of his life of faith relative to his experiences of conversion, suffering, discovery, and transformation. His narrative of these "turning points" was a unique occasion for one who admitted, "I have always spoken from myself, but I have never spoken of myself."[7] *Turning Points* revealed and developed DuBose's theological method in terms of the central role of human experience.

However, Donald S. Armentrout does not consider *Turning Points* to be a work "of major theological importance."[8] He states that *Turning Points* "was not a substantial theological work but was much more autobiographical and personal."[9] In effect, for Armentrout, DuBose's spiritual and theological autobiography does not count as real theology. In a review of an anthology of DuBose's work, Armentrout even refers to "DuBose's six published books."[10] It is interesting that two other historians, David L. Holmes and Ralph E. Luker, also follow Armentrout in counting only six theological works by DuBose.[11]

But the theological significance of DuBose's *Turning Points* has not been entirely ignored. The English theologian J. O. F. Murray begins his discussion of DuBose, entitled *DuBose as a Prophet of Unity*, in light of *Turning Points* and his "background of spiritual experience."[12] Accordingly, it is no surprise that Murray acknowledges that DuBose's thought was embodied in "*seven* volumes published between 1892 and 1911," along with other articles.[13] Murray recognizes the importance of experience in DuBose's theological method, and counts *Turning Points* among DuBose's seven volumes of theology.

The disagreement over the number of DuBose's theological works is no mere quibble over terms and definitions. The question goes to the heart of the meaning of personal narrative and the possibility of using personal narrative as a point of synthesis for pastoral experience and theological reflection. Can personal narrative count in the world of serious theology? Certainly we can benefit from the use of personal narrative to draw together what we have known in our life and church with theological reflection on the meaning of our experience.

It can be for us in the church today as it was for DuBose. Experience and theology went hand-in-hand for him. The important themes of his theology are rooted in his life experience. For example, his theology was deeply rooted in his personal religious experience, which was followed by theological reflection. His theology of the cross can be traced in the moments of suffering that he experienced, such as his shocked realization that he was going to be on the losing side of the Civil War. DuBose was a Confederate soldier, and his brigade was sleeping "under the stars" after being defeated in battle. At this moment he realized the impossibility of success for the Confederate cause and the world he had known all his life. He felt himself to be "alone upon the planet, without home or country or any earthly interest or object before me, my very world at an end," and "redevoted" himself "wholly and only to God, and to the work and life of His Kingdom, whatever and wherever that might be."[14] DuBose turned to God in the poverty and loss of defeat. In later years, he also endured the death of his wife and youngest child. Through his darkest hours and most painful losses, he came to experience that there is no divine forsaking. This was an experience of faith and trust in God for DuBose. It was as true for him in the face of defeat and destruction in war as it was for Jesus on the cross. It is apparent that he came through intense suffering and loss to know a deeper faith in God. This was the basis of his theology of the cross.

At eighteen, DuBose had a mystical experience of conversion. He got up to pray in the night, and then leapt to his feet trembling. He recalled that "a light shone about me and a Presence filled the room. At the same time an ineffable joy and peace took possession of me which it is impossible either to express or explain."[15] After this experience, for DuBose, "There was simply a New World without me, and a New Self in me—in both which for the first time, visibly, sensibly, really, God was."[16] DuBose mentioned his conversion experience to no one until the reunion with his students, some fifty years later.

At the time of his conversion experience, he had "no conscious sense of sin, nor repentance, nor realization of the meaning of the Cross, or of the Resurrection, or of the Church or the Sacraments, nor indeed of the Incarnation or of Christ Himself."[17] His conversion was the beginning of a saving process in which sin, repentance, cross, resurrection, church, sacraments, and incarnation would come to have considerable meaning for him. But he did not grasp all these realities and aspects of the Christian faith in their entirety at the moment of his conversion. The reality of God's saving presence was already present to him, fully and objectively, but he had not yet appropriated it and made it his own subjectively. That was to be the work of his lifetime. His experience was the beginning of a saving process that was to continue throughout his life. Its intended end was his fulfillment and unity with God. DuBose's experience of conversion reflected the "living kernel" of his life in relationship with God in a "New World."[18] The realizing of that "living kernel" was to be the work of his lifetime of faith.

DuBose's conversion experience informed his theology in many ways, especially his theology of salvation. It seems to have been the basis for his distinction of objective and subjective in a process by which God's objective reality becomes the subjective and saving reality of our faith. The difference between the objective truth for a person and the realized truth of a person calls for "the life-time process, as one can, of gradually digesting, assimilating, and converting that faith into one's own, and finding in it the full food and content of one's life."[19] This process of converting the faith into one's own involves many experiences and their interpretation—not just one experience at the inception of faith. The full meaning of DuBose's conversion experience was to be known through the "actual and active" process of its becoming his own. It was a process of salvation that was really saving him. It led him to appreciate how the objective gift of God's presence may increasingly be appropriated and realized subjectively in the life of the believer.

DuBose had experiences of discovery during his academic career as a student and a teacher. These experiences were formative for his life and theology, especially the openness to continuing revelation and discernment that characterized his vision for the church. As a junior (first year) seminarian, DuBose encountered a senior student who had strong Calvinistic and low-churchmanship views. This seminarian challenged DuBose as to "whether the language and argument of St. Paul did not necessitate all the essential principles, the five points, of Calvinism."[20] This encounter required DuBose to face and overcome his own prejudices, and commit himself to "follow the truth wherever it may lead me."[21] It was a turning point for him. Once he had faced and considered Calvinism with an open mind, he found that he was not obliged to accept it. The real issue for DuBose was the question of committing himself in openness to the truth. It involved his personal, spiritual, and academic integrity.

DuBose also experienced openness and discovery in his classroom teaching at Sewanee. There was a spirit of "free enquiry" in his classes. He lived his theological method in his classes. He explains, "Everything was to be tested and verified, according to our Lord's prescription, in the light and in the terms of human nature, human life, and human destiny."[22] The result of DuBose's theological method of open inquiry was visible in his students as well as in his life and published theology. His former students attending the reunion in his honor represented "all the sides and aspects of faith and opinion" in the Episcopal Church.[23] There were no "DuBosians." DuBose noted that the reunion of his former students included "all the ways of thinking and believing the Church." He urged that "we have learned here to think and live together without sense or recognition of parties or partisanship. All honest and reasonable difficulties or convictions have been met and treated with equal interest, sympathy, and mutual respect and understanding."[24]

DuBose's idealism concerning his gathered former students is understandable. Nevertheless, he clearly saw in them the potential of a church where members of different perspectives could share in living and discerning the truth. They were the living witness of the open forum that was his vision for the church. His understanding of the open forum was derived from his experiences of discovery as a student and teacher. It was likewise intended to be tested in light of the experience of others. Theology should "ring true" to the experiences of real life, making sense of experience and proving itself sensible in light of experience.

Indeed, DuBose's theological development of autobiographical and personal details in *Turning Points* provides the key to understanding the experiential basis of his theological method. The formative experiences for DuBose's faith and theology can be identified and categorized in terms of his experiences of (1) loss, (2) transformation, and (3) discovery. These experiences were related to his theological understanding of (1) the cross, (2) the process of conversion, and (3) the needed openness of the church. His experiences and understandings were formative for his Christology, soteriology, and ecclesiology.[25] These conclusions would be impossible without the use of DuBose's own theological and autobiographical reflections in *Turning Points.*

DuBose sought to communicate the truths of faith and theology that were rooted in his life experience, so that others could understand and live the saving process he had known. His experiences of loss, transformation, and discovery were integral to the Christian life he lived and the theology that he systematically presented through all his works. DuBose's theology can remedy the disjunction that tends to exist between the pastoral life of the church and serious theological reflection in an academic context. His emphasis on the role of experience—in salvation and in his theology—draws out in a very dynamic way the pastoral dimension of theological reflection and the theological dimension of pastoral life. DuBose's spiritual autobiography makes clear that human experience and theological reflection are deeply related. They must not be divorced from each other.

The Experience and Theology of William Stringfellow

The contemporary Episcopal theologian William Stringfellow also supports the importance of theological narrative in his autobiographical *A Simplicity of Faith, My Experience in Mourning.* He notes that the theological exploration of biography is "congruent with the definitive New Testament insight and instruction: the incarnation." Stringfellow adds that "biography (and history), any biography and every biography, is inherently theological, in the sense that it contains already—literally by virtue of the incarnation—the news of the gospel whether or not anyone discerns that. We are each one of us parables."[26] God's story is revealed in the outward and visible signs of our own story of faith. We can discover and share how God has been incarnated in our history as we reflect on the times and turning points of our lives.

Stringfellow's reflection on his experience in mourning his companion Anthony Towne is particularly significant in light of his ongoing engagement with the threat of death in his life and theology.[27] Stringfellow identified the power of death in the many forms (personal and social) that threaten to diminish humanity through fear, intimidation, bigotry, greed, hate, domination, or anything less than God that would become a "ruling idol" in human hearts.

With respect to the power and pervasiveness of death, he noted that "In the Fall, death reigns over men and nations and ideas, and over all that is, as a living, militant, pervasive and, apparently, ultimate power—in other words, as that which gives moral significance to everyone and everything else."[28] Death then becomes the ultimate idol as it takes the place of God, commanding its own worship and conferring its own ultimate meaning. Stringfellow resisted those threats in light of the victory of life over death in Christ. He was unwavering in the face of opposition and controversy, even when his support and assistance to the fugitive Daniel Berrigan brought the threat of federal prosecution.[29] Stringfellow would not be intimidated, silenced, or deterred from the Christian ethic of witness against death in all its forms. He encountered the forms and powers of death with a theological critique and personal witness that reached far beyond the issues of his time. The Christian witness against death was the theme in Stringfellow's theology. He notes that most of his books focus "upon the death/resurrection motif."[30]

Stringfellow also faced death squarely in terms of his own medical condition. He suffered greatly from a disease of the pancreas that brought him to the verge of death in 1968. He tried to resist the effects of the disease and maintain his active schedule. However, he underwent an extensive and radical surgery in November, 1968. Although Stringfellow came away from that operation with a "wildly erratic diabetes," he surprised many by surviving the surgery and the effects of the illness for many years.[31] Stringfellow describes his medical ordeal in *A Second Birthday.*[32] Towne recalls that, shortly before the surgery, Stringfellow went to Baltimore for the Berrigan trial: "On the evening of the third day of the trial, what remained of William Stringfellow did, in fact, appear. There were speeches being made to several thousands gathered in a Baltimore church. Stringfellow would utter (whisper) a few words, the last of them an admonition to remember that death has no dominion over us."[33]

Stringfellow perceived the power of death at work in his body and in his society. And he fought that power. One friend notes that "Stringfellow fiercely resented the ravages of disease upon his body. He fought them zealously and insisted on maintaining a travel, lecture, and writing schedule that defied their power—successfully for most of the time."[34] Concerning the federal charges for sheltering Berrigan at the Block Island home that he and Towne shared, Stringfellow felt he was "being threatened with death" by the American legal system.[35]

Stringfellow believed that the powers of death (in whatever form) must have no dominion over us. For Stringfellow, the Christian witness includes active resistance to the power of death. The crisis of personal confrontation with death "is the definitively humanizing experience."[36] The powers of death threaten the person with loss of identity, and the seductive undermining of moral and rational faculties. The powers of death offer idols in place of hope and trust in God. But resistance to the powers of death is humanizing, and a necessary aspect of Christian life. Stringfellow explains in *Dissenter in a Great Society* that the drama of history "is not a conflict between evil and good, as secular ethics supposes, but concerns the power of death in this world and how death is overpowered in this life by the power of the Resurrection."[37] Stringfellow's theology emphasizes that this victory of life over the powers of death occurs daily, in history, through the lives of Christians who also seek the fulfillment of that victory in the coming of the kingdom of God.

This theology of victory in Christ over the powers of death was incarnated in a very personal way for Stringfellow as he struggled with the sudden death of his beloved friend Towne. They had been companions for seventeen years, and Stringfellow felt that "Anthony's life was the closest to my own" of all the people he had known.[38] Stringfellow believed that the truth of his existence was "the drama of death and resurrection" as he confronted Towne's death.[39] Stringfellow faced and recognized a variety of temptations as he grieved the death of his friend. He faced "the issue of allowing grief, the atmosphere and activities of grieving, and the effort of grief, to define my living." He realized that, if he allowed this to happen, the "power of death would not only have claimed Anthony in the grave" but it would also "seize" him prematurely.[40] He also noted "the common temptation to follow the dead into death" by committing suicide, or by "resigning from living" instead of "making the effort to continue to live."[41]

Stringfellow also had to struggle with the temptation "to keep everything as it had apparently been" before his friend's death, "to freeze time by ritualizing the routine of household that had prevailed before his death."[42] He could not fill the gap that Towne left in the home, he could not do all the things that Towne did, and he could not give in to "the familiar temptation to pretend that nothing had changed."[43] Stringfellow also recalled bereaved neighbors who "keep the clothing and similar personal items, or the personal space, of the dead just so, as if in readiness for an imminent return of the dead." He concluded that this was "a morbid fantasy and a pagan practice." In light of this realization, he promptly removed almost all of Towne's possessions from the house. He also began to dismantle Towne's study, instead of allowing it to "become some sort of shrine."[44]

Stringfellow describes with some humor the suggestion by friends that he "locate some surrogate for Anthony." Different friends apparently described this surrogate as "a secretary, a paramour, a houseboy, a bride." Stringfellow responded to these suggestions, "Perhaps someday, somewhere, I will have a wife, a houseboy, a paramour, or even a secretary (or all of them at once), but in the midst of both grief and mourning I yearned, more than anything else, to be alone, to return to myself, so to speak, to conserve myself for awhile, and to be freed of entanglements." Stringfellow recognized the possibility of a "surrogate" for Towne as another form of denial. This was an instance of "morbidness" that seeks "to cling to the past, maintain things as they were, and indulge the pretense that the dead are not quite dead." On a trip to New York, where he first met Towne, Stringfellow even realized that he was retracing steps he had originally walked seventeen years earlier, and that he was "searching for Anthony." Once he "understood whom I was looking for, the search was exhausted, and this awful temptation fled from me." Stringfellow would not give in to the various temptations to deny the painful reality of Towne's death. He explained that such issues involve "learning to respect the freedom of the dead to be dead; honoring the dead in their status as dead people, and refraining from harassment of the dead by refusing to mythologize the dead or enshrine them."[45]

It was in facing the reality of Towne's death that Stringfellow also encountered the power of life in Christ. In this regard, Stringfellow's theology was based in his experience, and his experience provided the occasion for him to articulate his theology. His passage in grieving Towne is reflected in the chapter titles of *A Simplicity of Faith*: Dread, Conversion, Solitude, Joy. At a service celebrated with special intention for Towne on the anniversary of his death, Stringfellow shared the eucharist and knew that his tears were done.[46]

Stringfellow also understood that to be a "beneficiary" of the resurrection of Jesus Christ "means freedom now from all conformities to death, freedom now from fear of the power of death, freedom now from the bondage of idolatry to death, freedom now to live in hope while awaiting the Judgment."[47] As "the transcendence of the power of death, and of the fear or thrall of the power of death, here and now, in this life, in this world," resurrection "has to do with life" and "the fulfillment of life, before death."[48] This was not an abstract understanding of death and resurrection for Stringfellow. He lived this theology and perceived it relative to Towne's death. Stringfellow stated, "I rejoice that Anthony lived, while he lived, and that when he died he had already known the resurrection from the dead."[49] That was Stringfellow's belief, and his experience.

Personal Narrative and Theological Reflection

DuBose and Stringfellow provide examples of how lived experience can be formative for theology, as theological reflection can be formative for understanding the meaning of experience. And for both DuBose and Stringfellow, personal narrative was the point of synthesis for experience and theology. DuBose's theological understanding of the cross, conversion, and discovery was based in his experience. His theology was also expressed in terms of that experience. Stringfellow's theological understanding of the Christian duty to face and confront death, and the victory over death in Christ, was lived out and expressed in terms of his experience of Towne's death. DuBose and Stringfellow pointed to the deepest truths of their lives, and they spoke with power. Their stories engage us.

We need that kind of power in the Episcopal Church today. We need to engage the power of Christ's gospel. His gospel is life, and it gives life. We need to reflect on the meaning of that life for us, and share it with others. It is communicated through real human lives and experiences. We have had enough unreflective enthusiasm and latest fads. We have had enough special interests and agendas. We have had enough dry theology that leaves the hearts and lives of people untouched. Faith can seek understanding, and deepen with greater understanding. The living experiences of faith can also provide a defining point of reference for theology—especially the future unfolding of theology in the Episcopal Church.

We can know Christ in our lives, our parish, and our theology. The truths of our lives and our theology matter, and we can share those truths in terms of experience. We can tell the story of our faith community, and the story of salvation history. We can tell all that God has done for us, and share our understanding of what that means. We can speak from the depth of our own experience to the depths and needs of others' lives. We can articulate a theology that is powerful in Christ, as we use personal narrative to draw together the lived experience of faith and theological reflection.

Notes

1. See Augustine, *Confessions*, trans. R. S. Pine-Coffin (Harmondsworth, Middlesex, U.K.: Penguin Books, 1961); Ignatius of Loyola, *The Autobiography*, trans. Parmananda R. Divarkar, S.J., in George E. Ganss, S.J., ed.,

Spiritual Exercises and Selected Works (New York: Paulist Press, 1991), 65–111; *Story of a Soul: The Autobiography of St. Thérèse of Lisieux*, 2nd ed., trans. John Clarke, O.C.D. (Washington, D.C.: ICS Publications, 1976); *The Life of the Reverend Devereux Jarratt: An Autobiography* (Cleveland: Pilgrim Press, 1995); John Henry Cardinal Newman, *Apologia Pro Vita Sua* (New York: Modern Library [Random House], 1950); Phoebe Palmer, *Selected Writings*, ed. Thomas C. Oden (New York: Paulist Press, 1988); C. S. Lewis, *A Grief Observed* (Toronto: Bantam Books, 1980); Thomas Merton, *The Seven Storey Mountain* (New York: Harvest/HBJ, 1978); Rachel Hosmer, *My Life Remembered: Nun, Priest, Feminist*, ed. Joyce Glover (Cambridge, Mass.: Cowley Publications, 1991).

2. Athanasius, *The Life and Affairs of our Holy Father Antony*, in *The Life of Antony and The Letter to Marcellinus*, trans. Robert C. Gregg (New York: Paulist Press, 1980), 29–99; Bonaventure, *The Life of St. Francis*, in *The Soul's Journey into God, The Tree of Life: The Life of St. Francis*, trans. Ewert Cousins (New York: Paulist Press, 1978), 177–327; Anne Ayres, *The Life and Work of William Augustus Muhlenberg* (New York, 1894); Vida Dutton Scudder, *Father Huntington, Founder of the Order of the Holy Cross* (New York: E. P. Dutton & Co., Inc., 1940).

3. See, e.g., James Wm. McClendon, Jr., *Biography as Theology: How Life Stories Can Remake Today's Theology* (Nashville, Tenn.: Abingdon Press, 1974).

4. Portions of this discussion are drawn from Robert Boak Slocum, "The Lessons of Experience and the Theology of William Porcher DuBose," *Anglican Theological Review* 79 (Summer 1997): 341–368.

5. The six other books by William Porcher DuBose are *The Soteriology of the New Testament* (New York: Macmillan Company, 1892); *The Ecumenical Councils*, vol. 3 of John Fulton, ed., *Ten Epochs of Church History* (New York: The Christian Literature Company, 1896); *The Gospel in the Gospels* (New York: Longmans, Green & Co., 1906); *The Gospel According to Saint Paul* (New York: Longmans, Green & Co., 1907); *High Priesthood and Sacrifice: An Exposition of the Epistle to the Hebrews* (New York: Longmans, Green & Co., 1908); and *The Reason of Life* (New York: Longmans, Green & Co., 1911).

6. William Porcher DuBose, *Turning Points in My Life* (New York: Longmans, Green & Co., 1912).

7. Ibid., 15.

8. Donald Smith Armentrout, *The Quest for the Informed Priest: A History of the School of Theology* (Sewanee, Tenn.: The School of Theology, The University of the South, 1979), 111. Armentrout takes the same position in an introduction to his anthology of DuBose's writings, *A DuBose Reader:*

Selections from the Writings of William Porcher DuBose (Sewanee, Tenn.: The University of the South, 1984), in which he refers to DuBose's "six major writings" (25). In his article "William Porcher DuBose and the Quest for the Informed Priest," he also refers to DuBose's "six major books." In *Saint Luke's Journal of Theology* 31 (September 1988): 258–261.

9. Armentrout, *The Quest for the Informed Priest*, 112. Armentrout also takes the position that *Turning Points* was "autobiographical and personal" and not a "major book" in a signed entry on DuBose for the *Dictionary of Christianity in America*, Daniel G. Reid, coordinating ed. (Downers Grove, Ill.: InterVarsity Press, 1990), 367.

10. Donald S. Armentrout, "Review of William Porcher DuBose: Selected Writings," *The Saint Luke's Journal of Theology* 32 (September 1989): 295. See Jon Alexander, O.P., ed., *William Porcher DuBose: Selected Writings*, Sources of American Spirituality Series (New York: Paulist Press, 1988).

11. See David L. Holmes, *A Brief History of the Episcopal Church* (Valley Forge, PA: Trinity Press International, 1993), 123; Ralph E. Luker, "DuBose, William Porcher (1836–1918)," *Encyclopedia of Religion in the South*, Samuel S. Hill, ed. (Macon, Ga.: Mercer University Press, 1984), 211.

12. J. O. F. Murray, *DuBose as a Prophet of Unity*, Lecture I, "The Background of Spiritual Experience," and Lecture IV, "His Method-Spiritual Psychology" (London: Society for Promoting Christian Knowledge, 1924), 23, 46. These lectures were part of a series for the DuBose Memorial Foundation delivered by Murray on November 7–10, 1922, at the University of the South, Sewanee, Tennessee. This was the inaugural series of lectures for the DuBose Foundation. Murray's book was based on these lectures to the theology students at the University of the South. Murray was the Master of Selwyn College, Cambridge.

13. Ibid., 5 (emphasis added).

14. DuBose, *Turning Points*, 49–50.

15. Ibid., 18–19.

16. Ibid., 21.

17. Ibid., 21.

18. Ibid., 21.

19. Ibid., 23–24.

20. Ibid., 30–31.

21. Ibid., 32.

22. Ibid., 7.

23. DuBose, "Transfiguration Sermon," in *Turning Points*, 122.

24. DuBose, *Turning Points*, 8.

25. For further discussion of this position, see Robert Boak Slocum, "The Lessons of Experience and the Theology of William Porcher DuBose,"

Anglican Theological Review 79 (Summer 1997): 341–368; and Robert Boak Slocum, "Living the Truth: An Introduction to the Theological Method and Witness of William Porcher DuBose," *Saint Luke's Journal of Theology* 34 (December 1990): 28–40.

26. William Stringfellow, *A Simplicity of Faith: My Experience in Mourning* (Nashville: Abingdon Press, 1982), 20.

27. Portions of this discussion are drawn from Robert Boak Slocum, "William Stringfellow and the Christian Witness Against Death," *Anglican Theological Review* 77 (Spring 1995): 173–186.

28. William Stringfellow, *Dissenter in a Great Society* (New York: Holt, Rinehart and Winston, 1966), 136–137.

29. Daniel Berrigan, a Jesuit priest and a personal friend of Stringfellow, protested against American military involvement in Vietnam. Berrigan was arrested with others for burning draft records with napalm in Catonsville, Maryland, and put on trial in Baltimore in November, 1968. Berrigan was convicted of the federal charges against him, and his legal appeal was unsuccessful. However, Berrigan refused to surrender himself to federal authorities after his appeal was denied. He went into hiding "underground." In August, 1970, he fled to "Eschaton," the home shared by Stringfellow and Towne. They offered him hospitality. Berrigan was arrested at their home several days later. Stringfellow and Towne were indicted for "harboring and concealing" the fugitive Berrigan, but these charges were later dismissed on procedural grounds.

30. William Stringfellow, *Instead of Death, New and Expanded Edition.* (New York: Seabury Press, 1976), 3.

31. Melvin E. Schoonover, "Present and Powerful in Life and Death: William Stringfellow's Quest for Truth," *Sojourners* 14, no. 11 (1985): 14.

32. William Stringfellow, *A Second Birthday* (Garden City, N.Y.: Doubleday, 1970).

33. Anthony Towne, "On Sheltering Criminal Priests," in William Stringfellow and Anthony Towne, *Suspect Tenderness, The Ethics of the Berrigan Witness* (New York: Holt, Rinehart and Winston, 1971), 18.

34. Schoonover, "Present and Powerful in Life and Death ," 14.

35. William Stringfellow, *An Ethic for Christians and Other Aliens in a Strange Land* (Waco, Tex.: Word Books, Inc., 1973), 85.

36. Ibid., 138.

37. Stringfellow, *Dissenter in a Great Society*, 136.

38. Stringfellow, *A Simplicity of Faith*, 22.

39. Ibid., 69.

40. Ibid., 115.

41. Ibid., 117.

42. Ibid., 118.
43. Ibid., 120.
44. Ibid., 119.
45. Ibid., 120–122.
46. Ibid., 141–142.
47. Ibid., 113.
48. Ibid., 138.
49. Ibid., 140.

Knowing the Tasks

Gardiner H. Shattuck, Jr.

In his epic novel, *In the Beauty of the Lilies*, John Updike chronicles the lives of four generations of an American family he calls the Wilmots. A talented and theologically astute writer, Updike observes the interplay of religion and American popular culture through the eyes of this fictional family. The story begins in 1910, when Clarence Wilmot, an introverted and scholarly Presbyterian minister in Paterson, New Jersey, realizes that he has lost his religious faith and no longer believes in God. And the novel ends in Colorado eighty years later, when Clarence's rootless great-grandson, Clark, joins a millenarian religious cult and dies in a Waco-like apocalypse. There is a real ebb and flow in the beliefs that Americans hold, Updike suggests, and we tend to take what we believe—or do not believe—to extremes.

Updike describes in loving detail the moment when Clarence Wilmot, the minister, surrenders himself to atheism. He had been struggling for many months with the question of God's existence, we are told. Then suddenly it hit him "like a many-legged, wingless insect that had long and tediously been struggling to climb up the walls of a slick-walled porcelain basin; and now a sudden impatient wash of water swept it down into the drain. *There is no God.*" Having come to this realization, Wilmot feels for the first time a kind of intellectual peace, but, as a conscientious man, he senses that he must now surrender the pastorate he holds at the Fourth Presbyterian Church in Paterson. He decides to inform the moderator of his presbytery, Thomas Dreaver. When he meets him, he is impressed by his professional manner and by the "honeyed promissory timbre to his voice that marked him as an executive of Christian business." The two clergymen sit down to discuss Wilmot's status in the denomination, and Wilmot begs to be relieved of his ministerial vows. Dreaver, however, refuses to accept this plea. "Unfaith is a cohort of faith," he explains; "The No must be said, so that Yea can ring out." Dreaver observes, furthermore, that Wilmot's problems may well be a result of the particular theological training he has received. While Wilmot is a graduate of Princeton Seminary ("the old muscular tradition" of conservative Presbyterian orthodoxy), Dreaver was trained by more liberal theologians (including Charles Augustus Briggs, the great Presbyterian-heretic-turned-orthodox-Episcopalian) in the flexible intellectual atmosphere of Union Seminary in New York. At Union, he had learned that "everything is relative" and that "there is nothing in your beliefs or unbeliefs that can't serve as the basis for an effective and deeply satisfying Christian ministry." While Wilmot replies that he now views his ministerial vocation as merely "going through the motions," Dreaver advises him to interpret those duties in a more positive way—as "walking toward the light." Dreaver concludes, therefore, that the Presbytery of Jersey City will not accept Wilmot's resignation but will, instead, place him on a year's probation, during which he will be expected to continue his pastorate. Dreaver asks if that plan troubles him, and Wilmot replies: No—"I know the tasks; they are the only tasks I do know." Then, go back home and do them, Dreaver says. Don't become distracted worrying whether or not God exists; just "renounce your intellectual pride and give God's grace a chance to do its work."

Whatever the pastoral merits of Dreaver's advice, it was not able to restore either Clarence Wilmot's faith or his ability to preach about it. Indeed, there were many Sunday mornings during the course of the next year when he awoke to find that he could not speak at all. "He felt strangled, . . . a dry web stuck in his throat." On those occasions, he simply gave the pulpit to his wife Stella, whose sermons, "drawing as much upon her Missouri girlhood as upon the Bible, were increasingly admired and enjoyed by the initially skeptical congregation." Actually, the arrangement was a good one for most of the people concerned: Wilmot's family continued to live in the comfortable parsonage in Paterson; the congregation of the Fourth Presbyterian church enjoyed the homey pieties Stella preached when Clarence's throat closed up; and Stella felt empowered by the new responsibilities she had assumed. The only person who was not happy was Clarence himself. After the probationary period had passed, he returned to Thomas Dreaver, who reluctantly accepted his resignation from the ministry. Wilmot "knew the tasks," but he could not do them effectively when they were devoid of substance and no longer housed a solid theological core.[1]

I begin with this illustration from Updike's novel because it expresses well my sense of the role that theology has played in the Episcopal Church throughout much of its history. I use this story as a parable for a church that appears to regard theology as fundamentally irrelevant to its corporate life and development. Dreaver's pragmatism, Stella Wilmot's common sense, and even Clarence Wilmot's struggle with belief describe aspects of the Anglican heritage in the United States. The Episcopal Church functions as if "knowing the tasks"—whether "going through the motions" or "walking toward the light"—were sufficient, while engaging intellectually the truths that lie behind those tasks is, at best, of secondary significance. This is not to say that Episcopalians today have abandoned faith in God or turned against historic Christianity—far from it. Indeed, by stressing the experiential over the rational dimensions of the faith—by viewing the essence of Christianity as "a way of life" and a handful of "core doctrines" (as the majority in the recent heresy trial of Walter Righter suggests we do)—Episcopalians have, I believe, affirmed the essence of historical Anglicanism.[2]

The current situation in the Episcopal Church is the logical outcome of an evolutionary process that began in the distant and virtually forgotten past, when the Puritan movement emerged out of the Church of England. Puritanism, of course, had many manifestations, but central to its outlook was the demand for an orderly universe, the denunciation of superstitious beliefs and rituals, and the strengthening of the role of the Bible in church life. The Puritans also thought the future of English Christianity belonged to an educated church membership, lay and clerical, who could communicate their beliefs in a rational fashion. The "Anglican" adversaries of Puritanism, on the other hand, tended to stress what the modern world regards as the non-rational aspects of the faith, especially the interrelationship of theology, prayer, and communal experience.[3] Out of this Reformation-era controversy, an ethos based on the concept of *lex orandi, lex credendi* ("the law of worship is the law of belief") took shape, an idea that conveyed the precedence of worship over theology. This notion, now one of the hallmarks of Anglicanism, has tended to foster a utilitarian attitude toward the faith instead of a speculative one, and its expansive spirit has promoted stability and order while discouraging schisms and other divisions within the church.[4] Unlike the heirs of Puritanism (e.g., Wilmot's Presbyterians), Episcopalians have been able to remain a single, united denomination. And while we have enjoyed few periods of genuine theological renewal, such as occurred within mainline Protestantism during the struggle between fundamentalism and modernism in the early twentieth century, we have also demonstrated a remarkable penchant for muddling through our various internal conflicts.

One of the reasons for what I see as our current lack of interest in abstract theological reflection has roots, therefore, in the distinctive Anglican ethos (*lex orandi, lex credendi*) that came into being at a critical moment in the late sixteenth century. A second major factor relates to the impact of two important nineteenth-century religious movements—one American, one English—that further helped to shape (and blur) the intellectual identity of the Episcopal Church. The first movement, which occurred during the religious revivals of the Second Great Awakening, produced the phenomenon that historian Nathan Hatch calls "the democratization of American Christianity." Although many Episcopalians consciously resisted the religious awakening that swept through the United States in the early nineteenth century, our church has still been significantly influenced by it. The democratization that came in its wake had less to do with the specifics of church polity and governance than with the profound metamorphosis of all Christian denominations within the milieu of American popular culture. Revivalism in that period, for example, emphasized the role of the laity in religious life, and it called into question the need to defer to either a clerical or an intellectual elite. The awakening similarly encouraged ordinary men and women to accept their deepest spiritual impulses as divinely inspired. "Enthusiasm"—a concept often disparaged during the eighteenth century—became the essential touchstone of genuine religious conviction in the nineteenth century as more and more Americans came to believe that they had a right to think and pray in whatever way they chose.[5]

With the arrival of the Oxford Movement in the United States in the 1840s, just as the fires of the awakening were beginning to cool, Episcopalians cut themselves loose from theological rationalism even further. The sacramental emphasis of the Oxford divines, unlike the emotionalism of the revivals, was couched in distinctly Anglican terms but implied a similar approach to formal theology. When discussing baptismal regeneration, for example, Edward Bouverie Pusey and Robert Isaac Wilberforce stressed that the sacrament was a mystery that could not be fully apprehended by the human mind. Rational assent was of no significance, they argued, because baptism conferred sacramental graces upon infants and adults alike, whether they knew what was happening or not. Unlike the older High Church tradition, which had viewed faith in part as an intellectual exercise, the Tractarians insisted on the importance of holiness, piety, and religious *feeling*—a tendency that paralleled the contemporary Romantic revival in literature and art. Despite its ostensibly anti-modern posture, therefore, the Anglo-Catholic spirit that came to maturity in the Episcopal Church in the second half of the nineteenth century was at home in the Victorian world and thoroughly enmeshed in the culture of its day, even while striving to transcend it.[6]

So there is certainly nothing new about the divorce between theology and everyday religious life in the Episcopal Church because—for better or worse—it has been an inescapable feature of Anglican history. But having said this as a historian, let me now add two personal anecdotes that will further illustrate some of the stumbling blocks and complications that someone who values theological knowledge and reflection faces in the church today.

My first personal anecdote begins in the early 1970s when I was a senior at the General Theological Seminary. Although prior to 1970 each diocese conducted its own examinations to test the competency of candidates for the ordained ministry, the 1970 General Convention created the General Board of Examining Chaplains in order to standardize that process on a national basis. The Board eventually composed the General Ordination Examination (GOE), which is designed to test students in seven areas of expertise: Scripture, history, theology, ethics, contemporary society, liturgics, and ministry. Since the GOE was developed during a time when the term "relevance" was in vogue, its creators were concerned that students should apply the formal knowledge they had acquired in seminary to real-life pastoral situations, thus making theological learning (in their words) "*responsive* to the needs and demands of people in the world."[7] The first GOE was administered in 1972, but, like the original model of any new product, it contained numerous small flaws and defects. As historian John Booty notes, critics faulted early versions of the exam "for ignoring content knowledge, for less than adequate evaluation, and for situation questions that were contrived and to a degree false."[8]

I remember well how one of those contrived "situation questions" caused me trouble and embarrassment when I took the GOE in 1975. I was asked to imagine being a parish priest visiting a woman whose husband had just died suddenly from a heart attack. The widow is trying to make sense out of her husband's unexpected death. After a few minutes of general conversation, she asks the priest to explain the church's teachings about death to her. Based on the remarks I received from the people who evaluated my answer, I should have responded to the widow's concerns in the following way: as a priest on a pastoral visit, I would allow the widow to express whatever pain or anger she was feeling; I would reassure her that her feelings about her husband's death were understandable and normal; I would explain to her that death is a natural event; I would tell her that, despite her husband's death, God continues to love and care for him; and I would emphasize that one day she and her husband will be reunited in heaven. In other words, I would do everything *but* give a direct answer to her question about the church's teaching on death.

That theologically evasive but emotionally sensitive response was the one I should have given on the exam, according to my evaluators. The need for a pastoral approach to the widow's grief seemed so obvious, however, that I assumed the questioners were seeking something more—namely, a theological response. As a result, since students were being asked specifically to discuss the church's teaching about death, I decided to begin with an exegesis of 1 Corinthians 15, the biblical reading that had such a central place in the burial service of the 1928 Prayer Book. I got out various books that had been assigned in my seminary New Testament classes and began to explain the Pauline text I assumed had been read at the husband's funeral. The themes I discussed during this hypothetical "pastoral" call included: the link between death and human sinfulness; the nature of the place where the dead now "sleep"; their awakening when Christ returns; the attributes of the spiritual body; and so on.[9] Although I was proud of the biblical and theological acuity my answer displayed, I had actually made a disastrous mistake. As one of my evaluators remarked, she would have "thrown me out of the house" for mentioning such theology on a pastoral call. Another evaluator thought I sounded more like a fundamentalist or a Jehovah's Witness than an Episcopalian! Thanks to the knowledge I had gained studying the New Testament in seminary, as well as my own inexperience with the theological ethos of the Episcopal Church, I failed one of the GOE areas—namely, the theory and practice of ministry.

Luckily, the examining chaplains of my own diocese gave me a second chance, and, once I explained to them the reasoning that led to the answer I gave, they understood the problem and passed me along for ordination on schedule. I like to think they made the right decision, because in the parish ministry I quickly learned when and how to abandon my academic training in theology for the sake of a pastoral response. I learned that in real-life situations in the Episcopal Church "theology" always takes second place to "pastoral care." As the majority opinion in the Righter trial observed twenty years after I took the GOE, the doctrinal teachings of the church are related to "the lived experience of the people of God in particular times and places, under the guidance of the Holy Spirit."[10] I see that much better now than when I was in seminary. I have also come to understand that, if the Episcopal Church has any official teaching about death, it is not likely to be found in reading the apostle Paul. I realized this most clearly when I participated in a funeral at which the recessional hymn was a solo rendition of Frank Sinatra's "My Way" ("The record shows I took the blows / And did it my way"), sung by the granddaughter of the deceased. Although the theology of Sinatra's song is diametrically opposed to the text of 1 Corinthians, the priest who officiated explained that he had allowed the piece as a pastoral gesture to the family.

My second personal story starts in 1986, when I was called to be rector of a parish in Rhode Island. Because of my graduate school training in church history, I was asked to instruct students in the diocesan School for Deacons. My teaching role was expanded a few years later, when leaders in the diocese decided to integrate all aspects of its educational programs. In 1990, a new "School for Ministries" was formed, which combined the three former educational ministries of the diocese (the School for Deacons, the Lay Ministry Program, and the Diocesan Christian Education Committee) into one body. While the School for Ministries continued the task of training people who were studying for the diaconate, it also offered courses in biblical studies, theology, church history, and spiritual development, which were then required by the diocese for anyone who wished to be licensed as a lay reader or lay eucharistic minister. The courses were designed for people of all educational levels, ordained as well as lay, who were seeking a congenial forum in which to learn about and discuss religious issues and ideas. I was a member of both the governing board and the faculty of the school, and there was tremendous excitement when our first catalog was published in the fall of 1991. The curriculum, we said, was intended to provide courses and workshops by which adults in Rhode Island would be enabled to grow spiritually and intellectually, to learn about the Christian faith, and to become better equipped to live out their baptismal vows. Those of us who helped develop the curriculum believed we were offering not only a decidedly Anglican vision of theological education (an emphasis on growing spiritually and on exercising one's baptismal vows), but also a program that would be popular, accessible, and empowering for everyone in our diocese.

Early results were excellent. Several hundred lay people took courses in the school, and most of them expressed real enthusiasm about having the opportunity to learn more about their church. We thought we were onto a good thing. Yet in our pleasure and optimism about the initial feedback from participants in the program, we failed to appreciate the extreme skepticism with which many clergy view both theology and theological education, especially for the laity. As a rector who was one of the early critics of the school observed, people often "confuse theological sophistication with the ability to minister," and he wondered "if St. Peter would have emerged as a leader in the primitive church had he been required to attend a theological academy" like the School for Ministries. Of course, those of us who led the school intended it to occupy a point midway between "a theological academy" and *no* education at all. But our critic had touched upon a valid concern: in focusing on the question of openness and intellectual accessibility, we had forgotten how little Episcopalians value theological knowledge for its own sake. Furthermore, given the current emphasis on baptism as the sacrament that empowers lay people for ministry, it was obvious that no education was necessary: "If I am made a minister in the Episcopal Church by virtue of my baptism as an infant, why do I need to take *courses*? If I am already empowered by the sacrament of baptism, what more can education do? Isn't a simple desire to serve sufficient preparation for lay ministry?" We had no adequate answers for those questions. Not only were they inspired by the very same populist attitudes that had helped create our school in the first place, but they were also quintessentially Anglican: an approach to the faith that was both sacramental and pragmatic, rather than rational and intellectual.

Unfortunately, our diocesan leaders, too, began to espouse this viewpoint about the purpose of the School for Ministries. If you wish to be a minister, they argued, come to church on Sunday mornings and participate in services there. ("Know the tasks," then, and do them.) As a consequence, the training program for deacons was discontinued in 1996. The following year, requirements for both the education and licensing of lay ministers were dropped. The other principal educational resource, our diocesan bookstore, was closed at the same time. Although the school itself limped on for another academic year, offering a handful of courses, most of them were eventually canceled for lack of official support. Demoralized and disappointed, the governing board disbanded the school in the spring of 1998. We had gotten the point: "knowing the tasks" that involve worship and pastoral care is the basis of church life. Theological knowledge and understanding, on the other hand, are luxuries few Episcopalians seem to have time for.

Recently, Doug LeBlanc of Episcopalians United observed that liberals in this country hold "a powerful trump card" in their debates with conservatives over changing attitudes on controversial issues such as sexuality. While the right wing of the church today relies upon "propositional truth and often abstract theological principles"—i.e., traditional beliefs—the left appeals to "emotions through powerful storytelling and firsthand experience." In other words, conservatives speak theologically and liberals speak pastorally; one side addresses the head while the other inspires the heart.[11] I think LeBlanc's analysis is accurate and helps explain why members of Episcopalians United and others who are committed to "propositional truth" feel so embattled in the Episcopal Church of the late 1990s: they have not grasped the non-rational character of historic Anglicanism and thus find themselves adrift in a denomination embodying that ethos.

LeBlanc's head-heart dichotomy, furthermore, is a useful tool for understanding the manner in which Episcopalians have resolved past disputes. In the controversy over slavery in the nineteenth century, for instance, one side tended to invoke theological ideals and propositional truths (e.g., "All men are created equal," "The spirit of the Lord is upon me to proclaim liberty to the captives," and "In Christ there is neither Jew nor Greek, slave nor free"). Members of the opposite faction, however, appealed to the pastoral and cultural norms of the white elite and stressed that public worship and personal holiness were the church's only genuine concerns. As a result, the Episcopal Church, unlike other major American Protestant denominations, was comparatively untroubled by the antebellum controversy over slavery. When the Civil War itself came, the church essentially ignored the cause of the conflict.

As I have tried to suggest in the foregoing discussion, the future of theology in the Episcopal Church has to be an uncertain one because the past itself is so ambiguous. In order to have a future, there must be a past on which contemporary Episcopal theology can be based, and yet few Episcopalians have made a creative contribution to this discipline. William Porcher DuBose is the single figure who comes readily to mind, yet even he is best remembered for his emphasis on the role of personal experience in the development of his thought. By emphasizing the primacy of the sacramental life and conformity in matters of worship, moreover, Anglicanism has traditionally honored individual conscience and allowed latitude in matters of doctrine. It has also made few concrete demands on its members beyond simply "knowing the tasks." As someone who is committed to intellectual inquiry, I am often frustrated by this ethos even while, as a lifelong Episcopalian, I am thoroughly at home in it. In a way, my own ambivalence reflects that of my church and its history. Yes, I think there were times in the past when Anglicans and Episcopalians ought to have paid attention to their rational faculties and theological principles (as in the controversy with Puritanism or the debate over slavery). I also wish that the diocesan leadership in Rhode Island had placed more value on the theological education of lay people when deciding to close the school and bookstore here. Just as often, however, I am glad that feelings and intuitions have taken precedence, as in the growing openness and acceptance of lesbian and gay members within our church.

In the end, I believe that these paradoxes are at the heart of both human history and the Christian faith, for God comes to us at the point where reason fails. The church came into existence, after all, trying to explain the inexplicable: that both the depths of human sinfulness and God's redemption of humankind are revealed in a single event. God was made known when Jesus died in abandonment and rejection on the cross. God was most engaged in the world when, at Gethsemane and Calvary, there was no visible sign of the divine presence.[12] I have always been fond of Paul's first letter to the Corinthians, in part because it expresses one of the deep paradoxes of Christian theology: "God chose what is foolish in the world to shame the wise; God chose what is weak in the world to shame the strong" (1 Corinthians 1:27). Ultimately, theology takes place where human wisdom falters. By eschewing an overly intellectual approach to the faith, Episcopalians have shown an appropriate, though profoundly ironic, understanding of what Christian theology is all about. Of course, this failure to engage in serious theological discourse also shows that we have a long way to go before we can claim either to have reached the limits of human rationality or to have learned to distinguish clearly between what is wise and what is foolish. We as a denomination are, indeed, like the fictional Clarence Wilmot, who found himself unable to speak about the Christian faith. Despite "knowing the tasks" quite well, we have frequently seemed uncomfortable articulating and analyzing the theological ideas that lie behind them.

Notes

1. John Updike, *In the Beauty of the Lilies* (New York: Knopf, 1996), 5–7, 50–58, 71–83, 87.
2. "The Bishop's Trial: Excerpts from the Summary of Court's Opinion," *Episcopal Life* 7 (June 1996), 12.
3. A. G. Dickens, *The English Reformation*, 2nd ed. (University Park: Pennsylvania State University Press, 1991), 367–377.
4. W. Taylor Stevenson, "Lex Orandi – Lex Credendi," in Stephen Sykes and John Booty, eds., *The Study of Anglicanism* (London: SPCK, 1988), 174–183.
5. Nathan O. Hatch, *The Democratization of American Christianity* (New Haven: Yale University Press, 1989), 3–16.
6. For this discussion, I have relied upon the insights of the following scholars: Robert W. Prichard, *The Nature of Salvation: Theological Consensus in the Episcopal Church, 1801–73* (Urbana: University of Illinois Press, 1997); Robert Bruce Mullin, *Episcopal Vision/American Reality: High Church Theology and Social Thought in Evangelical America* (New Haven: Yale University Press, 1986); Allen C. Guelzo, *For the Union of Evangelical Christendom: The Irony of the Reformed Episcopalians* (University Park: Pennsylvania State University Press, 1994); and T. J. Jackson Lears, *No Place of Grace: Antimodernism and the Transformation of American Culture, 1880–1920* (New York: Pantheon, 1981).
7. Taken from a description of the proposed General Ordination Exam, worked out in December 1970 by the newly-constituted General Board of Examining Chaplains under the leadership of Bishop Stephen Bayne (emphasis added).
8. John Booty, *The Episcopal Church in Crisis* (Cambridge, Mass.: Cowley Publications, 1988), 47–48.
9. My discussion relied heavily upon Oscar Cullmann, "Immortality of the Soul or Resurrection of the Dead?" in Krister Stendahl, ed., *Immortality and Resurrection* (New York: Macmillan, 1965), 9–53.

10. "The Bishop's Trial: Excerpts from the Summary of Court's Opinion," 12.

11. Doug LeBlanc, "Heat and Light at Burning Issues," *United Voice* (March 1998).

12. Rowan Williams, *The Wound of Knowledge: Christian Spirituality from the New Testament to St. John of the Cross*, 2nd rev. ed. (Cambridge, Mass.: Cowley Publications, 1991), 1–4, 22–23, 149–151.

On Being Reasonably Theological

Charles Hefling

As I write, a very basic theological issue, the authority of the Scripture, is playing a controversial part in the bishops' deliberations at the 1998 Lambeth Conference. A few years ago that issue was identified by the bishops of the Episcopal Church as the focus of a project that would, it was hoped, enable the church to engage in a serious, sustained discussion of the theological foundations of its life and witness. Papers were commissioned, written, and circulated. Then the project died on the vine. The bishops as a body turned instead to other matters, like their own collegiality, and though the papers were published, they went largely unnoticed.[1]

This episode typifies the Episcopalian attitude towards theology. We do not, as a church, esteem theological reasoning very highly or pay it much attention. Much less do we support or foster it. We seem surprised when other Christians rely on theology in making their decisions; witness, for example, the Episcopal Church's 1997 Concordat negotiations with the Lutherans, during which many Lutherans used theological arguments as a basis for rejecting the proposal. There are exceptions, of course. An Episcopalian has just put out a book that makes a noteworthy contribution to the conversation about the Trinity now going on among Christian scholars.[2] From time to time a theologically articulate cleric is elected bishop. On the whole, however, the level of theological literacy in the Episcopal Church is modest, and we seem content to have it so.

It is sometimes suggested that indifference towards theology belongs to the ethos of Anglicanism. Ours is not, after all, a confessional church, or so we tell ourselves. We have no distinctive doctrines or theological axes to grind. We do have the Book of Common Prayer, and having it is what "makes it possible for the Episcopal Church to be a pragmatic church which understands its identity through participation in corporate worship."[3] So says a well-regarded handbook of church terminology. The inquirer or new Episcopalian who reads it will likely notice two implicit contrasts, which were no doubt meant to be noticed. First, a pragmatic church presumably differs from a church that takes its stand on theoretical principles and doctrinal statements, that is, on theology. Likewise, participatory self-understanding through corporate worship is presumably meant in contrast with intellectual self-understanding through concepts and definitions, that is, through theology.

That Anglicanism can be characterized by such contrasts as these is true enough, up to a point. Episcopalians commonly take things well beyond that point. In a recent issue of a national church journal, readers are told that "the very idea of 'theology' is ridiculous." Whether this laughable discipline takes its bearings from Scripture or tradition or reason makes no difference; "it is all the same thing, an attempt to find certainty." Intelligent discourse and rational reflection are ineffective, if not irreligious. "All that we can do is experience the mystery." How? Such experience is to be had "when we gather around the altar for the sacrament, without"—of course— "trying to explain it."[4]

The article I have quoted is not eccentric. It advances a position in which a more or less overt anti-intellectualism combines with the more or less categorical assertion that sacramental worship is the one thing necessary. From the combination, it follows that experience trumps reason and that theology is superfluous. It is a position which, with variations, I believe to be deeply entrenched in the Episcopal Church. In this paper I propose to explore it.

The first thing to say about such a position is that it is itself a theological position. It amounts to a theological argument against arguing theologically, which makes using it self-subversive, like sawing off the branch you are sitting on. To that point I shall return in conclusion.

The second thing to say is that the Episcopal Church has not always had a bias against theology. So it is fair to ask why we have one now. The explanations I will suggest do no more than touch on the complexities of the question. They may, however, serve to clarify a further one: is our distaste for theology benign?

Though it may be that Episcopalians do not now understand themselves in terms of theology, they once did. The formation of our church as an independent community with its own identity at the turn of the nineteenth century was in large part a matter of articulating a definite theological stance. It had to be. Anglicans were surrounded and outnumbered by Christians of persuasions different from theirs. Where they stood on the great questions of sin and salvation, grace and repentance, renewal and the life of the world to come needed to be made clear vis-à-vis these other churches' tenets.

To that end, after a good deal of discussion and some false starts, the General Convention adopted the Church of England's XXXIX Articles of Religion, without substantive change. At the same time, more importantly, it placed the Articles in the interpretive context of a canon of texts. This "Course of Ecclesiastical Studies," drawn up by Presiding Bishop William White, prescribed the education in divinity undertaken by all Episcopalian ordinands, and anchored the church in a tradition of theology that was unabashedly rational. Not that it aimed at logical proof of truths stated in the Articles, or tried to put apodictic certitude in the place of faith. That is not what its rationality consisted in. It was rational, rather, in its conviction that God's ways with the world are coherent and intelligible. We are apt to sneer at the Enlightenment's reliance on reason, used as it was for church-bashing; but reason could be, and in England had been, used in support of Christianity, and, as such, it was an important part of the early Episcopal Church's self-definition over against the irrationalism of revivalistic sects.

Nor should it be supposed that the theology which characterized Episcopalianism through most of the nineteenth century was narrow or inflexible. Bishop White chose his required texts judiciously, and the two parties, High Church and Evangelical, into which Episcopalians sorted themselves then as now, were able to live together with comparatively little friction. On the other hand, the church's theological synthesis did have boundaries. Nobody thought it should be all-inclusive, and, in fact, it was not. One bishop, for one set of reasons, left for Rome. Another, for another set of reasons, left to found the Reformed Episcopal Church.

This latter secession marked the end of consensus, according to Robert Prichard, whose account I have been drawing on. So it is worth mentioning the reasons that the bishop who seceded had for seceding. He, and those who followed him out of the Episcopal Church, objected to the intrusion of "erroneous and strange doctrine." Tractarian doctrine, to be more exact—the theology of the Oxford Movement—was now spreading from England to the United States. The precise doctrinal point at issue is less important, in the present context, than the fact that the point was doctrinal. For while the Oxford Movement is apt to be associated with elaborate ceremonial—more on that presently—it was in the first instance a theological movement. Its doctrines, strange and erroneous or otherwise, did not waft into the Episcopal Church on a cloud of incense; they came by way of Newman's learned lectures on justification and Pusey's yet more learned tract on baptism. In allowing those who embraced these doctrines a place at its table, the Episcopal Church in effect began to alter its own theological identity. By 1880, Prichard writes, the church was "well on the way to a broad theological pluralism that Bishop White would hardly have recognized."[5]

What the bishop would think after another hundred years is hard to imagine. Pluralism seems a mild word for the theological anarchy Episcopalians live with today. What happened in the meantime? An adequate answer would have to be at once a history of the Episcopal Church, a history of religion in America, and a history of Christian theology. All I can do here is point out two of the currents that have eroded the church's respect for, and reliance on, theology. One of these can be seen in the further course taken by the Oxford Movement in American Anglicanism; the other, in the course taken by Anglicanism in America.

It is not too much to say that everyone in the Episcopal Church today, not self-avowed Anglo-Catholics only, is heir to the Oxford Movement in some sense. But that sense needs to be specified, for—somewhat ironically—a movement that began in a university and propagated itself through academic tracts has left a legacy that is less intellectual than it is aesthetic and, in certain ways, anti-intellectual.

The doctrinal impulse that launched Tractarianism has for the most part dissipated; what remains is the liturgical enrichment introduced (or, if you like, restored) by the "Subtractarians" who belonged to the later, ritualistic phase of Anglo-Catholicism. The vestments and ornaments began, to be sure, as visible expressions of a very definite theology. Before long, however, they detached themselves and came to be valued in their own right. Today they are as likely to be found together with New Age spirituality or some species of Marxism as with ultramontanism or Thomist philosophy. What the original Tractarians meant by catholicism had a specific theological content, centered on the nature of the church and the ordained ministry. What the word has come to mean is a comprehensiveness with no theological center at all.

There is, thus, a way in which time has corroborated the way Anglo-Catholicism was described by Cardinal Manning, himself a former disciple of the movement. "Private judgment in gorgeous raiment," he called it, "wrought about with diverse colors."[6] Now that innovations which the ritualist party had to fight for are standard usage throughout the church, the cardinal's jibe ought to give Episcopalians pause. By private judgment, he meant individual opinion, unregulated by public, objective criteria. Thus, one target of his criticism was the notion that anything goes, theologically speaking, so long as it is liturgically correct. That way of putting things is, of course, a caricature. Still, to judge by its current Prayer Book, the Episcopal Church as a whole has become Anglo-Catholic, and there is reason to think that a preference of liturgy over theology, experience over intelligence, feeling and mystery over rational deliberation and sober judgment, has been bequeathed to the church at large, along with gorgeous raiment and diverse colors, by its catholic party. I do not mean that there is some mysterious affinity between a taste for liturgical spectacle and a distaste for serious thinking. I do, however, mean that the cultured suspicion of reason in general, and of theological reasoning in particular, that runs so prominently through Newman's writings has been magnified and passed on by his Anglican followers together with their emphasis on sacramental worship.

That line of explanation, however, ought not to be pressed too hard. If the Episcopal Church's attitude towards theology is the result of developments inside Anglicanism, outside pressures have to be taken account of as well. A good case could be made for thinking that the gradual adoption of a non-rational, experiential, liturgical mode of focusing its own identity has been one way for Anglicanism to adjust itself to a new environment. In some ways, what was happening in America as that shift took place parallels what happened in England when Pope Gregory first sent Augustine as a missionary. Instead of uprooting the folk religion he would find there, Augustine was told by the Pope to graft Christianity onto it, adapting and absorbing what people already believed and the way they already worshiped. This he and his successors did and, by doing it, helped make the Christian church English. In turn, something of the same process has helped make the Anglican church American.

Religion, in its broadest sense, is the way people orient their lives around what they deem most choiceworthy. In that sense, Americans have long had a folk religion, a loose and largely unreflective congeries of ideas and practices that bestow meaning and value on their individual and social living. These "habits of the heart" have been called the religion of democracy. They embody and reflect an unstated metaphysic of the human, an anthropology, whose core doctrine, said to be self-evidently true, is that everyone is created equal. It is not exactly a Christian doctrine. Arguably it is a Christian heresy, in which the equality of every person as a child of Adam on the one hand and as redeemed by Christ on the other becomes the interchangeability of persons in other respects. Be that as it may, the egalitarian ethos of the newly independent United States was shared, with more or less conviction, by those adherents to the Church of England who were left after the Revolution. Not surprisingly, it made itself felt in the fabric of the newly independent Episcopal Church.

The structural effects of absorbing the religion of democracy can be seen in our polity, official and unofficial; the intellectual effects, in the contribution that serious theological thought makes to the church's life and witness. If that contribution is small and ineffectual, one reason is that serious thought of any kind has not generally been esteemed in America. We admire know-how, not knowledge, and frown on intellectual pursuits as elitist. Applied to religion, this attitude favors do-it-yourself theology. Everyone is entitled to an opinion about what Christianity is and is not. Episcopalians share that view to the extent that, as Americans, we believe in an inalienable right to believe as we choose—in a right to private judgment, as Manning called it.

Private judgment, in itself, is not necessarily a problem. Every judgment is private, inasmuch as it is made by an individual mind. The problem arises when individuals who judge for themselves arrive at their judgments rashly, thoughtlessly, irresponsibly, out of ignorance or desire or fear. Judgments about religion clash—as they did so notoriously and painfully at the 1998 Lambeth Conference—not because they are individual but because they are fallible. When and whether and how and how far to resolve them—that is the problem. In the past, Anglicanism has customarily tried to deal with theological differences in a theological way, by appealing to publicly available authorities: to Scripture, reasonably interpreted in the light of the church's tradition of reasonable interpretations. Such an appeal was built into Bishop White's "Course of Ecclesiastical Studies." How the three elements of this triad cooperate is a very pertinent question. At the moment, it is more pertinent to point out that none of the three is egalitarian. Reading the Bible in any serious sense demands more than elementary literacy; interpreting it reasonably demands more than common sense; drawing on the vast riches of tradition demands a more than casual acquaintance with it. Anglicanism once gloried in a learned clergy, educated to meet these demands. But a learned clergy is not egalitarian, either.

So it is that in various ways and on various occasions American Anglicanism has had to face a dilemma. Given that everyone is entitled to an opinion (although not everyone is qualified to judge opinions by the customary Anglican standards), there seem to be two options. One possibility would be to override democratic ideals and defer to specialists whose training, gifts, and, perhaps also, graces put them in a position to help the church clarify its own mind. That possibility the Episcopal Church now avoids pretty consistently. The other possibility, which has gradually become a feature of the church's way of life, is much more egalitarian. This second option begins by acknowledging that theological opinions are many and disparate, but goes on from there by applauding the disparity as wholesome diversity, setting aside disputed issues in the interest of peace, discounting the importance of resolving them, and falling back on common worship according to the Prayer Book to hold things together. You may call this making the best of a bad situation. You may call it the genius of Anglicanism. Either way it comes down to an unwillingness to say that anyone is wrong. Where reasonable discussion is held to be incapable of settling disagreement, indiscriminateness becomes a duty. Decisions must needs be arrived at by counting heads.

I have been suggesting two sources of an eclipse of theology in the Episcopal Church: the internal influence of an Anglo-Catholic emphasis on liturgy, let loose from its doctrinal moorings, and the external influence of egalitarian sentiments that are bred in the American bone. These are not the only reasons for our corporate disregard of theological learning and scholarship. They do, however, appear to have played the most significant roles in the church's reversal of its once high estimate of the value of intelligence, as applied to matters of Christian faith.

There would be no great harm in writing off theology as ridiculous if it were true that the practice of Christianity—when we gather around the altar to "experience the mystery," for example—entails no theological issues. It is not true. Every eucharist presupposes and enacts the answers to a vastly complicated set of interlocking questions—unless we are willing to concede that any gathering of any group of people around any table to do and say anything whatever constitutes a eucharist. If we are not, then who are "we" who gather? Must we be baptized? If so, why? Shall one of us, alone, preside? If so, in virtue of what qualifications? May the presider be a woman? If so, may she be a lesbian? Must what is said by the presider conform with what is printed in the Prayer Book? If not, must it at least express certain ideas? If so, which ones? And so on.

These are elementary questions, most of them, which is not to say they are simple. Yet they scarcely touch on the real mystery, the paschal mystery, that the eucharist exists to enact and proclaim. That mystery, it is true, transcends anything human speech can say about it. But from this it does not follow that nothing can be said or that saying what can be said is worthless, for here too—here above all—questions arise and need to be answered intelligently and responsibly. To quote, by way of example, our liturgy's own statement of what the eucharist is all about, Christ "stretched out his arms upon the cross, and offered himself, in obedience to your will," that is, the will of God the Father, "a perfect sacrifice for the whole world." What does, what can, that *mean*?

Christian people do ask what it means. They cannot help it. That is how they are made. Nor should they try to help it. Asking questions is what comes of being made in the image of God. Wonder, the root of all inquiry, all questioning, is our native appetite for transcendence. In heaven there is no theology, because the saints in glory see God face to face. All their questions are answered. That is what being in glory *is*. But in this life, while we are on the way home, our restlessness to be there manifests itself, among other ways, in the raising and answering of further and further questions about where we are going and how we get there.

The problem, then, is not that we ask too many questions. It is that we do not ask enough. We are content to be pragmatic, averse to thinking things through. Orthodoxy, as one very Anglican bishop is reputed to have said, is reticence. But if reticence means refusing to raise and address relevant questions, it is quite the opposite of orthodoxy. It is more like the sin against the Holy Ghost, who, we have been promised, is to lead us into all truth. How does that leading occur, if not through wonder, inquiry, investigation, questioning?

I am emphasizing questions, theological questions, partly because it is sometimes supposed that theology is a matter of hard-edged answers that fit together like a jigsaw puzzle. That is one way to think theologically. Anglicanism has never been in danger of espousing it, least of all in this country. Still, questions are meant to be answered. That is what they are for, however partial and provisional the answers turn out to be. To return, then, to the question that might well occur to the worshiper at an Episcopal eucharist: what does it mean that Christ "on the cross . . . offered himself, . . . a perfect sacrifice"?

Bishop John Spong has made addressing that question the topic of one of the twelve theses that set out the agenda of his latest book. According to the traditional Christian story, as Bishop Spong reads it, God "needed the blood offering of his son to save the fallen creation." But that explanation of the cross is a "barbaric idea based on primitive concepts of God,"[7] and must be abandoned, the sooner the better. This is not the place to engage the bishop in what would have to be a lengthy theological discussion. Suffice to say that, if what he is repudiating is an identification of sacrifice with violent death inflicted on an innocent victim in order to stave off divine vengeance, I join in the repudiation, precisely because I would at the same time deny that such a soteriology is the normative content of *the* Christian tradition. But at present a different point needs to be made. Whatever else one may think of Bishop Spong's theses, there is this much to be said: he does not think theology is ridiculous. Christians, and persons who might become Christians, have minds. They apprehend the gospel in thoughts as well as feelings. How they are to understand the cross does matter. And not all answers to the question of what Christ's death means and does are equally right.

How to discriminate between answers that are right and answers that are not—how to arrive at theological judgment—is itself a theological question. Insofar as his theses raise it, Bishop Spong will have done something worth doing. I can think of no question for the Episcopal Church to take more seriously. To ignore it will mean, in the long run, acquiescing in the fashionable idea that there can never be right answers; in other words, acquiescing in nihilism. In the short run, ignoring it will mean that issues such as convulsed the 1998 Lambeth Conference will become more convulsive. They can be drowned out by rhetoric, perhaps, or stamped out by the usual machinery of power politics. But they are theological issues, like it or not, and so they invite the question of how theological issues are to be decided.

Experience will not decide them. An appeal to experience has been the hallmark of Christian theology in modern times, beginning with Schleiermacher. But the idea that experience is self-authenticating and unambiguous, that it comes "neat," unmingled with thinking, independent of circumstance—that very naive idea is no idea of Schleiermacher's. What he actually held had already been summed up in a Scholastic maxim: "Whatever is received is received according as the receiver receives it." Experience, in other words, is never sheerly "given." It is received by a receiver who is more or less sensitive, more or less instructed, more or less faithful. That is why, ever since the evangelist urged believers to "test the spirits, to see if they are of God," the church has maintained that no religious experience, on its own, is authoritative. On that, Christians as different as Ignatius of Loyola, with his "discernment of spirits," and Jonathan Edwards, in his treatise on religious affections, are at one. Experience is something to ask questions about. It does not deliver the answers.

Nor can liturgy decide theological issues. Liturgy *is* a theological issue. The Book of Common Prayer was once a kind of semi-sacred text that changed very seldom and never very much. Today, where it has not been abandoned altogether, it is in a state of perpetual flux. Consequently, to the extent that our identity is, as the handbook of terminology quoted earlier says, understood through participation in corporate worship, to that extent Stephen Sykes is quite right: the "basic seat of authority" for the Anglican churches lies in the process by which liturgies are altered. That is as much of a magisterium as we have. To change a liturgy is to change the way those who worship by it "experience the mystery"; it is to change how they understand themselves and their calling; and it is to change the whole pattern of relationships that is the church. Is liturgical revision itself, then, subject to any authority? Are there standards or criteria by which to decide whether a liturgy does whatever it is that liturgy should do? If sacramental worship addresses the worshiper's entire self, intelligence as well as emotion, if it is a vehicle of intelligible meaning, then once again the question of its norms arises, and it is a theological question, not an artistic one.

I said just now that I can think of no question worthy of more serious consideration by the Episcopal Church than the question of how theological issues are to be decided. And I have said that neither experience nor liturgy is enough to decide them. What remains? One formulation of the standard Anglican position was mentioned earlier. What remains is Scripture, reasonably interpreted in the light of the church's tradition of reasonable interpretations. As stated, that is a slogan, and no more. Every word calls for explication—particularly, as I have been saying in various ways throughout this essay, the word *reasonable*. We know what Scripture is, give or take a few syllables. We know what and how the church has learned from it in the past, though we may of course know it better. What is the most reasonable way to learn from it now?

A flight from reason has been one prominent feature of the twentieth century, certainly not in theology alone, but certainly there too. Freud and Marx and Nietzsche all cast doubt on the human mind's ability to know truly, and theologians have not been slow to join them. It was probably this recent surge of irrationalism in Christian thought that C. S. Lewis had in mind when he posed one of the riddles in *Pilgrim's Regress*. A traveler was journeying homeward, with an enemy going along close by. The house stood beyond a river that could be crossed neither by swimming nor by wading. From there a message was sent to the traveler: Should the only bridge be destroyed, lest the enemy cross it, or left standing for the traveler?[8]

The bridge is reason. It can be used for good or ill. Its use in matters of religious faith and practice is theology, and theology, too, can be done so that God is, or is not, glorified. As much fatuousness, spleen, naiveté, prejudice, and stupidity can be found among theologians as elsewhere. A lot of theology *is* ridiculous. Agreement on theological issues is notoriously difficult to achieve.

But we have no other bridge.

Notes

1. Charles Hefling Frederick Houk Borsch, ed., *The Bible's Authority in Today's Church: Papers on the Authority of Scripture presented to the Episcopal House of Bishops* (Valley Forge, Pa.: Trinity Press International, 1993).

2. David S. Cunningham, *These Three Are One: The Practice of Trinitarian Theology* (Oxford and Malden, Mass.: Blackwell Publishers, 1998)

3. John N. Wall, Jr., *A New Dictionary for Episcopalians* (Harper-SanFrancisco, 1985), 29. This book has gone out of print, but a second edition is currently in progress.

4. *The Living Church* 217 (5 July 1998).

5. Robert W. Prichard, *The Nature of Salvation: Theological Consensus in the Episcopal Church, 1801–1873* (Urbana and Chicago: University of Illinois Press, 1991), 171.

6. Quoted in L. E. Elliott-Binns, *Religion in the Victorian Era* (London: Lutterworth Press, 1936), 231; John Shelton Reed, *Glorious Battle: The Cultural Politics of Victorian Anglo-Catholicism* (Nashville: Vanderbilt University Press, 1996), 259. I have changed the original spelling.

7. John Shelby Spong, *Why Christianity Must Change or Die: A Bishop Speaks to Believers in Exile* (San Francisco: HarperSanFrancisco, 1998). The quotations are from Bishop Spong's Op-Ed Page, *New York Times*, 13 August 1998, and from his website, maintained by the Diocese of Newark. See also, John Shelby Spong, "Twelve Theses," *The Living Church* (17 May, 1998).

8. C. S. Lewis, *Pilgrim's Regress* (Grand Rapids, Mich.: Wm. B. Eerdmans Publishing Co., 1959), bk. 3, chap. 9.

Whither the National Church? Reconsidering the Mission Structures of the Episcopal Church

Ian T. Douglas

There is much said and written today on the nature and shape of American denominationalism and the organization of religious work at the national level.[1] On one side are conservatives and/or traditionalists who decry the errant ways of national church structures. To them national offices are bloated centralized bureaucracies, at best, or hotbeds of leftist radicals at worst. The goal for many in this camp is to close the national offices with a concomitant devolution of mission programming to the local level. On the other side are individuals who identify or are associated with the national offices and thus feel compelled to maintain and protect established programs in the face of growing dissatisfaction and decreasing dollars. The reality shared by both those who are for, and those who are against, nationally centralized church structures is that American Protestant denominationalism is undergoing profound change. Old ways of working and secure denominational identities are challenged as never before. The way forward is unclear and uncertain.

Within the last three decades, the historic missionary agencies and mission boards of American mainline Protestantism, in particular, have come increasingly under attack.[2] For a variety of religious, cultural, and economic reasons, the centralized denominational church structures that flourished in the first part of the twentieth century have given way to downsized, program-gutted agencies.[3] Long gone are the days of glory when big church organizations provided common educational and missionary programs for their denominations, nationally and internationally. Local churches today are more likely to go it alone or associate with like-minded congregations outside of their denomination than to look to their denominational headquarters for guidance, networking, and mission resources. What has resulted is a loss of denominational identity, cooperation, and cohesion, and an increasing splintering of the American Protestant experience. Any discussion of the future of theology and the Episcopal Church must therefore consider the past, present, and future of the mission structures of the "national church" in light of these changes in American Protestantism generally.[4] We must first look back in order to discern where God might be leading us in the future.

Craig Dykstra and James Hudnut-Beumler, in their article "The National Organizational Structures of Protestant Denominations: An Invitation to a Conversation," described changing patterns of American Protestant denominational life over the past century and a half. They suggest that the history of denominational organization and governance at the national level in American Protestantism can be described by a series of three metaphors: constitutional confederacy, corporation and regulatory agency.[5] These three metaphors are very helpful to understand institutional changes in the Episcopal Church over the last century in light of the rise and fall of the "national church ideal" as the major motivating force in the Episcopal Church's mission work.[6]

Constitutional Confederacy

The "constitutional confederacy" metaphor described by Dykstra and Hudnut-Beumler characterizes the Episcopal Church in the late eighteenth and early nineteenth centuries. The realization of nationhood at the end of the eighteenth century forced the emergence of a new understanding of acceptable forms of the church in the United States.[7] Dutch and German Reformed, Methodists, Anglicans, Presbyterians and Congregationalists no longer could look to their religious patriarchs in Europe, especially England, for their authority and identity. Each American church, in turn, had to develop its own standards of faith and ecclesiastical organization. The *Presbyterian Form of Government*, the *Methodist Book of Discipline*, and the *Constitution and Canons of the Protestant Episcopal Church* represent the organization of American Protestants independent from their mother churches in England.

During these early years of American Protestant denominationalism, the parish, presbytery, or diocese took precedence over national organization. Denominations were thus confederations of local faith communities organized under an agreed upon constitution.

> The formation of national-level church bodies in the earliest years of the republic did *not* involve the formation of large-scale bureaucratic denominations as we know them today. They responded to the ecclesiastical problems of ministerial succession, guidance, and governance brought on by the fact of America's emergence as a separate nation, but the forms they used were not bureaucratic; they were constitutional. Churches became national bodies by constituting themselves as confederations.[8]

The national organizing principle of American Protestant denominations during this period of constitutional confederacy was a loose affiliation.

> There was no perceived need for national action on social issues or even for collective coordination of charitable work. These denominations had no professional staff, nor were they charged with the production of any national goods or services, not even Sunday school materials.[9]

The main question before American Protestants at this time was: How do we get along as newly independent churches in a newly independent country?

Following the Revolutionary War, Episcopalians were primarily concerned with the contextualization and organization of an independent Anglican church in the United States. Early General Conventions were not interested in missionary outreach but, rather, diocesan organization, the forming of a national constitution, the adoption of a Prayer Book, and the need to secure and guarantee an American episcopate. Even after the Episcopal Church had set up the Domestic and Foreign Missionary Society in 1821, there was little interest in supporting missionary endeavors. During its first decade and a half, the Domestic and Foreign Missionary Society, as a voluntary society under the auspices of the General Convention, failed to capture the imagination and support of Episcopalians.[10]

Dykstra and Hudnut-Beumler indicate that from 1830 to 1860 American Protestants become increasingly interested in the world beyond their constitutional confederacies. They were responding to new political and religious stimuli in American society: first, there was a newfound faith in democracy—the belief that every person could and should take an active role in determining her or his destiny; second, Americans increasingly accepted evangelical premises brought on by the Second Great Awakening, especially the Arminian principle that each individual could respond to God by free will and thus effect her or his own salvation.[11] Dykstra and Hudnut-Beumler state that these two religious impulses, democracy and voluntarism, gave birth to voluntary societies in American Protestantism. They emphasize, however, that these societies were not, at first, nationally organized.

> [The voluntary societies] were, first of all, independent of local, regional, and national church bodies. Organized by groups of Christians to address needs unmet by Church or society, the antislavery societies, the tract societies, the Bible Societies, the prohibitionist societies, and even the home and foreign mission societies might or might not be associated with the members of a particular faith tradition.[12]

Thus, in the first half of the nineteenth century, American Protestants remained constitutional confederacies but began to embrace a larger social and missiological mandate through a variety of voluntary societies. Some of these voluntary societies would evolve into the modern denominations.

There were voluntary societies in many dioceses of the Episcopal Church in the early decades of the nineteenth century. Diocesan missionary societies, especially the Protestant Episcopal Missionary Society of Pennsylvania, contributed to the founding of the Domestic and Foreign Missionary Society in 1821. Episcopalians, however—because of their theological and social class traditions—were less affected by the piety of the Second Great Awakening.[13] As a result, the voluntarism that drove the majority of Protestant missionary societies in the first half of the nineteenth century was never fully realized in the Episcopal Church. Instead, Episcopalians followed a more catholic ecclesiology that saw the church—the church as a whole—as responsible for missionary outreach. After a decade and a half of struggling as a voluntary society, the Domestic and Foreign Missionary Society was reconstituted in 1835 as a society of the whole. Each Episcopalian, by virtue of baptism, was a member of the Missionary Society. Episcopal mission work was interpreted as advancing the church catholic as a corporate body, not as voluntary evangelism promoted by associations. As chief missionary and defender of the faith, a missionary bishop embodied the catholic calling to spread the church at home on the Western frontier and overseas in such countries as Liberia, China, and Japan.[14]

Corporation

The second metaphor presented by Dykstra and Hudnut-Beumler is the denomination as corporation. At the turn of the twentieth century, American government and businesses became increasingly centralized and bureaucratized. "This was the age of trusts, collectives, and, above all, vertically integrated corporations."[15] Clergy and lay leaders, many of whom were businessmen familiar with the organizational parlance of their time, worked together to bring the many and diverse ministries of a church under one central administrative structure. By 1900, for both practical and ideological reasons, the corporate bureaucratic form of organization that would characterize American Protestantism at the national level for most of this century had begun to take shape.[16]

Dykstra and Hudnut-Beumler point out that corporations are in the business of providing goods and services, and the modern denomination was no exception to this rule. The centralization of mission boards, social service agencies, and publishing ventures in national headquarters resulted in greater denominational reach at home and overseas for American Protestant denominations.

> [T]he first product . . . of the corporate denomination was a centralized mission effort, which compared to its predecessor efforts, was more broadly coordinated and more clearly identified with the denomination. Where there had been an Armenian mission appealing to every congregation within the denomination, there was now a unified giving campaign that highlighted the Armenian mission activities as but one part of the total overseas mission of the church.[17]

Other goods and services provided by the corporate church included, but were not limited to, oversight and financial support for educational institutions and social service agencies including hospitals, the production of Sunday school curricula and denominational magazines, clergy and missionary pension funds, and assistance with the building of church buildings. Annual conventions and assemblies of the denominations became, in effect, stockholders' meetings, and annual reports of the national church organizations resembled those found in the corporate sector.

The emerging corporate model in American Protestant denominationalism was exactly what was needed to further the Episcopal Church's mission work at home and around the world. The idea of church as corporation appealed to both the social and the theological predisposition of Episcopalians at the time. Episcopalians who had embraced the social gospel promoted the centralization of the church's various educational, social service, and mission boards. Greater coordination meant greater and more effective service to the world. At the same time, the Episcopal Church increasingly appropriated its British establishmentarian tradition. William Reed Huntington believed that the mission of the Episcopal Church was to unite all non-Roman Catholic Christianity in the United States and, thus, shape and mold the Christian character of the nation.[18] The Episcopal Church's experience of the social gospel coupled with a newfound establishmentarianism resulted in an increased common identity for the church: the national church ideal. Imbued with this ideal, Episcopalians increasingly saw their mission as spreading the richness of Anglican tradition and the riches of American democracy at home and abroad.[19]

The national church ideal, aided by the territorial advance of the United States following the Spanish American War, resulted in an expansion of the foreign mission portfolio of the Episcopal Church. In the first two decades of the twentieth century, the number of foreign and extra-continental missionary districts of the Episcopal Church grew from three to seventeen and foreign missionary appointments more than tripled from approximately 100 to over 370.

The crowning glory of the corporation metaphor for the Episcopal Church was the creation of the National Council with an elected Presiding Bishop in 1919. The consolidation of the Board of Religious Education, the Commission on Social Service, and the Board of Missions of the Domestic and Foreign Missionary Society under one administrative structure was inspired by Arthur Selden Lloyd, Bishop of Virginia. The merging of the Episcopal Church's work in education, social service, and missions fortified the national church ideal. The mission of the Episcopal Church, as represented by the National Council, was to provide a more abundant life to all people though Christian truths coupled with American democratic freedoms. The products of the new corporation were good schools, good hospitals, and right-ordered worship. A nationwide campaign which included an annual every-member canvass, also adopted in 1919, guaranteed that the corporation would have a constant supply of financial resources to accomplish its mission.[20] Under the banner of the National Council, the Episcopal Church extended its reach at home and abroad. Henry Knox Sherrill, Presiding Bishop from 1947 to 1958, would come to epitomize the role of chief executive officer of a vast national and international corporation.[21]

There were, however, significant flaws in the National Council's model for extension of foreign mission work. Foreign missionary districts of the Episcopal Church were treated as overseas subsidiaries of the larger parent corporation at home. Missionary bishops were elected by the House of Bishops in the United States. Their allegiance was more often to the directors in the United States than to their overseas constituencies. In addition, the product that seemed to sell so well in the United States (good schools, good hospitals, and right-ordered worship) was uncritically exported without genuine consideration of the needs and resources of the overseas church. As a result, missionary districts were saddled with large institutions and methods of production that they would not be able to support when separated from the parent corporation.

Flaws in the top-down corporate model of mission were not limited to the overseas subsidiaries. Because support for missionary endeavors were filtered through the bureaucratic machinery of the National Council, the people in the pew became increasingly separated from their overseas workers. In addition, support for National Council programs at home and around the world was predicated on parishes and dioceses embracing the national church ideal. The presuppositions of the national church ideal, however, would be challenged by new social and political realities in the United States and around the world in the post-colonial era. The corporation would experience a crisis in confidence after which business as usual no longer could continue.

Regulatory Agency

The third organizational metaphor described by Dykstra and Hudnut-Beumler is the regulatory agency. Beginning in the early 1960s, the corporate model for American Protestant denominational structures began to show signs of strain. This occurred for a variety of reasons. First, the general consensus between national administrators and the people in the pew on the nature of mission began to break down. Decisions were made by the national leadership that were not completely supported by the church at large. Dykstra and Hudnut-Beumler note as examples of such decisions the scaling back of overseas mission initiatives and the turning over of domestic missions to local groups.

> For some very good reasons, the mainline denominations began to call the missionaries home, dismantle their more evangelical enterprises, spin off overseas synods, conferences, and dioceses as independent churches, and invite the new sister churches to send their own missionaries to the United States.
>
> While done for valid reasons relating to self-determination, cutting these traditional foreign mission activities was unpopular with the rank and file. Similar decisions were made—with similar effect—in the late 1960s to turn national mission activity over to local groups working with Indians, orphans, alcoholics, pregnant teenagers, and African-American schoolchildren.[22]

The loss of consensus and the cutback in popular programs further alienated the national leadership from church members. Financial resources in support of the national denominational bureaucracies began to decline as the people in the pew held back their money. The loss in income was exacerbated by the fact that membership in the mainline denominations began to decline in the late 1960s. With reduced resources, the corporation could no longer provide its products. What emerged in response was a new model of denominational organization: the regulatory agency.

The regulatory agency model was born when denominational leaders discovered that they no longer had sufficient economic or programmatic power to influence social and ecclesiastical change. Long gone were the large staff and large promotional campaigns of the corporation. Denominational leaders thus turned to the only resource that they had left: the power to mandate change through regulation. Regulations were used to adjudicate the distribution of dwindling resources and control the budgets and activities of denominationally related institutions that the former corporation could no longer support.[23] The national organization in most mainline Protestant churches became an arbitrator to be tolerated or avoided rather than the keeper of the church's identity. Denominational headquarters increasingly fell out of favor with church members, and church officials became isolated from the wider church they had hoped to serve.

> Rather than producing valued and valuable goods and services, [church bureaucrats] find their time and energies consumed by participation in meetings and consultations internal to the bureaucracy itself, by engagement in conflicts among various parties in the larger system, and by the production of policy papers, regulations, sanctions, and inducements designed to keep the organization in a state of controlled equilibrium.[24]

Dykstra and Hudnut-Beumler conclude that the regulatory agency model, still found in most denominational structures today, is not working well enough to provide the kind of national institutional governance our time requires. A new model is needed to break the cycle of dissatisfaction that currently exists.[25]

The decline of the corporation and the advent of the regulatory agency characterizes the changes in the mission structures of the Episcopal Church in the post-colonial era. The social and political turmoil in the United States and around the world in the 1960s and 1970s profoundly challenged the assumptions of the national church ideal. The function of the National Council—to provide a more abundant educational, physical, and spiritual life to all people though Christian truths, coupled with American democratic freedoms—seemed sorely out of step with the times. The National Council struggled to discern a new *raison d'être*. In 1963, the name of the National Council was changed to Executive Council, reflecting a different portfolio. The new nomenclature was more than semantic, for it pointed to the increasingly administrative and regulatory function of the national leadership of the Episcopal Church in the face of the social and political turmoil of the post-colonial era.

Seeking to address the crisis in the inner cities of America, Presiding Bishop John Hines initiated the General Convention Special Program (GCSP) in 1967. GCSP signaled a sea change in the mission of the national church as the Executive Council turned over its resources to local groups working for the empowerment of ethnic minorities and other disenfranchised groups. Increasingly, the missiological mandate to provide good schools, good hospitals, and right-ordered worship at home and around the world—as encouraged by the national church ideal—began to wither. With the loss of the ideal and the ensuing change in function of the Executive Council, individual church members became increasingly alienated from the national church. Parishes and dioceses held back their financial support for the Executive Council, and historic programs of the national church were cut, never to be replaced.[26]

The foreign mission work of the Episcopal Church was one of the most obvious and significant losses resulting from the death of the national church ideal. The cutbacks in missionaries and the divestments of overseas missionary districts were justified by a redefinition of mission priorities for the Episcopal Church. Drawing on the priorities set forth in the 1963 Toronto Anglican Congress and its manifesto, "Mutual Responsibility and Interdependence in the Body of Christ," the Episcopal Church committed itself to inter-Anglican cooperation as the primary agenda in its overseas work. Mission partnership and international development became the guiding principles of the Episcopal Church's engagement in "world mission."[27]

Mission partnership and international development were embraced because they complemented the function of the national church as a regulatory agency. Under the Partners In Mission (PIM) program adopted by the Anglican Communion in 1971, the primary role of the Executive Council staff was to arbitrate negotiations between the Episcopal Church and other Anglican churches around the world.[28] National church functionaries spent their time insuring that PIM principles were followed and coordinating Episcopal Church representation at PIM Consultations and meetings of the Anglican Consultative Council. At the same time, the financial resources for the overseas work of the Episcopal Church became increasingly scarce as the national church fell further and further out of favor with the wider church. The number of appointed missionaries of the Episcopal Church continued to drop and financial grants to the church's remaining missionary dioceses and other Anglican churches were jeopardized.

The Episcopal Church could no longer support the many overseas institutions it had established during the heyday of the national church ideal. Cooperation with the United States government in international development projects temporarily alleviated the financial burden. The writing and execution of government grants fit the regulatory model, and new funds were channeled to Anglican churches around the world. The government grants, however, were made without the knowledge or control of the wider church. The new cooperation between the United States government, the staff of the Executive Council, and partner Anglican churches was open to abuse, and over time such collegial ventures were scaled back significantly.[29]

The commitment of the Episcopal Church to its few remaining missionary dioceses and other Anglican churches around the world has suffered as the church has become increasingly consumed with regulating ecclesiastical affairs in the United States. The Episcopal Church today is threatened by internal strife and division. Liberals and conservatives are fighting bitterly over many issues. Conflicts over women's ordination, inclusive language, the blessing of same-sex unions, and the ordination of homosexuals threaten a schism in the church. The preoccupation with domestic debates over these issues has blinded Episcopalians to the joys and struggles of sisters and brothers in Christ around the world. Another model, beyond the regulatory agency, needs to emerge or the Episcopal Church will become increasingly isolated from and peripheral to the ongoing life of the Anglican Communion and the wider world Christian community.

Network

In the last decade a new model or metaphor, not envisioned by Craig Dykstra and James Hudnut-Beumler, has arisen in the organizing of American Protestant religious work at the national level. The metaphor that best describes the emerging construct is that of the network. Like the electronic networks of the computer age (e.g., the worldwide web), the network metaphor is built on a series of multilateral relationships by which individuals or individual communities communicate and connect directly with affinity groups or affiliated parties. There is no one centralized organization through which all must connect like the hub and spokes of a wheel. Rather, each access point is free to link up directly with other constituencies depending upon its own needs and resources. There is thus no real identified center but, rather, a virtual center, a spider web of relationships that functions as a whole, a network of networks. Could such a network of networks describe a possible way forward in the future national mission structures of the Episcopal Church?

The world mission community within the Episcopal Church has been experimenting with a network model as a possible organizing principle to advance Episcopal mission engagement around the world. The development of the network idea has not been easy, but it has proved to be quite effective and positive. The roots of the network were first planted in rocky soil. In the late 1970s and early 1980s, several groups within the Episcopal Church, upset with the direction of the Executive Council and its programs, came together to found a variety of independent voluntary missionary societies free from the regulatory hand of the national church. Such new agencies as the Episcopal Church Missionary Community (ECMC), the South American Missionary Society, USA (SAMS-USA), and Sharing of Ministries Abroad (SOMA), while generally embracing a more evangelical theology of mission, saw themselves as alternatives to the missionary programs of the Executive Council. The split between the more liberal theological positioning of the Executive Council and the more evangelical position of the new independent mission societies was representative of a larger missiological rift in American Protestantism generally.[30]

To the credit of both mission administrators at the national headquarters of the Episcopal Church as well as new leadership in the voluntary societies, a series of attempts was made to heal the theological and organizational difficulties that existed between the two groups. In the late 1980s a series of annual mission education gatherings was held at the University of the South in Sewanee, Tennessee. Sponsored jointly by the World Mission Department of the national church, SAMS-USA, ECMC, and the university, these events produced the conversations and the trust-building that eventually would result in the network idea. Episcopalians across the theological and organizational spectrum came to discover that their common commitment to God's mission was greater than the issues that divided them.

In St. Louis, Missouri, in 1990, the many and diverse world mission organizations of the Episcopal Church that had participated in the earlier mission education conferences came together voluntarily to form the Episcopal Council for Global Mission (ECGM). The ECGM soon grew to be a network of over forty organizations in the Episcopal Church. The aim of ECGM is to promote the unity and effectiveness of the various world mission initiatives in the Episcopal Church through shared covenants and open communication and dialogue. Arguably one of the most diverse and eclectic networks in the Episcopal Church, the ECGM embraces a wide variety of mission theologies and strategies: there are the independent missionary societies—some committed to mission education, others to mission funding, and still others to the actual sending out of missionaries; in addition, parishes, dioceses, seminaries, funding agents (such as the United Thank Offering and the Presiding Bishop's Fund for World Relief), and constitutional bodies of the church (such as the Standing Commission on World Mission) also participate in the Council.[31] Affirming that each organization has an important role to play in the world mission of the Episcopal Church, ECGM brings all members to the table as equals. Decisions are made by consensus, and leadership is built on a circular model. Rather than electing officers and naming committee chairs, the membership each year chooses a new steering committee by lot and creates new action teams of volunteers to work on special projects.[32] These special projects range from educational conferences on mission to people who have not yet had access to the gospel to the plight of persecuted Christians around the world.

The strength and vitality of the Episcopal Council for Global Mission was manifest boldly in 1994. In February of that year the Executive Council proposed that the Domestic and Foreign Missionary Society "no longer fund appointments of Missionaries and Volunteers for Mission on a regular basis."[33] The reasons given for ending the Society's direct support of missionaries were the combination of declining financial resources at the national level and the relinquishing of missionary programs to local dioceses and independent voluntary societies. Such a move, however, would signal the end of the Episcopal Church's 173-year commitment to the sending of missionaries as a unified national organization. In response, the ECGM, at its 1994 annual meeting in Ridgecrest, North Carolina, crafted resolutions for the 1994 General Convention that would continue the missionary-sending function of the Domestic and Foreign Missionary Society and challenge the whole Episcopal Church to a recommitment to world mission. The lobbying of the ECGM and its related mission activists at the 1994 General Convention in Indianapolis not only played a major part in the maintenance of the world mission program of the Executive Council but also resulted in a challenge to the Episcopal Church to re-vision its mission structures at the national level.[34]

Following the mandate of the 1994 convention, the Standing Commission on World Mission of the General Convention and representatives of the ECGM worked together over the following triennium to come up with a proposal that would implement new strategies and structures for world mission in the Episcopal Church. Resolution A-204 to the 1997 General Convention in Philadelphia proposed the creation of a new Episcopal Partnership for Global Mission that would bring together the voluntary association of the mission organizations in the ECGM with the legislative and executive functions of the church as represented in the General Convention and Executive Council.[35] The proposal, ultimately, was too far-reaching and radical for the 1997 General Convention to endorse in an unqualified manner. Old-guard liberals and reactionary conservatives, both of whom are invested in the current culture wars of theological and ecclesiological debates, could not envision a new way of working. The idea of an open and inclusive network where power is shared and a diversity of opinion is voiced in a free exchange of ideas across differences seems to be as threatening to the status quo power structures of the regulatory agencies as it is to their detractors. The legislative and executive structures of the church were not yet ready to embrace the network model as the primary means by which Episcopalians organize themselves for mission.[36]

The coming together of the various world mission organizations to form the ECGM does point to a new way of working in the Episcopal Church and also to the promise of possible ECGM successors. The future, of course, is unknown. The world mission community, however, is committed to working together as sisters and brothers in Christ in a mutually responsible and interdependent manner. World mission activists do believe that the emerging network model offers the possibility of unity as the body of Christ in the world today beyond the either/or dualities of current church organization. The hopeful and grace-filled manner in which world mission organizations have been able to work across their differences for the greater glory of the gospel bodes well for the future of the Episcopal Church. The future of the national church may lie not in maintaining old structures but—following the lead of the world mission community—in evolving into a network of networks, a spider web of voluntary associations that affiliate with one another but still retain their primary commitment (world mission, domestic mission, urban ministry, evangelism, stewardship, etc.). Such a future offers a rich new wholeness and oneness in the body of Christ; a future where the church's mission to restore all people to unity with God and each other in Christ is truly lived out and realized.[37]

Appendix A

1997 Member Organizations of the Episcopal Council for Global Mission

African Team Ministries, Inc.
The American Committee for the Kiyosato Educational Experiment Project
Anglican Frontier Missions
Anglican, Global and Ecumenical Studies of the Episcopal Divinity School
Christian Eye Ministry
Church of the Apostles, Fairfax, Virginia
Church Periodical Club
Committee to Assist the Episcopal Diocese of Honduras
Companion Diocese Network
Companions in World Mission
Diocese of Indianapolis—National and World Mission Committee
Diocese of Massachusetts—Commission on Wider Mission

Diocese of New York
Diocese of San Diego—World Mission Committee
Diocese of Southern Ohio—National and World Mission Committee
Diocese of Virginia—Committee on World Mission
Diocese of Western Massachusetts—World Mission Commission
Domestic and Foreign Missionary Society of the Episcopal Church
Episcopal Church Missionary Community
Episcopal Church Women—Women to Women Program
Episcopal World Mission, Inc.
Global Episcopal Mission Network
Missions to Seamen, North America and the Caribbean
The Order of the Daughters of the King
The Presiding Bishop's Fund for World Relief
The Programs Centers, School of Theology, University of the South
Province V, Companions in Mission Program Unit
Russian Ministry Network
St. Peter's Church, Cambridge, Massachusetts—Wider Mission Committee
Seamen's Church Institute International Training Center
Seminary Consultation on Mission
The Society for Promoting Christian Knowledge/USA
The Society of St. Margaret
South American Missionary Society-USA
Standing Commission on World Mission of the General Convention
Stanway Institute, Trinity Episcopal School for Ministry
Trinity Parish in New York Grants Program
United Thank Offering
Volunteer Oklahoma Outreach Mission

Appendix B

"Theological Affirmation" The Partnership for Global Mission Proposal

God has lovingly and joyfully created heaven and earth. Human beings, however, have become alienated from the Triune God, turning away from God and one another. God, in love, seeks to heal the divisions that drive us apart. In the incarnation, death, and resurrection of Jesus Christ, God provides the way by which all creation can be reunited with our loving and merciful Creator. In dying for us, Jesus Christ redeems us to new life. In him the Reign of God is made real and accessible for all. Empowered by the Holy Spirit, the Body of Christ present in the world today proclaims and lives out Jesus' work of reconciliation and redemption. The mission of the Church is thus to restore all people to unity with God and each other in Christ (The Catechism, The Book of Common Prayer, 855). As God sent Jesus into the world, we too are sent into the world.

The history of salvation from creation to the present day demonstrates that God is a sender. The Holy Scriptures are the definitive chronicles of the work of the sending Triune God. They tell of prophets and apostles, women and men of faith, impelled to speak and act in God's mission. The truth of Scripture is that from the Triune God, Creator of all, God the Word is sent and made human to accomplish reconciliation and redemption, and God the Holy Spirit is sent to empower God's people to participate in and bear witness to God's Reign.

God's mission of reconciliation and redemption is the work of the Church. In mission God the Holy Trinity takes God's believing people as a partner. Commissioned in Baptism, and enabled by the Holy Spirit, Christians are invited to be recipients and channels of God's transforming grace. We do this through: prayer and worship, repentance and forgiveness, the proclamation of the Good News of God in Christ, loving service, and struggles for justice and peace (The Baptismal Covenant, The Book of Common Prayer, 304–305).

God's mission carries us across frontiers to encounter the new and the unfamiliar in our own communities and beyond. Every Episcopalian is called to cross frontiers, local or global. Mission is both "domestic" and "foreign." We thus participate in God's mission in the Episcopal Church, in the United States, within the Anglican Communion, and beyond. As we are called to go, so are others called to come and bear witness to Christ among us. We are both givers and receivers in God's mission.

As missionaries, Christians are nourished by God's Word and sacraments, and sent into the world in God's name to bring hope, healing, and justice to a sinful, divided, and broken world. The God who is known in the Old and New Covenant works both through the established and through the surprising and unpredictable. The variable strategies and structures of the Church have always been a response to new circumstances. As the world and its cultures change, so too should the vehicles by which God's people present the Gospel at home and to the ends of the earth.

Notes

1. The Center for Social and Religious Research of the Hartford Seminary, one of the foremost institutions of religious research in the country, has recently embarked on a significant study of eight American denominations entitled: "Organizing Religious Work for the 21st Century: Exploring Denominationalism."

2. The loss of stature and cultural power of mainline American Protestantism in the last few decades has led some writers to describe them today as "old-line" or "sideline" churches rather than "mainline.

3. For two of the best discussions of the changes in the denominational structures of American mainline Protestantism, see Craig Dykstra and James Hudnut-Beumler, "The National Organizational Structures of Protestant Denominations: An Invitation to a Conversation," in Milton J. Coalter, John M. Mulder, and Louis B. Weeks, eds., *The Organizational Revolution: Presbyterians and American Denominationalism* (Louisville: Westminster/ John Knox Press, 1992), 306–330; and Russell E. Richey, "Denominations and Denominationalism: An American Morphology," in Robert Bruce Mullin and Russell E. Richey, eds., *Reimagining Denominationalism: Interpretive Essays* (New York: Oxford University Press, 1994), 74–98.

4. As there is no provision for an established state church under the Constitution of the United States, "national church" will generally refer to the structures and programs of the Episcopal Church historically associated with the Domestic and Foreign Missionary Society, the National Council, and the Executive Council. These programs are popularly understood as "815," the street number of the national offices of the Episcopal Church at The Episcopal Church Center, 815 Second Avenue, New York, New York.

5. Dykstra and Hudnut-Beumler, "The National Organizational Structures of Protestant Denominations," 306–307.

6. For a full discussion of the "national church ideal," specifically as it relates to the foreign mission work of the Episcopal Church, see Ian T. Douglas, *Fling Out the Banner: The National Church Ideal and the Foreign Mission of the Episcopal Church* (New York: The Church Hymnal Corporation, 1996).

7. Dykstra and Hudnut-Beumler, "The National Organizational Structures of Protestant Denominations," 308.

8. Ibid., 310.

9. Ibid.

10. Douglas, *Fling Out the Banner*, 23–33.

11. Dykstra and Hudnut-Beumler, "The National Organizational Structures of Protestant Denominations," 311.

12. Ibid., 312.

13. See Robert Bruce Mullin, *Episcopal Vision/American Reality: High Church Theology and Social Thought in Evangelical America* (New Haven: Yale University Press, 1986).

14. Douglas, *Fling Out the Banner*, 33–38

15. Dykstra and Hudnut-Beumler, "The National Organizational Structures of Protestant Denominations," 314.

16. Ibid., 315.

17. Ibid., 316.

18. See William Reed Huntington, *A National Church* (New York: Charles Scribner's Sons, 1898), and *The Church-Idea: An Essay Towards Unity* (Boston and New York: Houghton Mifflin Company, 1899).

19. Douglas, *Fling Out the Banner*, 81–124.

20. Ibid., 149–184.

21. Ibid., 222–236.

22. Dykstra and Hudnut-Beumler, "The National Organizational Structures of Protestant Denominations," 318.

23. Ibid., 320–322.

24. Ibid., 327.

25. Ibid., 329.

26. Douglas, *Fling Out the Banner*, 288–300.

27. Ibid., 300–323.

28. For an overview of Partners in Mission and its processes, see Anglican Consultative Council, *Giving Mission its Proper Place: Report of the Mission Issues and Strategy Advisory Group*, ACC Mission and Ministry Study Series, 2nd ed. (London: Anglican Consultative Council, 1985).

29. In *Terry Waite and Ollie North: The Untold Story of the Kidnapping—and the Release*, Gavin Hewitt documents the cooperation between officials of the Episcopal Church and the United States government. He demonstrates how the Executive Director of the Presiding Bishop's Fund for World Relief, Samir Habiby, became the conduit for Oliver North's recruitment of Terry Waite in the Iran-Contra scandal (Boston: Little, Brown and Company, 1991).

30. For a good overview of this conciliar evangelical debate over mission, see Donald McGavran, ed., *Eye of the Storm: The Great Debate in Mission* (Waco, Texas: Word Books, 1972).

31. See Appendix A for a list of current ECGM organizations.

32. From ECGM promotional flyer, "The World to Christ We Bring."

33. J. Patrick Mauney, Executive for Partnerships, Episcopal Church Center, to Appointed Missionaries and Volunteers for Mission, 20 January 1994.

34. Resolutions D-107a, "Continuing the Volunteers for Mission

Program," D-032s, "The National Church and World Mission," and D-108, "Reinstatement of 5% Reduction of Funding for Overseas Dioceses," turned back the cutbacks proposed by the Executive Council. Since each of these resolutions had significant budget ramifications, all three resolutions had to receive funding approval by the Program, Budget, and Finance Committee (PB&F). Ultimately these three resolutions were part of close to twenty resolutions that passed the House of Deputies and received funding from PB&F but were inadvertently omitted from the legislative concurrence calendar of the House of Bishops. This mistake left the three resolutions in legislative limbo, although the overwhelming support by the House of Deputies in favor of funding assured that these actions of General Convention were efficacious in the 1994–1997 triennium. As with resolutions D-107a, D-032s, and D-108, resolution D-016a, "Developing New Missionary Structures," was also mistakenly left off the concurrence calendar by the House of Bishops. Ratification of D-016a by the Executive Council in January 1998, corrected this oversight.

35. Report of the Standing Commission on World Mission, *Report to the 72nd General Convention: Otherwise Known As "The Blue Book"* (New York: The General Convention of the Episcopal Church, 1997), 524–533.

36. Resolution A-204s of the 1997 General Convention does call on the Executive Council to create a modified Episcopal Partnership for World Mission, building on many of the networking priorities of the original resolution. As of the end of 1998, the Executive Council had not moved significantly on this resolution. See *Journal of the General Convention of the Episcopal Church: 1997* (New York: The General Convention, 1997), 199–200.

37. From the Catechism, The Book of Common Prayer (New York: The Church Hymnal Corporation, 1979), 855. The missiological principle that God's mission is one of reconciliation and redemption leading to the unity of all people with God and each other in Christ is consistent with the theological affirmations for the networking model developed by the Standing Commission on World Mission and the Episcopal Council for Global Mission for the 1997 General Convention. See Report of the Standing Commission on World Mission, *Report to the 72nd General Convention*, 526, and Appendix B.

Liturgy and Theology

Leonel L. Mitchell

The last half of the twentieth century has seen a proliferation of new, revised, and reformed liturgical materials unequaled since the sixteenth-century Reformation. It is not simply Anglicans; the entire Christian world is involved in liturgical change. It has been suggested that this is by no means coincidental. In the sixteenth century the late medieval culture was rocked by the invention of the printing press; and in the twentieth century, Western culture has been dramatically changed by television and the computer. In many ways the prophet of these changes was the mid-century media expert Marshall McLuhan. In 1962 he wrote, in *The Gutenberg Galaxy*,

> The invention of typography confirmed and extended the new visual stress of applied knowledge, providing the first uniformly repeatable *commodity*, the first assembly-line, and the first mass-production.[1]

His point is that the invention of printing—which, among other things, made possible both the production of prayer books and liturgical uniformity—"taught men how to organize all other activities on a systematic lineal basis." He concludes:

> . . . the assumption of homogeneous repeatability derived from the printed page, when extended to all the other concerns of life, led gradually to all those forms of production and social organization from which the Western world derives many satisfactions and nearly all of its characteristic traits.[2]

For McLuhan, the advent of television and the computer have brought an end to the passivity and linear regimentation produced by the invention of printing. He sees the effects of this in the changes that have so altered Western civilization during this last century:

> The new electric galaxy of events has already moved deeply into the Gutenberg galaxy. Even without collision, such co-existence of technologies and awareness brings trauma and tension to every living person. Our most ordinary and conventional attitudes seem suddenly twisted into gargoyles and grotesques. Familiar institutions and associations seem at times menacing and malignant.[3]

Many contemporary Christians will respond to McLuhan's description of the age in which we live. His book *Understanding Media,* dealt with the contemporary effects of this "new electric galaxy":

> The electric technology is within the gates, and we are numb, deaf, blind, and mute about its encounter with the Gutenberg technology, on and through which the American way of life was formed. . . . Our conventional response to all media, namely that it is how they are used that counts, is the numb stance of the technological idiot. . . .
>
> The effects of technology do not occur at the level of opinions or concepts, but alter sense ratios or patterns of perception steadily and without any resistance. The serious artist is the only person able to encounter technology with impunity, just because he is an expert aware of the changes in sense perception."[4]

Most of us have at least a passing familiarity with McLuhan's ideas, frequently summed up in the phrase, "the medium is the message," but we shall simply note here the disruptive effect of this paradigm shift on culture, values, and institutions, and leave them aside to consider the effects of these massive changes on liturgy and theology.

McLuhan quotes Roman Catholic liturgists Louis Bouyer and Joseph Jungmann to show how the Roman mass of the Middle Ages "was increasingly misunderstood by the clergy as well as by the faithful," and how "it began to disintegrate through the fault of the medieval liturgists themselves."[5] Bouyer, in turn, cites Dom Ildefons Herwegen, abbot of Maria-Laach until 1946:

> Far from demonstrating an ideal understanding and practice of the Catholic liturgy, the Medieval period in fact paved the way for the abandonment of the liturgy by Protestantism and its final disgrace and neglect in so much of post-Tridentine Catholicism. . . .

> The fundamental error of the Middle Ages, when they are compared with Christian antiquity, would be, according to the former Abbot of Maria-Laach, in their turning from an objective kind of piety to a subjective one. Here, he thinks, is also to be found the root of all subsequent errors, since the true and authentic spirit of the liturgy is forthright objectivity, while that of medieval and post-medieval piety tends more and more to an all-absorbing subjectivism. This tendency goes along with a shift of emphasis from the union of the whole Church with God to an emphasis on the union of the individual soul with Him.[6]

It is precisely this shift in piety, coming out of the late Middle Ages, which McLuhan identifies with the coming of typography. It substitutes a visual text for the oral word. McLuhan quotes Thomas More's complaint that John Frith understood the whole of the Bible to be continuous, uniform, and homogenous,[7] a complaint which might be made about contemporary fundamentalists. He comments:

> The new homogeneity of the printed page seemed to inspire a subliminal faith in the validity of the printed Bible as bypassing the traditional oral authority of the Church, on the one hand, and the need for rational scholarship on the other. It was as if print, uniform and repeatable commodity that it was, had the power of creating a new hypnotic superstition of the book as independent of and uncontaminated by human agency.[8]

The Reformation was, if anything, more of a child of the Gutenberg revolution than Counter-Reformation Catholicism. The liturgical community of the early church was not restored in either the English or Continental Reformation, in spite of the reformers' good intentions. The church tended to become a schoolroom, studying the sacred text, rather than a community celebrating liturgy. The Bible and, for Anglicans, the Prayer Book became sacred objects. Worship became privatized and individualized. Congregations become aggregations of individuals reading from books, watching a liturgico-theatrical spectacular, or listening passively to an ordained minister.

Liturgical Renewal

It would as clearly be an exaggeration to claim that the invention of printing is responsible for the decline of the liturgy—which stretched over the first nine centuries of the second millennium—as it would be to claim that the invention of electronic communication will be responsible for its renewal. There are deep theological causes at work in both decline and renewal, but, in McLuhan's estimation, the cultural phenomena he examines account primarily for the popularity of the ideas:

> Later medieval visual stress muddied liturgical piety as much as electronic-field pressure has clarified it today. . . . With regard only to our new electronic technology, it might baffle many to explain why there should be such a profound liturgical revival in our time, unless they were aware of the essentially oral character of the electric "field". . . . The merely individual and visual aspects of worship no longer satisfy.[9]

Traditional Christian liturgical worship is an interactive rather than a spectator event. It is "the work of the people," a public corporate activity. The liturgical movement of the twentieth century has had as a major goal the "full, informed, and active participation" of the Christian *laos* in the celebration of the liturgy. The Vatican Council II *Constitution on the Sacred Liturgy*—citing 1 Peter 2:9, "But you are a chosen race, a royal priesthood, a holy nation, God's own people, in order that you may proclaim the mighty acts of him who called you out of darkness into his marvelous light"—describes this participation as "their right and duty by reason of their baptism."[10] The words may be those of Vatican II, but the idea is important to Christians in a wide spectrum of churches. Liturgical worship is an action in which the people of God participate. The Book of Common Prayer is primarily neither a sacred text to be worshiped nor a codification of laws binding the worshiping community, but a script for the celebration of the divine drama of salvation in which all have their part.

Anglicans have traditionally spoken of their liturgy as participatory, but often this has not been the case in practice. Congregations have frequently been mere audiences, while clergy, acolytes and semi-professional choristers performed the liturgy. While it is certainly true that there is a sense in which "watching" and "listening" are participatory, if that is the full extent of congregational participation, it falls far short of the full and active participation which is "their right and duty by virtue of their baptism." Anglican worship has also retained much of that late medieval piety of which Ildefons Herwegen complains. Worship is seen as a time for the individual to offer his or her own prayers, and the complaint is frequently made that the new emphasis on corporate participation takes away the opportunity for such prayer. Indeed Herwegen and his followers in the Maria-Laach school were accused of indifference to personal religion. Bouyer is certainly correct when he comments:

> Would not, then, an authentic way of returning to tradition be found in the rediscovery of the inherent and mutual relation of the "subjective" and "objective" in piety, and, in consequence, of the person and the Church, rather than in fruitlessly opposing either subjective to objective, or person to Church?[11]

Yet, a great deal of the conflict surrounding the introduction of the 1979 Prayer Book had its roots precisely in this opposition. Like the Benedictines of Maria-Laach, the Anglican liturgical reformers of the late twentieth century often seemed to oppose corporate worship to personal religion. "I don't have time for my own prayers," was a complaint frequently heard about the Rite Two eucharist. The summons to greet one's neighbor in the peace of Christ grated against the piety which prescribed "knees on the ground, eyes on the cross, and hearts in heaven,"[12] as the proper attitude in which to approach the eucharistic mystery. Often eucharistic celebrations of the 1960s and 1970s were so corporate as to seem to lack any referent outside the celebrant community. The often-heard exhortation to "celebrate life!" seemed to some to refer not to the community's life in the body of Christ, but to a comfortable existence in the suburbs for which we gave corporate thanks. Bouyer is certainly correct in suggesting that the "true tradition" does not oppose corporate worship and personal piety but lies in "the rediscovery of the inherent and mutual relation of the 'subjective' and 'objective' in piety, and in consequence, of the person and the Church."[13] In practice, this is often difficult to achieve, and the pendulum seems to swing between "liturgical prayer" and "personal devotion."

Certainly there has been a renewed understanding in this last half-century of the church as the eucharistic community and of the eucharist as the central activity of the church. The active participation of the individual worshiper in the corporate offering of the liturgy has been stressed and a great deal of movement in this direction has occurred. The tension between this and the more static medieval view has been both real and painful. We have also seen a renewal in "spirituality," a recovery of the interiority of not only worship but of Christian life, as the pendulum seems to swing back. This recovery of the primitive understanding of liturgy as action is based on solid scholarship and represents a recovery of an authentic theology of worship, but we need to remain aware of the role that the change in outlook epitomized by the television and computer screens in popularizing this piety. Certainly liturgy in the twenty-first century will become more participatory.

The renewal of spirituality shows signs of keeping pace with it, which should result in the deepening of the interiority of liturgical worship. We are a sacramental church committed to the view that outward and visible signs are the means by which we receive inward and spiritual grace. As Presiding Bishop Frank T. Griswold has written:

> It is our hope that praying and singing the prayers and canticles [of the liturgy] will deepen and strengthen our encounter with Christ and make it possible, with ever increasing conviction, to cry out with St. Ambrose, "You have shown yourself to me, O Christ, face to face. I have met you in your sacraments."[14]

Moving Forward

Finally, the church has begun to come to terms with the "electronic galaxy." A resolution of the 1997 General Convention read:

> *Resolved,* That the Standing Liturgical Commission be directed to prepare a plan for liturgical revision and enrichment of the common worship of this Church to be presented to the 73rd General Convention, and be it further
>
> *Resolved,* That this plan include forms of worship reflective of our multicultural, multiethnic, multilingual, and multigenerational Church while providing rites and structures that ensure the unity of Common Prayer, and be it further
>
> *Resolved,* That any new or revised rites when authorized be available for distribution in a variety of forms, including multimedia and electronic options.[15]

Since the resolution also calls for amendment of the constitution to permit the authorization of "alternative liturgical materials" and for the materials themselves to be presented to the 2003 General Convention, it seems to set a liturgical agenda for the beginning of the twenty-first century.

The Unity of Common Prayer

What does the resolution actually call for? First, it sets forth the unity of common prayer as a value to be preserved. It does not propose that everyone be permitted to do his or her own liturgical thing, or even that each congregation or diocese be permitted to do their own. The liturgical unity of the church in common prayer is a part of our tradition which we do not wish to abandon. The word used is *unity* not *uniformity*. Anglicans have sometimes talked liturgical uniformity, but it has seldom been realized, and never without tremendous cost. Today, it is commonly recognized by Anglicans that liturgical uniformity is both unattainable and undesirable. The myth that the English Book of Common Prayer of 1662 set a liturgical and theological standard for Anglicanism has been abandoned, even by the Church of England, and has had few American adherents since 1789, when the first American Prayer Book was adopted. The 1988 Lambeth Conference passed two resolutions putting the myth to rest:

> This Conference . . . urges the Church everywhere to work at expressing the unchanging Gospel of Christ in words, actions, names, customs . . . [and] liturgies, which communicate relevantly in each contemporary culture.[16]

and

> This conference resolves that each Province should be free, subject to essential universal norms of worship and to a valuing of traditional liturgical materials to seek that expression of worship which is appropriate to Christian people in their cultural context.[17]

Most of the member provinces of the Anglican Communion have used this freedom to issue new prayer books or alternative service books. The International Anglican Liturgical Consultation has, in fact, affirmed that it is not common texts, but a common structure for our worship and a common understanding of what we are doing that unites us.[18]

Liturgical Inculturation

I wrote recently in *Anglican Theological Review:*

> Anglicanism has often described itself as having no distinctive doctrines or practices, but holding the faith of the undivided Catholic Church. If it is true that Anglicanism is simply a particular expression of the Catho-

> lic Church, then we shall be hard pressed to find things which are distinctively and essentially Anglican. . . .
>
> If we take our own theology seriously, and believe in the Incarnation of the Word of God and in the catholicity of the Church, then not only Christianity, but Anglicanism is set free from the bondage of any one cultural expression. In fact, an Anglican liturgy rooted and grounded in the Gospel and in the indigenous culture is more Anglican than an imitation of Canterbury Cathedral in Ghana or of King's College, Cambridge, in Fiji.[19]

This is "our multicultural, multiethnic, multilingual, and multigenerational Church" at work, being and worshiping as the body of Christ in a particular place. Inculturation is the technical term for this, and we shall see more of it in the new century, as Anglicans ask themselves how much of the English culture which nurtured the church is a part of being Anglican. On the world stage, the answer is, "Not very much." Anglicans are freeing themselves from their identification with British colonialism.

Episcopalians will find this question asked within our own borders as well. Why should the Spanish Prayer book be simply a translation of the official English-language Book of Common Prayer? Are there not ways in which it should reflect Latino culture? Must African American congregations ignore the vital traditions of African American worship to be real Episcopalians? Native American liturgies have begun to reflect their culture, and this will become more widespread as the new century unfolds. In the hymnal supplement *Wonder, Love, and Praise,*[20] we begin to see some of these riches unfolded.

Expansive Language

Another example of this awakening cultural consciousness is *Enriching Our Worship.*[21] In one sense this is simply a continuation of the process of liturgical revision which began in the nineteenth century. "Liturgical enrichment" was a stated goal of both the revisions of 1892 and 1928. The recognition that the Reformation's "simplification" of Anglican worship was often overdone has combined with the ecumenical climate of the present to open the entire liturgical repertoire of East and West to potential use. Not just ancient Catholic liturgies can be mined, but modern Protestant ones as well. The Canadian *Alternative Service Book,* for example, includes in its Good Friday liturgy a version of the ancient

"Reproaches" from the supplemental worship resources of the American United Methodist Church,[22] and the Revised Common Lectionary is a primary example of cooperative work by Christians of different churches.[23] But there is another aspect of contemporary liturgical enrichment. Frank T. Griswold states in the preface to *Enriching our Worship*:

> One of the considerations in choosing or developing the texts included in this collection has been the prayer experience of women, and the desire to honor that experience while remaining faithful to the constituent elements and norms of liturgical prayer as this Church has received and understood them.[24]

This concern represents more than a desire by the Episcopal Church to be politically correct and to reflect current concerns. The problem it is seeking to solve is theological. Liturgical language is theological language, but it is not the language of academic theology. It is the language of primary theology, of address to God. It embodies the images and metaphors in which we think of and speak to our God. This language of prayer and hymn shapes our theological understanding much more surely than articles in theological journals. Anglican theology as much as Anglican piety has been shaped over the years by the liturgy of the Book of Common Prayer.

It is almost impossible for human beings to avoid using anthropomorphic terms in thinking about God and, therefore, in addressing God in prayer. The more "real" and "personal" our notion of God is, the more anthropomorphic our language is likely to be. As Christians we properly justify the use of such language in terms of the incarnation and the *imago Dei.* Christ is "the image of the invisible God" (Colossians 1:15), and we are all, male and female, made in the divine image (Genesis 1:26).

But when we use human language to speak of God, as we must, we use it metaphorically. This is instantly recognizable when we say things like, "The Lord is my shepherd," but we tend to forget that "Lord" is as much a metaphor as "shepherd." The constant use in the liturgy of masculine metaphors for God has caused some people to attribute maleness to God. This tendency has been aggravated by the unwillingness of contemporary speech to use masculine pronouns for persons of both sexes. The problem is easy to state but difficult to solve: without betraying either the gospel or our sense of continuity with the worship of the church of the ages, we must find ways to affirm our theological belief that God is both personal (in fact, tripersonal) and without gender. In English most of our gender-free words are also abstract and impersonal. The quest will take an important place in the immediate future of liturgical revision, and it is a theological, not simply a politico-pastoral one.

Liturgical Convergence

Ecumenically, we are in a period of what has been called liturgical convergence. Starting with the same documents of the early church and with a high degree of agreement about sacramental theology, as evidenced by the "Lima Document," *Baptism, Eucharist, Ministry,*[25] and the Anglican-Roman Catholic and Lutheran-Episcopal agreements,[26] contemporary liturgical books tend to resemble each other more than they do their sixteenth-century predecessors. Whether this theological and liturgical agreement will result in intercommunion remains unclear, but both eucharistic theology and praxis will continue to develop along the lines expressed in the Book of Common Prayer 1979.

Sacramental Theology and Praxis

The Book of Common Prayer calls the eucharist "the principal act of Christian worship on the Lord's Day and other major Feasts,"[27] and it has become so in fact as well as in theory. It is the service most Episcopalians attend on Sunday morning. It is a service of word and sacrament in which the reading and preaching of the Scripture leads to the celebration of the eucharist with general reception of communion. This was the tradition of the early church and was the ideal which Cranmer, Luther, and Calvin equally sought to revive, now realized more fully than at any time since the fourth century.[28]

Striking as the eucharistic revival of the last quarter century has been, the changes in baptismal practice brought about under the impetus of the 1979 Prayer Book are even more sweeping. The implementation of the changes in baptismal practice has been slower and less universal, but they will continue to gain ground, as the church recognizes their implications for various aspects of its practice.

Most obviously, baptism has ceased to be a "private" service. It has been restored to the public liturgy of the church. Baptisms are regularly held at the Sunday eucharist, and are seen as constitutive of the life of the church and of the congregation. The baptismal feasts[29] are becoming regular occasions of public baptisms, and the "Baptismal Covenant" is being renewed by congregations when there are no baptisms. This is leading us to a new awareness that it is baptism which makes us members of the church, "the Body of which Jesus Christ is the Head and of which all baptized persons are members,"[30] as the catechism teaches. There is still reluctance to accept the full implications of the statement, "Holy Baptism is full initiation by water and the Holy Spirit into Christ's Body the Church."[31] All who have received the one baptism are members of the one church, regardless of age, sex, or denominational preference. Communicating baptized members of other churches has become routine, and the communion of children is becoming more usual, but the Ghost of Confirmation Past[32] lingers, and there is a reluctance in many to communicate the unconfirmed.

The place of confirmation in Christian initiation is unclear, and clarifying it will be important for the church. This task is complicated by a lack of clear ecumenical consensus on the meaning of confirmation, and, to some extent, by the manner in which baptism and confirmation are celebrated. Although baptisms are now generally celebrated at the Sunday eucharist, they cannot match the pomp associated with the bishop's annual visit for confirmation. Clearly, our actions indicate that this is a most important occasion. The solution to this part of the problem is for bishops regularly to celebrate baptism at their visitations, and to make the confirmations secondary.

Ministry

This is one symptom of a larger problem. We need to rethink not only the celebration of confirmation but of ordination as well, in order to make clearer our understanding of the primacy of baptism. It is difficult to participate in the ordination of a bishop without assuming that the church considers the ministry more important than baptism, and this is often reflected in the "top down" manner in which parishes and diocese operate.

The opening statement of the 1997 conference on Ordination of the International Anglican Liturgical Consultation reads:

> We affirm a baptismal ecclesiology as the proper context for understanding the nature of Christian ministry, as expressed in the ecumenical document, *Baptism, Eucharist, and Ministry.*[33]

In their second statement the conference reaffirmed the statement made by the International Anglican Liturgical Consultation in Toronto in 1991:

> Baptism affirms the royal dignity of every Christian and their call and empowering for active ministry within the mission of the church. The renewal of baptismal practice, with a consequent awareness of the standing of the baptized in the sight of God, therefore has an important part to play in renewing the church's respect for all the people of God. A true understanding of baptism will bring with it a new expectancy about the ministry of each Christian.[34]

The primacy of baptismal ministry as the foundation for all ecclesial ministry is taught in the Book of Common Prayer as follows: in the catechism, by naming lay persons first among the ministers of the church; in the ordination rites, by requiring the candidate for ordination to appear in a white vestment (i.e., a baptismal robe); and in baptism, by the words used in welcoming the newly baptized, "Confess the faith of Christ crucified, proclaim his resurrection, and share with us in his eternal priesthood."[35] Admittedly, this could be clearer, and there will be attempts to make this baptismal foundation of ministry clearer in the rites themselves, for the liturgy here lags behind the theological insight. The ministry is the ministry of the church, and attempts to isolate the theology of ministry from ecclesiology result in distortions. We have sometimes seemed to speak of the ministry, especially the episcopate, as if it were constitutive of the church, instead of the other way around. It is our common baptism that binds us to Christ and to the church, and which empowers us to confess the resurrection faith and proclaim the gospel of salvation. Ministry only exists within the community of the baptized. Texts of rites and the manner in which they are celebrated will change to make this relationship clearer.

Another issue which has been raised in connection with ministry is that of direct ordination. The pastoral impetus for direct ordination is the perception that the restoration of the diaconate is impeded by the treatment of deacons as apprentice priests. The proposal is that we abandon our tradition of sequential ordination and ordain people directly to the order to which they are called, diaconate or presbyterate. While candidates for bishop almost always would be priests or deacons, this would not be formally necessary. It would be possible to follow the example of St. Ambrose and elect a lay person bishop. The arguments for restoring this ancient practice are powerful, but the discussion is by no means concluded, and it is uncertain whether this will happen. If it does not, there will undoubtedly be some revision of the rite for ordaining deacons to make it more appropriate for transitional deacons, and some rethinking of the relationship of the orders.

The New Electric Galaxy

Finally, the General Convention resolution calls for the distribution of "any new or revised rites when authorized . . . in a variety of forms, including multimedia and electronic options." This is the first official indication that the publication of texts in a book is not all that is required. The technological changes are lagging far behind the theological, but there is at least some recognition of them, and it will be the availability of new texts in a variety of media that will make them usable. The "book liturgy" which Gutenberg made possible, while not yet obsolete, is giving way to liturgy crafted on a computer and distributed to the people for a specific occasion, without benefit of printing press or the formal authorizations previously given to the church's printed worship resources (e.g., the imprimatur of the bishop(s) or the certification of the Custodian of the Standard Book of Common Prayer).

Many of us who lived through the revision process which produced the Book of Common Prayer 1979 thought that the period of constant liturgical change was behind us. Actually it is accelerating as the church moves into the new electric galaxy. Liturgy is changing; the world is changing; theology is changing; but the gospel is not. The church is still called to proclaim it to the world.

Notes

1. Marshall McLuhan, *The Gutenberg Galaxy* (Toronto: University of Toronto Press, 1962), 124.
2. Ibid., 144.
3. Ibid., 278f.
4. Marshall McLuhan, *Understanding Media: The Extensions of Man* (New York: McGraw-Hill, 1964), 32f.
5. Louis Bouyer, *Liturgical Piety* (Notre Dame, Ind.: University of Notre Dame Press), 16.
6. Ibid., 15, 17.
7. Thomas More, *English Works* (1557), 835, cited in McLuhan, *Gutenberg Galaxy*, 143–144.

8. McLuhan, *Gutenberg Galaxy*, 144.

9. Ibid., 137f.

10. Vatican Council II, *Constitution of the Sacred Liturgy* (Collegeville, Minn.: Liturgical Press, 1963), §14.

11. Bouyer, *Liturgical Piety*, 17.

12. I have no idea what is ultimate source of this dictum. It was taught to me in confirmation class as the proper way to participate in corporate worship.

13. Bouyer, *Liturgical Piety*, 17.

14. Frank T. Griswold, preface to *Enriching Our Worship* (New York: Church Publishing Incorporated, 1998), 7.

15. Resolution C-021s, 72nd General Convention (1997).

16. Resolution 22: Christ and Culture, Lambeth (1988).

17. Resolution 47: Liturgical Freedom, Lambeth (1988).

18. "In the future, Anglican unity will find its liturgical expression not so much in uniform texts as in a common approach to eucharistic celebration and a structure which will ensure a balance of word, prayer, and sacrament, and which bears witness to the catholic calling of the Anglican communion." David R. Holeton, ed., *Renewing the Anglican Eucharist: Findings of the Fifth International Anglican Liturgical Consultation, Dublin, Eire, 1995* (Cambridge, U.K.: Grove Books, 1996), 7.

19. "Essential Worship," *Anglican Theological Review* 79 (1997): 499, 502.

20. *Wonder, Love, and Praise: A Supplement to The Hymnal 1982* (New York: The Church Pension Fund, 1997).

21. *Enriching Our Worship: Supplemental Liturgical Materials prepared by The Standing Liturgical Commission* (New York: Church Publishing Incorporated, 1998).

22. *The Book of Alternative Services of the Anglican Church of Canada* (Toronto: Anglican Book Centre, 1985), 314–316. The source is *From Ashes to Fire*, Supplemental Worship Resource 8 (Nashville: Abingdon, 1979).

23. This ecumenical version of the lectionary has been authorized for trial use in the Episcopal Church by 1974 and 1979 General Conventions. Resolution A-072a of the 1979 Convention directs the Standing Liturgical Commission (now the Standing Commission on Liturgy and Music) to prepare legislation to adopt the Revised Standard Lectionary in Advent of 2003.

24. Frank T. Griswold, preface to *Enriching Our Worship*, 6.

25. *Baptism, Eucharist, and Ministry* (Geneva: World Council of Churches, 1982).

26. Anglican-Roman Catholic International Commission, *The Final Report*

(London: SPCK/Catholic Truth Society, 1982); "The Windsor Statement," *An Agreed Statement on Eucharistic Doctrine* (1971): 9–25; *The Report of the Lutheran-Episcopal Dialogue, 2nd Series*, 1976–1980 (Cincinnati: Forward Movement, 1981), 25–29, 145–148.

27. The Book of Common Prayer (New York: The Church Hymnal Corporation, 1979), 13.

28. While the celebration of the eucharist remained normative in both East and West until after the Reformation, the reception of communion by the congregation, except on Easter, had become uncommon. Zwingli's establishment of quarterly Communion at Zurich actually quadrupled the number of annual receptions of the sacrament for most people.

29. The Book of Common Prayer, 312: "Holy Baptism is especially appropriate at the Easter Vigil, on the Day of Pentecost, on All Saints' Day or the Sunday after All Saints' Day, and on the Feast of the Baptism of our Lord (the First Sunday after the Epiphany). It is recommended that, as far as possible, Baptisms be reserved for these occasions or when a bishop is present."

30. Ibid., 854.

31. Ibid., 298.

32. The rubric found in earlier prayer books forbidding the communion of the unconfirmed is in the minds of many Episcopalians. This is a place in which church discipline and presumably doctrine have changed, and many people either do not realize this, or find the concept of change in this matter difficult to accept.

33. David R. Holeton, ed., "Anglican Orders and Ordinations: Essays and Reports from the Interim Conference at Jarvenpää, Finland, of the International Anglican Liturgical Consultation, 4–9 August 1997," *Joint Liturgical Studies* 39 (Cambridge, U.K.: Grove Books, 1997), 50.

34. David R. Holeton, ed., *Growing in Newness of Life: Christian Initiation Today* (Toronto: Anglican Book Centre, 1993), 236.

35. The Book of Common Prayer, 855, 524, 308.

Who is like God? On Not Mistaking the Pointing Finger for the Moon

Robert M. Cooper

I beseech you, in the bowels of Christ,
think it possible that you may be mistaken.
—*Oliver Cromwell*[1]

"Michael" is a name. It is the name of an archangel. "Michael" is also a question: "Who is like God?" "Michael" or "Big Michael," the bell, sounded that preemptive question, the wonderfully Hebrew challenging question at least three times daily to those of us who spent some years among the oaks, hickories, sugar maples, sumacs, and birches of the lovely woods along the eastern shore of Upper Nashotah Lake. This briefest suggestion of a description of a place, in which only a few species of trees are named, is so powerfully important because it is always the particulars of our lives that are dear to us. Alfred North Whitehead spoke of this in terms of "the incurable 'particularity' of a feeling" in his *Process and Reality.*[2] I offer this example of particularity: nobody else smells just like the persons we love and touch. We do not recall generalities in order to dwell upon them even if it were possible to do so! We dwell on particularities. Such a marvelous word is "dwell": "poetically man dwells on this earth," says Friedrich Hölderlin, "*dichterisch, wohnen der Mensch auf dieser Erde*" (from his "*In Lieblicher Bläue*").[3] Good poetry gives us back again the particulars of our irreducibly, "incurably particular" individual lives, and having, in the exchange, enhanced them in such ways as to convince us that we'd never truly seen or known them before deepens our lives in amazement and gratitude. Now we recognize them anew as though we had never seen our lives before. We remember what composed our dwelling places, and we hold on to our memories of them, however frail and "wrong" (inaccurate) they may be.

Our memories may figure powerfully in our fantasies but we never fantasize about abstractions, or about what I have just referred to as "generalities." (Against such putative generalities, I would, in another idiom, oppose Aristotle's "eachnesses.") We may *think* in general, but we *fantasize* about, with, and by means of particulars. For example, I fit at least these classes or categories: male, ordained, married, parent. I was born from a particular mother in a particular time and place, ordained in a particular communion, am married to a particular woman, and am father of particular children. I do not—and no one else does—live a life in the abstract or in general, and that fact alone is one reason why so much theology is jejune; it too often doesn't attend to particulars. Everything that I and we do and everything that happens to us happens to us in the particularity of my flesh, your flesh. The sentimentalist and the ideologist, as we shall see further on, pretend to be exceptions to this. Sigmund Freud demonstrated a strong sense of this truth when he vouchsafed to his sister-in-law, Minna Bernays, "Money doesn't make us happy as adults because we never fantasized about it as children (*Kinder*)." He was right, of course, because we can do nothing directly practical with abstractions, a truth Shakespeare knew long before Freud drew a breath across his lips at his mother's breast. The words are Othello's concerning the comparative worths of his purse and his name: " 'tis [his purse] something, nothing / 'Twas mine, 'tis his and has been slave to thousands."[4] Money, because it is an abstraction, cares for nothing and for no one, and it isn't even a practical thing until it is exchanged. Recall the opening words of the speech from which the two lines quoted above were taken: "Good name in man and woman, dear my lord [Iago], / Is the immediate jewel of their souls." This is an essay, among other things, about God as "the poet of the world," as Alfred North Whitehead says in *Process and Reality*.[5] God is the poet of the world, fashioning us through the desire we pursue in our particular existences. Whitehead claimed that God "is the poet of the world, with tender patience leading it by his vision of truth, beauty and goodness." Further, this essay concerns the widening fissures in the "jewel of our souls." Soul is the inexplicable and irreducible interiority of each of us or, as Owen Barfield says in his widely influential *Saving the Appearances*, "that inner life of feeling and memory . . . constitutes"[6] the soul. I will argue later that soul finally is God's knowledge of each of us.

Now our emblematic question is "Who is like God?" It is a question with more than a single proper answer. The God whose word (*logos*) is pitched in the tent of human flesh is the God who continues to come to us (certainly, an odd image.) It is God who comes from the future, who beckons today, even while at the same time coming certainly toward us. It is God's Jesus who set this expectation for us, who told his messengers to tell us that he is ahead of us, going before us into Galilee. While God's prophet, Moses, may have come down from the dreadful mountain with tablets of the law, the God who is coming to us even now is not coming with an armful of propositions, sentences, or confessional statements, stuff that we are supposed to believe, under pain of death—or worse. God gets to be God. That is awesome enough, and there are more than enough death-dealing propositions already—left over from the Hebrew camp and calf ranch at the foot of Sinai—to continue to build an unfailing supply of idols (an unending fountain of idols springing forth from the human mind, according to John Calvin). We—not God—are the fashioners of creedal statements, the writers of creeds and confessions, the framers of "personal belief statements," and on and on. But propositions have their uses, and the principal one of them we see in Whitehead's insistence that "propositions are lures for feeling,"[7] lures of God, we may say, for our feeling the world and finding God in the midst of our experience. Hence, human discourse—theological or otherwise—cannot well do without propositions (statements, declarative sentences, etc.). I doubt that I can get though a single day without, say, five or six of them.

There is an exhaustion in the land, an exhaustion with propositions about what (usually) personal behavior God is alleged to approve or disapprove, and the proposers always find powerful founding propositions for their views in the translations of certain ancient Hebrew and Chaldee texts or in more recent Greek ones. And there is another problem here, too, in attempting to find the right way to put these ancient Near Eastern texts into a plethora of tribal languages and come up with a Christian lingua franca. (We never could get it right even in the centuries between the years of Jesus and Chalcedon in 451, when we couldn't quite find the right words to yield the exact formulation of very important Greek ideas about a Triune God, the person and natures of Jesus, etc.: *traduttore e traditore, davvero*: the translator is a traitor, indeed.)

How long will it take millions of African Christians to decide that a relatively small group of North American and European sisters and brothers have the right, orthodox, arrangement of propositions about "gender," "sexual orientation," and "sexual preference" when it's taken many of them a century and a half to disabuse themselves of the deadly concept that God is a European—preferably an English—white man? And it doesn't oversimplify terribly to note here that Constantine ordered the bishops of the Christian world (his Empire) to decide what is orthodox and what is not in the controversies raging over the views of the presbyters Arius and Athanasius, etc. Decide the matter. Tell him their conclusions. He would enforce "right opinion" in the world.

There was extraordinary pressure both imperial and ecclesiastical-theological to settle the matter, to achieve a conclusion that purports to be what was believed always everywhere and by all: a fatuous, inhuman, ungodly and death-dealing notion. Lionel Spencer Thornton, C.R., made the claim over eighty years ago in a sermon in Cambridge, England, that the New Testament "is a literature of experience." What had it been like to try in the earliest years of Christian believing to feel the power of the Jesus movement in the Near East? Thornton's insight was that those earliest experiences produced a literature, "a literature of experience."[8] The early ecumenical councils also, doubtless, produced a host of various experiences, but their greatest products were documents comprised of human claims, mostly in propositional form, and we still try to take them for what they are (were?). Such propositions have to be voted on, and so we count and we purport to quantify what cannot be quantified (viz., experience).

It is God who comes to us from the future. And if God has a language, there is nearly nothing in the Bible to lead us to believe anything other than that it is the language of poetry, poetry framing and fashioning mystery, images, metaphors, myths, songs, and—yes—also the blessings and the excoriations and denunciations of the prophets. Much of what I shall have to say here will perhaps be found by some to be only a re-vision of the differences between apophatic and kataphatic language about God. Were I expected to choose, I choose apophatic. I also prefer an icon over a blueprint any day ("by the breath of my mouth were the heavens made"). I opt for faith before belief. (It is a great loss that we cannot say in proper English "I faith you" or "I faith God," but if we could, it would be something like, "I 'heart' you.") But belief isn't faith, and never will be.

Always watch out when "believe" is followed by one of the deadly prepositions "that" or "in." Continuing to try to be an Anglican is not easy, but the effort does provide a strong possibility to go for the inclusive ("catholic") over the exclusivity of confessional statements which lead into party spiritedness, spiritual sloganeering, cant, and the re-laying of the foundation for a new flat-earth society where we worship an untranscendent God. Don't we already know that neither liturgy nor ritual thrive on propositions, except those of an endeictic (demonstrative) or ejaculatory sort? We will find our only lasting life-giving unity in the solemn and playful actions of the liturgy and in our constantly caring for Jesus' "little ones," and not in theological (propositional) concordats. There simply never can be a truthful unchanging set of statements about anything, and none about the God whose very Hebrew name is a verb form. Whatever is not changing is dying or is dead already. We've known this in the West since Greek antiquity when much was deeply understood about "generation and decay." It took Western fascists thousands of years to bring us a human institution, a Reich, that would last 1,000 years, i.e., forever. Hitler's architect, Albert Speer, brought the world buildings of monumental ugliness to display to the world the ossified, unchanging and, therefore, dying souls of its builders.

Propositions are more fragile than buildings—let's say that they are tabernacles, booths, tents of a sort. But propositions, however accurate they may be, destroy the interplay of light and shadow in our lives as we actually live them; they can remove altogether the penumbra and the chiaroscuro. Here propositions would displace us from, dislocate us from, where we feel the blood pound, where we can feel our very own mothers and fathers, and where we sense God's rhythm already alive in our world and, at the same time, coming to us anew from the future; the God who gestures one moment toward everything we never saw before in "most this amazing"[9] creation and in the next moment arms open to gather us close and say to us something so wonderful and so ordinary as, "Now. Let's go eat and drink. You can't imagine how much all of you delight me!"

As I write these words, finer ones—in my judgment, among the most splendid sentences in the English language—are coming to my mind. From the penultimate paragraph of Flannery O'Connor's story "Revelation":

> Until the sun slipped finally behind the tree line, Mrs. Turpin remained there with her gaze bent to them as if she were absorbing some abysmal life-giving knowledge. At last she lifted her head. There was only a purple streak in the sky, cutting through a field of crimson and leading, like an extension of the highway, into the descending dusk. She raised

> her hands from the side of the [hog] pen in a gesture hieratic and profound. A visionary light settled in her eyes. She saw the streak of a vast swinging bridge extending upward from the earth through a field of living fire. Upon it a vast horde of souls were rumbling toward heaven. . . . Yet she could see by their shocked and altered faces that even their virtues were being burned away.[10]

My own image, of course, is that of God coming to us from the future. The God who comes to us is a God who embraces us, who has killed the fatted calf, who calls us to eat and drink together, and be taken delight in. After all, we are earth's dust with breath (*nephesh*) in it, and such a dust the coming God continues to take delight in! This it is a very odd God indeed who does these things with us as with friends and yet remains a God revolted by likenesses.

Nothing else is God but God (*YHWH*) and no idol can be brooked among the Jews. The God of the Jews is a God whose name is in a verb form, and that is so because the nature of that God is never to stand or be still. Every verbal formulation must also be understood to be either actually or potentially an idol. In our centuries-long *odium theologicum*, what we have actually witnessed is a war of idol with idol in the clash of theological propositions. The swords of such clashes don't just make theological sparks fly; they have terribly been used also to kill the living would-be faithful. (When you have won an argument, what have you won? Your life itself or mine comes to be wanted in satisfaction.) Every theological form(ula) or formulation is already well on the way to idolatry as soon as it is off of the lips of any living creature. In Arnold Schoenberg's unfinished opera, *Moses und Aron*, Moses comes down from the mountain and —finding the "miraculously" and spontaneously formed golden calf in the Hebrew camp—stammers out these words to Aaron and to the others, "*unsichtbar unvorstellbar Gott*," invisible [and] unrepresentable God! "*Unvorstellbar*," yes, even in speech. George Steiner writes:

> *Unvorstellbar*, that which cannot be imagined, conceived, or represented (*vorstellen* means, precisely, to enact, to mime, to dramatize concretely), is the key word of the opera. God is *because* [Steiner's emphasis]. He is incommensurate to human understanding, because no symbolic representation available to man can realize even the minutest fraction of His inconceivable omnipresence. To know this, to serve a Deity so intangible to human mimesis, is the unique magnificent destiny which Moses envisions for his people.[11]

For us English speakers, this is an unbearable God, always beyond human conceptualization and articulation: an intolerable austere God for whom poor we find ourselves craving fleshly, human form for our sakes. Yet, this is not a counsel of despair, for there is another necessary biblical perspective, and, so, we come 'round now to the second of our answers to the question posed by the name of "Michael," who is like God? That answer, of course, is: we are—each of us is—like God, and I began to see that truth with a special clarity in my years of work as a pastoral psychotherapist.

In the course of carrying out those years of work, I once found myself writing in my personal notes (not for the person's official file) the following:

> It comes over me today with a sickening recognition that too often I am baffled by what/how a patient presents herself, that I have found myself asking myself, "What am I looking at here?" That is, I had been looking for a diagnosis, a classification, a safe place to store data and order it. The truth that sickens is the realization that the question is altogether wrong. The life-giving question is, rather, "Who am I looking at there?" or better "Who am I with?" Hence, whatever else is at stake here is a secondary issue at best. Above all, I am looking at a person. None of the persons with whom I work fits any "what?" no matter how many of the diagnostic categories they meet. I've always known that, of course, but what has stunned me today is that my perceptions have evidently been too frequently fitted to a template of diagnosis, and worse, done so with the knowledge that insurance will not pay without there being a diagnosis.

"Who is like God?" She is and I am; "my patient" and I are like God. We are godlike. Each of us is an irreducible mystery. Neither of us is, nor will either of us ever be, more than partially known. It may be that it is my business, my profession to be the knowing one with regard to her life, to lead her more and more into self-knowledge. We all learn that, in the good (the life-giving) therapeutic encounter, the two persons are continuing to be born. These encounters are profoundly Socratic, maieutic, midwife-ish. Martin Buber was right that in conversation the bread of human compassion is passed from one person to another, but we also give (re-)birth to each other. (We can, of course, be death-dealing also, but that is not our topic here.) For my part, I have wanted to understand myself to be God's agent in the therapeutic encounter and try to live into the understanding that it is God in every instant who is continuing to fashion us out of chaos into creatures who are forming further into the likeness and the image of the innermost divine nature—male and female at the heart of God (Genesis 1:27).

Important values are contained in what has just been said. Let me state the principal one directly: there is nothing on earth, nothing in the world, more important than a human being. Kant used the term "thing-in-itself," averring correctly that persons have worth (because they cannot be replaced) while things have price (because they can be replaced), and H. Richard Niebuhr, in his *Radical Monotheism and Western Culture*, referred to people somewhat coldly as "value centers." Niebuhr's crucial turn on the concept of value, however, had come earlier in his *Christ and Culture*, where he claimed that with Jesus Christ we encounter in later Christian life and behavior "a principle that presents itself in the form of a person."[12] Niebuhr is addressing two difficulties which we face in trying to "define the essence of . . . Jesus Christ": "The first is the impossibility of stating adequately, by means of concepts and propositions, a principle which presents itself in the form of a person." Here, of course, is our by-now familiar theme of the relative poverty of propositions. It is, nonetheless, essential to notice how principle is a value wearing a particular recognizable kind of clothing. Every value can be dressed—and they always are dressed—as a principle. Among other things that we use principles for is to enable us to judge correctly the policies (maxims) by which we purport to lead our lives by those principles which we claim to be our highest values. One important venue in which these values appear so prominently is in the therapeutic encounter. Here is how that works, in the terms of our preceding discussion. Persons are mysteries and they are the most valuable entities in the world. That sentence (proposition) expresses our highest value. So what policy may warrantably (by that principle) be seen to be consonant with it?

An example from my previous work will lend a useful reply to our question and will indicate a worthy policy. Here I understand that a worthy policy will guide my behavior, much as would what Kant called "the maxim of my action." My questions here are not rigorously but rather rhetorically, suggestively framed. What would it be like if the person with whom you are counseling experiences you as God? What kind of God would he find you to be? Consider how he would tell of you, recount his time with you. (We readily see here lineaments of the golden rule, of course.) What do you consider that his recounting of your aspects, qualities, defects, and characteristics would come to? Could you recognize yourself and him in his recounting? Would you be revolted, awed, or charmed by how you are seen? What would it be like for you if you—and perhaps the rest of us—had a God like you, like you are in your behavior? Yes. Ad hominem pleading? Charles Saunders Pierce's remark must be considered. He writes, "In the light of the successes of science to my mind there is a degree of baseness in denying our birthright as children of God and in shamefacedly slinking away from anthropomorphic conceptions of the universe."[13]

Martin Gardner, writing many years ago in the magazine *Scientific American*, remarked, "Statistics are people with the tears wiped off." Statistics express quantification, and, in that expression, they undergird the criterial categories of the *Diagnostic and Statistical Manual of Mental Disorders IV*, which figured strongly in my earlier quote from my professional notes. The quote echoes the poignant hollowness in that lifelessness that Wordsworth gestured toward in showing us how we must murder in order to dissect a life. In analyzing (literally, a loosening and taking-apart) our inner life, we destroy the very life we would examine. "Though nothing can bring back the hour / Of splendour in the grass, of glory in the flower."[14] We seem not to be able to dispense with diagnostic categories (and that is not completely a bad thing, of course). Persons cannot be reduced to diagnostic categories or criteria; at best, such terms can yield only a partial truth. They are akin to that vulgar partial truth that we human beings are (only) what we eat. An apparently sophisticated cousin of this vulgarity circulates among those who insist that our current knowledge of the neuro-chemico-physiology of the brain adequately explains the complexities of human love, eros, and sexual behavior. Years ago, C. S. Lewis referred to such as "men without chests."

William James gives us a special clarity of insight when he writes in *The Varieties of Religious Experience* (1902) that "Knowledge about a thing is not the thing itself." I would add that all ideologists mistake their ideas for the world, for what James called "the thing itself," just as I would go on to say, the sentimentalist—who is the ideologist's first cousin—mistakes a thought or an idea for a feeling. Roger Shattuck has said that, "Hard as we may try, we cannot be both inside and outside an experience or a life—even our own."[15] The sort of knowledge that James is speaking of is, after all, knowledge formed as propositions. A proposition is never the thing itself. A world of propositions does not make a world. We only reduce a certain proposition to another proposition or to a set of propositions.

Wordsworth understood this in a special way by showing us how we can miss the very world in which we walk about, in his poem "Peter Bell":

> A primrose by a river's brim
> A yellow primrose was to him,
> And it was nothing more.[16]

The Zen way of putting this matter of propositions and things is the most trenchant, the most elegant, cautioning us against mistaking the pointing finger for the moon. Yet quite wonderfully, as Whitehead has it, a proposition "is a lure for feeling, [is] the eternal urge of desire."[17] Otherwise, propositions are only *about* the world.

Ludwig Wittgenstein in his seemingly laconic, diffident, almost Zen-like way has tried to show us that a given proposition about the world, e.g., "the moon is shining brightly this morning" leaves unsaid (i.e., not put into propositional form) all else that might be said about the world. One sentence is not everything that can be said about the world. We can think of it this way: all of the inarticulate world craves at any moment to come to voice ("The whole creation is longing [Whitehead's "desire"]" to come to voice). In human speech and gesture the world does come to voice. This we can also see in psychoanalytically oriented psychotherapy: the "patient's" body is, in the course of the therapeutic process, coming to voice; as each one finds words for her life, her body speaks, and to that small extent at least, each of us becomes the unique, the singular, incurably particular life, the irreducible life that each of us is, who each of us is beyond the diagnoses, categories, propositions—and yes—even beyond that binding language of internal and external realities, subjective and objective knowledge. We can recover an ampler view of our experience than our varieties of knowledge afford.

The most trenchant way of putting these matters of knowledge, proposition, experience, etc., came from what, for me, was a pleasantly surprising source; it has become my *locus classicus.* In Book IV of *Institutes of the Christian Religion*, John Calvin, concerning himself with "the true nature of the corporeal presence in which believers partake through the Spirit" of communion bread and wine, writes,

> Now, if anyone should ask me how this takes place, I shall not be ashamed to confess that it is a secret too lofty for either my mind to comprehend or my words to declare. And to speak more plainly, I rather experience than understand it.[18]

In Calvin's Latin text of this passage, these are the words of the last quoted sentence: *experior magis quam intelligam* ("I experience more than I understand"). I do not have the French text, but the Latin will bear the two translations which I have given. I simply prefer the latter for the sake of euphonious English, and, in either rendition, the claim is both powerful and important. Our experience is greater, ampler, than our knowledge. Our experience is other than our knowledge because experience cannot be reduced to it.

Our Western epistemologies have for at least 2,000 years come to wreckage again and again upon one rock or another until we have despaired of ever finding a seaworthy craft. We've been like Odysseus despairing of ever again coming home to Ithaca and the place of his heart. Some of us have despaired of dwelling ever again "poetically on this earth." I do not pretend that Paul Roubiczek, in his important 1969 book *Ethical Values in the Age of Science,*[19] settles all epistemological problems. It was written in part to stand in the face of what he claimed about our age, that it lives by "a tacit agreement to exclude the absolute." Roubiczek's book does arrange and then effect a marriage between Kant and Kierkegaard.[20] Although I am neither recapitulating nor reasoning through his long argument, I hold that Roubiczek enables us to avoid being destroyed either by Scylla or Charybdis. Let us say that Scylla (the Rock) is objective knowledge of external reality and that Charybdis (the Whirlpool) is subjective knowledge of internal reality. Say further—to stay with our Homeric metaphor—that Roubiczek is Aeolus who gives us the bag of winds, which bag, let us say, contains his "essential knowledge" of "primary reality." Calvin himself was a scholar of the classics and of Seneca in particular, so it is not too great a stretch to claim that Calvin may have had a glimmer—by his own age's remarkable light—that essential knowledge is coming forth from his encounter with primary reality, and that the occasion for its occurring was the Lord's Supper: "I experience more than I understand."

While I have adverted here to some images from Homer's *Odyssey,* I have found myself in very good company indeed. Paul Scherer said years ago, in an address at Yale Divinity School while speaking of certain passages in the letters of Paul, "where grammar cracks grace erupts." So I began to learn that when literary and philosophical business-as-usual breaks down, we find ways to go on. What else can be done when, as Whitehead puts it, "philosophy may not neglect the multifariousness of the world—the fairies dance, and Christ is nailed to the cross."[21] It is no failure to go to metaphor and image, for they can restore deep breathing when we are exhausting ourselves in thin air. Whitehead, in his turn, had long observed how his own greatest mentor, Plato, turned to metaphors and myths at crucial times in the *Dialogues*, when dialectic had played itself out and become lost or floundering. Plato turned, on the one hand, to the metaphor of the cave and the sun and, on the other hand, away from the light altogether and to the darkness of the underworld where Minos and Rhadamanthus are consulted[22] or where the ring of Gyges the Lydian is used to illuminate certain issues about justice that might otherwise have remained opaque.[23]

There is a final turn to make before I close. In 1 Corinthians, Paul claims that our present knowledge (*gnosis*) is partial knowledge, knowledge in part (*ek merous*, as in *meros*, the joint of a finger or toe), but then he says—in God's time "I will know even as I am now known" (*de epignōsomai kathōs kai epegnōsthen*) (1 Corinthians 13:12). I take this to mean, at least, that the best that you and I can hope for is to know ourselves as God knows us, that that will be the highest knowledge attainable here or hereafter. It is how God knows me that matters most, now and always, how God knows you. Experience is greater than knowledge and can never be reduced to knowledge of any sort or degree. We have access to the primary reality of each other through essential knowledge. Perhaps we can use John Henry Newman's motto here: *cor ad cor loquitur*, heart speaks to heart, speaking of the heart's own knowledge and in the heart's own language.

This essay began in the woods, so to speak, and perhaps it is fitting that it conclude there. Here is a portion of a poem written in those same woods on the eastern shore of Upper Nashotah Lake, and published twenty-five years ago:

> A nose he has for what lives in the dead.
> I have felt it play upon my dimmed face
> The cumulated bundles of its sour breath:
> The banded wisdom breathed by all my race.
> I have almost been—been understood to death.[24]

And I have been understood! I can say now that I have also been understood (partially) to life. A patient for five years of psychoanalytically oriented psychotherapy comes to understand much and to be much understood. But none of us in this world is ever altogether understood except by God. From a human worldly point of view, psychoanalysis will be ended, of course, by death. As long, though, as one remains alive, his psychoanalysis can or must, indeed, go on. Sigmund Freud understood this well as his 1937 paper "Analysis Terminable and Interminable"[25] shows. During my practice of pastoral psychotherapy, I used to propose—more as a playful "thought experiment" than as something fully serious—to several persons with whom I had met weekly for from five to seven years, that they try to imagine what it would be like to tell someone else what those hundreds and thousands of hours over our years together had been; what we discussed; the dead-ends; the insights and the changes that they had experienced. Instantly, they saw it as impossible, an endless undertaking.

This thought experiment never failed to put me in mind of one of the ways in which Kierkegaard ridiculed the preposterously inadequate systematic theological efforts of some of his Danish Hegelian antagonists. Thomas C. Oden, in his *The Parables of Kierkegaard*, calls one selection from that author's works "The Dog Kennel by the Palace": "A thinker erects an immense building . . . that he himself does not live in . . . but [he lives] in a barn alongside of it, or in a dog kennel, or at the most in the porter's lodge."[26] And while we may live in "the household of language," as Heidegger has taught us, and while it is the case that no longer do we write large-scale systematic or dogmatic theologies, we all know—we're smarter than the three little pigs—that our houses of straw and of sticks are constructed of propositions.

The turbulent wake of the always-coming-to-us God is always loosening our propositional houses, shaking their foundations. This is the much heard expression, "in the final analysis." But note well, this is the final loosening, which is happening all of the time and always challenging the security of our every dwelling place. This God of turbulence is "the poet of the world," "the great companion—the fellow-sufferer who understands."[27] "Thus God in the world is the perpetual vision of the road which leads to the deeper realities."[28]

Notes

1. Cromwell to the Church of Scotland, August 3, 1650.
2. Alfred North Whitehead, *Process and Reality: An Essay in Cosmology*

(New York: Harper and Bros., 1960), 420. This volume is Whitehead's Gifford Lectures 1927–28 at the University of Edinburgh.

3. Friedrich Hölderlin, *Poems and Fragments: A Bilingual Edition*, trans. Michael Hamburger (Ann Arbor, Mich., 1967), 600–601.

4. William Shakespeare, *Othello*, 3.3.157–8.

5. Whitehead, 526: "[God] is the poet of the world, with tender patience leading it by his vision of truth, beauty, and goodness."

6. Owen Barfield, *Saving the Appearances: A Study in Idolatry* (New York: Harcourt, Brace and Co., 1954), 124.

7. Whitehead, 522: This "lure for feeling [is] the eternal urge of desire". In Whiteheadian language, "This doctrine of 'feeling' is the central doctrine respecting the becoming of an actual entity" (356). Whitehead said somewhere that *Process and Reality* is "a critique of pure feeling," but I can no longer find the reference.

8. Lionel S. Thornton, "A Sermon in Great Saint Mary's Church," *The Cambridge Review* 47 (1927): 256–258.

9. e. e. cummings, *Poems 1923–1954* (New York: Harcourt, Brace and Co., 1954), 464.

10. Flannery O'Connor, *Everything That Rises Must Converge* (New York: The New American Library, 1967), 185f.

11. George Steiner, *Language and Silence: Essays on Language, Literature, and the Inhuman*, (New York: Atheneum, 1974), 135. For a helpful recent discussion of the matter of idolatry and the Jewish people, see Moshe Halbertal and Auishai Margalit, *Idolatry*, trans. Naomi Goldblum (Cambridge: Harvard University Press, 1992). The reader who has a particular care about these matters will want to consult Avivah Gottlieb Zornbierg, *Genesis: The Beginning of Desire* (Philadelphia: The Jewish Publican Society, 1995).

12. H. Richard Niebuhr, *Christ and Culture* (New York: Harper and Bros., 1956), 14.

13. Charles Saunders Pierce, *Collected Papers of Charles Saunders Pierce*, vol. 1, ed. Charles Hartshorne and Paul Weiss (Cambridge: Harvard University Press, 1931), 316. Pierce was a North American contemporary of Whitehead.

14. William Wordsworth, "Ode: Intimations of Immortality," st. 10.

15. Roger Shattuck, *Forbidden Knowledge: From Prometheus to Pornography* (New York: St. Martin's Press, 1996), 334.

16. William Wordsworth, "Peter Bell," st. 50

17. Whitehead, *Process and Reality*, 522.

18. John Calvin, *Institutes of the Christian Religion*, ed. John T. McNeill and trans. Ford Lewis Battles, vol. 21, bk. 2 of *The Library of Christian Classics* (Philadelphia: Westminster Press, 1960), 1403.

19. Paul Roubiczek, *Ethical Values in the Age of Science* (Cambridge: Cambridge University Press, 1969).

20. See Robert M. Cooper, "Plato and Kierkegaard in Dialogue," *Theology Today* 31 (October 1974): 187–198. In this article I "map" Roubiczek's schema sketched here upon (1) Plato's "divided line" and (2) Kierkegaard's *Stadier* ("stages").

21. Whitehead, *Process and Reality*, 513.

22. See Plato, *Apology*, 41A; also *Gorgias* and *Laws*.

23. See Plato, *Republic*, 2.359Dff. Extraordinary myths also are found in other works by Plato, *Symposium*, *Phaedrus*, and elsewhere.

24. Robert Cooper, "I Understand," *The Greensboro Review* 13 (Winter 1973): 12.

25. Sigmund Freud, Standard Edition, vol. 23, ed. James Strachey (W. W. Norton & Co., 1976), 209–253.

26. Thomas C. Oden, *The Parables of Kierkegaard* (Princeton: Princeton University Press, 1978), 21. The source is Kierkegaard's pseudonymous Anti-Climacus, *The Sickness Unto Death*.

27. Whitehead, *Process and Reality*, 532.

28. Alfred North Whitehead, *Religion in the Making* (New York: Meridian Books, 1960), 151. I have, in a related manner (though with a different focus), treated some of these matters of poetry, place, language, and God in my "The Native Tongue of God," *Anglican Theological Review* 76 (Spring 1994): 197–211.

The Crack in the Heart

Alan Jones

When Helen Keller was asked if there was anything worse than being blind, she said, "Yes. Having no vision!" Perhaps it was ever thus, but there is some truth to our having the end-of-the-millennium jitters about the fate of the human project. How does one find and embrace a vision of life which is true and sustaining in a world where old boundaries, from those of the nation state to those of the religious traditions, are breaking down? There's a great deal of talk now about conversation (not idle chat, but "deep listening"). In times of radical upheaval, radical attentiveness is called for. There's a Tibetan saying: "The crack in the heart lets the mystery in." One of the major themes of the spiritual life has to do with how the heart is cracked open by compunction and repentance. They ready the heart for renewal.

What is behind the concern for the future of theology and the Episcopal Church? People within a particular tradition—in our case, Anglican—are often tempted to think of themselves as especially beleaguered or especially privileged. We hear of dwindling numbers, read of scandals and controversies, and think these things peculiar to us. It is closer to the truth to say that something larger and more far-reaching is going on in all the great religious traditions. It is a mark of narcissism that we think we have been singled out by some peculiar virus designed specifically to attack the Episcopal Church.

In the Sunday edition of *The New York Times*, we read: "There's a striking change in the nature of faith and worship in America. There's a new breed of worshiper . . . looking beyond the religious institutions, and integrating spirituality into ordinary, everyday life . . . God is being decentralized."[1] This decentralizing has left many of us puzzled, confused, and angry. What does one do when the religious divisions are not so much *between* the traditions as *within* them. A recent survey by the Fetzer Institute estimated that there are about 44 million Americans who belong to a growing constellation of people who link their own spiritual growth with a life of service and social action. (Anglicans might take comfort in the fact that only six percent could be considered New Age!)

How do Anglicans talk to each other? Some retreat into a kind of boutique-Anglicanism and call it traditional; others seem to have no historical imagination at all. I preached some time ago in a conservative parish and was castigated at the coffee hour by a woman who wished Eisenhower were still president and that she were still thirty years old. "Before you people came along with the new Prayer Book, women priests, and all these homosexuals, we had this *darling* little church!" "The darling little church" (if it ever existed) has gone forever. The disgruntled wealthy can still buy their "traditional" religion and the ahistorical liberals can spin off into space. But what about the rest of us?

I believe that we need to recover a sense of the sacred and embrace a mystical and experiential approach to the life of faith—a new traditionalism. I also believe that Anglicanism has yet to come into its own. It's the only tradition that enables me to be a Christian. In spite of all the unfair jokes about the *via media* making us flaccid and bland, Anglicanism is capable of sustaining the kind of critical conversation needed in these times. Anglicanism is confusing to extreme Protestants and Roman Catholics. I have tried to explain it as the Zen Buddhism of the West because we believe that schism is a greater sin than heresy. We need antidotes both to fundamentalism and to liberal reductionism, and a sustained and faithful conversation will bring us to a new place.

There are several levels of discernment we need to examine. First, the context: what is it like to be a human being at the end of the twentieth century in North America? Are we committed to an unchanging reality or to the possibility of the radically new? Do we believe more in the "perennial philosophy" than in the "evolution of consciousness"? How far should we respond to the culture and how far should we contradict it? I live in San Francisco, and every Saturday morning that I'm in town I go to the local farmers' market for fresh produce and for a salmon-BLT sandwich. I look over the crowd and wish my own congregation were as colorful and diverse. I struggle with the challenge of how a cathedral in a highly secular city can be true to itself while being wildly hospitable to the culture. I think of myself as a traditionalist but am distressed by people whose views of the tradition are limited to their own narrow experience. Writing of the church as being like Noah's ark, one of the eighteenth-century English bishops confessed that he was "as much distressed by the stink within as the tempest without." So it is for many of us.

Secondly, we need to develop a good sense of smell with regard to where life really comes from. "O God make us truly alive!" was a prayer of the early church. We now live in a time of terrible disconnections, and one of these is the separation of theology from life. The ancient wisdom made a connection between prayer and theology. Theology was experimental. Theology made a difference in everyday life. Theology pushed one into conversion. The temptation is always to retreat behind a merely *verbal* orthodoxy which kills lively conversation. Words: the area where we cause the greatest harm and feel the most vulnerable; and real and imagined wrongs poison our social life. Theology makes no sense outside liturgy. Conversation is a form of worship. We do not know how to worship and pray together and that's why the church fails to engage in true theological debate.[2]

What makes us behave the way we do? How is our sense of self and our behavior transformed? The spiritual life is the drama of the soul's choice and the work of the theological imagination is an important discipline to help us choose how we are going to live. Not long ago Emperor Akihito of Japan was snubbed and insulted during his visit to England by lines of veterans with their backs turned. In contrast, Eric Lomax, a war veteran with good cause to hate the Japanese, sought out the man who had tortured him for operating a forbidden radio set as a prisoner of war. Together he and his torturer visited the museum at Nagasaki in memory of one of the torturer's relatives who had died when the city was destroyed by an atomic bomb. What made Eric Lomax work for and effect a costly act of reconciliation? What makes others nurse and live from their resentments? Another veteran of the Japanese conflict wrote of his conversion experience after the bombing. Peering at the charred bodies of the dead and not completely dead in a Japanese dressing station, he felt pity. He was able to pray for the Japanese dead as well as for his own. "Humanity, however distorted, is one," he said, echoing the words of Irenaeus: "There is one human race wherein the mysteries of God are fulfilled." The work of the theological imagination (which, in turn, shapes the conversation) is for the restoration of our loveliness—the likeness of God in each of us. The theological enterprise is for the sake of the conversion of mind and heart in our confrontation with God and with ourselves.

Our way forward, then, will be by attentive conversation—"by prayer and fasting." If this sounds too idealistic, we should remember that transformation doesn't require everyone or even the majority to take part. A critical mass will change the world. Eleven or twelve will do. Sometimes the miracle of true theology happens—the miracle of integration when the words cease to be mere words and a true transformation occurs and one's moral sense is inflamed by beauty and joy. God, then, is not a matter of debate but of love, and in the process we are changed. Theology truly becomes *experimental.*

Jan van Ruysbroeck tried to describe this in *The Adornment of the Spiritual Marriage*:

> In this storm of love two spirits strive together: the spirit of God and our own spirit. God, through the Holy Spirit, inclines himself towards us; and, thereby, we are touched in love. And our spirit, by God's working and by the power of love, presses and inclines itself into God: and, thereby, God is touched. From these two contacts there arises the strife of love, at the very depths of this meeting; and in that most inward and ardent encounter, each spirit is deeply wounded by love. These two spirits, that is, our own spirit and the Spirit of God, sparkle and shine one into the other, and each shows to the other its face. This makes each of the spirits yearn for the other in love. Each demands of the other all that it is: and each offers to the other all that it is and invites it to all that it is. This makes the lovers melt into each other. God's touch and his gifts, our loving longing and our giving back: these fulfill love. This flowing back and forth causes the fountain of love to brim over; and thus the touch of God and our loving longing become one simple love.[3]

Experimental theology is as much concerned with *how* beliefs function in the psyche as with the beliefs themselves. I am not as sure as I once was of the gulf that is supposed to exist between the believer and unbeliever, between the Christian and the non-Christian. There is plenty of evidence of the cruelties of the so-called orthodox. Are there Christian truths and Buddhist truths? Or, are there simply truths? St. Thomas Aquinas reminds us that truth, from whatever source, is of the Holy Spirit. It is important to know why we cling to certain beliefs. It isn't always for reasons of "orthodoxy" (even if we think it is so) that we hold certain beliefs dear. They serve a purpose, often a dark one—perhaps, to make us feel safe or superior. This is an insight that many of the non-Christian traditions (especially Buddhism in its American form) have grasped better than we have.

I find myself pulled in two ways. I am propelled back into Christianity by many of my growing non-Christian contacts and friends. I am pushed away from Christianity by those who profess such a repellent form of the faith that I cannot find a place for myself in it. Two recent examples of contact with non-Christians will serve to illustrate my first point. I was invited to take part in a video presentation under the general title of *Compassion* at the Esalen Institute at Big Sur. The subject matter was hardly controversial, and the other two panelists sounded interesting. They were both monks: one Benedictine, the other Thai Buddhist. The Benedictine monk was an old friend, and I was looking forward to meeting a monk from Thailand. Ajahn Amaro turned out to be an Englishman from Kent who had been confirmed by the Archbishop of Canterbury. Traveling in Thailand as a student, he exchanged his dry and lifeless Christianity for the life of a Buddhist monk. We have since become good friends, and two issues come up for me when we talk. One is the fact that he has a deeper and more intuitive grasp of the gospel (and, by the way, of the practice of the Christian life) than he had as a formal Christian.

As the speaker at a big one-day conference sponsored by the Vedanta Society, I felt welcome and very much at home. However, I was brought up short by a statement that reminded me that I am, after all, caught up in the Christian tradition. The swami from India let slip a statement that drove me to my Christian roots. In answer to a question about the nature of evil in reference to the Holocaust, he said, in passing, "Of course, the creation itself is evil." Whoops! Suddenly, I knew who I was without judgmentalism and with a clarity that would have eluded me if I had avoided the conversation with people from another tradition. If it is true that the deep divisions in religion nowadays are not between the great religious traditions but within them, what do we do about the real differences that do exist? My experience with the Vedanta Society (hospitable and edifying) that pointed out to me in no uncertain terms that I was firmly in the Christian tradition. Nevertheless, both within and between the traditions, a deep division exists between the contemplatives and literalists, between those committed to tribalism and those dedicated to transformation.

What, in the end, do we have to tell each other? I would like us to reassure each other that we can trust each other enough to meet in the silence and dare to enter our own shared solitude. Thomas Merton wrote that you will then "truly recover the light and the capacity to understand what is beyond words and beyond explanations because it is too close to be explained: it is the intimate union in the depths of your own heart, of God's Spirit and your own secret inmost self, so that you and He are in all truth One Spirit."[4]

As for my being repelled by other Christians, examples, alas, are legion. Two minutes of TV evangelism is sufficient. Pat Robertson suggesting that God will send hurricanes and even a meteor to punish the city of Orlando, Florida, for being hospitable to gay people, is enough to send me back to Buddha. God, protect me from my fellow Christians. At Pentecost last year (God has a sense of humor), Grace Cathedral in San Francisco was picketed by members of a Baptist church in Kansas. The church has a website called www.godhatesfags.com.

There is nothing in what they do or who they are that touches me in the area of faith. What passes for much of the Christian religion in our culture is nothing but pervasive paranoia and pathology. One of the "negative" tasks of the theological imagination is to make us aware of the way in which our view of the world and of each other is distorted by the contagion of our own obsessions, aggressiveness, and ambition. Thomas Merton tells us: "If we attempt to act and do things for others or for the world without deepening our own self-understanding, our own freedom, integrity, and capacity to love, we will not have anything to give to others. We will communicate nothing but the contagion of our own obsessions, our aggressiveness, our own ego-centered ambitions."[5]

Iris Murdoch wrote, "Man is a creature who makes pictures of himself and then comes to resemble the picture."[6] We rightly worry about the external world—with the environment and ecology—but what of our neglect of our own inner nature? Jacob Needleman writes, "Along with the obvious crimes our culture is committing against the natural world, we would be wise to remember that the main crimes are the crimes against our inner nature. From these inner crimes all the outer evil arises."[7] Our unacknowledged despair for the world and its future erupts into violence —both outward and inward.

We are all into making pictures. How do we know in which movie to invest? Are we willing to take on the psychological and social risks of "the examined life"? The unexamined life, we are told, is not worth living. If this is so, we will all be in for a time of discomfort as we open ourselves up for examination. We won't see what's there without "attention" and "wonder"—the instruments of true moral perception. Again, Iris Murdoch reminds us, "Love is the extremely difficult realization that something other than oneself is real. Love . . . is the discovery of reality." Which brings me full circle to the issue of the church needing to recover and, in some cases, discover for the first time, the mystical and the experiential—what was disparagingly referred to in the seminary where I taught as "piety." The prevailing view was that, since it cannot be taught, it should be left to the individual to come to some private arrangement with God. Hence, the vast majority of the clergy have had to muddle through to find some kind of focus and discipline for their lives. Our lack of discipline and training now uncovers new forms of spiritual poverty.

Transforming conversation to break the heart open has its price but is easier than we think. We are not totally lost. We do have a place to stand. For example, we may recall G. K. Chesterton and his struggle with depression, a two-year period of internal darkness.

> When I had been for some time in these, the darkest depths of contemporary pessimism, I had a strong inward impulse to revolt; to dislodge the incubus or throw off this nightmare. But as I was still thinking the thing out by myself, with little help from philosophy and no real help from religion, I invented a rudimentary and makeshift mystical theory of my own. It was substantially this: that even mere existence, reduced to its most primary limits, was extraordinary enough to be exciting. Anything was magnificent compared with nothing. Even if daylight were a dream, it was a day-dream; it was not a nightmare . . . or, if it was a nightmare, it was an enjoyable nightmare.[8]

Chesterton found encouragement in Robert Louis Stevenson's refusal to go mad:

> He stood up suddenly amid all these things and shook himself with a sort of impatient sanity; a shrug of skepticism about skepticism. His real distinction is that he had the sense to see that there is nothing to be done with Nothing. He saw that in that staggering universe it was absolutely necessary to stand somehow on something . . . he did seek for a ledge on which he could really stand. He did definitely and even dramatically refuse to go mad; or, what is much worse, to remain futile.[9]

Perhaps it's all simpler and harder than I thought? Our task is straightforward. All we have to do is rehabilitate language with the development of a new epistemology. The question now is not "What can I know?" but "Who can I trust?" We know that words can be both pathetic and poisonous. We learn painfully that we can say true things falsely. The word is either spiritual truth or verbal excrement. With us it is often the latter. The truth without love is a lie. Trust is undermined by narrow intellectualism as well as anti-intellectual emotionalism. We think words are robust. We like the cut and thrust of debate, the malicious and irresponsible cleverness of the academic, the rabble-rousing rhetoric of the demagogue, the rigid precision of ideologues. But is there anyone or anything I can trust? Does language have to be the prison and prism of ideology, with issues of gender, class, race, and sex eviscerating and decentering our humanity? Must all our conversations be reduced to a battle for power?

Think about what kills the conversation for you. What about myth versus fiction? Are we simply to exchange the old patriarchal myths for the new feminist fictions? Think of the ever-increasing list of things we *can't* talk about: abortion, euthanasia, homosexuality. We not only need a good dose of irony in our conversations but also an awareness of its abuse. Sometimes (as happened with Chesterton), we need to doubt our doubts. Julie Burchill tells us, "Life is much easier to deal with if you strain it through Irony—the muslin of the mind." As we "swim in the rubbish-filled tide of popular culture," perhaps we need a thick skin to bear the new sarcasms, the kind of mind that records everything but understands nothing? I hope not. The new commandment seems to be, "Above all, be unaware of the ideological squint through which you see the world." The cultured despisers among us tell us, "It is safest to believe in nothing at all, or at least place all beliefs in quotation marks, and so live your life through a posture of ironical detachment." The slogan is, "Intellectuals of the world unite; you have nothing to lose but your brains."

Have we reached the historical moment in which all beliefs are suspended? Is the church in a last gasp of the past with its bossy precepts and its claim to know who we really are? Haven't we moved from Christianity to "Christianity"—the movie version? Life is merely episodic, like a soap opera:

> Any part can be replaced by an equivalent which will "do just as well," and the attachment of people who try to live by faith, that is people who are attached to particulars—to wives and husbands, and lovers, to projects and ambitions, to sacred places and "imagined communities" —begins to seem faintly comic, especially in playback.[10]

Perhaps we have to risk looking faintly comic and take the risk of trust in the light of our commitment to renew the public conversation?

There are two marks of someone caught up in the godly conversation: a commitment to self-knowledge and an acknowledgment of dependence on others. Our fear of the dark shadows thrown on the wall by bright lights has paralyzed us. We know how horrible "enlightened" people can be, but no matter how hard we try to live in a world in which "everything is relative," we almost always manage to smuggle a few unannounced universal values through the back door. Then, a different kind of silence is imposed on us—the silence of impotence rather than the silence of new possibilities. The first silence kills the conversation and can end in violence. The second silence is a kind of pregnancy which allows the Word to come to term in us so that it can be born in due time.

What are the conditions of the passionate conversation? We come back to the risk of trust and love. Roberto Unger writes, "Trust is the climate in which the passions flourish. Forgiveness is the antecedent and preserver of trust."[11] The conversation, marked by love, is "an act of grace devoid of condescension or resentment"[12] and mutually reinforces our dependence on one another while giving us proper self-possession. In short, this kind of conversation builds up the body of Christ.

Listen to Roberto Unger:

> In the course of social life people shoot at each other in an endless flurry of poisoned arrows: all the accumulation of these real and imagined wrongs progressively reduces the area of free movement in social life; we feel drastically limited in the initiatives we can take by our earlier history of animosities and resentments. By the same token we are prevented from running the risks of vulnerability that render faith, hope, and love possible. The experience of empowerment, of listening to and contemplating one another . . . makes it easier to tear the arrows out. It weakens the force of mean-minded concerns founded upon fear and self-contempt. It enables us to imagine ourselves connected in untried ways to other people, even those who have harmed us or whom we have harmed.[13]

Finally, I want to emphasize that my aims are very modest. They are based on the conviction that God's generosity and abundance always triumph. God reigns. The last thing I want to do is to be part of a movement to "save" the Episcopal Church or the Anglican Communion. There's an old adage: "Pursue integrity and identity will follow." This is as true for institutions as it is for individuals. One of the hardest lessons for us to learn is that mere empowerment isn't enough:

> [Empowerment] cannot deliver the happiness it promises. It does not teach forgiveness of others because it is blind to the imperative of self-forgiveness. It fails to accept the real, exposed, tottering individual, housed in a dying body and dependent on uncontrollable others for all the tangible and intangible supports that enable him [or her] to sustain a presence.[14]

Aldous Huxley wrote, "Even among those whom nature and fortune have most richly endowed, we find, and find not infrequently, a deep-rooted horror of their own selfhood, a passionate yearning to get free of the repulsive little identity to which the very perfection of their 'adjustment to life' has condemned them."[15] Is not our culture infected with what Huxley called, "The partial damnation of everyday life"? Many of us are horrified by our own selfhood. This is one of the dark things we share in common—the one thing that the gospel addresses with uncompromising joy.

Helen Keller was right. Having no vision is worse than being blind. Vision comes when the crack in the heart lets the mystery in. It's time for the cracking open of hearts.

Notes

1. *New York Times*, 7 December 1997.

2. It is a great blessing that Episcopalians have in Frank Griswold a Presiding Bishop with a theological imagination grounded in a strong liturgical and prayer life. However, if recent exchanges between Bishop Spong and his detractors are anything to go by, we still have a long way to go in modeling the "great conversation" demanded of us.

3. See the E. P. Dutton edition (London: 1916), alt.

4. Rob Lehman (The Fetzer Institute), *The Heart of Philanthropy* (paper privately circulated).

5. Ibid.

6. See the essay, "Metaphysics and Ethics," in Iris Murdoch, *Existentialists and Mystics* (New York: Allen Lane [Penguin], 1998), 59.

7. Jacob Needleman, *Time and the Soul* (New York: Doubleday, 1998), 147.

8. See Dudley Barker, *G. K. Chesterton: A Biography* (New York: Stein and Day, 1973), 61–62.

9. Ibid., 61.

10. Roger Scruton, *Times Literary Supplement*, 18 December 1992, 3–4.

11. Roberto Unger, *Passion: An Essay on Personality* (New York: The Free Press, 1984), 73.

12. Ibid., 221.

13. Ibid. (paraphrase).

14. Ibid., 75.

15. Aldous Huxley, "Substitutes for Selfhood" in Jacqueline Hazard Bridgeman, ed., *Huxley and God* (San Francisco: HarperSanFrancisco, 1992), 117.

When Worlds Collide: A Comment on the Precarious State of Theology in the Episcopal Church

Philip Turner

Introduction

What relation is there, or ought there to be, between theology and the everyday life of the church? Proper as the question may appear, it is not high on the agenda of very many Episcopalians, clerical or lay. It is sad but also true that we have witnessed over the past years a steady decline in the place of theology at all levels of the life of the Episcopal Church. Attention has moved steadily away from instruction that draws the baptized members of the church more deeply into a *common* knowledge and love of God (which is the proper subject matter of theology in all its forms) and toward various forms of social action or pastoral practice designed to address either the perceived ills of society or the experience and perceived needs of individuals. In this matrix of social concern and personal need, theology tends to become at best a "tag on"—a way of justifying a particular set of social concerns or a way of giving religious meaning to a personal history. Its focus is not primarily the knowledge and love of God as mediated through the common life of the church but the provision of ad hoc justifications for pursuing a limited range of personally selected and very earthly goods.

In our present ecclesial culture, theology tends to follow along behind commitment and experience and is trotted out, if the occasion demands, to provide a blessing for what our commitments and experience have already told us is right and good. It is no wonder, therefore, that theology is something of an orphan child in the parish, allowed to make only limited public appearances. It is no surprise, either, that theology in its more formal and academic guise is, on the whole, viewed from within the parish context as remote, abstract, and of no real value for the everyday life of the church.

I have spoken thus far of the Episcopal Church, but generalizations of this sort apply across the spectrum of American Christianity. In his book, *Kicking Habits*, Thomas Bandy notes five theological motifs that characterize what he calls the "thriving" churches in America.[1] Although these theological motifs are characteristic of churches outside the established denominations, Bandy describes motifs increasingly common to all forms of American Christianity, Episcopalianism included. The striking thing about these "theological motifs" is how widespread they are and how remarkably anti-theological each of them turns out to be.

Bandy terms the first motif "sentinel theology." Sentinel theology is more of a stance than a thematic account of Christian belief and life. It urges believers to adopt the stance of "a watchman on the ramparts" proclaiming, not impending doom, but "the *experience* of a proximate holiness (or state of health) that is just over the horizon."[2] The second motif is "healing." The new theology does not emphasize the imitation of Christ and the suffering such imitation involves. Rather, it holds out a promise that, by walking with Christ daily, life can be transformed in a way that will allow one to "kick the habits" that ruin life's pleasures. It follows that the third motif is "walking with the risen Lord." The emphasis of the new theology is neither an exploration of basic Christian doctrine nor an ethical imitation of Christ. Its focus is rather "healing *in association* with Christ."[3] Given this emphasis on the daily experience of healing and the constant presence of the Christ in one's personal life, it is not surprising that the fourth motif is a "return to Eden." Salvation does not involve dying and rising. It consists of the return to a state that "combines final and complete insight into one's own unique selfhood, affirmation, and cleansing of that selfhood, and taking one's appropriate place in the eternal scheme of the universe."[4] The final motif is "the Damascus road." In Bandy's words, "Authentic religion is not about information [read theology]. It is about experience."[5] It is better to speak of this experience as a transformation in the direction of life than as a conversion in which one has to assimilate new information or an adequate and full account of Christian belief and life.

Here is an understanding of the Christian religion that has little need for theology. Indeed, Bandy insists that thriving churches will downplay the importance of doctrine (and, more broadly, theology) altogether. They will, in fact, reserve such teaching for those who may develop an interest in that sort of thing. Theology in a "thriving parish" thus becomes the preserve of a special interest group—one that has rather rare tastes.

Theology: What in the World Is It?

Now if circumstances are even close to the way in which I have described them, one must ask, as Bandy does, if parishes have much need for theology. Is there any sense in which theology might have importance for parish life that is more fundamental and more extensive than the ad hoc, limited, and rather instrumental role it now seems to play? The answer to this question depends on what we understand the nature of theology to be. If it turns out that theology is in fact what most people now take it to be, the answer certainly is "no." However, if—as I believe—theology is properly a very different sort of enterprise than our popular notions display, then a renewed and reformed presence of theology within parish life will bring about nothing less than a collision of worlds!

One can get a sense of the force of the collision by asking how we *ought* to understand the nature of theology. In his book, *The Nature of Doctrine*, George Lindbeck asks what we mean when we speak of church doctrine.[6] He notes that theological theories of religion and doctrine can be divided into two primary types: the first "emphasizes the cognitive aspects of religion and stresses the ways in which church doctrines function as informative propositions or truth claims about objective realities"[7]; the second focuses on what Lindbeck calls the "experiential-expressive" dimension of religion, according to which doctrine is comprised of symbolic expressions that display "inner feelings, attitudes or existential orientations."[8]

Lindbeck suggests what he considers a more excellent way—one he calls the "cultural-linguistic" approach to religion and doctrine. Religion and doctrine can best be understood as analogous to languages and the forms of life to which they are tied. Thus, doctrine should be understood in the first place not as a set of truth claims nor as a set of expressive symbols (though it contains both) but as a form of culture that is comprised of "idioms for the construction of reality and the living of life."[9] In this view, doctrine may be compared to the grammar of a language. It comprises a set of "communally authoritative rules of discourse, attitude, and action."[10] Accordingly, doctrine is, not a means of personal communication, but the necessary medium for becoming part of a culture. As one cannot be a person apart from a culture, so one cannot be a Christian person apart from the language and forms of life that give identity to such a reality.

The Place of Doctrine in the Life of a Parish

Bandy's picture of the theological motifs characteristic of what he calls a "thriving church" all suggest that an "experiential-expressive" view of doctrine is now dominant within the churches. I have suggested that such a view of doctrine is the most pervasive one within the Episcopal Church as well. However, one must admit that there has been a negative reaction to the recent ascendancy of experience over received teaching. Disturbed by what they hold to be a too-frequent dismissal of classical Christian doctrine by those who refer first to experience as the basis for their theological positions, a growing number of Episcopalians are turning to yet another Lindbeck option, the view that doctrine is simply a number of propositions that convey objective truths about God and the world. The problem is that this strategy—while it does uphold a notion of truth that is more objective than the subjective views of the "experiential-expressivist" school—tends to substitute assertion for convincing argument and, consequently, does little to convince those for whom experience constitutes the primary avenue to truth. More seriously, the propositional view tends to turn doctrine into a sort of theological border patrol whose *sole* function is to keep out illegal (theological) immigrants.

If these two views of doctrine are inadequate and if Lindbeck's third view of the nature of doctrine is, in fact, more adequate, how, then, does giving theology its proper place in the life of a congregation bring about this dramatic collision of worlds to which I referred? If doctrine is best understood as definitive of a culture, as comprising its language and forms of life, then the chief pastoral function of a parish is to provide a place in which those who believe in Christ learn how to speak the Christian language well and how to inhabit more fully the forms of life that go along with it. It is not the parish's chief function to provide a religious idiom for the expression of personal experience and commitment. Neither is its chief function to provide a series of propositions that serve to ward off falsehood. It is doctrine that allows people to have the sorts of experiences Christians have and so become adults who, as members of a single culture, both speak as Christians ought to speak and care responsibly for the forms of life that give Christian people their distinct identity.

The learning of doctrine (which includes both the ability to read the Bible as Christians read it and the ability to give expression in word and deed to the witness to God contained therein) is not the preserve of a special interest group, or simply a vehicle for giving religious expression to personal commitments and experience, or some surgical mask designed to keep out religious germs; at the most basic level, the learning of doctrine is—along with worship, witness and communion—the primary means of forming a distinct people.

Viewed in this way doctrine (which is the most basic, but not the only, form of theology) comes to resemble, as in the movie *Armageddon*, an asteroid that threatens to annihilate the parish as we know it. On the whole, Americans do not view the congregations to which they belong as assemblies in which one must be reborn into a new people and then learn, like a little child, a new language, a new form of life, and a new range of experiences. They tend instead to view their congregations as service organizations whose function is to meet their spiritual needs and provide for them a medium for the expression of their particular sensibilities, talents, and commitments. Because of their liturgical nature, Episcopal churches may seem an exception to this rule for the simple reason that liturgy tends to focus attention on common forms of belief and life. More often than not, however, Episcopal parishes do not follow up on this apparent emphasis in their programmatic offerings. In fact, their programs go in a rather different direction, providing a range of options that serve more to satisfy individual tastes and interests than to draw people into a common form of belief and life.

If one adopts a cultural-linguistic view of the nature of doctrine, however, one's view of the proper function of a parish must change, and the nature of one's programs must change as well. Theology is a word with multiple denotations and connotations. At its most fundamental level, for Christians, it refers to those common beliefs and practices that yield the knowledge and love of God as made known to us in Christ Jesus and mediated through the common life of the church. It is comprised, as Lindbeck says, of those "communally authoritative rules of discourse, attitude, and action" that give definition to God's people. If the New Testament is to be believed, one cannot learn those rules apart from others who share them; and one cannot learn them unless one becomes once again a little child who must be brought to maturity through the tender care of those who have a more mature grasp of the language and its attendant forms of life.

At its most fundamental level, therefore, theology is, or ought to be, a form of pedagogical practice by means of which Christian belief and practice are handed over and by means of which Christian experience is opened up. The congregation is clearly the primary locus for this incorporating and community-forming activity. It is the "place" where many become one body, not only because they share one meal, but also because they learn to speak one language and live one form of life.

A Practical Proposal about Theology in the Parish

The minute one begins to look at the place of theology in the parish in this way, one is confronted with enormous challenges. In the first place, until recently and despite a constitutional insistence on the separation of church and state, the grammar of Christian life and belief was passed on from generation to generation in a very diffuse manner through a broad spectrum of social institutions, not all or even most of them ecclesial ones. As time has passed, Christian content increasingly has been excluded from public forms of communication and education. In the second place, as I have said, the spirit of the age awakens ever and ever more private views of religious belief and practice. Despite the longing for community, the very notion that common forms of language and life take precedence over individual taste and opinion seems increasingly unacceptable.

American religion, like most other American institutions, has a real genius for marketing and so has responded creatively to these circumstances. It has more or less gracefully accepted its dethronement as the provider of a common moral and religious foundation for American society and has thrown its energies into developing "program churches" which market a wide range of religious and social activities that appeal to a wide range of distinct "publics."

The fact that church attendance has remained as high as it is in America is a testimony to the success of these efforts. Nevertheless, they have resulted in a splintering of congregations and churches into subgroups based on interest. As a means of justifying this sort of inner segmentation, appeal is made increasingly to an "experiential-expressive" view of doctrine and theology. Counter appeals to theological proposition—propositions that carry the authority of the ages and supposedly are binding on all—do little to diminish this experiential view of the nature of religious truth. In fact, the result is little more than a stalemate between contending forces.

If, however, doctrine is best understood as the grammar of a language and form of life that is definitive of a common culture, then we must not view the reaction of the churches in America to their changed social circumstances as a creative adjustment, but as a misconception of, or even defection from, what they ought to be up to. Strange as it may seem, the 1979 Book of Common Prayer suggests a very different view of the place of theology in the parish than either of these common points of view—one that lies far closer to the "cultural-linguistic" view of theology than to either the "experiential-expressive" or the "propositional" view.

The 1979 Book of Common Prayer gives the sacrament of baptism a far more prominent place than that accorded by the 1928 Prayer Book. In doing so, it highlights its public rather than its private nature. It seeks in numerous ways to focus attention on the fact that one does not enter upon a personal and very private journey in baptism. Rather, one becomes part of a people who share one Lord, one faith, one baptism, and one God who is father to all. The promises contained in the baptismal covenant unite all Christians in a common affirmation of faith that Jesus is both Lord and Savior.[11] United in this faith, Christians define themselves as those who "continue in the apostles' teaching and fellowship, in the breaking of bread, and in the prayers."[12]

It is this promise that defines what it means to accept Christ as Savior and follow Christ as Lord. It is this promise that makes faith in Christ as Savior and obedience to Christ as Lord a common rather than an individual enterprise. It is this promise, also, that implies that doctrine and theology are best understood on the basis of Lindbeck's "cultural-linguistic" model. After all, to continue in a teaching and form of life means, at a minimum, to have a grasp of this teaching and its attendant forms of life. Consequently, it is this promise that makes theology central rather than peripheral to the life of a congregation. The promise suggests that, first of all, congregations ought to be asking themselves, not how to appeal more adequately to individual tastes and commitments, but how they can become a body of people who faithfully pass on (in forms suitable to their own time and place) that language and those forms of life that comprise the apostles' teaching and fellowship, the common meal they shared and the prayers they prayed. If the question of the place of theology in the life of a congregation were posed in this way, the present agenda for the life of most congregations in America would have to change almost beyond recognition.[13]

Other Dimensions of the Place of Theology in the Life of a Parish

To this point I have spoken of theology in its most basic form—as church doctrine. Theology has other forms that naturally grow from and supplement this most basic one. Doctrine must be explored, explained, and defended. If indeed doctrine provides a grammar on the basis of which one can learn to understand and live out a form of belief and life, it is important to explore the full range of its implications, to clear up the confusions it may produce and to respond to the objections it may call forth. Consequently, theology properly takes on more complex forms. We know these as historical, dogmatic, systematic, philosophical, and apologetic theology.

This essay is not the place to go into the differences between the forms that theology can take. It is enough to say that doctrine, which is intended to provide access to the knowledge and love of God, must be explored, explained, and defended if it is to be convincing and life-forming. Theology in these forms, thus, also has an important place in the life of any congregation, and it is not one that can be left to "interest groups." Continuing in the apostles' teaching and fellowship, in the breaking of bread, and the prayers will inevitably draw all Christians at one point or another toward theological questions that can be avoided only at the cost of spiritual health.

There is no reason for it, but Anglican churches have, from a time shortly after the initial stages of the Reformation, tended to place in the hands of their clergy the major responsibility for seeing to the presence in the parish of theology in these more complex forms. Indeed, at their best, Anglican clergy have seen this sort of theological knowledge and pedagogy as a central aspect of effective pastoral care. However, thirty-seven years as a seminary professor have convinced me that, despite assertions to the contrary, theological knowledge of this kind is infrequently considered central to pastoral care. The vast majority of theological students now come to seminary because they want "to do ministry." The churches and dioceses that send them want the same thing, and by "doing ministry" they do not mean passing on, exploring, explaining, and defending the language and forms of life that define Christians as Christians. They mean responding sensitively to the needs and interests of others as these needs and interests are presented. They mean "feeling the pain" and offering empathy and concrete help to those who perceive themselves in need. The ordained ministry thus becomes a therapeutic profession and, given this view of the ordained ministry, it simply follows that an "experiential-expressive" view of doctrine is about all one needs.

Theology and Episcopal Authority

If indeed theology in the parish has to do with passing on, exploring, explaining, and defending the language and forms of life that lead to *common* knowledge and love of God, then it becomes important for the church as a whole to see that the theological knowledge passed on, explored, explained, and defended at the parish level is not out of accord with the teaching and forms of life passed on by the apostles.

History displays various arrangements by which the church has sought to insure that, in the countless times and places its traditions are passed on, it remains of one mind in a bond of peace. Anglicans guard the fidelity and unity of the church through the office of the bishop. Through the office of the bishop, theology in the parish is related to theology in the church universal. The job of a bishop is complex, but its primary aspect is to see that its language and forms of life of the local church are in accord with those of the apostles. It is, however, just this aspect of the office of bishop that has moved steadily out of sight within the life of the Episcopal Church. The inability and unwillingness of our bishops to take the steps necessary to see that the passing on, exploration, explanation and defense of the language and forms of life that constitute Christian identity have been displayed plainly by their inability and unwillingness to address the various theological crises that have come before the Episcopal Church in the last fifty years, and by their insistence that respecting difference is more fundamental to the life of the church than finding a common mind. They have not taken the steps necessary to see that the passing on, exploration, explanation, and defense of the language and forms of life that constitute Christian identity are in accord with the mind of the church universal.[14] The result of this abdication is a sort of theological congregationalism at the level of both parish and diocese—a form of congregationalism that has an affinity for the "experiential-expressive" view of doctrine and theology and a preference for a form of dialogue that leads to the recognition that each person, each parish, and each diocese may hold its own truth no matter what such diversity might do to the unity of the mind and life of the church, rather than a form of dialogue that leads (as did Plato's) to the overcoming of falsehood.

A Conclusion

As its subtitle suggests, the conclusion of this essay is that theology occupies a very precarious place in the present life of the Episcopal Church. Its place is precarious because an inadequate view of the nature of theology has taken hold of the mind of the church. This inadequate view, which Lindbeck terms "experiential-expressive," has taken hold, however, because of a false understanding of the nature of the church itself—an understanding of the church that pictures it as a service organization designed to meet human need and interest. In the course of displaying these inadequate notions of church and theology, I have suggested that they cannot be met adequately by a propositional view of doctrine designed to provide a protective shield against invading armies. It is more adequate to hold that the church comprises a people and that theology is a practice meant to carry, over time and space, the language and forms of life that make this people distinctive. I have suggested as well that, should the Episcopal Church decide to adopt the view of theology in the parish I have proposed, its adoption would involve a collision of worlds that would set the Episcopal Church at odds with both the general and the ecclesial cultures of the American people. It would involve a change in the way we view the congregation, a change in the way we view the ministry of the church, and a change in the way we view the exercise of authority within the church. Our history has not prepared us for changes such as these, but they are changes that I believe are required if we as a church are to be faithful to vows that we took or that were taken on our behalf at baptism.

Notes

1. Thomas Bandy, *Kicking Habits: Welcome Relief for Addicted Churches* (Nashville: Abingdon Press, 1997), 213–226.
2. Ibid., 215 (emphasis added).
3. Ibid., 218 (emphasis added).
4. Ibid., 220.
5. Ibid., 222.
6. George Lindbeck, *The Nature of Doctrine: Religion and Theology in a Postliberal Age* (Philadelphia: The Westminster Press, 1984).
7. Ibid.,16.
8. Ibid.
9. Ibid.,18.
10. Ibid.
11. The Book of Common Prayer (New York: The Church Hymnal Corporation, 1979), 302–303.
12. Ibid., 304 (cf., Acts 2:42).
13. For an account of how the agenda might change if theology, understood as I have sought to display it, became central to a congregation's understanding, see Philip Turner, *A Rule of Life for Congregations Based Upon the Baptismal Covenant,* (Cincinnati: Forward Movement Publications, 1997). For information about a group of parishes seeking jointly to make this rule the basis of their parish program, write St. John's Episcopal Church, 134 North Broad Street, Lancaster, Ohio 43130. Or you may contact the following E-mail address: jmreade@computech-online.net.
14. For accounts of the decline of the episcopal office in respect to doctrine and theology in the church, see Philip Turner, "Authority in the Church: Excavations Among the Ruins," *First Things* (December 1990): 25–31; "Communion, Order and the Ordination of Women," *Pro Ecclesia* (Summer 1993): 275–284; "Episcopal Oversight and Ecclesiastical Discipline" in Ephraim Radner and R.R. Reno, eds., *Inhabiting Unity: Theological Perspectives on the Proposed Lutheran-Episcopal Concordat* (Grand Rapids: Wm. B. Eerdmans Publishing Co., 1995), 111–133; "Episcopal Authority in a Divided Church," *Pro Ecclesia* (forthcoming). See also R. R. Reno, "An Analysis of the Righter Decision," *Pro Ecclesia* (Summer 1996): 271–281.

Source of Light and Life

John M. Gessell

> For you are the source of light and life, you made us in your image, and called us to new life in Jesus Christ our Lord.
> —*Preface of the Lord's Day 1, The Book of Common Prayer*[1]

Anglicanism, as a way of being Christian in the world, is characterized by at least three principles: recognizing the distinction between what is necessary to salvation and what are, though important, matters of indifference; repudiating infallibility; recasting essential formulations of dogma in light of continuing experience in the world. These are the bases of the comprehension we should value as Episcopalians of Anglican inheritance.

The Rev. Dr. Rowan Greer recently observed that Anglicans

> must seek to be honest. And to be honest requires us to understand the whole of our tradition with all its contradictions and failings and above all with its reluctance to adopt any clear earthly authority. Perhaps what Anglicans of all stripes ought to have in common is a willingness to place infallibility where it belongs, in God and His Christ.[2]

In this way, Anglicanism was freed from carrying the weight of infallibility on its shoulders. Since its separation from Rome, the genius of Anglicanism has resided in its struggle with the "development of doctrine." While this phrase is borrowed from John Henry Newman's famous 1836, *Essay on the Development of Christian Doctrine*, it characterizes the theology of many of the best-known English and American Anglican divines.

Newman's *Development of Christian Doctrine* wrestled with the tension between historical consciousness and the revelatory self-disclosure of the transcendent God to human faith in finite time. With the growth of the objective understanding of the tradition by the church, faith has always had to be revised in light of the growing insights of reasons and experience which lie beyond conceptual thought and plain language. Newman's was the most thorough and original attempt to explain the development of doctrine, an analysis of how reason works and the way ideas develop historically in society.

F. D. Maurice sought to reinterpret the meaning of baptism in the social ethics of his time (social ethics that Charles Gore would later call the "social question"). Gore himself issued three volumes in his *Reconstruction of Belief* series. The Lux Mundi School contributed profoundly to late-nineteenth-century Anglican theological consciousness by framing the questions to be addressed by serious scholars of faith.

Following in their train into our own day, we can note constructive Anglican theologians including William Temple (in his last years), J. A. T. Robinson, James A. Pike, Gibson Winter, William Spurrier, John Shelby Spong, Norman Pittenger, and William Stringfellow, this last, arguably the most influential Anglican biblical theologian of our time.

In his 1971 address to the annual convention of the Diocese of Southern Ohio, Bishop John Krumm stated, "Basic to all our considerations in the church these days is a recovery and re-statement in contemporary language and in the light of the new human situation in our time of the timeless Gospel of Christ." In calling for the engagement of theology with contemporary life, Krumm was writing one more paragraph in the Anglican development of doctrine.

On reflection, I am persuaded that the contemporary reluctance and refusal to heed Krumm's admonition has contributed to the intractable conflict in the Episcopal Church today. Opposing the Anglican tradition of the development of doctrine is a crude theological fundamentalism cherished by undereducated bishops and clergy who seem unable to understand church history, the function of the theology, and the project of moral theology, ethics, and moral discourse. The current attempt to raise moral precepts (inevitably and by nature temporally and topographically conditioned) to the level of unchanging doctrine is perverse and arises out of cultivated theological ignorance. The future of theology in our church must open the way forward beyond this unnecessary conflict and impasse.

Frederick Buechner, in the introduction to *The Sacred Journey*, writes "that all theology, like all fiction, is at its heart autobiography, and that what a theologian is doing essentially is examining as honestly as he can the rough-and-tumble of his own experience with all its ups and downs, its mysteries and loose ends, and expressing in logical and abstract terms the truths about human life and about God that he believes he has found implicit there."[3]

To further this discussion, then, I shall begin with the premise (amply demonstrated in the history of doctrine) that theology is autobiographical, the effort to make sense out of life, which otherwise would be nonsense (to paraphrase Archbishop Temple).

To point the way ahead I shall indicate a foundational theology extruded from my own experience of wrestling with the gospel and reflecting on its meaning in my life in the world and my life shared with companions in my world. I trust that these foundations are securely anchored in Scripture and faithful to the tradition forged in nearly two millennia of theological reflection. Applying the three principles adumbrated at the head of this essay—distinguishing essentials from adiaphora; foreswearing any temptation to ascribe infallibility to created beings; and attending to the serious task of continuous revision of the forms of belief in light of reasoning faith and of faithful reason—we can continue the theological task given to each generation: the development of doctrine.

Doctrine

What does it mean to live theologically as the people of God in the world? What does it mean that we are a people gathered by his Spirit to be a people before him, to worship and to serve him all our days and to serve his creatures everywhere, responsive and responding to his world as it comes upon us? The following nine points constitute a theological outline for grappling with these questions.

1.

Where the Word of God is spoken and heard, there is the church, the faith community. The church is constituted as the people of God called out from the world, gathered by God's grace, to be in his service as his people in the world. Within this tension of being called out in order to be, they are called to hear and to respond to his Word addressed to them. The church is constituted by this Word of God, where this Word is spoken and where it is heard and responded to. It is the community of the resurrection faith: there the church is (and nowhere else), witnessing to the fact and presence of the risen Lord and to the fact that only in him is the inexorable power of the law of sin and death destroyed.

Theologically, the church is a gathered people and not a voluntary society. The mode of regarding the church sociologically as a voluntary association leads to the privatization of Christianity, where faith becomes a purely personal matter and where the tension and conflict between gospel and the world are avoided. But the gospel, as witnessed by both Old and New Testaments, does not distinguish private and public virtue—personal and social ethics. They are inseparable; and the privatization of the gospel does violence to the body of Christ, becoming an occasion of its secularization. The increasing secularization of the church occurs, further, as the church conforms to the "American way of life" and studies institutional survival instead of the revelation of God's judgment and reconciliation with the world. The church's uncritical relationship to capitalism, imperialism, and militarism has sapped its virtue and its vital relationship to its own gospel tradition. The result has been its loss of credibility and integrity. The secularization of the church only reduces the anxiety of those who claim its membership and who have been programmed for living in a secular society, its sensual self-indulgence, and its redundant evil. Further, the church's growing alliance with the drift toward the conservative right unwittingly secularizes its life as Christian values become confused with secular values and the church's well being becomes synonymous with the welfare of the nation.

2.

There is only one Word of God, one principle by which all other words must be heard and criticized—Jesus, the Christ, the Son of God, and Lord. The question arises for the church, what does it mean to confess Christ in our day? The church is not to confess itself, nor to confess others. The church's confession is that Jesus Christ is Lord—as witnessed by Scripture as the one World of God which we hear and obey and in which we trust in life and death.

The one word which the church is most in need of hearing today is the warning against apostasy. "You did not return to me, says the Lord" (Amos 4:6). This is the life-and-death church struggle today.

3.

This Word, which is from the beginning and is everlasting, calls all human words into question and puts all human words under judgment. Even though all human knowledge and truth are historically conditioned and their forms continually changing, this Word—the object of our faith and the subject of our knowing and that by which all things are made—is unchanging.

4.

Holy Scripture, which witnesses to the cross of Christ as the foundation of our faith and that by which our faith is tested, is God's self-disclosure of his purposes in the events of our history. Its subject is the eternal Word in the world reconciling the world to himself, and the sending of his Holy Spirit into the world as his continuous presence.

While Scripture must be read and interpreted anew in each generation and while the church receives Christ anew in each generation, these historical tasks are always to be interpreted by the Word of God in Holy Scripture. The church's own experience as well as secular wisdom as sources of reflection in the life of faith are to be interpreted in the light of this Word revealed in Scripture and not autonomously or *a priori* as assumptions of reason.

5.

The church's faith is its calling into the future, which God has prepared since before the foundations of the world. The church professes that God is making all things new in Christ, and confesses that, as a pilgrim people, we have no permanent city in this world but look ever toward that heavenly Jerusalem where he will draw all people to himself and bring them to the perfection of his elect. This pilgrim church is the prophetic remnant which, after all earthly powers and pretensions pass away, will continue to find its service to God in his world.

6.

The church confesses the absolute centrality of the cross both for faith and for history, both as the sign of the covenant of the kingdom and as the revelation of God's power and of his full and final intention for his creation. This is, at the same time, a confession of a radical and monotheistic faith calling into question all pluralities, all provisional loyalties, all principalities, all finite creatures—anything, in short, that has any power to qualify God's claim on us of absolute loyalty to himself and to his cause, his kingdom, and its justice. For, "My ways are not your ways, says the Lord" (Isaiah 55:8), and God's ultimacy must relativize all human claims. The church confesses in The Shema a lively hope in the coming of the kingdom, even though its time is not known.

The church must be willing to accept and to face the reality that the suffering of pain and powerlessness—as revealed by the cross, which is the subject of the church's gospel—stands at the very center of human existence. Theological existence is, in part, the sharing of the suffering of others and responding appropriately to it; not covering it up, but acknowledging it and meeting it. The church's obsessive concern with the management of conflict and pain must be called into question. Personal discomfort and inconvenience are escalated to the level of pain, and pain is trivialized as discomfort and inconvenience; consequently, language is confounded, and the church is bewildered by feelings that literally have become nameless. The church no longer has the power to handle them and rushes to adopt strategies for "reconciliation" before there is anything to reconcile, before confusion is dispelled, before the problem has been named, before confession has been made, and before forgiveness is requested. On the contrary, the gospel calls the church to participate in the suffering of God in the world.

7.

Radical monotheistic faith is the ground for the church's righteousness, not the cause. We are saved by grace. The church's faith cannot be separated from the requirement it acknowledges for obedience. Loyalty, faith, and obedience are inseparable, and, likewise, are inseparable from justice and social concern. This obedience is a call to suffering. It is not a guarantee of success or that the problems and conflicts which are experienced in the world and in the church will be resolved.

The church's obedience in the gospel is not to be confused with or equated with loyalty to any historical principle that might claim transcendent authority over individual conscience. Present controversies within the church generate many such instances of erroneous and misapplied appeals to conscience. These represent a perverse refutation of the church's polity and a denial that the Spirit of God works through the political processes of the church's bicameral councils. The gospel refutes this kind of ecclesiological permissiveness.

Personal feeling recently has been elevated to the level of principle and the locus of authority and obedience. Consequently, the authority of the church is no longer internalized by many. Their obedience is offered only when it feels comfortable and when it appears to be agreeable.[4]

Faith and obedience are inseparable but they are not identical. How does faith in the one God and in his divine, incarnate Word determine our actions? They are not determined by an invariable rule, but by the fitting response of faith to Him who is present in all of our actions and in all actions upon us. This obedience requires a steady and constant faith, informing all of our decisions and actions; and it is the mode of Christian spirituality in the world.

8.

Christian faith is a concrete way of being in the world. Faith and obedience are the grounds and prerequisites for all ethics, for all moral knowledge, and for living life as citizens of the kingdom. The Christian life is one of listening and responding, actively and publicly, acting in the present in faith, not knowing the outcome.

9.

The ministry of the church, both to itself and to the world, takes place where the Word of God is spoken and heard in faith.

Narrative: Autobiography, Imagination, Poetics, Politics, and the End of Epistemology

The transition from propositional theology to the way forward happens through autobiographical narrative, reflecting on experience as shaped by imagination, literature, and politics.

Incarnation

My own life as theologian is not defined by my lifelong struggle with providence and theodicy and meaning. Theology is not merely a logic-centered discipline combined with reflection; it is also framed by passion, feeling and emotion, what Walt Whitman called "passional affection."

Specifically, my theology is formed also out of my sexuality. Providence and theodicy as such are, by themselves, without passion, mere husks, mental notions adventitiously applied as defenses against the threat of unanswerable questions. Even probability theory does not avail here. Theology without passion is bloodless, exquisite Tinkertoy constructs rattling in the chambers of the mind. Theology must come from the heart —from loving and from the cross-grained existence which questions every human convention.

One Christmas Eve from heaven high, love came down and graced me. I knew a beloved companion, and we recognized, responded to, received, and forged the bonds of love. Together, silently, we opened ourselves to one another, and, in that joy, life was transfigured for me, now shot through with passion. The husks were filled, and the frozen snow banks of mid-winter melted in a spring freshet. The adamantine walls, like molten steel, dissolved. I was freed to live and love, a new being. In loving another and being loved, I knew, with a knowing beyond words and theological formulae, the loving mercy of God, transcending paradox and contradiction. It was my sexuality that fully opened for me the work of theologian; I had finally come into my vocation. Love that is unmerited, love that is freely given and taken unconditionally, teaches more than any definition. At last I *knew* that I was loved, infinitely, forever.

Søren Kierkegaard's urgent paradox concerning the point of intersection of time and the timeless can be held in tension, as it must be, only in the context of this unsearchable love. But T. S. Eliot also gives a clue. The apprehension of that point of intersection, he wrote, is "something given / And taken, in a lifetime's death in love, / Ardour and selflessness and self-surrender."[5] God's gift of his only son on the cross is the paradigm. There can be no theology without this passionate love and suffering, and Kierkegaard reminds us that religion *is* suffering.

The theologian's task, then, as I see it, must mark his progress beyond theology, beyond ideas, to the priority of desire and love which charts his daily struggle against those contextual constraints which cabin and confine thought and imagination. His struggle is to break free of the cultural conditionings which saturate us all and, yet at the same time, to recognize his debt to the culture which nurtures him. The theologian must be able to respond to God in all actions which come upon him in the concrete daily experience of living. In other words, the theologian's task is to acknowledge his existential context and, at the same time, to transcend it.

John M. Gessell

Redemption

Redemption was originally a gutter word, from the world of commerce, the market place, an ambiguous word. You buy back an article that is in hock; you pay money to redeem a slave into freedom. It is the price of release for a prisoner, a ransom. It is the violent action of a thug who races through and snatches a piece of goods out of a merchant's stall in the bazaar.

Christians saw it as a metaphor for the work of Christ, as in "ransomed, healed, restored, forgiven," the rescue of the soul from the devil's snare. The trouble is that it became viewed as a transaction, difficult to explain rationally; and cumbersome atonement theories developed with clanking, mechanical explanations. If it did not remain a mystery of faith, it was—for most people, anyway—incomprehensible. I remember a friend in my parish who asked me at the coffee hour (the dread time that figures so prominently in the hypothetical question portion of canonical examinations) what atonement meant. I was speechless.

The idea, of course, is that souls are rescued from sin and death by God's act in Christ. Early Christian theological reflection insisted that God had acted in some decisive way by sending his son into the world and that his death on the cross had forged a new objective relation between God and humanity.

This language stays somewhat impersonal and transactional (as when I am invited to engage in "interaction" with someone rather than a "conversation"). I think that Milton was closer to it in the opening lines of *Paradise Lost* in which he speaks of "Man's First Disobedience" which brought death into the world until "one greater Man" restored us, and he concludes the stanza with the lines, "I may assert Eternal Providence / And justify the ways of God to men."

The connotation of redemption has traditionally meant some sort of rescue of the believer from the clutches of sin, the bonds of death—an evocation of Bunyan's "Vanity Fair" or even Thackeray's novel of the same title. But I believe that a more useful analogy for us is that of Jesus' encounter in the house of Simon the Pharisee. The incident appears in all four gospels (an indication of the story's critical importance), but Luke's account (Luke 7:36–50) is the most potent and paradigmatic reflection. We see an unnamed woman (identified only as a "woman of the city who was a sinner") who clearly was poor and marginalized, on the fringes of Judaism, outside the law because she was too poor to observe it, reduced to prostitution. In other words, she was held to be contemptible and unclean, not worthy of consideration.

In the presence of Jesus, her immediate response was astonishing and contrite: she knelt and bathed his feet with her tears and wiped them with her hair, anointing and kissing them—acts of punctilious hospitality. Matthew and Luke commend this action as "a beautiful thing," appropriate and fitting. In Jesus' presence she is accounted a woman of grace. Nonetheless, Simon condemns her before Jesus, but Jesus praises her acts to Simon—who himself has not fulfilled his obligations of hospitality. Jesus insists that her sins, though many, are forgiven and set aside, for "she has loved much." He concludes by telling the woman that she may go in peace, for her faith has saved her. The bountiful love which she has poured out is accounted to her for faith, and, crucially, Matthew (26:13) and Mark (14:9) add that, wherever the gospel is preached, what this woman has done will be told in memory of her.

An unknown, unnamed, contemptible woman becomes for us an icon of faith, remembered wherever and whenever the gospel is proclaimed. What is this power of transformation? It is no mystery, but it is scary and unnerving, if only because divinity comes too close to us in Christ Jesus, as Martin Luther said. God was in Christ reconciling us to himself, Paul wrote. Paul was no naif; he was a "God-dazzled" man (to borrow J. D. Salinger's word used in another context to describe Seymour Glass). The sign of the transforming power of which Paul spoke is the sacrament of baptism, in which we become what we are declared, children of God and inheritors of the kingdom. In Jesus, God comes to us. The poisonous things that we have put into our hearts, God has dethroned. This is the "great reversal," as Charles Williams put it. We are enabled to change the old for the new because we are God's chosen, and he comes to us in a blinding, overwhelming, unconditional love. We discover that, at the heart of the universe, there is one who loves us with a terrible love. As the woman at Simon's house discovered, he encounters us face to face in our sinfulness with intense, unwavering, candid eyes, the reconciling God in Jesus piercing our addicted souls with the arrows of his love, and making us his own.

Wherever the gospel is preached, there will be a memorial to the woman at Simon's house, a memory across the millennia, an anamnesis in which the unsearchable love of God is brought into our present with healing in its wings, making us mindful of the love that bought us once and for all on Calvary's tree. In blazing light, that cross reveals to us the redemptive suffering of Jesus whose absolute obedience to the Father is the source of the power which transforms, a radical kind of rebirth.

One of my shaping theological influences is the nineteenth-century Anglican, F. D. Maurice. His life and work reiterates this redemptive and transformative work of God in the world. Maurice begins with the fact that Christ, who comes into the world, comes to his own, for in Christ as the center, all things were created to live in union with God and with each other. Men and women are created for community with God and with one another in God. The sign of this for Maurice is baptism, in which we become what we were created to be.[6]

Reconciliation

Paul's insistent theme is that "God was in Christ reconciling the world to himself" (2 Corinthians 5:19). Here there is no metaphysical speculation, but the irreducible experience of meeting God directly in the person of Jesus as the Christ, the second person of the Blessed Trinity. This meeting does not boggle the mind with the task of explaining through substance metaphysics how Jesus could be God and man. It is a witness and a testimony that in Jesus we meet God face to face and that this meeting is earth-shaking, transforming, saving. Paul testifies the simple fact and the fact that he was never the same again. In Jesus, God and man are reconciled.

But what must be reconciled? Presumably the ravages of sin which, in the shattering consciousness of the confession, allow us to realize that there is now no health in us, that is, no faculty remains untouched by disability, and we are unable of ourselves to heal ourselves. The problem for us is that sin is destructive and prevents us from possessing that necessary insight about ourselves and the power to be able to stay anchored in reality. We are beguiled.

What is the cure? The trouble with sin is that it is really sinful and creates in us a delusional dysfunction, splitting us from reality and from the well-spring of our soul's life. It creates adamantine walls of self-preservation behind which we think all is well, when, in fact, the *Titanic* is sinking. The will is atrophied and misguided. It is directed toward destructive ends.

Sin is the opposite of faith; sin is in opposition to faith. Reconciliation means coming into balance, harmony, the settling of difference. If we can know it, it is God who can do this for us. In his commentary on the Book of Revelation, Bruce Metzger invokes the dramatic imagery of St. John the Divine:

> The profound religious insight that lies behind these kaleidoscopic pictures is that men and women worship some absolute power and if they do not worship the true and real Power behind the Universe, they will construct a god for themselves and give allegiance to that. In the last analysis, it is always a choice between the power that operates through inflicting suffering, that is, the power of the beast, and the power that operates through accepting suffering, namely, the power of the Lamb.[7]

What needs reconciling is the howling emptiness of the sinner in himself or herself. Cut off from God by our faithless rebellion, we suffer the unassuageable thirst of loneliness without a comforter. We try to cleave for comfort to the earthly things that seem so readily at hand. It is the loneliness of Lucifer, cast out of God's presence in emptiness without end. The need to seek earthly remedies arises out of the clamor of fear and despair, and in our desperation these remedies promise to fill this emptiness. But we then fall into the clutches of idols, beguiled by false promises and false hopes, addictions which we think we cannot live without. We become like addicts who refuse to enter the program of recovery. We seek the wrong, the destructive power.

One seventeenth-century New England preacher captured this situation with uncanny precision: "We are dethroned, become slaves to those things that were made to serve us. We put those things in our hearts that God has put under our feet."[8] This is to turn the natural order of things upside down. The only remedy is what Charles Williams called "the Great Reversal" in which God and man are reconciled, where God meets us in our need, where, as the "Hound of Heaven," he continuously offers us his depthless, astonishing love, eternally on offer without condition. In Jesus as the Christ, God and man are reconciled.

Religion means suffering, as Kierkegaard pointed out; and the overcoming of difference is the fruit of reconciling love so powerful that—in it, by it, and through it—we become the new creation.

Salvation, the New Creation

The reference here is to health and wholeness of body and soul. Paul Tillich's powerful metaphor is "the new being," a reference to 2 Corinthians 5:17, "Therefore, if anyone is in Christ, he is a new creation; the old has passed away, behold, the new has come." Salvation comes in the sacrament of baptism whereby we are made one with Christ, a child of God and a citizen of God's kingdom. Salvation means becoming what we were created to be and is the gift of God's love and grace, his holiness and goodness. We are what we have been made by our baptism. We are not sinners; we are forgiven sinners, a new creation through water and the Word, in the visible signs of bread and wine, in eucharist. This cannot be earned nor can we become deserving of it by conforming to some model of moral behavior. As Ephesians says, "For it is by grace you are saved, through trusting him; it is not your own doing. It is God's gift, not a reward for work done" (Ephesians 2:8–9).

Or, as it is written in Titus, "But when the goodness and loving kindness of God our Savior appeared, he saved us, not because of deeds done by us in righteousness, but in virtue of his own mercy . . . so that we might be justified by his grace and become heirs in hope of eternal life" (Titus 3:4–7). Of course, this seems outrageous to those who wish to control others by dictating moral norms, for it seems to them that there are no norms to be enforced. But God's ways do not enter into our human calculus, and God's mercy is not conditioned on our righteousness.

The loving kindness of God has appeared to all. He lets each nation go its own way. He is evident to them in the happiness he gives them. Thus, has Lambeth so grievously misunderstood.

Clearly, salvation ushers in a new moral life, but it is constituted, not in human reason, but in the virtue of Jesus' love based on his single-minded devotion to God. As H. Richard Niebuhr says, it is the virtue of the love of God and of the neighbor in God.[9] In the so-called parable of the good Samaritan, Jesus shifts the discussion from the legalistic or moralistic question of "who is my neighbor" to the question of who proves himself a neighbor. It is clear that being a neighbor is fitting for those who are members of the household of God. It is not necessary to sort out those who are to be loved and those who are not. The point of the parable is not the man who is in need, but the man of compassion, not a rule or law to be fulfilled, but the redeemed who come to the neighbor as to Christ present in the neighbor.

The key to the moral life—indeed, to the life of theological existence—is the response to the neighbor in loving compassion: to those who starve because they cannot buy food, to the naked because they are unclothed, to the imprisoned who are in want of justice, to the bereft who have no shelter. This is a daunting task, because it means changing our hearts and working to change government policy and cruel social structures. This is being Christ to the neighbor, and the act of compassion of the redeemed precedes and is the precondition to any theory of justice, whether fairness, or desert, or remedial.

Conclusion

This, then, the reflection on the experience of incarnation, redemption, reconciliation, and salvation, constitutes the reality of the beloved community, the household of God. Through the autobiographical consideration of my life, I try to make the words of Peter my own: "You are a chosen race, a royal priesthood, a holy nation, God's own people. . . . Once you were no people but now you are God's people; once you had not received mercy but now you have received mercy" (1 Peter 2:9–10).

This essay has been written in a time of personal turmoil. Several beloved companions have entered the gates of larger life and have tested severely "the sure and certain hope of the resurrection to eternal life." And the disasters of the 1998 Lambeth Conference seem to signal balefully the twilight of the Anglican Communion. Earlier above I referred to "the intractable conflict in the Episcopal Church today" and that the future of theology "must open the way forward beyond this unnecessary conflict and impasse." I hope that I have assisted in this effort.

Notes

1. Preface of the Lord's Day 1, The Book of Common Prayer (New York: The Church Hymnal Corporation, 1979), 377.
2. Webpage, St. Peter's Church (Charlotte, N.C.), October 1997.
3. Frederick Buechner, *The Sacred Journey* (New York: Harper & Row, 1982), 1.
4. For a fuller discussion of "conscience" and "permissiveness," see my discussion in "The Iker Consecration, the 'Conscience Clause,' and the Function of the Law," *Sewanee Theological Review* 38 (Michaelmas 1995): 363–366.
5. T. S. Eliot, "Dry Salvages," *Four Quartets* (New York: Harvest, 1971), 44.
6. See H. Richard Niebuhr, *Christ and Culture* (New York: Charles Scribner's Sons, 1948).
7. Bruce Metzger, *Breaking the Code: Understanding the Book of Revelation* (Nashville: Abingdon Press, 1993), 76.
8. Urian Oakes, *A Seasonable Discourse* (Cambridge, Mass.: Samuel Green, 1682), 27.
9. Niebuhr, *Christ and Culture*, 16–17.

Supporting the Spiritual Depth of the Church

Tilden Edwards

In recent decades I have noticed more and more clergy and laity in the Episcopal Church claiming their hunger for a deeper personal and collective sense of connectedness with God. This echoes the general spiritual awakening that we find across the country and in much of the world today. During one of the great spiritual awakenings in nineteenth-century New England, the Episcopal Church had the reputation of sitting on the sidelines and absorbing some of those who fled the movement. Today, however, the response seems very different. Today I sense humility and vulnerability—as well as confusion—in the face of the spiritual movements within and around us. Episcopalians today often are part of the awakening.

In the Shalem Institute's many ecumenical spiritual formation programs, Episcopalians are usually one of the largest groups. When they (and everyone else) share their spiritual yearnings and experiences, the general sense is that a full understanding of these yearnings and experiences finally transcends the theological responses available in any denominational tradition. Together, these ecumenical groups share a foretaste of the great church to come and a theological ground broader than that of any current denomination.

Tacitly, that great church already exists to the extent that the readings required of seminarians in every mainstream theological school today include authors from many Christian traditions. Also, judging by their church-shopping habits, the laity often assume that there aren't many (if any) *fundamental* differences between one church and another—at least not among the mainstream churches—and, in any case, they believe they can choose to ignore those differences or doctrines that they don't agree with. The resulting mix of denominational backgrounds apparent in most congregations inevitably erodes any sense of a "pure" denominational tradition and slowly changes it toward something more inclusive.

Other significant influences add to the mutual fertilization and lowering of denominational boundaries: (1) the growing knowledge of non-Christian traditions; (2) the more questionable, yet nonetheless powerful, influences often referred to as "New Age"; and (3) the bits and pieces of scientific, psychological, and cultural influences that shape our awareness via mass media, including the worldwide web. Together these influences create a context for the future of theology and life of the Episcopal Church that is far larger than the context in which the church and its theology were formed. Today we are part of a vastly expanding, popularly available body of knowledge that challenges the assumptions and boundaries of every religious tradition.

Given this expansive, sometimes mutually reinforcing, sometimes conflicting and confusing global context, what does the spiritual heart of our church need most from Episcopal theologizing and from our church life together? Let me highlight three possible responses: (1) reverence for the mystery of the divine; (2) practicing the presence; and (3) the contemplative connection.

Reverence for the Mystery of the Divine

Long ago I heard someone say that the most important task of theology is to protect the mystery of God. Our Anglican tradition at its best has not tried to overdefine the nature of God and the world. We have affirmed Scripture, reason, experience, the great early Councils, and other watersheds of tradition as privileged sources of wisdom about spiritual reality, and yet we have done so in a way that accommodates widely different views and allows for the possibility of additional sources of wisdom. We have had our closed-down moments, but these often have been less intense and enduring than those of many other Christian traditions. For the most part, Anglican tradition has not tried to submit personal spiritual experience to rigid doctrinal tests; instead, human experience is given a spiritual context that includes a respect for the mystery of God's ways.

Theology in Anglican history has been primarily an "essay" tradition rather than a systematic one, reflective, I think, of an Anglican sense that reason can offer insightful speculations about the nature of the divine/human relationship but cannot produce definitive statements that capture the essence of the mystery. Anglicans assume that there will be a valuable, ongoing, theological dialogue about the nature of spiritual reality in the context of evolving historical events and personal experience; however, this dialogue always will surround a vast mystery that we never will be able to domesticate with our minds. The tradition is carried, then, not by a hard "party line" but by an ongoing "party dialogue" within certain broad parameters.

Such an existential stance serves us well today, during the exponential increase in available and evolving human knowledge. We are not saddled with a confessional theological heritage into which all reality must be squeezed. Even the broad heritage that we do "confess" is kept open to ongoing interpretation, providing us with a respect for and willingness to learn from the radiant gleanings of our ancestors, although not restricting us to them. New learning—when it is broadly compatible with the mainstream historical dialogue—is welcomed.

The Episcopal Church does not belong to the Bible and to tradition. Rather, the Bible and tradition belong to *it*. Both Bible and tradition are "opened" in the light of the living Spirit in our individual and corporate experience today. The Bible and tradition are carried by a church committed to the living breath of God in our time, a church that fundamentally connects with, yet transcends, all past formulations. The Bible and tradition are not straightjackets that confine our understanding, nor are they univocal in what they offer us. They are, rather, unique gifts that speak of the mystery of God's reality and Good News among us, historical markers that help us orient our lived experience individually and collectively.

Anglicanism's historical theological emphasis on the incarnation reinforces a respect for the mystery of God's presence in the world. If we see the incarnation, among other things, as revealing the mystery of the intimate involvement of God's energies with all created matter, then we pave the way for a sense of the great cosmic mystical body of Christ that finally includes all that is of God. Such a theological view connects well with the contemporary hunger for embracing the sacredness of all dimensions of life and including all forms of life in God's oneness. Jesus Christ becomes a welcomer, revealer, and empowerer of the great banquet table of life at which all creatures are meant to sit and find reconciled kinship and joy.

The Benedictine influence seen in the Book of Common Prayer also shows respect for the intimate mystery of God in our midst. God is embraced through the day, through the year, through rites of passage, through joys and sorrows, without theologically overdefining what is happening. The mystery of God's presence is embraced, and the goodness of God is affirmed through all times. The words of the liturgy convey both broad ancestral *and* contemporary hope in God and have a way of surrounding the moment or human event without dominating it with overly interpretive language. The silences that often surround the common prayer times reinforce the mystery of the occasion; we may say some things, but other things are left to the inclusive silence, and to the swell of the music that can open us wordlessly to the larger presence.

Theology might serve this great liturgical tradition better if future revisions of the Prayer Book demonstrate more sensitivity to the spiritual intent of the prayers that are included. Many of our current prayers feel impersonal, as though they were written for their theological and aesthetic correctness, not their personal spiritual impact. A prayer's theological "correctness" becomes questionable when the dualism implied between divine action and human response begins to shortchange the incarnational spiritual intimacy of the divine/human relationship. Such a prayer leaves us sensing God "out there" somewhere to be brought "in here" (as if God weren't already inside of everything real). A prayer should help us recognize that God's Spirit has always been incarnationally alive and at work "in here," in us, in this situation, in this time. It is for us to embrace this amazing reality of the image of God being lived in our form.

Liturgical theology might also serve our tradition by helping churches to be in touch with what I would call the "foundational intent" of gathering in the name of Christ; of being open to what is given in the living presence. At their best, the distinguishing marks of formal liturgical worship—using the "right" words, rubrics, and behaviors—guide churches toward a collective opening to the presence of the living Spirit. At their worst, these marks of formalism become an unconscious conspiracy to evade God in the name of God, as though we really didn't trust what might happen if the living Spirit really did "take over" once in a while in an unpredictable way. Order in liturgy, ever since the chaos in some of the church services overseen by St. Paul, has been rightly valued by Anglican tradition. A liturgical structure is needed as a steady vehicle for the Spirit of God in Christ and as a protection against the dominance of the personalities of liturgical leaders. Liturgical structure is a container for something other than itself, and openness to that "otherness" is crucial. Ongoing experimentation with and theological reflection on the possibilities of liturgy as an immediate divine/human meeting ground needs to be encouraged in our liturgical life so that the church may better fulfill its promise.

Practicing the Presence

The most sustaining spiritual practice, and the most elusive one, is summarized by St. Paul in 1 Thessalonians 5:17: "Pray without ceasing." I interpret this to mean praying for the empowerment of our trust in God's immediate guiding presence throughout the day, or—in a more specific sense—leaning back into the spacious, personal presence of God's Spirit in Christ, trusting that this eternally living Spirit is ready to free us for whatever is of God in any given moment.

We could say that liturgical and other intentional prayers are invitations to, or celebrations of, this foundational orientation to God's presence in our lives. The proliferation of prayer groups, quiet days, and retreats in churches also touches this core desire to practice the presence. As more and more people seek a deeper spiritual life, this orientation to God in the moment may lead the way. It is especially important for religious leaders to demonstrate this foundational orientation if they are to be true spiritual leaders. However, since everyone is called to be a spiritual leader in various ways (i.e., to let the Holy Spirit lead them in various work, family, community, and church situations), this orientation is basic to all mature Christian living.

Theological perspectives need to inform the orientation of the spiritual life to the living presence, just as the experience of presence provides data that informs a fuller theological perspective. The American spiritual tradition on the whole is experience-oriented rather than theory-oriented. For theology to be valuable and "heard," it needs to stay close to human experience. What the process needs is a theological anthropology, one closely connected with the movements of the spiritual life, one with a strong focus on our human nature in God. Some theologians have said that all theology is really anthropology, seeking the ultimate in our own experience. Perhaps what we need is a more precise anthropology that takes into consideration the incredible divine/human intimacy implied by the incarnation, and expressed by the great mystics of the tradition. Anglican tradition has often upheld the theological insights derived from the deep experience of great mystics of the early, medieval, and later church. But the more academic theologians of the last few centuries, up until very recent decades, have often veered away from theology derived from their own deep, radiant experiences.

The connection of radiant personal experience and the radiant experience found in the tradition is crucial. We could say that we have not cultivated a careful tradition of sharing the mind of Christ, out of which his words and acts flowed. It is in that mind, his pristine awareness of life in God, that he sees us doing greater things than he, in the power of the Holy Spirit. Episcopal theology and liturgy have helped people to appropriate a certain meaning and practice that orients them somewhat to their true being in God, but the deeper call to holiness—the sharing of the mind of Christ, the movement from the image to the likeness of God which the early church fathers saw as the heart of our human calling—has not yet found sufficient help from the church's theology or practice.

We need an anthropology that reflects the movement of the Spirit in us toward realization (not just conceptualization) of our true nature in the image of God, and the realization of life flowing from the divine wellspring moment by moment. Such a realization reveals our true nature: like a membrane that is constantly permeable by God (as opposed to an insulated box that occasionally might be broken into by God). Our ultimate identity will be seen in God and not in our psychic and physical identity. Our psychic and physical identities will be gifted, unique carriers of that larger identity in the image of God.

A woman once told me about a greeting ritual that is used in her Christian ashram in India. She said that whenever the members greet each another, they always bow and precede the person's given name with "om," such as "om Jane," "om John." The Sanskrit word "om" could be thought of as the largest name for God, beyond definition (in English we have—from the Greek—such words as "omnipotent" and "omniscient" which convey some sense of the Sanskrit word). This apophatic name beyond definition is followed by our particular cataphatic given name, constituting a powerful way to reinforce a sense of our full identity: each of us as a very particular, unique expression of the image of God; each of us with a personality meant to carry divine qualities of creativity, love, freedom, etc., into the daily life of the world. The world itself is soaked in divine presence and therefore to be reverenced, as we reverence one another.

How are we able to know God? That epistemological question represents another dimension of the anthropology we need for the sake of the practical spiritual life of people in the church. One of the tacit assumptions of the curricula of our theological schools is that we can know God by thinking in a cognitive, academically-oriented way about God and our experience. Whatever else is done—prayer, worship, and service, which are related to will, devotion, and feelings—may be essential to the church but is not considered a distinctive way of knowing that can be learned or cultivated.

I suspect that our theological schools are subject to some unexamined, post-Enlightenment, secular assumptions about how we know, assumptions that are reflected in their accreditation standards (standards which are tied closely to those of secular universities and colleges). These standards normally assume that essential knowledge comes from a detached analytical process. The contemplative process, on the other hand—participation in discerning prayer, worship, and service—has not had (according to Robert Bellah) a significant place in higher education as a means to authentic knowledge since before the Enlightenment. Contemporary science, philosophy, and theology today clearly are challenging the adequacy of Enlightenment thinking, which views the contemplative way of knowing with contempt.

To my knowledge, the participative way of knowing hasn't been *explicitly* rejected by theological school faculties; it just hasn't been consciously and collectively considered. As a result, the same implicit Enlightenment academic norms persist in every aspect of theological education, including the preparation and selection of most faculty members. Any other way of knowing is marginalized.

This impoverishment of our ways of knowing results in a curriculum that is dominated by an epistemology that cultivates a sophisticated knowledge "about" things but does little in the formation of what I call the "spiritual heart," which receives spiritual truth through participative knowledge. The analytical process can reflect upon participative knowledge and thereby help to understand and communicate it in its own cognitive terms. However, the essence of contemplative knowledge cannot be translated directly into cognitive terms. Participative knowledge does not require cognitive reflection for it to become "knowledge." It has its own distinctive qualities of awareness that are noncognitive. Real respect for participative knowledge would lead to a curriculum and teaching method that would assist the process of living out of the mind of Christ, not just providing words about the mind of Christ.

I realize I am saying things that fly in the face of a system of theological education that is well-established, extensive, and consistent across most denominational lines in this country. And yet I believe that other ways of knowing need to be seriously considered. We impoverish the spiritual formation of our seminary faculty members and, through them, our clergy and, through them, our churches when we cultivate cognitive understanding of spiritual reality apart from the careful cultivation of a contemplative way of knowing that reality. Their mutual cultivation would allow a more integrated, "head in heart" approach to the mystery and subtlety of spiritual knowledge. Integration is key here: I am not talking about valuing the two ways of knowing at separate times. I'm speaking of a quality of presence that comes from the head and heart's joint "givenness" to God in the moment.

A cautionary note here: "knowledge" is a paradoxical affair in the spiritual life. Knowledge of God in any form is not something to be grasped; it is something that is given. In the *Cloud of Unknowing*, we hear that God can be known directly by love alone, a participative kind of knowledge. In other classical writings we hear that we cannot really know God at all. We can only let ourselves be known by God's Spirit in Christ, and, from that vulnerability, a paradoxical kind of obscure but substantial knowledge arises.

Here is another application for the theological anthropology of the future: we need to become better informed about non-Christian traditions. While we continue to ground our understanding of human nature in biblical views and in the interpretations of the divine/human relationship drawn from the experience of great mystics of Christian tradition, we should engage, test, and enlarge this understanding through contact with the understandings of human nature found in other deep religious traditions. Sadly, the church has shown much more openness to the relatively recent psychologically developed understandings of human nature in this century than it has ever shown toward the understandings of human nature that have been evolving in other religious traditions for centuries.

Increasing numbers of people in our churches are involved with the practices of and readings from these other traditions. Many Roman Catholic theologians, especially those in religious orders, have taken this phenomenon seriously and written a great deal about the stimulus of Eastern/Western contact and its practical effects upon the church. There does not appear to be anything similar to this level of attention in Episcopal theological circles, but perhaps that is because the Episcopal Church has fewer theologians by comparison, and because our smaller size tempts us toward a more insular position. In any case, we need to be equipping our leaders to be more helpful when people ask for a discerning exploration of our human nature in the Christian tradition and how that understanding is enhanced or contradicted by other traditions and practices. Few of us have time for a major exploration, but even a light exploration can open the door to learning and free us from the danger of a smug provincialism that simply ignores the existence or relevance of any other tradition.

Historically, the Anglican church has seen itself as an interim church on the way to the great catholic church. Today the Episcopal Church might widen its vision and see itself as an interim church on the way to discerning connectedness with whatever is wise and compassionate in all human traditions that have been formed by divine inspiration. Just as our ecumenical "opening up" has occurred without essential loss and, often, with great gain, our opening up to interfaith can be accomplished without loss of the integrity of the Episcopal Church's own depths and contributions. As we open up to other faiths, we will continue the process begun during our ecumenical opening: discerning what is compatible with our understanding, what will stretch our understanding, and what truly is in conflict with our understanding.

So many people yearn today for a spirituality that explores, discerns, and appreciates whatever is of God in the world. Too often what they find, however, is a spirituality that is overly sectarian and continually narrows the search for God and truth. Such narrowness can appeal to people who have a great need to secure themselves amidst life's fearful uncertainties, but in the end they are cheated of the larger truth. If such people come to dominate the life of a congregation, they can discourage those who are ready for a deeper search and lead them to affiliate elsewhere.

We need to embrace a spiritual tradition that truly keeps open to the truth of God, wherever it is found. We would do well to draw upon the writings of Simone Weil, who reminded us that Christ is the truth, and that wherever the truth is found, Christ can't be far away; Christ doesn't belong to Christians; Christ belongs to God. Our theology needs to affirm both his revealed personalness and his mysterious largeness that is beyond our capacity to capture fully in any tradition. At its best, the Good News of God's Spirit in Christ—as it is offered to us through the particularities of Anglican tradition—gives the people life-giving and discerning ways to connect with the universal truth of divine reconciling presence in human life. As we see this happening, we will know that we are not cultivating a narrow, self-securing, sectarian entity, but rather a well-built platform for a truly universal church. As a monk-theologian once asked, "How can the church be truly catholic, truly universal, unless it is willing to accommodate the fullness of the truth given to humankind?"

The Contemplative Connection

The theologian Monica Hellwig says that the essence of a contemplative attitude is vulnerability:

> Allowing persons, things, and events to be, to happen, allowing them their full resonance in one's own experience, looking at them without blinking, touching them and allowing them to touch us without flinching. . . . It is a constant willingness to be taken by surprise. It is a deep existential grasp of the truth that all our theory is a critique of our praxis and that evasion of experience means distortion or alienation in our theory.
>
> Further, she says:
>
> Contemplation is an attitude pervading all aspects of life, all experiences, activities, and relationships. It is also a way of prayer. It is a way that allows the ultimate to reveal itself in the immediate that is given to us when we do not try to escape the silence at the roots of our own consciousness or the emptiness at the center of our being. The ultimate reveals itself when we do not try to escape the immediate or to distort it in self-defense or to subvert it to our pettiness.[1]

Such a view of contemplation—especially, as Hellwig says, with a sense of the "silence at the roots of our own consciousness" and "the emptiness at the center of our being"—allows us to burrow beneath the postmodernist critique of objective interpretations of reality and find a substantive place where we live before the conditionings of our consciousness that "postmodernists" find so suspect.[2] Hellwig's view also allows us to burrow beneath many of the controversies in the church to a deeper common well from which the life of God flows into the world. It is a fundamental way of seeing, discerning, and praying that has found a growing audience in and out of the church, even if its subtleties are not always grasped. Increasingly, a contemplative orientation has been seen, not as something in contrast to social action, but as the foundation for authentic action, which in turn fertilizes the inner life.

Theologically speaking, a contemplative orientation attends the immediacy of divine presence and seeks to live out of the guidance of that presence rather than from an insular sense of reality. God is not an object in the air or in our consciousness to be contacted; God is the trusted subject of our existence, in and beyond all forms, whose Spirit animates every moment. Or at least this is one way of speaking about the ineffable, before whom all words finally collapse in the mystery of the Word out of silence. The Episcopal Church has a spiritual tradition that can accommodate such a contemplative view more easily than the traditions of many other churches, even if the Episcopal Church doesn't have much experience in acknowledging and expressing it in any careful or ongoing way.

In the future, spiritual theology, informed by "the head in the heart," can be very helpful to the church in looking more carefully at spiritual experience and where it seems to be moving. Particular attention should be paid to individual and collective movements toward freedom in God (in contrast to those who seem stuck in ego-securing stasis). In the ministry of one-on-one and group spiritual direction, spiritual theologizing is happening all the time, although an enlargement of this dialogue is needed, one informed by the tradition and by a more careful and dynamic understanding of our human nature in God. This dialogue might assist the process of looking at the intents and outcomes of particular spiritual practices and experiences. It would encourage people's critical honesty and their connectedness with the full life and callings of Christ's Spirit in the church and the larger society.

The serious divisions in the church today can find (and often have found) a common meeting ground in the spiritual hunger that people have to go deeper into God. However, the fault lines between liberals and conservatives will reappear in the spiritual life of the church when there is not an adequate theology of sanctification, when there is not an evolving spiritual life, alive and understood.

Such a theology is needed to help people look discerningly at their experiences, practices, and attitudes in the light of an ongoing process of sanctification that has no finishing point in this life, only stepping stones. With a full lifetime perspective of the spiritual life supporting them, potential adversaries might demonstrate a more accommodating sense of humility and a respect for one another's points of difference along the way.

Sometimes the differences between spiritual movements are not nearly so real as they might seem on the surface. For example, charismatic and contemplative orientations are not opposites. Both give weight to the immediacy of the Holy Spirit's presence. One emphasizes an expressive, effervescent form of presence, the other a calmer, clearer form of presence. There is no reason why both couldn't exist under the same roof and enrich one another—that is, if they can respect the mystery and goodness of the Spirit at work among them in different ways without having to assert any particular theological position to which everyone needs to conform in order to be spiritually authentic.

Many people come to the church in search of an orientation that can accommodate their first-hand experiences in a loving sense of God, provide enough security to keep them going, and inspire a way of trusting the always mysterious process of growth and calling that we are given in the ups and downs of life. The evangelical future of the Episcopal Church depends on finding ways to attract and hold such people by providing them with a spiritual theology concretized in spiritual practices and in opportunities for the kind of sharing that meets the spiritual hungers people bring to church (including the spiritual hunger to care for the world in countless forms of social service and advocacy).

The Episcopal Church is a small church needing to resist the temptation to hold to a defensive theology and practice from the past as a way of preserving itself. That would be a sure way to impotency and death. A true future for the church involves mutual listening to the living Spirit in Christ alive today, and living in the guidance of that fire, the same eternal fire that has burned itself into historical moments and saints and left an indelible memory of the nature of divinity. We need to attend that living flame and not settle for the ashes of the past that once were fire but now are only cold clues to the living nature in our midst. Theology can help us see the qualities of that fire, and the church's life can evolve from its mysterious light.

Notes

1. Monica K. Hellwig, "Theology as a Fine Art," *Interpreting Tradition, The Art of Theological Reflection*, The Annual Publication of the College Theology Society, vol. 29, 1983 (Chico, Calif.: Scholars Press).

2. See Paul D. Murray, "Theology after the Demise of Foundationalism," *The Way*, Spring 1998.

Searching for the Beloved: Today's Spiritual Hunger and Jesus

Mark McIntosh

She had already begun to dabble in the occult, and by the time she was in her mid-twenties, she was voraciously experimenting with the esoteric and the exotic of every brand. Today she would probably be listening to Gregorian chant on her car tape player while rushing out to buy the latest bestsellers on angels and near-death experiences. One wonders if, had she lived in our day, Evelyn Underhill would ever have found her way back to Christianity at all, let alone Anglicanism. And yet by God's providence she did. Indeed, Underhill became one of the great spiritual teachers and counselors of the Anglican tradition. Archbishop Michael Ramsey remarked that she very nearly single-handedly rescued English Christianity between the two world wars from the kind of tedious somnolence and superficiality which might have damaged it forever.

How many Evelyn Underhills are we losing today? Listen to a 1994 *Newsweek* cover story:

> From Wall Streeters to artists, from Andre Agassi to David Mamet, millions of Americans are embarking on a search for the sacred in their lives. Whether out of dissatisfaction with the material world or worried about the coming millennium, they are seeking to put spirituality back into their lives. For careerist baby boomers, it's even OK to use the S words—soul, sacred, spiritual, sin.[1]

And the interest in "spirituality" has continued to blossom since then. What could be a more auspicious moment to share the prayerful depths of Christianity with others?

And yet ever since I read this article I've had a sinking feeling, because, over and over, the authentic yearning of our culture seems to be directed towards spiritual junk food. The rich spiritual life of Christianity is easily misunderstood when it is considered from the standpoint of individualistic quests. The doctrinal and scriptural sinews of the spiritual journey can be misinterpreted as oppressive or antiquarian or simply unrelated to the longings of people in a hurry to find the "sacred" or a little tranquility. So it is disarmingly easy, especially in a season of desperate measures, for the church itself to convert faith into a form of therapy and to recast theology as merely a culturally limited metaphor for the supposedly far deeper and universal "spiritual" experiences that all people everywhere are assumed to have.

It is a very serious question, however, whether such forms of facile self-transcendence are capable of truly setting people free for God, or whether they only pacify the deeper longing, numbing it into a demoralized resignation to the status quo. Mark Edmundson notes with considerable accuracy the uneasiness and sense of insufficiency that afflicts so much of the contemporary search for spiritual nourishment.

> The very insubstantiality of the easy transcendence scenarios, their status, acknowledged even by some of their consumers, as simple wish fulfillment, testifies to the absence of plausible hope for many Americans. The fact that the devotees of easy transcendence—the self-help programs, the spiritual journeys, the New Age philosophies—move so rapidly from one to another, as though an endless carousel, a spiritual lazy Susan, were forever turning, and know that they will leave channeling for primal-scream therapy, and screaming for orgone treatment, suggests the despair that often underlies the current quest for self-renovation.[2]

Of course the dark flip side of this spiritual vacuity is the kind of dead-end despair and cynicism that leaks out in much of the music favored by American youth. A craving for true spirituality cannot be fed with vicious and socially alienating computer games for very long before it begins to turn sour.

The popular culture of "have a nice day" and pet angels has no room for the deep and dangerous longings in our hearts, especially our children's hearts. But the price we are paying for pushing such longings aside —and, in church, for disconnecting them from the demanding mystery of faith—is becoming clearer.

> Tattoos—which one architectural modernist derided as body ornaments, saying they were the mark of the killer-to-be, the urban savage—are now all the rage among our Gothic, tribal young. They wear Poe-esque brands, indelible marks of the intention (or hope) to sin. And they come decked out in chains, their bodies variously pierced to signify limit, capture, enclosure, or perhaps their awareness that the drives are in command and that the erogenous zones—preferred sites for piercing—hold one in Gothic thrall. The kids look like stylized dungeon escapees, which is pretty much the point.[3]

The sanitized, homogenized religion of modernity—so rational, so well-meaning—has little resource for coping with such a situation. But the mystical heart of Christianity knows all about the mysterious piercing, the wound that infinite love makes in frail human flesh.

I'm suggesting, then, that the spiritual hunger in contemporary America will never be adequately met by anything less than God's own life, for it has been aroused in the first place by God's desire for us. And Anglicans, if anyone, ought to know how to invite the hungry to the only banquet really worth tucking into: "Whoever comes to me will never be hungry, and whoever believes in me will never be thirsty." We must somehow make our way into the labyrinths and mazes of our culture's dark search for spiritual life and leave signs there of the One whom so many seek without knowing.

What exactly can we do? A little more plainchant in the liturgy and more unashamed celebration of the angels? It wouldn't hurt, but my hunch is that what will really make the difference, strange as it may sound, is some sustained practical reflection on the doctrine of Christ. As Anglicans, we have a rich tradition of devotion to the Word made flesh, the lover of souls. We ought to let our society in on the most luminous secret, namely, that the true source of today's spiritual hunger does not lie in the vacillating fads of pop culture but in the abiding yearning of *God* for *our* companionship.

This is the secret that we must unveil behind the present frantic search for crystals, channelers, and new ways to meditate: that these longings have been aroused in humanity by God. And this is, of course, where Christology fits in and why it is so important at this critical moment. For God has not left even our acquisitive age to its own glittery but forlornly vacuous devices. Jesus of Nazareth approaches our age, too, with heart-rending compassion, a gaze which speaks of infinite sorrow yet infinite mercy, hands wounded yet dangerously determined to pull us out of hell. Can we not help this living Christ to make himself known to our hungry culture? Can we not speak of him—so much more tangible and fraternal than an angel, so much more engaging and lively than the most sumptuous totems of our inner selves—can we not speak of him as the true beloved whom our age is seeking, in whose breast pulses the secret of that unquenchable and eternal love which has come to find us and rescue us?

Back to Evelyn Underhill. In 1921 she turned to the great Roman Catholic thinker Friedrich von Hügel for spiritual direction. He listened to her ardent talk of the "absolute" and of her untiring (though, in truth, quite depleting) search for union with "ultimate reality," and he suggested three spiritual projects: she should spend some regular time with the poor, visiting and helping those whom God loves in the most humble, mundane details of their daily lives; she should reconnect with some very real, faithful, Christian community, not shying away from whatever she might find distasteful or tiresome there; and she should begin to open herself more directly to Christ as opposed to the unknown deity of her day's popular spiritual quests. Some years later, Underhill wrote these intriguing words to a friend:

> Until about five years ago I had never had *any* personal experience of our Lord. I didn't know what it meant. I was a convinced theocentric, [I] thought most Christocentric language and practice sentimental and superstitious and was very handy to shallow psychological explanations of it. I had, from time to time, what seemed to be vivid experiences of God, from the time of my conversion from agnosticism (about twenty years ago now). This position I thought to be that of a broadminded and intelligent Christian, but when I went to the Baron [von Hügel] he said I wasn't much better than a Unitarian! Somehow by his prayers or something he *compelled* me to experience Christ. He never said anything more about it—but I know humanly speaking he did it. It took about four months—it was like watching the sun rise very slowly—and then suddenly one knew what it was. . . . More and more my whole religious life and experience seem to centre with increasing vividness on our Lord.[4]

Gradually, coinciding with her growing personal encounter with the living Jesus of Nazareth, Underhill found herself back at prayer and work within the Church of England.

Year after year she went on working with the poor in London and was in ceaseless demand to lead retreats and give spiritual direction. She often warned those who consulted her against "a sort of arrogance" which may find Jesus too earthy, too time-bound, thereby "missing some of the loveliest, deepest and most touching parts of Christianity."[5] She told one correspondent to "face the fact" that Christ is not simply one of the great spiritual lights thrown up by evolution. And after recommending *Belief in God* and *Belief in Christ*, by the Anglican Bishop Charles Gore, she added, "My own idea is that it is really better to face up at once to what a genuinely Catholic religious philosophy teaches, than to temporize with half-Christian pantheistic-immanentist books."[6] Yet she knew well that simply being frustrated with what seems wrongheaded accomplishes nothing: "When [some people] bring out all this stuff about Christ being a World Teacher, or the parallels of the Mystery religions, the high quality of Buddhist ethics, etc., I just feel what shallow, boring unreal twaddle it is! *But feeling that doesn't win souls for God.*"[7] Shrill denunciations and a retreat to one's cozy right-thinking ghetto will advance the cause not at all.

How can we make known to our own age the Christ who won back the heart of Evelyn Underhill? By revealing the secret of Christ which permits him again and again to convert to himself those who long for re-creation. This is his secret, that—in the very least detail of his utterly human life—he enacts the mission, the identity, the personhood of God's eternal Word to us. This is the power of his attraction, that in his humble human struggle to go on loving even at the cost of his own life, he is acting out in our time and space the eternal self-offering of the divine Trinity. And, therefore, our own struggles to give our lives to his mission bear within them this unbelievable hope of glory: for, in living into the mystery who is Christ, we are living into the mystery of God's own life.

It is true that I am evoking here the claims of a high Christology, that is, an understanding of Jesus which affirms his divinity as well as his humanity. I want to suggest that such a fully incarnational Christology, one which knows of God speaking to us, loving us, precisely by *being human*, makes the most sense of a long historical continuum of experience. This is the experience that demonstrates that what is so compelling about Jesus is not that God has spoken to us through him—after all, God speaks to us through other people all the time—but that, in this life and destiny, as this particular historical individual, God chooses to be God *humanly*. As Jesus, God reveals to us that it is of the very essence of God's life, God's passion, to be God in a way which includes human life within

God's life. The mystery of Christ is the mystery of God's eternal desire to be God in this way and in no other, to be God as our beloved.

I believe that this is the experience of Jesus which so captivated his friends and disturbed his foes. This is the experience which, in continual communion with him, the church has groped to understand. It is certainly the experience of Christ which was powerful enough to call Evelyn Underhill back to the Christian church, even to the Church of England. And this, I would also argue, is the experience of Jesus which could today shed light upon the dark spiritual searching of our culture. This is the mystery we must invite our society to draw close to—that in meeting this particular human being, in sharing ever more deeply in his joy and commitment and love, one is actually living in companionly fidelity with God.

The paramount question then becomes: have we the resources to make this case, to witness to this encounter? Or perhaps more pertinently, what kind of parish communities do we need to be if we are to foster this witness? There will be other occasions to discuss how we might live out the incarnation more intentionally in our liturgy, our outreach, our youth ministry, etc. But in order to do any of these things with clarity and insight, we need to be sure that the basic outlines of the doctrine of the incarnation make sense to us, that we can talk about them among ourselves without confusion or awkwardness. Why not take the next chunk of the adult forum or the Lenten series or even announcement time and really look carefully at the Chalcedonian Definition in the Book of Common Prayer?[8] Find there an itinerary for a profound, life-giving spiritual journey, an encounter with the Word made flesh. Talk about the definition together, not just in terms of history but in terms of a spiritual invitation.

Here you have the stupendous news that the identity of this very human historical individual, Jesus of Nazareth, is actually that of the divine Word or Son. Note carefully, the Chalcedonian Definition is not saying that Jesus is some kind of mixture of God and humanity: a "human being" is *what* Jesus is. But every human being acts out her or his identity in different ways, different patterns. If you go around in a fire truck rescuing people from burning buildings, that's quite a different pattern of personal identity than lying around on a couch watching television and eating cheese puffs all day. And in a real sense, the identity of such very different individuals (*who* they are) is determined by the quite different patterns of activity they each live out. The pattern of activity, the identity-giving life that Jesus enacts is the identity or personhood of the eternal Word of God. That is *who* Jesus is.

How often I've noticed at a vestry meeting or a parish picnic how a particular member of the congregation comes to life in certain circumstances. There are these public moments when all the central identifying traits of a person seem to shine, and, with that one generous gesture or light-hearted retort, we catch a glimpse of *who* this person really is—indeed, sometimes we even catch a glimpse of who such a person may yet grow to become. And then, when I get to know this same person when visiting at home or talking over a meal, I realize how intrinsic and fundamental these identifying traits of personhood really are. The person who soothes a child's fears or calms a family argument at home is the very same person who calls a vestry meeting out of its paralyzing anxiety. It is the same person, enacting the same pattern of identity, but the "material" in which that personhood comes to expression will change in different circumstances.

Consider the helpful clarification of that great Anglican thinker of our century, Austin Farrer:

> God cannot live an identically godlike life in eternity and in a human story. But the divine Son can make an identical response to his Father, whether in the love of the blessed Trinity or in the fulfillment of an earthly ministry. All the conditions of action are different on the two levels; the filial response is one. Above, the appropriate response is a co-operation in sovereignty and an interchange of eternal joys. Then the Son gives back to the Father all that the Father is. Below, in the incarnate life, the appropriate response is an obedience to inspiration, a waiting for direction, an acceptance of suffering . . . a willingness to die. For such things are the stuff of our existence; and it was in this very stuff that Christ worked out the theme of heavenly sonship, proving himself on earth the very thing he was in heaven; that is, a continuous perfect act of filial love.[9]

Jesus is certainly all the more human for giving himself away to those who need him, for suffering their sorrows with them, for dying beside them. And yet the miracle stammeringly exclaimed by Chalcedon is that, exactly in being so very human, Jesus *is* the divine Son carrying the Father's love to the most alienated depths of existence and never ceasing to return that love in the power of the Spirit.

That is *who* he is, the Father's beloved—both in heaven and in the broken circumstances of our world. If it is the Son's eternal role, his personhood, to be the Word, the speaking forth of the Father's love, what could be more divine than to carry it forth infinitely, to carry forth the Father's love into the midst of that which is not only *other* than God (i.e., human life) but actually antagonistic towards God (i.e., sin), and so, from Golgotha and even in hell itself, to offer that divine love back to God?

All this should help to overcome the theological confusion about Jesus that so easily prevails in congregational life. In some places, there is an incarnational minimalism of the "right": here you can find the stained-glass divinity who shimmers magnificently but aloofly beyond the struggles of our common life. In other places, there is an incarnational minimalism of the "left": and here you find the suffering man who preaches an appealing gospel but affords us little intimate communion with God. It is just this division in our thinking about Jesus that the doctrine of the incarnation, lived into, rejoiced in, and taken as a spiritual guide, is meant to overcome. For the mystery of the incarnation draws us into an encounter with the one who is divine precisely by being human, and who exists at all as a human being precisely because he is divine. For in Jesus, our humanity has been drawn into life, become personal, by the direct and immediate outpouring of the Father's love.

We all become persons because someone has aroused our wants and desires. Our parents waved a fuzzy bear before our eyes, and, suddenly, it wasn't enough anymore to lie gurgling in our cribs. Pretty soon we were reaching out our hands for a lot more than cuddly toys. Our desires have drawn us from the bare biological persistence of human nature up into individual personhood. But in our world, our deepest desire, namely our desire for communion, has been warped and misdirected. We've grown up in cultures in which our desire, instead of passing through the world, has become stuck. And so our personhood has become a kind of caricature of the personal identity God has been desiring for us. God desires me eternally to be myself by being attracted up into personhood, by being drawn through the beauty of the world and the compassion of others and the love I pour out to become an authentic person. But sin stunts this journey into personhood. Instead of sensing the intimacy of God in the joy of human loving, I want to turn love into a manipulable possession of my own. Soon the world and my life are opaque, no longer radiant signs of God's presence. The people and places around me become dull idols, arresting my gaze which was designed to go on infinitely desiring and being drawn into God.

But Jesus, as the doctrine of the incarnation tells us, grows toward full personhood through all the conflicting voices and dull obsessive idols of this world. He struggles through all these magnets of desire by hearing the call of the Father in them and beyond them all. His personhood is not trapped by distorted desire. The Father's love, whom we call God the Holy Spirit, draws Jesus' humanity into full personhood by placing the whole world before him, not as a potential object of his own possession, but as gift to be cherished, healed, blessed, broken open, and offered in the perfect communion of love.

And because that is who Jesus is, it is possible for him to draw us also into his communion with the Father, to heal our desire, to make us the authentic persons God eternally desires us to become. If the world distracts us or hypnotizes us into desiring in a self-defeating way, Jesus—like a *good* hypnotist—calls us forth into a new personhood. Jesus offers to us his own mission, his own personal relationship with the Father. And this becomes the setting free of our desires, their deepening, and making pure and whole. James Alison puts it this way:

> Our identity is formed by the desires and currents of this world . . . and it is normally a fragile identity, tangled up and full of contradictions, as are the desires by which we are shot through and which have formed our consciousness. In fact the conscious "I" of each one of us has very little idea of who we are, very little capacity to understand what we are, in point of truth, doing, what hidden dramas of self-punishment, of vengeance, and so on, we are creating. That is, our level of self-deception is pretty high. Jesus understands very well that to this "me," God does not even speak, because it is a mask "me" which only has the ears and eyes of this world. Because of this Jesus doesn't speak to this "me" either, but calls into being another "me," rather as a hypnotist does, a "me" which apparently has nothing to do with who we are, and may be its complete reverse, but which is calling into becoming something we do not even suspect, entering into the process of the creation of a different story.[10]

It is because Jesus is a being who is fully human, whose personhood is given him through his relationship with the Father, that he is able to call us also into that person-making communion. We oughtn't to think of Jesus' divinity, in other words, as a kind of weirdly inaccessible item whose relevance to our congregational life is rather ambiguous. Jesus' divinity is not a kind of divine "stuff" always hovering just beyond our reach. No, what makes Jesus divine as well as human is that he lives out his humanity as the person of God's beloved. It is his relationship with the Father that makes Jesus *who* he is, and that relationship, the power of the Holy Spirit, can become the very pattern of our corporate life. As Christian congregations who live into this mystery of the incarnation, we ourselves become, as St. Paul saw, the body of Christ. And in that way his personhood, his call into relationship with God, becomes available (through our corporate life) to a world hungering for divine communion.

This is the Christ who has power to re-create human lives and to speak directly to our culture's spiritual seekers. It is true that the reality of Christ is a great mystery, but this does *not* mean that Christ's being is unintelligible or that it must be uninviting to our contemporaries. Clearly Evelyn Underhill believed that the spiritual hunger of her contemporaries would be best assuaged within a framework of basic clarity about the one whom they were seeking. Here is a great mission for Anglicanism today: to help the men and women of our own age discover the secret of the beloved, the one whom they are aroused to seek precisely because he has come to seek them first. It is a journey that requires us to recognize how our theology and our spirituality are intrinsically related and mutually informing. It is a journey in which our inchoate desires are named and clarified and cleansed through the corporate mind of the Christian community—including by means of the community's teaching about the incarnation—and then offered as cherishable gifts for the growth of all.

Notes

1. *Newsweek*, 28 November 1994, cover story.
2. Mark Edmundson, *Nightmare on Main Street: Angels, Sadomasochism, and the Culture of Gothic* (Cambridge: Harvard University Press, 1977), 82–83.
3. Ibid., 119.
4. *The Letters of Evelyn Underhill*, ed. Charles Williams (Westminster, Md.: Christian Classics, 1989), 26.
5. Ibid., 234.
6. Ibid., 183.
7. Ibid., 27 (emphasis added).
8. "Historical Documents," The Book of Common Prayer (New York: The Church Hymnal Corporation, 1979), 864.
9. Austin Farrer, *The Brink of Mystery* (London: SPCK, 1976), 20.
10. James Alison, *Raising Abel: The Recovery of the Eschatological Imagination* (New York: Crossroad Publishing Co., 1996), 89.

The Future of Anglican Theology: In Dialogue with the Theology of John Shelby Spong

Reginald H. Fuller

In his latest book Bishop Spong has set out a clear program for the future of Anglican theology and, indeed, all Christian theology.[1] He believes that, unless radical changes are made, amounting to a new Reformation, Christianity will die.

If we are to formulate an alternative view for the future of Anglican theology, as I believe we must, it behooves us to do so in "dialogue" with Bishop Spong. His challenge deserves to be taken seriously and not to be dismissed as the wild ravings of a heretical bishop. The questions and issues he raises are inescapable, but his answers are problematical for those of us who have striven to combine, in an acceptable synthesis, a fearlessly critical treatment of the New Testament with a faithful adherence to its basic message, as formulated in the apostolic kerygma and summarized in the creeds (in other words, a critical orthodoxy).

The necessity of this dual approach was impressed upon me by my successive experiences of New Testament study at Cambridge and Tübingen. At Cambridge I learnt critical methods; at Tübingen I was plunged into the German church and its theologically grounded resistance to the challenge of National Socialism, a challenge that could only be met by a faithful adherence to the word of God as attested in Holy Scripture. It is in loyalty to that double inspiration that I enter here into my examination of Bishop Spong's call for radical change.

Theism

Bishop Spong argues that, if Christianity is to have any future, we must abandon what he calls "theism."[2] By this he does not mean we should all become atheists, but that we should abandon a particular kind of theism: the view of God as a "personalistic deity," located in an external place "up there." Such a God was thought to "intervene" in the cosmic process and human history. It is the Bishop's contention that the modern worldview, shaped successively and cumulatively by Copernicus, Galileo, Newton, Darwin, Freud, and Einstein, cannot possibly accommodate the traditional view of the deity. In place of "theism" thus understood, Bishop Spong proposes that we substitute Tillich's idea of God as the "ground of being."

Caution, however, is advised here. The view of the world as a closed system of cause and effect is not nearly so secure today as it has been since the Enlightenment. There is an increasing openness to the possibility of dimensions of reality not susceptible to scientific observation. Marcus Borg calls attention to this when he writes, "The world view that rejects or ignores the world of the Spirit, is not only relative, but is itself in process of being rejected. Not only is there no intellectual reason to suppose this second order of reality to be unreal, but there is much experimental evidence to suggest its reality."[3] Borg is not speaking of another world up there, but of a dimension or depth to observable reality transcending scientific observation and perceptible only to spiritual vision.

Much of what Bishop Spong treats as traditional theism is called "mythology" by Rudolf Bultmann. That is true, for instance, of the concept of "God up there" and of "God coming down." Such mythological language certainly must be "demythologized." By that, Bultmann meant that the language is neither interpreted literally nor eliminated, but rather interpreted existentially. While we would question the adequacy of Bultmann's existential interpretation of the biblical mythology, we would agree wholeheartedly that, when the Bible says God is "up there" and "coming down," neither literal interpretation nor elimination will do, because the language is saying something important about God. It is attesting to an experience of God as a reality transcending the ordinary level of reality. Biblical passages such as this one attest to this: "Thus saith the high and lofty one who inhabits eternity, whose name is Holy: I dwell in the high and holy place, and also with those who are contrite and humble in spirit" (Isaiah 57:15). The passage speaks of the Spirit world as the dimension of God's being. It speaks of another dimension of reality not accessible to scientific observation. It speaks, not of the location of God, but of the quality of God's being.

The Bible speaks in mythological language of God "coming down," especially at crucial points in Israel's history. Thus at the Exodus:

> Then the Lord said, "I have observed the misery of my people who are in Egypt; I have heard their cry on account of their task masters. Indeed I know their sufferings, and I have come down to deliver them from the Egyptians, and to bring them up out of that land to a good and broad land, a land flowing with milk and honey" (Exodus 3:7–8).

And again, at the return from exile: "O that you would tear open the heavens and come down" (Isaiah 64:1); and of the Christ event: "He who descended is the same one who ascended far above all the heavens" (Ephesians 4:10); or this, "The one who comes from above is above all" (John 3:31).

The language of "coming down" is indispensable for the biblical view of God. This language is not to be taken literally, but speaks of the divine condescension, what Luther called God's *Herablassung*, God's letting God's self down. In these crucial events of salvation history, God became graciously involved with the suffering of his people. Reject this and you have rejected what the Bible means when, ultimately, it declares that God is love. Surely Bishop Spong does not want to deny that!

As for the Tillichian language of God as the ground of being, such a concept is all right as far as it goes, but it is precisely the transcendent deity —the God who is "above all heavens" and who "comes down" in the Exodus, the return, and the Christ event—who is the ground of our being. It is a question of *both/and*, held in paradoxical tension, not of *either/or*, either the God "up there" or the God in the depths of our being. In short, theism is not to be abandoned, if we are faithful to the biblical message, but expanded to include both "hyper-pantheism" and "pantheism" (God *above* all things and *in* all things).

We call this God personal not because God is a person like ourselves, but because the biblical God addresses humans in God's word. By that word, God calls us into an "I/thou" relationship with God's self. The concept of the Word of God, so central throughout the Bible, forbids us to deny, as Bishop Spong would do, the imagery of personhood to the deity.

But can this claim that God has intervened in the history of his people,

Israel, be sustained, faced with a view of the world as a closed system of cause and effect? Some would now argue that the modern worldview has been modified by the discovery of a factor of indeterminacy in the cosmic process, and some Christian apologists have not been slow to exploit this revision. However, this indeterminacy appears to be confined to the microcosmic level of subatomic particles, and we should use caution before applying the possibility of indeterminacy to historical events. It would be more helpful for the theologian to appeal to the two levels of reality already mentioned. At the level of historical-critical observation, all historical events are, in principle, explicable in terms of cause and effect. This is true even of the central biblical events. But these events may be seen from a different perspective and at a different level. The great biblical events are accompanied by prophetic declaration. Moses declares the Exodus to be God's intervention, the second Isaiah declares the return to be an act of God, and the apostles bear witness to Jesus Christ as God's redemptive act. In each case the Word is proclaimed and either received by faith or rejected in unbelief. It is the Word and faith that make it possible for Christian theology to speak of acts of God, of God's interventions in history, in events which, at the ordinary level, are understood in terms of cause and effect.

Human Sin and the Law

Is Bishop Spong correct in rejecting the whole concept of human sinfulness, what traditional theology has called original sin?[4] Is it true, as the Bishop argues, that our view of the world and our understanding of human behavior are very different from what they were only fifty years ago, to say nothing of New Testament times? We understand a great deal more about human behavior since Marx, Freud, and Jung, and yet human beings still exploit and kill one another.

These considerations open up the question of law. Of course, the story of Moses going up the mountain to receive the Ten Commandments on tablets of stone is a myth, as Bishop Spong correctly recognizes.[5] But like all the great biblical myths, it expresses an important truth. Human beings generally have some sort of sense of right and wrong. They usually feel themselves to be under what Kant called a "categorical imperative." That sense of right and wrong was sharpened by Israel's experience of their God. They knew themselves to be responsible to Yahweh, answerable for their conduct. They realized that their sense of right and wrong was not just their own imagination. Of course, their formulations of the commandments were, as Bishop Spong points out, culturally conditioned.[6] That was true of the fourth (for Roman Catholics/Lutherans, the third) commandment enjoining the observance of the Sabbath. It is true, too, that the prohibition of adultery had more to do with property rights than with sexual morality. But we have to interpret the Ten Commandments (or at least the second table) in terms of Jesus' radicalization of them in the Sermon on the Mount, and in terms of the double commandment of love. Even the fourth (third) commandment is not entirely irrelevant: the Sabbath finds its eschatological fulfillment in the coming of the kingdom of God, and we celebrate the coming of the kingdom and participate in it in the weekly observance of the Lord's Day. Thus, for Christians, Sunday is not the Sabbath, but its eschatological fulfillment.

There is another reason for insisting on the divine origin of the moral imperative: sin is seen as sin only in the light of the demand of God. Paul saw this when he spoke of the law as a summons to repentance (Romans 7:7–25). Only if it is the transgression of a divine imperative is it really exposed as sin, i.e., rebellion against God and the perversion of our relationship with God. And until that happens, the need for divine deliverance is not perceived. It is in response to this situation that God's redemptive act in Jesus Christ occurred. And to that we now turn.

The Christ Event

We can agree with Bishop Spong that parts of the Jesus story in the gospels cannot be taken literally. This is especially true of the infancy narratives and of the resurrection appearance stories.

I have argued elsewhere[7] that the birth stories in Matthew and Luke are in the main narrative expressions of Christology, and that Christian belief means accepting the Christology they express. Bishop Spong is on the right track when he treats them as "midrash," though "midrash"—which usually is understood as an expanded interpretation of an Old Testament text—probably is not the right technical term in this connection.[8] Perhaps the birth stories contain a little more factual history than Bishop Spong is prepared to allow. Certain points of agreement between Matthew and Luke make it clear that some of the factual traditions enshrined in the stories are of pre-gospel origin and may indeed be historical. Such items include the names of Mary and Joseph, the claim that Joseph was of Davidic descent, the dating of the birth of Jesus toward the end of Herod's reign, and perhaps also the curious timing of the conception,[9] and the location of the birth at Bethlehem. In reading these stories, however, we must listen to the proclamation which they enshrine—that Jesus Christ is the interventive act of God, fulfilling the hope of Israel's restoration.

Bishop Spong is highly allergic to "blood theology," i.e., the interpretation of Jesus' death as a sacrifice.[10] (Ironic that he should be squeamish on this topic, given that this century may be the bloodiest in human history!) We may agree with him that the language of cultic sacrifice is meaningless in contemporary culture. But the following points should be borne in mind:

1. Cultic sacrifice provides only one of several images with which the New Testament presents the meaning of Christ's death. For Paul, it plays only a minor role, and that in citations from traditional hymnaic formulae.[11] Other important images are taken from international/personal relations (reconciliation), the law court (justification), and the battlefield (victory over the cosmic powers of evil).
2. The cross is central to the Christian message, the heart of the act of God in Jesus Christ. Theologians must not lay it aside as incomprehensible but find adequate imagery for contemporary understanding.
3. "Blood" in Hebraic thought means, not just the physical reality, but life itself, especially life given over to death.
4. The idea of self-giving love, poured out to the point of death, is surely not alien to our culture or any other. We can appreciate Paul's meaning when he speaks of Christ who "loved me and gave himself for me" (Galatians 2:20).

The Easter Stories

The Easter proclamation summarized in 1 Corinthians 15:3–8 is generally recognized by scholars to be pre-Pauline and probably a very early tradition. The people listed in this formula had visionary experiences that may be susceptible at one level to psychological explanation.[12] However, at the level of proclamation and faith, the New Testament claims them to be revelatory encounters. Through these revelations the recipients came to believe that God had raised Jesus from the dead and exalted him to God's own transcendent mode of being. The appearance stories at the end of the gospels are, however, later. In a manner similar to the birth stories, they are narrative expressions of the Easter message enshrined in the earlier tradition. They bring out the revelatory character of the appearances, and their implications: the inauguration of the kerygma, the foundation of the church and its mission, and the origin of Christian baptism and some aspects of the eucharist.[13]

Much more disputed is the story of the empty tomb. Many scholars would agree with Bishop Spong and, following Bultmann, dismiss it as a "late legend."[14] They may be right. However, I have argued elsewhere that there is a historical nucleus to the story from which the later "legends" could have been developed; this is the fact that Mary Magdalene, perhaps with some other women, found the tomb in which Jesus had been laid inexplicably empty. Like all other historical facts, it is susceptible of natural explanations, and a number of these possibilities are mentioned or suggested in the gospels. For instance, Mark is at pains to emphasize that the women noted the location of the tomb on Good Friday evening, thus hinting at the possibility that the women went to the wrong tomb on Easter morning. Matthew speaks of the rumor that the disciples stole the body. John suggests that some other person (e.g., the gardener) had removed the body. No doubt there are other possible natural explanations, but the synoptic accounts offer the literary device of an interpreting angel (*angelus interpres*). Here, the faith community is providing a revelatory interpretation of a historical event.

Another argument frequently adduced against the historicity of the empty tomb is its absence from the pre-Pauline kerygma of 1 Corinthians 15:3–8, and from Paul's subsequent discussion in that chapter. Not only is it arguable, however, that the sequence, "was buried—was raised," implies the reversal of the burial, but, more importantly, Paul's subsequent argument about the resurrection of the faithful implies a bodily resurrection. The resurrection of Jesus and the general resurrection of the believers involve the transformation of the body. This, of course, does not mean—as is frequently insisted upon today—the resuscitation of the corpse, but the transformation of the physical. The empty tomb tradition is a reminder that the Christian hope must embrace the glorification of the material cosmos.

The Ascension

The Ascension is narrated only twice in the New Testament, each time in the Lucan writings (Luke 24:50–51 [longer text]; Acts 1:6–11). The second version is clearly what Bishop Spong would call a midrash based on the similar story about Elijah in 2 Kings 2:1–12. It puts into story form a belief that was generally held in the early church, namely that Jesus—being raised from the dead—is now exalted to God's transcendent mode of being. Bishop Spong, in my opinion, is quite right to insist that the story not be taken literally.[15] But neither should the truth it enunciates be eliminated. "Ascension" is mythological language for the essential faith-truth that Jesus is Lord, removed from the restrictions of space and time and constantly available and present in Word and sacrament.

The Parousia

Similarly, the Parousia is not to be regarded as a literal event, during which Christ descends with his angels on the clouds of heaven at the end of history. It is a symbolic expression of what Pierre Teilhard de Chardin called the "omega point," the goal of human history and the cosmic process. Once again, Bishop Spong is correct in insisting that it cannot be taken literally. However, once again it must be interpreted, not eliminated.

Jesus as Spirit Person

Bishop Spong has picked up from Marcus Borg the description of Jesus of Nazareth as "Spirit person."[16] This idea certainly has its attractions. Jesus can be presented intelligibly to the modern world as one of a class of figures who had an unusual experience of that higher dimension of reality, the sacred or the world of Spirit. But that understanding fails to capture what is unique about Jesus. It is like the description of him as teacher and prophet—true as far as it goes.

It is interesting that, in support of this view of Jesus as a Spirit person, Marcus Borg cites the Lucan version of Jesus' inaugural address in the synagogue at Nazareth (Luke 4:18–19), during which Jesus quotes from Isaiah 61. So impressed is Borg by the appropriateness of this quotation on the lips of Jesus that he is tempted to accept its authenticity, despite its being a Lucan expansion of Mark 6:1–6 and, therefore, probably redactional (i.e., an editorial addition). Be that as it may, there are other passages to support the notion of Jesus as a Spirit-filled figure, e.g., Mark 3:28–29; Luke 11:20; and Luke 7:22, which echoes Isaiah 61:1. These are passages whose authenticity is less open to doubt than Luke's version of the sermon at Nazareth. Accordingly, we may agree that Jesus understood himself to be empowered for his mission by the Spirit. But Spirit, in this context, is something more precise: it is the eschatological power of God coming in a unique way upon his unique eschatological agent. Here, in Jesus' self-understanding, we find the pre-Easter genesis of post-Easter Christology.

Conclusion

Anglican theology has always striven to be faithful to kerygma and creed, yet open to new knowledge. To achieve such a synthesis is a difficult task and a constant challenge. It is always easier to adhere rigidly to the literal meaning of the Bible and to reject new knowledge. It is equally easy to capitulate unreservedly to contemporary thought and thereby surrender the truth of the gospel. But ever since *Lux Mundi*,[17] Anglicanism has preferred the "both/and" rather than the "either/or"—both fidelity to the revelation and openness to new discoveries of truth. To continue along that road will be the challenge facing Anglican theology in the third millennium.

This essay is dedicated to the memory of Raymond E. Brown, SS, priest, scholar, colleague and friend, whose death occurred while these lines were being written.

Notes

1. John Shelby Spong, *Why Christianity Must Change or Die: A Bishop Speaks to Believers in Exile* (San Francisco: HarperSanFrancisco, 1998).
2. Ibid., 43–55.
3. See, e.g., Marcus J. Borg, *Jesus: A New Vision* (San Francisco: HarperSanFrancisco, 1987).
4. Spong, *Why Christianity Must Change or Die*, 84–99.
5. Ibid., 150–155.
6. Ibid., 152–154.
7. Reginald H. Fuller, *He That Cometh* (Harrisburg, Pa./Wilton, Ct.: Morehouse Publishing, 1990), 94–96.

8. See John Shelby Spong, *Born of a Woman: A Bishop Rethinks the Birth Narratives* (San Francisco: HarperSanFrancisco, 1992), and *Resurrection: Myth or Reality?* (San Francisco: HarperSanFrancisco, 1994), 3–22, passim.

9. Raymond E. Brown, *The Birth of the Messiah* (New York: Doubleday, 1993), 526–528, 697–712 (historicity of the timing between betrothal and marriage; virginal conception through the Holy Spirit, a Christological interpretation); John P. Meier, *A Marginal Jew: Rethinking the Historical Jesus* (New York: Doubleday, 1991), 220–230 (a theologoumenon without certain historical basis in the timing of the conception).

10. Spong, *Why Christianity Must Change or Die*, 88–99.

11. C. Kingsley Barrett, *Paul: An Introduction to His Thought* (Louisville: Westminster/Knox, 1994), 114–117.

12. So Gerd Luedemann, *The Resurrection of Jesus: History, Experience, Theology* (Minneapolis: Fortress, 1994).

13. Reginald H. Fuller, "The Resurrection of Jesus Christ," *BibRes.* 4 (1960): 8–24.

14. So Gerd Luedemann; Spong, *Resurrection: Myth or Reality?* On the other hand there are scholars like Raymond E. Brown, *The Virginal Conception and the Bodily Resurrection of Jesus* (New York: Paulist, 1973), and John A. T. Robinson, *Can We Trust the New Testament?* (London: SCM, 1976).

15. Spong, *Why Christianity Must Change or Die*, 13, 33, 82.

16. Borg, *Jesus: A New Vision*, 39–46; Spong, *Why Christianity Must Change or Die*, 100–117. Borg has more to say on the possible authenticity of Luke 4:18–19 in a later book, *Meeting Jesus Again for the First Time* (San Francisco: HarperSanFrancisco, 1994), 44, n. 40.

17. Charles Gore, ed., *Lux Mundi: a Series of Studies in the Religion of the Incarnation*, 12th ed. (London: John Murray, 1902) [first published 1889].

A Retro-Future for Theology in the Episcopal Church

Paul F. M. Zahl

Introduction

The subject of theology's future in the Episcopal Church could make for a very short essay. First, there is the conditional character of the very possibility of any future to human experience in a positive sense. Can we really speak with solid hope of a promising future for the human race? To this first, constraining question, a Christian is bound to answer, "yes."

Second, there is the question of *theology*'s future? Does theology as an authentic, independent science still possess a charter? In a few years will there exist academic departments of theology at all, save in Roman Catholic universities and Protestant seminaries? We honor the University of Durham for sticking to its guns and maintaining a Department of Theology against the trend—as seen at Uppsala, for example—to transform ancient Christian faculties into departments of religious studies along American lines. Will we in a few years witness the American model coming into being at Marburg or Heidelberg, the "phenomenological" approach replacing systematic theology as such? One does well to wonder. Theology's future as a validated discipline is not assured.

Third, there is the specific question of theology's future in the Episcopal Church. We have not proven a particularly fertile ground for theological thinkers. We remember DuBose way back then, and—more recently—Hans Frei (who wore his Episcopalianism so lightly as to be almost invisible), and John Macquarrie, and Stephen Sykes. And there are many others. But if you asked most Episcopalians, they would probably not understand our church as a theologically driven institution. One would hear more likely that we "do" theology through the liturgy, *lex orandi, lex credendi*. Is there a widespread, serious desire among Episcopalians to think theologically, to think systematically, about God, to follow an argument to its logical conclusion, to venture, even to go all the way with an idea? Is our church, in fact, emancipated in the intellectual sense? Or does our touted roominess stretch nowhere so far?

So, this could be a short essay. It could shipwreck from the start on the shoals of a questionable future for the human race, a general supplanting of academic theology by "religious studies," and an inherited queasiness in the Episcopal Church itself regarding the very independence and validity—let alone the intellectual drive—of the enterprise.

Alternatively, we could propose a brighter future. We could set out a more hopeful agenda. This, in fact, is what we can do. If we think "retro" for a moment, if we adjust our perspective to celebrate important moments of theology within Anglican history—most of those moments being attached to distant thinkers and events—we might yet be able to take courage. There are tracts, some considerable tracts, of theological precedent within Anglicanism, which are venturesome, even daring. Our church does, I believe, have more than a little to go on. A retro-future for theology in the Episcopal Church is what this essay proposes: that is, a future of re-envisioning theology on the basis of radical breakthroughs that have already taken place in the past. Our future is bright, or at least brighter, if we are able to grasp where we have come from.

At least four moments in our theological tradition create a foundation on which to build, or build again, in the new millennium.

The Freedom Moment of 1688

When the Glorious Revolution of 1688 overthrew King James II in favor of William and Mary, the church was able to represent an exemplary moment in the struggle for intellectual freedom. The Whig divines and Latitudinarian bishops who came to power under the House of Orange have been much maligned ever since the rise of the Oxford Movement, and well before that by High Churchmen such as Dr. Sacheverell. They have been criticized for selling out "church prerogatives" and accommodating church truths too easily and lubriciously to political and cultural pressures of their day. But the Latitudinarians had something! They were conscious ecumenists before their time, Bible critics in the context of faithfulness long before their time, and much less *Anglican* thinkers than *Christian* thinkers. They believed in intellectual and theological freedom, as did the King who preferred them. They were comprehensive, rather than exclusive, thinkers. The moment represented by Tillotson and Stillingfleet and Tenison and Sherlock is a "freedom moment," possibly *the* freedom moment for Anglican theology. The intellectual and civil emancipation they wrought is a pillar for the future of theology in the Episcopal Church.

The Church Moment of 1549

The Episcopal Church still takes its inherited core shape from the Book of Common Prayer of 1549. It has received its mainframe theological shape from the collects that Cranmer edited, collected, and composed for the Prayer Book. The church's theology has put down deep wells within the insights that permeate the collects. The collects are able to function for us almost credally. Even one of Cranmer's collects is sufficient to demonstrate this, the collect for the First Sunday after Easter:

> Almighty Father, who hast given thine only Son to die for our sins, and to rise again for our justification; Grant us so to put away the leaven of malice and wickedness, that we may always serve thee in pureness of living and truth; through the merits of the same Thy Son Jesus Christ our Lord.[1]

This collect ties the church's teaching concerning justification indissolubly to the critical area of the church's worship as reflected in the set prayers. It is the high point, within Cranmer's collects, of a conscious Protestant theology of the Christian life.

Similarly, the collect for the Second Sunday of Advent is the high point within the liturgy of Protestant methodology or, better, of Protestant hermeneutics:

> Blessed Lord, who hast caused all holy Scriptures to be written for our learning; Grant that we may in such wise hear them, read, mark, learn, and inwardly digest them, that by patience and comfort of Thy holy Word, we may embrace, and ever hold fast, the blessed hope of everlasting life, which Thou hast given us in our Saviour Jesus Christ.[2]

This collect's focus on the Bible, to which human reason and church tradition are subordinated in the search for truth, is clear beyond any conceivable rationalization of an alternate priority. Justification and the Bible define the "church moment" in its Prayer Book form.

The second pillar of our creative retro-future for theology in the Episcopal Church is the "church moment" of 1549. It is Reformation theology set in liturgical form and thereby connected organically to the institution of the church.

The Grace Moment of 1595

The Lambeth Articles of 1595 mark a point of almost unexampled courage in the history of English church thought. Fashioned by Dr. Whitaker of Cambridge and formally approved by Archbishops Whitgift and Hutton, these nine articles, or theses, were an attempt to grapple with and settle confessionally the question of God's grace in the ultimate design of history. The "doctrines of grace" constituted the apple of discord in the late Reformation period. These doctrines referred in 1595, not to the crux question of God's grace versus human works in the disposition of salvation, but rather to a second, derivative question, the question of predestination or the motive force and spring behind the divine plan expressed in Christ. As grace versus law had been the first point of contention and as the eucharist had been the second point of contention (particularly among English Protestants and the Reformed), so, in the 1580s and 1590s, predestination was the third point or lightning rod for controversy.

Archbishop Whitgift moved with astonishing timeliness to settle the question for the sake of unity within the church. He and Matthew Hutton very mildly edited William Whitaker's draft, which stated the doctrine of double predestination and, in fact, most of the main points of classic Calvinist teaching concerning the doctrines of grace. The two archbishops, together with the Bishop of London and others, endorsed the amended draft on November 20th. These Lambeth Articles were not approved by the Queen, however, because the bishops had failed to consult her before they met. The Lambeth Articles are found in the Irish Prayer Book of 1615. They stand as a unique and enduring monument in our tradition to the necessary process of going all the way with an idea in hopes thereby of reaching the truth about it.

The nine propositions reflect absolutely not one trace of the so-called "Anglican" (i.e., deliberate) ambiguity of expression and ethos. Here are the Lambeth Articles as translated by Thomas Fuller:

1. God from eternity hath predestinated certain men unto life; certain men hath he reprobated.

2. The moving or efficient cause of predestination unto life is not the foresight of faith, as of perseverance, or of good works, or of any thing that is in the person predestinated, but only the good will and pleasure of God.

3. There is predestinated a certain number of the predestinate, which can neither be augmented nor diminished.

4. Those who are not predestinated to salvation shall be necessarily damned for their sins.

5. A true, living, and justifying faith, and the Spirit of God justifying (sanctifying), is not extinguished, falleth not away; it vanisheth not away in the elect, either finally or totally.

6. A man truly faithful, that is, such a one who is endorsed with a justifying faith, is certain, with the full assurance of faith, of the remission of his sins and of his everlasting salvation by Christ.

7. Saving grace is not given, is not granted, is not communicated to all men, by which they may be saved if they will.

8. No man can come unto Christ unless it should be given unto him, and unless the Father shall draw him; and all men are not drawn by the Father, that they may come to the Son.

9. It is not in the will or power of anyone to be saved.[3]

I give the Articles in full, because they are such an unambiguous production. They give the lie to any assumption that "Anglicanism" is *by nature* equivocal and two-faced. To the contrary, they reveal the spirit of a "road less traveled," a road to unmistakable assertion in the face of seemingly overwhelming and deterring paradox and mystery.

The key moment, or central premise, is Article 9. This thesis upholds God's grace as the only hope for human "success" in the ultimate sense. We can in no way save ourselves. All is God's movement towards us.

This is the third pillar of the retro-future for Episcopal theology in the new millennium: God's grace as the unique change-agent for the human condition and, moreover, God's grace as both the alpha and the omega for our doctrine of God.

The Mission Moment of 1811

On May 29, 1811, Alexander Viets Griswold was consecrated Episcopal bishop over Massachusetts, Vermont, Maine, Rhode Island, and New Hampshire. During the service, he was awakened "to more serious thoughts of duty as a minister of Christ; and in consequence I . . . with more earnest zeal preached 'Jesus Christ and him crucified.' "[4] We can date the renewal of evangelical missionary vigor in the Episcopal Church to that day in May, for it parallels almost exactly the renewal of such zeal in Virginia. With Griswold working in the Northeast and Richard Channing Moore and William Meade working in Virginia, the stage was set for what we may now see as the fourth pillar of a retro-future for Episcopal theology. This is the "mission moment."

An ardent and explicit desire to bring the nations to Christ is not un-Episcopalian. The nineteenth-century missionary signal emitting from England was fueled heavily by men and women from both High-Church and Low-Church Anglican sectors. In the United States, the Episcopal Evangelicals *built* the church, or rather rebuilt it following the Revolution, from South Carolina to New Hampshire, then to Ohio, Kansas, Iowa, and Nevada. The 1858 hymn "Stand Up, Stand Up for Jesus," written by George Duffield, is a pregnant symbol and signature of the vigor of the evangelicalism of the Episcopal Evangelicals. The cross was the focal point, together with its then universal interpretation as a substitutionary atonement.

George Bernard Shaw's having to deal with the atonement (in his preface to *Androcles and the Lion*) as the one inescapable theme in the Christianity he had known growing up, is one extremely telling indication of the character of nineteenth-century Anglican Christianity (and not just in England and Ireland but even more robustly in America). The fervor of Anglicanism's evangelical strand is so well attested by sources stemming from our church in the pre-Tractarian, post-Revolutionary decades that it is almost unbelievable in hindsight how universally this strand was isolated and forgotten after the Civil War. It is as if a group psychosis of focussed amnesia had settled over the Episcopal Church, at least regarding its "mission moment."

Here, then, is the fourth of four pillars supporting a retro-theology of the Episcopal Church: the "mission moment" of May 29, 1811.

Conclusion

"Retro" does not spell "reactionary." "Retro" spells "rethink." We are due for a rethink, based on sublimated moments of former theological aspiration. One moment is the "freedom moment" of 1688, in which intellectual emancipation was embraced theologically and politically, and at the very highest level in the church. One moment is the "church moment" of 1549, in which justification and the Bible were codified within the liturgy as confirmed necessities and irreducibles. One moment is the "grace moment" of 1595, when the archbishops took a central idea as far as it could go, both for truth's sake and for unity's sake. They did, thereby, hope to comprehend rather than exclude the Calvinist insight. A further moment is the "mission moment" of 1811, a moment essential for Episcopal survival and moreover for our great expansion within the American Republic. This fourth moment, like the other three, is not well enough known. Together with the other three, however, it carries a burning coal of hope (Isaiah 6:6).

Freedom, church, grace, and mission: four pillars of a propulsive theology of hope. This theology of hope is Anglican in tradition and catholic in breadth, Protestant in its passionate free search for truth, evangelical in regard to the Good News of grace, and evangelistic in relation to the missionary urge to tell. This is a radical retro-theology for the future of the Episcopal Church.

Notes

1. The Book of Common Prayer (New York: The Church Hymnal Corporation, 1928), 170.
2. Ibid., 92.
3. Thomas Fuller, *Church History of Britain*, vol. 3 (London, 1837), 147.
4. William Stevens Perry, *The History of the American Episcopal Church*, vol. 2 (Boston, 1885), 183–184.

Theology in the Service of the Church's Pastoral Life: A Proposal

J. Robert Wright

What would it mean for theology to be more closely related to the pastoral life of the church, and, in particular, to such life in the Episcopal Church? I write as a church historian who also "does" theology—especially historical and ecumenical and ascetical and liturgical theology—but also as someone who is interested in the more "pure" topics of systematic theology, such as God, Christ, Trinity, as well as ethical and moral questions.

When any kind of theology is "done," it would seem to me that it is either talked, written, read, or lived. In the first and fourth of these modes, everyone is a theologian; in the third mode, many are theologians; but only those who write (and, often, publish) are theologians in the second sense. It is theology in this second mode, written theology, to which I shall give primary attention in this essay, although I would also remark in passing that my own primary theological occupation deals most frequently with theology in the third and fourth modes (as a church historian, I read, chronicle, research, and analyze the lives of Christians, most of whom never write anything at all and many of whom read very little).

Now my question becomes the following: what would it mean for those theologians who do not merely talk and read and live but also write theology to write their theologies in ways that are more closely related to the pastoral life of the Episcopal Church? And my answer is that such theology should be written with closer reference to the questions that the majority (who do not write theology) are asking, and that theologians who will attempt to write with closer reference to such questions should make a greater effort at seeking agreement among themselves, and that the Episcopal Church itself should make a greater effort to encourage them in this enterprise. This is the thesis and thrust of my argument, although I readily concede that there still must be much room left for individual theologians to write their individual specialized articles, and for those with the greatest minds to construct their own particular and unique *summas*.

In my experience of the pastoral life of the Episcopal Church, most of the questions asked about this church are requests for greater clarity as to what the Episcopal Church teaches about various matters. Most persons are less interested in abstract theological "head-trips" than in clear answers; not necessarily simple answers, but clear answers, or at least answers that lay out the spectrum of belief that does exist and explain clearly the issues involved in reaching an answer. "What does the Episcopal Church teach?" they ask. Why does it teach what it teaches? How is what it teaches related to the Bible, to the Book of Common Prayer, to the historical tradition of the church, to contemporary life today, to the parallel teachings of other churches and other religions? Does it make sense, and how does it make sense? Is it important, and why is it important? Or should it be changed and, if so, why?

Similar questions are being asked of us, I might add, from ecumenical quarters, as those in other churches, especially those engaged in ecumenical dialogues and conversations with us, want to know what we as the Episcopal Church actually teach about particular matters. And it will just not do, either pastorally or ecumenically, to reply simply that there can be no answer but "ambiguity" and that, as Anglicans, we are in the business of celebrating ambiguity! I have actually heard such statements made, but I submit that they are usually a cop-out from facing questions where truth is involved and *can be ascertained*. If I as a professor find an instance of ambiguity in a term paper, I mark it down, and often I think that ecumenical representatives from other churches as well as the rank and file of the Episcopal Church tend likewise to mark down such answers when they hear them given. Of course, there are times when ambiguity will seem honestly necessary if no single answer seems possible, but too often an answer that urges a celebration of ambiguity merely represents a failure to address the question in a responsible and carefully thought-out way.

Now it is also my experience as a lifelong Episcopalian that, in the strict, professional sense of those who write and publish theology, our theologians are by and large very well qualified to address such questions, which they often do, and even to give clear answers to them, but that they usually do this individually and seldom collectively. There is very little impetus in the Episcopal Church—or in the Anglican Communion, for that matter—for theologians collectively to turn their energies towards the joint exploration of such questions with a view toward reaching some responsible, sufficiently nuanced, agreed answers that might be said to constitute our "doctrine" as such. Instead, everyone remains more or less a "lone ranger," at times even wallowing in the ambiguity of contradictory and unreconciled truth-claims. When collectively agreed answers occasionally are produced, they are likely to be rather simplistic and based upon inadequate preparation and reflection. Cases in point might be some of the resolutions of some recent Lambeth Conferences.

The Lambeth of 1998 has been accused of seeking a "Christianity of clarity," but to draw such an inference is, I believe, to miss the point. Surely there is nothing wrong with seeking clear answers to questions that arise from the pastoral life of the church, nothing wrong with seeking a Christianity of clarity. Indeed, clarity is the elimination or, at least, reduction of ambiguity through patient and thoughtful reconciliation of differences. The problem, rather, lies in a failure to take the collective theological enterprise with sufficient seriousness. With every Lambeth Conference proclaiming that its resolutions have no binding significance upon any province, and with only a minimum of collective theological preparation that involves only a very small number of theologians who write and publish, what else can one expect? I am not speaking of any one Lambeth resolution, but of most of them! There is nothing wrong with seeking or giving clear answers to straightforward, pastoral questions. But such answers must be extensively, collectively, adequately prepared by a deliberate theological process that involves more than the usual commitment of a handful of people doing a few months of work—usually part-time work while they are doing many other things as well. For theology to be more closely related to the pastoral life of the church, the collective enterprise of theology must be taken much more seriously than Anglicans have traditionally done.

Note the situation that the bishops of the Episcopal Church now face in the light of the 1998 Lambeth Conference resolution 1.15 on "International Debt and Economic Justice" (which, presumably, most of them voted for). This resolution calls for "cancellation of unpayable debts of the poorest nations" and a commitment from our dioceses "to fund international development programmes, recognized by provinces, at a level of at least 0.7% of annual total diocesan income." The bishops have also pledged themselves, in public support of this same resolution, "to highlight the moral and theological implications." But how are they going to do this? If such high-sounding words in support of so noble and needful a cause are not to be dismissed by the intelligent world as mere platitudes, our bishops very soon will need to have produced the moral and theological case for taking these actions—certainly by the time that the book containing this essay is published. If the issue is as pressing as they say it is, then one can reasonably expect them, all of them, to go public on the home front, at least by the early fall following the conclusion of Lambeth, with the moral and theological case. But the bishops are not specialists in this area, and I suspect that few of them will have said much about it, except for, perhaps, a few generalities. But we have theologians, especially some moral and systematic theologians (not to mention qualified economists) who can think from a Christian perspective, who are specialists in such matters, and they need to be brought into the process now, although, of course, it would have been better to have called them together to work on this task a couple of years before Lambeth met. Now, our bishops need to reflect with our theologians and other specialists: How are we to determine, on any Christian principle, which nations are the "poorest" ones and which of their debts are "unpayable"? As this essay is being written, Russia is on the verge of financial chaos. Which of its debts, from the moral and theological implications of which the bishops have spoken, are agreed to be "unpayable"? And who decides? Or take Africa, where Anglicanism exists and is growing and whose bishops were present and voting at Lambeth. Are the nations of Africa understood to be "poorer" than Russia and, so, do they take precedence? Who decides? What "moral and theological" resources will our bishops utilize, say, within the first year following Lambeth in order to convince their diocesan conventions that international development programs should now be funded by our church to a level of at least 0.7% of annual total diocesan income? These are noble Christian goals, but I suggest that our bishops will need the collective enterprise of our theologians and other qualified experts if they are to convince the rank and file of Episcopalians that Lambeth has given the right answer and that the Episcopal Church should now direct its funds for this purpose.

And so, from this specific example, I return to the question: What might it look like for the Episcopal Church (not to mention the Anglican

Communion) to make a greater effort to encourage a more collective enterprise in the service of doctrine in order to seek a more responsible and sufficiently nuanced clarity of answers to the many questions that arise from the pastoral life of the church today? For starters, over the past eleven years in the Church of England there has arisen a collective official procedure involving bishops, theologians, and other specialists for the consideration and determination of such questions when they are put; its structure is still in process of development. In many ways, the Roman Catholic Church tends to have an even better such process, though I, for one, would not always agree with the answers it produces, nor do I welcome the way in which the current doctrines of papal primacy and infallibility seem to impede that process.

I would suggest that what the Episcopal Church needs is the establishment of some sort of central clearing-house or, better, enabling-office (along with the necessary funding) that would promote such an enterprise. It should be sponsored under the aegis or *episkope* of the House of Bishops (as is the case in the Church of England), whose responsibility of oversight (as set forth in our Prayer Book's catechism) is to see that the church's faith is guarded and taught.[1] The bishops should recognize, encourage, and mobilize our theologians and other qualified specialists as their allies in this duty. Procedures might be developed as follows: the questions that need to be faced should be identified; a number of competent theologians representing many different viewpoints should be invited to work on each question; a series of collective theological study-projects should be launched for each topic; papers should be written; conferences or consultations should be held; national commissions and interim bodies of the church should be involved; accounts of the work in progress should be published; and position papers should be drawn up for discussion at all levels of the church's life, not unlike the churchwide process of revision that preceded our 1979 Prayer Book. Eventually, of course, and after further consultation with the House of Bishops, the most important matters should be referred for discussion and vote in the General Convention (and perhaps even at the Lambeth Conference, if there could be any agreement that its decisions are to be received on anything more than a pick-and-choose basis). What is needed, therefore, is not to dismiss those who seek "a Christianity of clarity," but rather to provide such clarity in a responsible way that takes account of the complexity of the questions addressed and also of the spectrum of answers that might be offered.

All this would probably need some vote of the General Convention in order to get underway. Such a mechanism could not emerge full-blown or appear overnight. And it would cost money. All the seminaries would need to be involved, as well as other centers of theological learning. The *Anglican Theological Review* might be a vehicle for publication of the work in progress. A bishop might be appointed to oversee it, or even a theologian consecrated to oversee it (i.e., consecrated to that particular form of *episkope*, oversight in the service of the church's doctrine), as is done, for example, in the Coptic Orthodox Church today. The Roman Catholic Church has its Congregation for the Doctrine of the Faith, which would not be all bad as a starting model for us, especially if the collective enterprise of theology were to be emphasized rather than individualistic pronouncements based upon absolute authority. Just as the 1998 Lambeth Conference recognized the need for, and growing significance of, "instruments of Anglican unity" such as the Lambeth Conference, the Anglican Consultative Council, the meeting of Primates, and the Canterbury Archbishop, so, perhaps, it is time for the Episcopal Church to establish some sort of national enabling-office and commission on theology for the sake of a more responsible and collective approach to doctrine in the service of its pastoral life.

Note

1. The Book of Common Prayer (New York: The Church Hymnal Corporation, 1979), 855.

Avoiding the Dangers of a Monumental Church

William C. Morris, Jr.

> . . . God, who might perfect his people in a moment, chooses not to bring them to manhood in any other way than by the education of the Church.
>
> —*John Calvin*[1]

The sixteenth-century reformers, once overrated, are now under-appreciated. We know their names, but we rarely read their works attentively anymore. We suppose that we and they have different concerns and different ends. They sought to rescue Christianity from the effects of the church's medieval successes. We are more often worried about the church's modern institutional failures. Hence, we assume that they have little to say to us.

However, reform and renewal do not depend upon a certain cultural setting or even upon the character of the impending crisis. Many of the issues in the church which perplexed the reformers also perplex us—anxiety, confusion, arrogance, a declining grasp of the gospel, historical and theological mendacity, a sense of disorientation and exhaustion.

The church which both nurtured and perturbed the reformers was the product of remarkable successes. It lingers in the Western imagination as an epitome of faith, with the result that we tend even now to equate spiritual authenticity with institutional power. The parish system put a priest and an altar within walking distance of almost everyone in Europe. Ecclesiastical institutions owned a third to a half of the means of production and received tithes from the rest. Cathedrals and parish churches loomed as large in people's lives as in the landscape. Everyone was baptized. In theory at least, everyone participated in the church's disciplinary and sacramental life. It was an outpost of learning and order, and a major employer in an impoverished society. In some parts of Europe, one man in twenty was ordained. Religious orders offered shelter and meaningful work to many others. The church administered education, welfare, and care of the sick. Clerics formed the nucleus of the civil service. The church was everywhere and did everything.

However, critics noted significant shortcomings: the clergy were ignorant; the people were superstitious; the church exploited spiritual anxiety to increase its power and revenues, but failed to deliver what was promised. Particularly after the onset of the Black Death, people were assailed by doubts. Had they done amiss or done too little? Did the church's grandeur conceal an emptiness or veil a hostile God? Kings and their ministers often saw the church as an obstacle or a rival. When scholars began to note the differences between what the clergy taught and what Scripture and the ancient fathers said, criticism intensified. Reform began to seem essential. However, the customary agents of change, popes and councils, were ineffectual. The ages of faith seemed to open upon despair.

Theology opened a way to renewal, less by saying what the church should do than by asking what Christianity is. It answered the question by using a careful and comprehensive reading of Scripture and tradition to challenge current practices and customary teachings. It was a fresh approach. It awakened people to the actualities of the situation and proposed reforms which connected with popular concerns, especially the longing to know a gracious God.

The reform movement gathered such strength that even today we refer to it as *the* Reformation. It was not a mere neatening up. It was audacious. It questioned much that was commonly received as true, developed a new theological vocabulary, investigated unknown and neglected areas, and rediscovered the roots of faith in word and sacrament. It called forth heroes and martyrs, who shared insecurity, sleepless nights, hard work, vilification, and, often, imprisonment or death.

Reform was costly. The church, once Europe's teacher and unifier, was dismembered and relieved of considerable wealth, power, and self-determination. The papal church became a compromised fragment of Christendom. Nationalized state churches became vehicles for the implementation of policy. Institutions upon which people depended were diminished or destroyed. Critics of reform also became heroes and martyrs.

Nevertheless, the whole church received a new lease on life through the recovery of the gospel. The diminution of temporal power revealed Christ as Lord and Savior and the church as servant. Simplification freed the church for ministry and allowed her eventually to become an advocate for justice and liberty as well as for faithfulness and integrity. If the Reformation was flawed, it was also sufficient, often in ways that the reformers themselves probably never envisioned.

The reformers suggested that reform should be continuous. However, people and governments wanted a predictable church, not a volatile one—more a monument than an organism. The vulnerability of Christ, and of a reforming church, are fearsome. That's why we often equate mission with the extension, defense, and preservation of the church. Like the first disciples, we do not want the Lord to go to Jerusalem, to wash our feet, or to be servant and sacrifice for the redemption of the world. We want him for ourselves.

Monumental thinking is pernicious. It appears to be constructive, but it frequently causes theology to become disconnected, trivialized, or demonized. Its presenting symptoms are the anxiety, blaming, and fragmentation which develop when something of central importance has been avoided or denied.

Anxiety. Life in the church becomes vexed and tiresome. Programs don't work. Leadership becomes depressed. Enthusiasm wanes while gimmicks abound. Ministry continues, but excitement about mission fades. People remember the past but fear the future. Giving may not decline, but it is often restricted. There is an undercurrent of fatalism and disappointment, but it is rarely discussed openly.

Blaming. Controversy and division emerge, often taking bizarre or random forms. People may express alienation by targeting matters which have upset them personally, such as liturgical reform, social ministry agendas, the ordination (or not) of certain categories of people, sexual ethics, worldliness, ineptitude, immorality, unspirituality, or generic bad attitudes. Groups may form around single issues—television programming, for example, or abortion, sexual ethics, or finance—which seem to offer clarity and unity amidst ambivalence. Managing the blaming (called, in political parlance, "damage control") can become a full-time occupation. Growth may slow or stop. Attempts to address significant issues may be abandoned as too risky. Communication becomes superficial. Then a silent church wonders what happened to its vitality.

Fragmentation. When the anxiety and blaming become too intense and destructive, fragmentation occurs. It is especially popular in the United States, where diversity is accepted as a self-evident good and division is a common remedy for conflict. Frustrated? Angry? Go west. Start a new church. Move. Begin a hate group. Say that you didn't leave the church; it left you. That's why America has 500 Christian denominations and why faith is often regarded as a mere eccentricity. Much that is foolish and destructive in American Christianity arises from anti-intellectualism and a suspicion of theology which prevents it from coping effectively with new problems and difficult differences.

However, theology, properly conducted, is a remedy, not an affliction. Were it not for theology, none of us might be Christians. In the first-century church, gentile converts were controversial and gentile culture was derided as hopelessly pagan. The changes necessary to communicate with the gentile world prompted bitter fights. The results are now defended as "the faith once delivered to the saints." However, people often fail to observe the painful process of deliberation and debate by which the delivery took place. Similarly, it was not obvious to everyone that Christ wanted to draw to himself the barbarians of northern Europe, but mission prevailed. It was there that Christian practice assumed much of the individuality and rural orientation that we now regard as normal. Significantly, too, it was the progeny of the barbarians who accomplished the reforms which equipped Christianity for Europe's journey into modernity. New people, unfamiliar cultures, and different perceptions evoke controversy but often prove to be occasions for renewal because people see Christ and his church through fresh and appreciative eyes.

Theology contains hidden treasures and amazing possibilities. When the church avoids it, she is thrown back on her habits, history, and cultural context, and her mission is not appropriately perceived, articulated, and renewed. If people cannot think about their faith, they cannot share it. If they do not share it, spiritual isolation will make them increasingly passive and disillusioned. If there is a theological vacuum at the heart of the church, demons will come in and fill it. Lust for power and delusions of grandeur will lead us to revisit the temptations of Christ and say "yes" where he said "no." Then the church becomes a means for keeping things safe for ourselves and our kind, and Christ is crucified again, deserted by his friends—again.

Ideally, thirst for the knowledge of God should move us toward theology. In actuality, it is often trouble which does it. We are driven into the wilderness so that we might know, not only our need for God, but also our need to think and speak about him. That's why the immediate future of theology in the Episcopal Church may be promising. We have troubles. We have passed through a series of disestablishments—constitutional, cultural, and practical—which affect our identity and self-awareness. We long ago ceased to be a state church. More recently, we ceased to be culturally dominant. Now, we are not even on some people's mental maps. The statistically typical American congregation is Roman Catholic or inerrantist Protestant, not Episcopal. We may have become more like the church we pray to be, but many Episcopalians feel frustrated and diminished. Since the 1960s, much of our attention and energy have been spent on domestic squabbling, not mission. The unarticulated agenda often includes the question, "Who dropped the ball, and what can be done about it?"

In fact, nobody dropped the ball, and nothing can be done about it. No one now occupies the niche once allotted to the Episcopal Church in American society. The cadre of East Coast friends and relations once referred to as "the Establishment" has been displaced by westward migration, meritocracy, and immigrant success. In any case, the now-customary scrutiny of people in high places inhibits the influential relationships which used to exist. Billy Graham, probably the last of the unofficial White House chaplains, was uniquely prominent in his generation. However, some critics see him in retrospect as too willing to pander and too slow to prophesy. In a media-dominated society, nearness to power is temporary and usually dangerous. Today, you're hot. Tomorrow, you're not. Then you're a target. As far as communicating life's deeper meanings along the way, don't count on it!

We think of contemporary American culture as, in some sense, our child. But it might be more accurate to think of it as our grandchild. It is independent, involved with strangers, and has surprising ideas and passions. It often mingles aggressive secularism and uncritical religiosity. Our problem, someone observed, is not that we don't believe anything, but that we believe everything. Prognosticators have spent most of the twentieth century predicting the demise of religion, but it persists. Secularism does not slake our thirst for the transcendent. However, "religion" does not necessarily mean classical Christianity. Often, it means New Age inventions, Pentecostalism, offshoots of Eastern religions, inerrantist bodies centered upon powerful personalities, Islam, or something whipped up in a bar. We dose ourselves with seaweed, practice yoga, bash the church, and find pictures of Jesus on our tortillas. We are fearful of commitment, but we are also afraid to close out any options. We embrace diversity partly because we are afraid of being knocked out in a culture war. Consequently, we exist in a context increasingly characterized by theological nonsense. Self-reported religious participation remains surprisingly stable, but, behind the bland numbers, religious diversity and controversy are growing. The political left flirts with repressing the churches in the name of liberty. Some in the religious right want a *de facto* overthrow of the republic to keep the churches safe. In the middle are a lot of people pushing religion as a hobby, a magic remedy, a cottage industry, or a political power base. We need theology—but theology which can speak to this churning mishmash of speculation and aspiration.

Defining a theological task has been difficult, as though the situation is so overwhelming that we cannot think about it coherently. Some of what is being done is disconnected, theology for the academy rather than for the church. Some of it is political, intended to win votes rather than to educate the church. Some of it revisits the comfort of favorite ideas without reference to current questions. However, we are better-equipped than most churches to undertake a communal theological revival. Some churches are, in practice, inhospitable to theology. They may be worried about error or obsessed with control. Independent thought and new ideas frighten them. They think of faith, not as trust, but as submission.

In contrast, the Episcopal Church is, by design and persistent intention, a theological community. We are decentralized. Our institutional presence is modest, subsisting through parishes, dioceses, some loosely connected colleges, and small seminaries. Power is distributed. We are suspicious of grandiosity and over-zealousness. We are not interested in managing everything and everyone from the top. We trust people. That enables theology to be part of our common life rather than the special province of a few. We do not have the hostility toward theology which develops in some communions, nor do we have a custom of identifying spirituality with ignorance. We do not think that theology is too fragile to touch. Everyone may do it. Theology is deeply embedded in our common life—in worship, prayer, community, and ministry. Our major theological document is our liturgical book. Sermons are expected to have a theological facet. Governing bodies frequently engage in theological discernment as part of their decision-making process. We talk about it. We can also laugh about it.

Christianity, based on revelatory transactions in human history, blends stability and flexibility. How much of each is allowable has been the topic of many long debates. It has philosophers, but it is not a philosophy. It exists in many cultural settings without being a product of any of them. Theology does not create it, but interprets and applies it. It is occasional, even when it takes a systematic form. On the whole, the ancient theological problems are also the modern ones: how to have integrity without isolation, communication without capture, how to advocate both mystery and rationality, critical trust, and candid love. It is easy to get sidetracked —to attempt marriage to a certain culture, or to grasp an opportunity too firmly. However, theology is always a means, not an end. The end is the knowledge of God.

The knowledge of God is also the chief end of the church. The church is a sacrament of Christ, not an instrument of convenience. Theology as a means of edification requires, as a foundation, giving up the idea that division promotes godliness or knowledge of the truth. In fact, division undermines the theological task by removing the most painful questions from the agenda, leaving us with something which reflects our wants, not our needs, and whose relevance to our situation is therefore illusory. In his *Institutes of the Christian Religion*, Calvin makes his case for sticking together by asking how St. Paul treated the church in Corinth:

> Does he seek separation from them? Does he discard them from the kingdom of Christ? Does he strike them with the thunder of a final anathema? He not only does none of these things, but he acknowledges and heralds them as a Church of Christ, and a society of saints. If the Church remains among the Corinthians, where envyings, divisions, and contentions rage; where quarrels, lawsuits, and avarice prevail; where a crime, which even the Gentiles would execrate, is openly approved; where the name of Paul, whom they ought to have honoured as a father, is petulantly assailed; where some hold the resurrection of the dead in derision, though with it the whole gospel must fall; where the gifts of God are made subservient to ambition, not to charity; where many things are done neither decently nor in order: If there the Church still remains, simply because the ministration of word and sacrament is not rejected, who will presume to deny the title of Church to those to whom a tenth part of the crimes cannot be imputed?[2]

Actually, many will so presume. Cult formation is tempting amidst the diversity and ambivalences of pluralistic society, because it seems to offer stability and peace. However, theology is not chiefly for that. It is for mission and ministry. It is a vehicle for engagement, not for flight. That is why it is essential for us to relate faith and history to contemporary culture and intellection—areas in which the church often becomes mired in its own rich past.

The old wars between faith and science are ending. Both now converge upon mystery. However, we have not been paying attention if we assume that the battle lines are as they were when they were first drawn.

The rise of scientific views and methods eroded the dominance of Christianity, partly because these views and methods functioned as an alternative faith, and partly because they disputed the connections between religion and truth, particularly through the following four propositions:

1. The universe is self-contained. God is not necessary to the existence of things and people.
2. Morality and society are based on reason. Religion is not necessary to social existence or to personal goodness.
3. Progress is inevitable and inevitably beneficial. What *can* be done *should* be done, so that the benefits of progress may be realized.
4. Knowledge is inherently good. Evil is to be identified with ignorance.

These assertions did not so much refute Christianity as attack popular assumptions about the necessity and benefits of religious conformity. Further, they provided a foundation for pluralism, and justified an unfettered pursuit of knowledge and change. The subsequent development of the West shows how stifling older attitudes had become, and how often religion was invoked to control economic and social change.

Christians responded in diverse ways. Some opposed the new understanding forthrightly. Protestants made inerrantist claims for the Bible. Roman Catholics adopted infallibility. More liberal Christians adapted to it by treating the Bible and theology as referring to the inward and subjective, rather than the outward and objective. Both surrendered much of the field by seeing religious knowledge and experience as separate categories of human endeavor. That diminished the unifying and integrative role of religion. Conversion often came to mean a flight from the world, or surrender to an alternative view of the universe.

This bifurcation of understanding and knowledge meant that neither the religion-oriented nor the science-oriented saw the world whole. Christianity, often preoccupied with self-advancement, did not raise difficult questions. Science, lacking a religious perspective, forgot how to treat the universe or human life with reverence. This era ended with suffering and destruction on an unprecedented scale. The experience denied the modern world's confident assertions about the reasonableness of morality and society, the goodness of humankind, the inevitability of progress, and its identification of evil with ignorance.

Now, our modern understanding is suffering the kind of doubt that clobbered Christianity earlier. We see that the scientific method cannot be verified by its own rules of evidence but rests upon an act of faith, namely, that careful observation and repeatable experiments can produce an accurate knowledge of certain things. Its sweeping optimism rested on hope, not knowledge. As it turned out, the scientific method could make the world worse as well as better by enlarging human capabilities without changing the human condition. Nothing—not religion or science or revolution—offers immunity from the vicissitudes and contradictions of this life. Much of the malaise that Western culture is presently experiencing is due as much to a collapse of modern views and scientific methods of understanding as to a failure of religion. Some call our era "postmodern," and note that it seems to be marked less by clashing faiths than by a diminished capacity for faith, and by a corresponding rise in superstition.

Science—the real thing, not the popular caricature—has grown, matured, and moved on. It no longer sees the universe as necessarily self-contained and self-renewing. The possibility of God is not excluded. Religion, culture, language, and spirituality are increasingly seen as valuable ways of knowing that complement science. We are more suspicious of claims to objectivity and more aware of the human role in how knowledge is discovered, developed, and used. We are also more aware that power does not necessarily increase wisdom and insight, and that we need to pay more attention to the fundamental concerns which have always been part of the agenda of religion.

However, churches preoccupied with survival and internecine squabbling are poorly equipped to minister to the world's concerns about life and truth—things which are, at bottom, theological questions. Is there one true religion? Are any religions true? Communicable responses may say more about grace and the incarnation than about classic systematic propositions. We are effective when we proclaim what we know—Christ—but not when we start minding other people's business for them.

Theology might also make us less defensive about change. There are reasons not to change some things, but it is also true that Christianity has always changed, as anything will which seeks to be, and is, present in every culture. We are an incarnational, historical, and relational faith, not an immutable system. It is in the midst of change that we encounter the effectual signs of God's faithfulness: incarnation, ministry, crucifixion, resurrection. Life leaps up where death was. When all seemed lost, then was all won. Redemption is a transaction—a change. When the apostle Paul writes about hope, he says, "We shall all be changed!" Change has an apocalyptic effect. It is a seeming disaster which reveals the presence of God who gives us life and liberty.

The fact that Christianity could cope with change was persuasive in converting the Roman Empire: When the quasi-divine Empire failed, there would be, not nothing, but the City of God. Such a hope would be helpful in a country which is increasingly worried about its own institutional unraveling. America came together around family, church, school, politics, and commerce. The presence of those institutions distinguished civilization from the wilderness and the frontier. That is why their apparent decline causes such acute anxiety. It is not mere change, in a neutral sense. It is the kind of change which seems to signal the destabilizing of our society. That is what prompted the development of the neo-conservative movement, and, even if one disagrees with the remedies it proposes, it is difficult to refute the analysis.

- Many families have a tattered and temporary character. The divorce rate is the symptom most frequently cited as evidence of decline, but what appears to be the increasing number of dysfunctional families may in the end be more significant. It means that, even if the form of the family is preserved, the benefits of family life will not be forthcoming. People will be effectively alone, not learning to love and be loved, and not gaining the skills and insights which equip people for life—the traditions, if you will, of civilization.
- Once-dominant churches are also in decline. It is not merely a matter of lost members. We fear that they have also lost momentum,

their place in American society, and their ability to communicate with the larger culture on behalf of the public good. That role has not passed to other bodies. It is missing. It vanished during the privitization of religion in the 1960s, and has not reappeared.

- Public schools, long thought of as a foundational American institution, are also in trouble. We probably broke them by expecting too much of them—that they could educate everyone while performing many tasks which are not immediately related to education. They did better when they were selective and focused. However, many Americans now want education to replicate a class system instead of forming a democracy.
- Politics is also in trouble, poisoned, many say, by television and money. That is illustrative of the postmodern problem. New means of communication seemed to render old institutions obsolete. Then we discovered how much we need their culture and discipline. Electronics is not simply an easier, faster medium for communication and interpersonal relationships. It is something new that we must learn to use, something with pitfalls and foibles, limits and temptations that we must come to understand.
- Commerce is increasingly dominated by large corporations which exist independently of particular social and political contexts. They present both opportunities and threats. They purvey cheap and attractive products and processes, but they also have power to plunder our resources and alter our lives in ways we would not choose if we were asked—which, increasingly, we aren't.

So we find ourselves, not in some cozy world closely connected with the past, but in some new place in which we must learn to live. We must recover our theological language, our biblical familiarity, our practice, and our universal view of things. Otherwise, we may be unable to do much with the opportunity which now presents itself. It has never been enough to be comfortable and cute, and we're being shown why it is not enough.

Notes

1. John Calvin, *Institutes of the Christian Religion*, vol. 2, trans. Henry Beveridge (Grand Rapids: Wm. B. Eerdmans Publishing Co., 1993), 284.

2. Ibid., 293.

A Hope for Theology in the Episcopal Church

James E. Griffiss

We Episcopalians are often heard to say that we are not a very theological church and that, for us, liturgy is what matters. Thus, we often say, "If you want to know what we believe, come and worship with us." An Archbishop of Canterbury once said that Anglicans have no theology of their own, only the theology of the Catholic Church. Indeed, we are more likely to think of theology as it is done *by* Anglicans, rather than of a distinctive Anglican theology.

Such statements may be made with a certain amount of smugness or with sadness, but there is a reasonable justification for them. We have neither a magisterium, as does the Roman Catholic Church, nor a confessional statement, as do some of the Reformed Churches, to which we can appeal for a teaching authority in matters of doctrine. Nor have the great majority of Anglican theologians, preachers, and pastors appealed, as some evangelical church groups claim to do, to Scripture exclusively as an authoritative source or standard in matters of belief. Anglicans generally have acknowledged the necessity of an intentional, if not always consistent, method for interpreting the Bible, although the methods may vary from one Anglican to another.

The provincial system of the Anglican Communion further complicates our lack of a clear and consistent approach to theology. The provinces of the Anglican Communion, of which the Episcopal Church is only one, often move in different directions as they respond to local situations. Thus, while the Episcopal Church and some other provinces have allowed for the ordination of women to the presbyterate and episcopate, other provinces have regarded such a move as theologically wrong and as a possible cause for schism. Now, considerations of sexuality, such as the ordination of non-celibate homosexual persons, are proving to be even more divisive. A central teaching authority for the entire Anglican Communion, which could at least make judgments about such theological questions by appealing to common theological tradition, does not exist for us.[1]

Furthermore, Anglican theologians, since the very beginning of our self-conscious theological history, can be found all over the theological spectrum. Academic theologians who are Anglicans draw quite easily upon Roman Catholic, Orthodox, and Reformed theologians and theological traditions. At the present time in the Episcopal Church—at a more pastoral, less academic level—there are divisions between "traditionalist Episcopalians" and "liberal Episcopalians" who disagree about what the church teaches on a variety of questions, and even how it should worship.

It is also difficult sometimes for outsiders and participants alike to discern how theology functions in the decision-making process of General Convention, diocesan conventions, or other quasi-official gatherings. Much theological work may be done in committees and private conversations, but public debate is limited by time and circumstances, as well as by the oratorical gifts and limitations of speakers. Observers of the process, and even participants, may have difficulty in understanding what theological considerations have gone into the votes which are taken. (On a personal note, I was once pleased and slightly startled to be told by a delegate to the General Convention in 1979 that he had read an article of mine, favorable to the ordination of women, and that it had changed his mind and vote.) All this gives the, perhaps, wrong impression that the process is only political and devoid of the kind of theological debate which, we like to think, took place at the councils of the early church, such as the Council of Nicea, when creeds were formulated and doctrines developed. Of course, those who know something of the great councils of the past and even some of the more recent councils in the Roman Catholic Church and the deliberations of Lambeth Conferences, will know that political maneuverings played no small part in those debates! The Holy Spirit does *sometimes* work through political process, but it is also true that our politics may sometimes drown out the Spirit.

Of course, it can be argued that Anglicanism, even while it does not have a clear dogmatic or doctrinal theology, does have a certain tradition, spirit, or ethos, a way of going about determining and giving theological expression to the faith which we have received in the apostolic witness and the ecumenical creeds. Michael Ramsey, who was no theological lightweight, argued, for example, that Anglican theology is "a method, a use, and a direction," something which has been and will be proved by its fruits.[2] And a leading historian of theology in seventeenth-century Anglicanism located what he called "the spirit of Anglicanism" in "the principle of mediation in regions of doctrine and discipline," rather than in "vicious extremes of exclusion."[3] But there remains some justification for the complaint sometimes made of us by our friends in other ecclesial traditions (as well as by Anglicans themselves[4]) that our theology, when we have it at all, is trendy, politically driven, uninformed, and incoherent. We are even willing at times to tolerate very public figures who seem to deny such a fundamental Christian belief as the resurrection of Christ or even the reality of God.

It is important, therefore, as we think about the future of theology in the Episcopal Church, to recognize the confusion and to accept some of the honest criticism which is made of us. While it is true that our forms of liturgical worship are deeply important for us, there are those who believe that, if we are to resolve the serious problems facing all Christians today, then we must have a deeper theological foundation in matters of doctrine.

However, it is also important, I believe, to look more deeply into what we mean when we talk about a church as *not* being "theological" (that is, one which is lacking in serious theological reflection at the institutional level) and what we might mean if we were to say that it *is* "theological" (that is, I want to suggest, one which is in the process of being formed in and shaped by Christian faith, worship, and practice). I want to draw upon my experience as a teacher of theology in church seminaries in order to suggest that perhaps we are more theological than we and our critics sometimes think, and I shall also suggest that the future of theology in the Episcopal Church is not without hope, if we think of theology as a process of formation, one of living into the mystery of God in Christ, and not only as the articulation of doctrinal positions by decision-making bodies.

First, a bit of personal background in order to explain why I believe as I do about our theological future and hope. I began the serious academic study of theology in 1951 at the General Theological Seminary after four years at a university which prided itself on its completely secular academic foundation and commitment. Unlike some other private universities, it had never had any involvement with a church, and its only concession to religion was the academic study of Near Eastern languages, which included the biblical languages. I had majored in philosophy as an undergraduate, and so when I entered General Seminary I was very conscious of the need to see the connections between the academic humanistic and scientific tradition in which I had been educated and Christian faith and its theological articulation. Quite fortunately for me, the faculty of General Seminary had the same concern. Most members of the faculty at that time were in the tradition of what was called "Liberal Catholicism," a movement begun at the end of the nineteenth century and committed to understanding the Christian tradition in light of the then-radical developments in the physical and biological sciences and in historical criticism of the Bible, all of which seemed to shatter, or at least to shake, the foundations of Christian belief about God and the Bible.

We students read and profited deeply from the volumes which had come from that movement, in particular *Lux Mundi* (first published in 1889 and frequently reprinted) and *Essays Catholic and Critical* (first published in 1926 and also frequently reprinted). We studied such biblical scholars and theologians as F. J. A. Hort, Brooke Foss Westcott, Charles Gore, A. E. Taylor, William Temple, Michael Ramsey, K. E. Kirk, among many others, all of whom in various ways carried on the Liberal Catholic tradition. They were concerned to show how belief in the incarnation of God in Christ so grounded Christian belief and practice that the theological interpretation of the Christian faith could be understood in terms of development and change as it entered into conversation with "the new social and intellectual movements of each age."[5]

Perhaps the best summary of what the Liberal Catholic movement represented for us in those days was expressed in the preface to *Essays Catholic and Critical*:

> For the two terms Catholic and critical represent principles, habits, and tempers of the religious mind which only reach their maturity in combination. To the first belongs everything in us that acknowledges and adores the one abiding, transcendent, and supremely given Reality, God; believes in Jesus Christ, as the unique revelation in true personal form of His mystery; and recognizes His Spirit embodied in the Church as the authoritative and ever-living witness of His will, word, and work. To the second belongs the exercise of that divinely implanted gift of reason by which we measure, sift, examine, and judge whatever is proposed for our belief, whether it be a theological doctrine or a state-

> ment of historical fact, and so establish, deepen, and purify our understanding of the truth of the Gospel. The proportion in which these two activities are blended will vary in different individuals and in relation to different parts of our subject-matter: but there is no point at which they do not interact, and we are convinced that this interaction is necessary to any presentment of Christianity which is to claim the allegiance of the world today.[6]

For my generation, after World War II, when even more radical social and intellectual challenges for Christian belief were emerging, these were encouraging and helpful words. They encouraged us to believe that the ancient sources of Scripture and creeds did not stand in opposition to new developments in secular learning, especially the sciences, but rather that they could be interpreted and understood in light of those developments. They also helped us to see, just as importantly, that all those new developments themselves could be enlightened and informed by Christian faith. The conversation went both ways: secular learning could inform theology and theology could inform secular learning.

For those in the Liberal Catholic tradition, the foundation for the conversation between Christian theology and this emerging "modern world" in the 1950s was the classical doctrine of the incarnation, as it had been formulated in the definition of the Council of Chalcedon in 451.[7] That definition, although modified and changed in terms of its conceptual language, provided a foundation for such an understanding of theology because it sought to give intellectual coherence to the belief that the transcendent God—the God of the Bible and the God of the philosophers — had become personally present in the completely human and historical life of Jesus of Nazareth, and, therefore, that our humanity with all its ambiguity, change, and development had been taken up into God and is present to God. For such a way of understanding Christian faith, the developments in scientific and historical learning could not, the Liberal Catholics maintained, be thought of as alien to God or to a doctrine of divine revelation in Holy Scripture.

This understanding of the relationship between theology and "the modern world" was carried out in the way we studied theology itself. There was a basic course in dogmatic theology in which we studied, quite thoroughly, the theological tradition, that is, the Bible, the Greek and Latin fathers, the doctrines expressed in the historic creeds, and their subsequent development in classical Anglican theologians such as Hooker and Andrewes and in the Articles of Religion (which were still taken as authoritative for Anglican teaching even though they were not binding). But in addition, we also had courses in apologetics which sought to show how the ancient faith could be expressed in contemporary terms and how it could meet the challenges posed to it by secular learning. Norman Pittenger, who was at that time Professor of Christian Apologetics, opened up for many of us the new and exciting developments in philosophy, science, and humanistic studies which were taking place outside the somewhat cloistered walls of General Seminary.

Liberal Catholicism had its limitations, as does any theological movement: it assumed too much for the coherence of Christian faith and secular learning; it tended to baptize secular, scientific reason; and it was overly optimistic about the human condition. In his study of Anglican theology in the early twentieth century, Michael Ramsey cites William Temple, writing in 1939 at the outbreak of World War II, as one of the great exponents of Liberal Catholicism who saw its limitations quite clearly:

> There is a new task for theologians today. We cannot come to the men of today saying, "You will find that all your experience fits together in a harmonious system if you will only look at it in the illumination of the Gospel" . . . our task with this world is not to explain it but to convert it. Its need can be met, not by the discovery of its own immanent principle in signal manifestation through Jesus Christ, but only by the shattering impact upon its self-sufficiency and arrogance of the Son of God, crucified, risen and ascended, pouring forth that explosive and disruptive energy which is the Holy Ghost . . . . We must expect the movement of His spirit among us to produce sharper divisions as well as deeper unity.[8]

It took a while for Temple's words to affect theology as it was taught in seminaries of the Episcopal Church, and, even after the changes began, the spirit of a theology centered in the incarnation continued to have an influence upon how many of us in that generation after World War II went about teaching, preaching, and otherwise exercising pastoral care; and so, it influenced how my generation affected the ways in which the Episcopal Church made many of its pastoral and theological decisions. We—who had been formed in the spirit of *Lux Mundi* and *Essays Catholic and Critical* and under the influence of Norman Pittenger and others like him—continued to be convinced of the importance of knowing and living in the catholic tradition which had developed out of the revelation of God in Christ as witnessed to in Holy Scripture, a tradition which, at its best, remained in conversation with other forms of human learning even when they seemed to be in opposition to our belief as Christians. This was our foundation as Anglicans. It not only gave us a particular sense of our identity as Anglicans within the larger Christian community, but it also affected how we understood our relationship to an increasingly secular world.[9]

After seminary and several years in parish ministry, I went off to graduate school and returned to the study of philosophy at Yale University, where the Department of Philosophy at that time (the late 1950s and early 1960s) was still dominated by a metaphysical and historical approach to philosophy, and so I was able to continue my interest in the relationship between philosophical and theological questions. While I began to move beyond the Liberal Catholicism of my seminary education, the doctrine of the incarnation, as my mentors had understood it, remained central to my own concerns and offered a way for carrying on the conversation between theology and the questions and dilemmas with which philosophers and other thinkers outside the Christian tradition were concerned.

Of course, during the turbulent three decades which followed the 1950s, William Temple's prophecy was fulfilled, and both theology and philosophy began to explore new areas. Also, the Episcopal Church, and all other churches, faced challenges and threats which were, in many ways, even more serious than those which had faced Anglicans at the beginning of the century. There were major cultural and political changes in American society itself—the war in Vietnam, the struggle for racial justice, the emergence of feminism, changes in sexual mores, an increasing secularism and decline in ecclesiastical allegiances, and a much more multicultural and pluralistic society. Membership in the Episcopal Church began to decline, as it did in most of the mainline churches which did not offer clear-cut and absolute authority in faith and morals. The theological and pastoral leaders in the Episcopal Church struggled to see how the church could relate to this changing world, and many times they did not succeed terribly well. We sometimes ended up in an unhappy middle ground between the desire for an other-worldly transcendence and a vapid liberalism and secularism.

But in all this confusion I do believe, as I look back upon it, that we were struggling to understand how a community, which is grounded in the incarnation of God in Christ, can express—both in its teaching and in its practice—the authority of God incarnate in the messiness and ambiguities of human history. And I think that the Liberal Catholic tradition, with all of its limitations, helped us to hold onto some things of fundamental importance to a community which believes itself to have a mission in the actual world and not to a world of its own imagining. The questions which Liberal Catholicism asked, if not all the answers which the movement supplied, have a way of returning for any church which holds to its center in the incarnation, and I think many of those questions remain with us even today.

Because the theology of Liberal Catholicism was centered in the mystery of the incarnation, it had two points of focus. First, as I have indicated, it did attempt to engage in a serious academic conversation with the scientific and historical culture which began to emerge at the beginning of the twentieth century and to address the questions which that culture posed for Christian faith. Now, of course, the questions have changed and so, therefore, has the approach which theologians must take in responding to and challenging a vastly changed world—those movements and themes which are loosely called postmodernism. A new generation of academic Anglican theologians must take up this new work, for this mission is always before a community of faith which believes in the God incarnate in the history of our humanity.

Finally, I want to consider another aspect of the Liberal Catholic movement which is certainly of equal importance in the complexity of the relationship between the church and the world today. It is the question which I posed at the beginning of this article: How does a community of faith which is grounded in the incarnation *live* as a theological community. For it is not exclusively in theological pronouncements by decision-making bodies or even in the academic work of theologians that theology is given expression in the life of a community of faith. The theology which guides and governs a community must also find expression in how that community of people grows into and enters into the consequences of its belief in the sovereignty of the incarnate Christ in those areas which are central to its life and faith: worship and pastoral care for the world in which it lives. In this process of growth into Christ, certain aspects of the heritage of Liberal Catholicism have affected our life together as a community of faith and can continue to speak to us and to form and shape how theology can be a vital force in the Episcopal Church.

Chiefly, Liberal Catholicism—by its emphasis upon the incarnation and upon the continuing relation of the biblical and theological tradition to the culture which was contemporary for it—made possible, in a significant way, the recovery of the sacramental life in Anglicanism which had begun with the Oxford Movement earlier in the nineteenth century. The Oxford Movement began the recovery of a sacramental spirituality in Anglicanism, but it was a spirituality which tended to be both individualistic and archaic, one which emphasized the individual's relationship to God and which sought to return to a romanticized past. The Liberal Catholic movement was able to move beyond that rather narrow focus and to begin the development of a sacramental theology which emphasized the importance of the sacraments for the contemporary ecclesial community and for the extension of the church into a culture that was becoming increasingly secular. This development of a sacramental spirituality paralleled the more academic concerns of Liberal Catholicism because it, too, was grounded in the belief that the incarnate Christ is present with us, redeeming all the human history of alienation and separation from God. The catholic movement made it possible for us to see that the sacraments offer us that gift of grace which is our participation in the divine life of God and, for that very reason, the gift that also directs us to our work in the world which is God's creation.

As a consequence there has continued to develop, slowly but also certainly, a sacramental spirituality in the Episcopal Church through which we are coming to see that the incarnation expresses the mystery of the coming together of God and all human concerns and hopes in Christ. William Stringfellow, a social and theological prophet in the Episcopal Church, expressed forcefully the relation between the incarnation and the sacraments when he wrote:

> The Body of Christ lives in the world in the unity between God and the world wrought in Christ and, in a sense, the Body of Christ lives in the world as the unity of God and the world in Christ. . . . [W]hen a congregation gathers in sacramental worship, the members of the Body are offering the world to God, not for His sake, not for their own sake, but for the sake of the world, and the members then and there celebrate God's presence in the world, and on behalf of the world, even though that world does not yet discern His presence.[10]

This incarnational and sacramental theology which resulted from the Liberal Catholic movement has found expression in the renewal of the worshiping life of the Episcopal Church in its liturgy, namely, in the 1979

Book of Common Prayer. The 1979 Book of Common Prayer is the result of many years of liturgical and theological reflection upon the biblical foundation of worship and its significance for the contemporary church. In particular it has given to the church a theology of baptism and eucharist which is centered in the paschal mystery of the death, resurrection, and exaltation of the incarnate Christ. The paschal mystery calls us to enter into the transcendent mystery of God's act of salvation in Christ even as we live in the human reality of the church in the world. Through our worship, the theology of the incarnation can become, not just a doctrinal affirmation, but also the pattern of our life as a believing community. It may well be that the most important question which the incarnational and sacramental theology of the Liberal Catholic movement raises for the church today concerns how we continue to respond to the call of entering more deeply into the incarnation through our worship. As we do so and if we do so, perhaps we shall know more clearly what we mean when we say, "If you want to know what we believe, come and worship with us."

Just as our liturgical renewal has developed out of our increased awareness of the significance of the incarnation for our life together, so also has it led to an increasing awareness of our pastoral and social witness and mission. This awareness has been and continues to be a prophetic and challenging one for the Episcopal Church. The Episcopal Church began historically as the church which represented the ruling powers in American society, and it was long considered a supporter of the rich and powerful. Gradually, too gradually some would say, we have been changing. In the decades since World War II, we have begun to move away from an identification with the political and economic status quo towards a greater identification with the political and social movements which have been so important in the development of public policies in this century. In the 1960s and 1970s, the Episcopal Church began to awaken to the cause of racial justice, and many in the Episcopal Church have been active in that struggle. Likewise, we have been able increasingly to affirm in our life together the equal humanity of women and men. In both of those movements it has been an increasing awareness of a theology of the incarnation that has helped us to recognize and to work for the full incorporation of all human beings into the life of the church and society.

Now, there are many other issues facing us in our contemporary postmodern culture: new struggles for social justice, sexuality, pluralism and the conflict of cultures, and a rampant materialism and greed in society—all of which call for a new pastoral theology and mission. I would suggest that, as we are faced with all these issues, it will continue to be our deepening awareness of the incarnation and the sacramental life which will lead us, at all levels of our life together, to ask ourselves an old question in new ways: if we believe that God has in Christ become one with our humanity, then how does this belief affect our way of living in the complexity, alienation, and pain of human beings? What, in other words, is the pastoral and theological mission of a community of faith which is living into the incarnate Christ? These are questions which will always be before us and which ought to call us into the mystery of the God who is incarnate in Jesus of Nazareth.[11]

As I said at the beginning of this brief reflection, Anglican theology is multifaceted. There is no one Anglican way or approach for expressing the depth of Christian faith. Liberal Catholicism was one way which helped to move the Episcopal Church from the securities and ingrained convictions of the last century into the complexities which we now know. Other theological approaches have made their own contributions. But, like all movements in theology, it should not be seen as something dead and gone, a movement to be forgotten. Not only has it left its mark upon us in the ways which I have suggested, but it continues to hold before us a fundamental question: What are the consequences of believing that in Christ we are called into the life of the world because we are called into God? It is my hope for the future of theology in the Episcopal Church that this question will continue to confront us as we live into the mystery of God in Christ.

Notes

1. See the analysis of this matter in "The Virginia Report: The Report of the Inter-Anglican Theological and Doctrinal Commission," published in 1997 for the Anglican Consultative Council. It may well be that a new form of central teaching authority may be developed for the Anglican Consultative Council as a result of the Lambeth Conference 1998.

2. See James E. Griffiss, ed., *To Believe Is to Pray: Readings from Michael Ramsey* (Boston: Cowley Publications, 1996), 44.

3. Paul Elmer More, "The Spirit of Anglicanism," in Paul Elmer More and Frank Leslie Cross, eds., *Anglicanism: The Thought and Practice of the Church of England, Illustrated from the Religious Literature of the Seventeenth Century* (London: SPCK, 1962), xxiv.

4. See, for example, Stephen Sykes, *The Integrity of Anglicanism* (London: Mowbray, 1978).

5. Charles Gore, ed., preface to *Lux Mundi*, 1st ed. (1889), xliii.

6. E. G. Selwyn, ed., preface to *Essays Catholic and Critical*, 1st ed. (1926), xxviii.

7. "Historical Documents," The Book of Common Prayer (New York: The Church Hymnal Corporation, 1979), 864.

8. Cited in Michael Ramsey, *An Era in Anglican Theology* (New York: Charles Scribner's Sons, 1960), 160–161.

9. The spirit of Liberal Catholicism to a considerable degree also dominated the teaching of theology in other Episcopal seminaries during this period, even at the Virginia Seminary and Nashotah House, which represented the Evangelical and Anglo-Catholic wings, respectively, of the Episcopal Church.

10. William Stringfellow, *A Private and Public Faith* (Grand Rapids: Wm. B. Eerdmans Publishing Co., 1962), 40–41.

11. For a moving account by an Episcopal bishop of one way of answering these questions, see Paul Moore, *Presences: A Bishop's Life in the City* (New York: Farrar, Straus and Giroux, 1997). For a succinct account of the history and problems of Anglican social teaching see Robert E. Hood, *Social Teachings in the Episcopal Church* (Harrisburg, Pa.: Morehouse Publishing, 1990).

II.

Ministries for the Future of Theology and the Episcopal Church

Christ: The Sovereign Word

Frank Tracy Griswold

In the ordination rite for a bishop, according to the Book of Common Prayer, the bishop-elect is bidden "to testify to Christ's sovereignty as Lord of Lords and King of Kings." The sovereignty of Christ is so thoroughly a biblical and Anglican notion, that I was struck by one of the resolutions promulgated by the 1998 Lambeth Conference which speaks, not of the sovereignty of Christ, but of the sovereignty of Scripture. Does the sovereignty of Scripture supersede the sovereignty of Christ, or is Scripture a manifestation of Christ's "most gracious rule" which is articulated in the life of the church under the aegis of the Holy Spirit?

Scripture itself helps us to answer the question inasmuch as it bears witness to the sovereignty of God in Christ whose work, as we are told in the Letter to the Ephesians, is to gather up all things—"things in heaven and things on earth"—in himself (Ephesians 1:10). What follows, therefore, are some reflections upon the risen Lord, who is named in the Book of Revelation, "The Word of God" (Revelation 19:13), and the word of God as it is addressed to us in Scripture, through the sacraments, and the circumstances of our lives.

The power to strike and pierce to the heart, the inner core and center of our being, is always present in the word of God as it confronts us in Scripture. As the writer of the Letter to the Hebrews observes, "The word of God is living and active, sharper than any two-edged sword, piercing until it divides soul from spirit, joints from marrow; it is able to judge the thoughts and intentions of the heart" (Hebrews 4:12).

Christ is the minister of the word in Scripture as is made clear in the gospel of Luke. Having encountered two of his downcast disciples on the road to Emmaus, the risen one proceeds to interpret to them "from Moses and all the prophets . . . the things about himself in all the scriptures" (Luke 24:27). Later, having recognized him in the breaking of the bread, they exclaimed, "Were not our hearts burning within us while he was talking to us on the road, while he was opening the scriptures to us?" (Luke 24:32). Christ continues to open the Scriptures to us in our own day causing our hearts to burn with the urgent immediacy of recognition, so that a particular passage becomes truly a word of life, and we find that we are convicted, illuminated, and embraced by the word all at once. In this regard, St. Ephraem of Edessa speaks of Scripture opening its arms to receive us and leading us by the hand from verse to verse.

The word is also developmental in character. "I still have many things to say you, but you cannot bear them now," Jesus tells his disciples (John 16:12), thereby indicating that they are not ready to receive the fullness of what he seeks to impart to them. The word is progressively unfolded by the Spirit of truth—who "will take from what is mine and declare it to you" (John 16:15)—in fidelity to Christ's intention.

This process of "unfoldment" cannot be rushed. It can only be lived over time, in union with the risen Christ. "You speak in my heart and say, 'Seek my face.'" And the psalmist replies, "Your face, Lord, will I seek" (Psalm 27:11). It is Christ who speaks in our hearts through the words of Scripture saying, "Seek my face," thereby drawing us into the ambit of his grace and truth. "Oh, Lord, thou didst strike my heart with thy word and I loved thee," exclaims St. Augustine of Hippo. All of which points to the fact that Scripture is sacramental in nature: through the outward and visible word, the one who is the Word addresses each of us in the very depths of our being. "Oh, that today you would hearken to his voice!" we are reminded, day by day, in the daily office. Here I might note that those of us who have been taught to use Scripture for preaching and teaching often have a difficult time letting Scripture accost and address us freely and speak in our hearts. We are so accustomed to being its master and making it serve our own homiletic and didactic ends that, before the word in Scripture can have its way with us, we have wrestled it to the ground and made it our prisoner.

"Christ is present and active, in various ways, in the entire eucharistic celebration," declares the Anglican-Roman Catholic statement on the eucharist, which we have received as consonant with the faith of Anglicans. There have certainly been times when the liturgical proclamation of

Scripture has caused my heart to burn within me, and the homily has been a real breaking of the bread of what has been set before us in the readings for the day. On such occasions, my subjective experience of Christ's presence has been mediated by the word rather than the sacrament.

Having said this, I believe the familiar distinction of word and sacrament is somewhat misleading. It suggests that the two stand in tension, if not opposition. In fact, Scripture is profoundly sacramental, just as the sacraments and sacramental rites are profoundly scriptural. The scriptural word is not simply *about* Christ. It actually *conveys* Christ and mediates Christ's real presence to the community and to the believer.

I have been led by the Spirit over time to confess the sovereignty of Jesus Christ as Lord of Scripture, not as some sort of abstract truth, but in an intimate, immediate, and personal way. For some of us, this confession is provoked by our life circumstances, our being riven through by a distinct word uttered in a sermon or proclaimed in Scripture which has been life-changing. For me, however, the Spirit's leading has been largely through the sacraments understood as enacted words of Christ rather than ritual forms.

Since I was confirmed at the age of fifteen, the eucharist has been the consistent and primary place of my encounter with the risen Christ. The liturgy has been the place of my deepest intimacy with the Lord, the place where my poverty and my burdens can be most truly acknowledged because of Christ's own desire: "Come unto me . . . and I will give you rest" (Matthew 11:28).

The eucharistic prayer of the 1928 Book of Common Prayer had a profound effect on me. The Johannine emphasis upon Christ dwelling in us and we in him laid hold upon my consciousness and determined the core of my spirituality. In good times and in bad times, filled with joy or anxiety, peace, or an agitation of spirit, the Lord of the eucharist, who is both host and guest, has been ready to welcome me and draw me out of myself and into his abundant life.

Several years ago I was speaking to a well-known and highly respected evangelist who was about to conduct a mission in Chicago. He said to me that Catholics have a much stronger sense of intimacy with Christ than Protestants do. The reason he gave was that Catholics are accustomed to receiving Christ in the eucharist, which is an act that both proclaims and mediates intimate relationship. I was surprised by his observation but, upon reflection, saw its truth, at least in my own life.

Over the years, I have been a frequent if not daily communicant for the simple reason that opening my hands to receive the bread of life is the most concrete way in which I can say: "Here am I Lord," and hear deep within, as the bread is delivered into my hands, "My grace is sufficient for you, for my power is made perfect in weakness" (2 Corinthians 12:9). There have been moments when the physical act of reaching out to receive the one who is the truth of my life has been the only expression of faith I have been able to manifest.

From participation in the eucharist, I have come to understand something of the paschal mystery, which is the fundamental law of our life in Christ. Through the eucharist, Christ draws us into the ongoing and ever unfolding dynamic of his dying and rising, which is played out in our lives in all their concreteness and specificity. Nothing I have to face, no decision I am obliged to make, no word of criticism or judgment I am bidden to hear, no telephone call or seemingly random encounter lies outside the paschal pattern of sharing the sufferings of Christ in order to know the power of his resurrection (Philippians 3:10). All things without exception are the stuff whereby the Spirit conforms us to the image of Christ in ways that have nothing whatsoever to do with notions of our righteousness or how we think we should be or ought to be.

Here I am consoled by the white stone in the Book of Revelation (2:17), on which is written a new name. The new name will be revealed to us only when our participation in Christ's suffering has brought us to that state of transparency which, in spite of our lingering limitations and imperfections, reveals the image of God, not to us but to others. In the Eastern Christian tradition, this is the mystery of the uncreated light, the transfiguration of the human person "until he shines again with the glory of God" (St. Isaac of Syria).

The eucharist has led me, therefore, back to the mystery of baptism, the sacrament which reveals who we are and are called to be. Here I have some difficulty with the prominence given to that portion of the baptismal rite in our present Prayer Book titled "The Baptismal Covenant." The difficulty comes not because I disagree with it, but because, in our teaching and preaching, the baptismal covenant frequently overshadows the fundamental action of the rite itself, namely our incorporation into the church, the body of the risen Christ. It is the function of the eucharist to support and develop this essential baptismal act of identification with Christ. "You are Christ," early bishops were not shy to declare to the newly baptized. "Become who you are," said St. Augustine to those who were newly incorporated into Christ. The whole of our lives is a process of *becoming* as we are molded and shaped by the circumstances of our lives, and drawn by Christ through the eucharist into an ever deeper companionship and identification with him.

Baptism and the eucharist are, therefore, an enactment of the gospel, a kind of lived Scripture. In baptism we are made one with Christ and through the eucharist we "grow up into Christ." But baptism and eucharist also point beyond themselves to the sacramental nature of life itself. If Christ can use water, oil, and bread and wine as the medium of his self-disclosure, Christ can make himself known through all created things without exception, including the ambiguous and paradoxical realities of human life and relationships. Here we are brought face to face with the fundamental expression of all that is sacramental: incarnation. T. S. Eliot, that most sacramental of poets, describes the incarnation as "the hint half guessed, the gift half understood."

> These are only hints and guesses,
> Hints followed by guesses; and the rest
> Is prayer, observance, discipline, thought and action.
> The hint half guessed, the gift half understood, is Incarnation.[1]

One of the places in which incarnation is most real is in the sacramental rite of reconciliation. This ministry of the church has brought me to a deeper appreciation of how Christ meets us and mediates his reconciling word through the words and welcoming compassion of another person, another member and limb of Christ's risen body. Standing undefended before a brother or sister in Christ in my poverty and veniality, with my whispering sins and my shouting sins, my shattered efforts to construct or maintain my own righteousness, and hearing over and over again in that thin place a human voice speak Christ's mercy—often accompanied by a gesture or look of "quick ey'd love"—has taught me more about the nature of Christ's companionship and compassion and boundless patience than I can ever put into words.

This awareness has taken a great deal of time to evolve. And I have come to the somewhat jarring awareness that what passed for repentance and a genuine opening to Christ and coming "before the throne of grace" when I first started to make my confession many years ago was actually wounded pride and disappointment with myself. Absolution was more a way of being restored to a state of purity and righteousness in my own eyes, and less a yielding of myself into the arms of God's welcoming forgiveness. It is amazing to me how the Spirit of Christ can overrule and expand our understanding and use of the sacraments, as well as catch us off guard, and thereby reveal that the sacramental actions of the church are preeminently acts of Christ, the deeds and gestures of the Lord of Lords and King of Kings. Here I am put in mind of some wonderful words of St. Ambrose: "You have shown yourself to me, O Christ, face to face. I have met you in your sacraments."

One of the great treasures of the Anglican tradition is the daily office of morning and evening prayer. The office has been the primary way in which Christ, the Word, has been able to address me and speak to my heart, on good days and bad days, in joy and sorrow, in turmoil and peace. And it is largely through the office that I have come to appreciate how the scriptural word shapes and forms us over time. What occurs in our lives, along with "the thoughts of our hearts," predisposes us to hear a particular word within the words of Scripture as a personal address, an invitation, a conviction, an illumination, and a summons that belongs uniquely and unequivocally to us at this juncture in our lives, in the urgent immediacy of the present moment. Why, we might ask, is it that on one occasion a passage of Scripture will seem remote when on another it will be to us as "a consuming fire"? It is because the real presence of Christ the Word is multidimensional. Christ is present and speaks through the world around us and in the concrete circumstances of our lives. "The world is word," observes the Jesuit poet, Gerard Manley Hopkins.

Christ is also present in the existential depths of our personhood as "the word which is near to you . . . in your heart for you to observe" (Deuteronomy 30:14), or again as the "implanted word" (James 1:21). This interior word is what, I believe, St. Paul is alluding to when he speaks about the Spirit praying within us "with sighs too deep for words" (Romans 8:26). It is this inner dimension of the word that is provoked into consciousness and born into freedom by Christ as he manifests himself in event and circumstance, and addresses us through the word of Scripture. "If you continue in my word, you are truly my disciples; and you will know the truth, and the truth will make you free," declares Jesus (John 8:31–32). It is the function of the risen Christ—through the agency of the Spirit who draws from what is Christ's and makes it known to us—to draw the various dimensions of the word together into one. This unified word has an immediate force and energy that can only be described as definitive and all embracing: it is called forth by the word of Scripture but includes all the experienced and lived dimensions of the word as well.

"Will you testify to Christ's sovereignty as Lord of Lords and Kings of Kings?" I return to where I started: the sovereignty of Christ. Through the incarnation and the paschal mystery, Christ is revealed to us as Lord and Word of God. As such, he addresses us through his many dimensional word which includes Scripture and the events of our lives. Christ's word is all embracing; it speaks to us personally and as a community of faith. Our courage to hear and receive it is the measure of our faithfulness.

Note

1. T. S. Eliot, "Dry Salvages," *Four Quartets* (New York: Harvest, 1971), 44.

A Theological Compass for a Local Church

Arthur A. Vogel

When I was first called to Nashotah House to teach theology, a small parish less than two miles away needed a rector. The parish had been founded by Bishop Jackson Kemper, who had also served as its rector for a time. The congregation was listed as a parish in the diocese, but its canonical status was possible only because, at very little cost to the congregation, a professor at the seminary had offered it pastoral services. With such a favorable arrangement available, the congregation had long avoided devolving to mission status.

Eager to teach theology in a manner relevant to the ongoing life of the church, I became the Rector of St. John Chrysostom's in Delafield, Wisconsin, thinking that it would give me a splendid opportunity to test ideas in the parish that we talked about in class. I told my students that we would no doubt be the first seminary of the church to offer an experimental laboratory course in theology.

In order to set up our experiments, the first thing we needed to determine was what we had to work with and the operative conditions for our work. We canvassed the town to discover how many Episcopalians and unchurched people lived in the community. When the results of the survey were in, our population profile revealed twice as many single women over sixty-five in the congregation as any other group, a community trait that had prompted my predecessor in the parish once to remark that, if he ever had a baptism to perform, it would be either a scandal or a miracle! My theological experiments in the congregation began with various series of sermons and courses, about which I duly reported to my students. After two years of such effort, our consistent laboratory findings were that there was absolutely no correlation between anything I did and church attendance!

After twenty-two years of teaching, I was elected Bishop Coadjutor of the Diocese of West Missouri. The election brought a number of unknowns to ponder and pray about, as I tried to discern God's will. It is a commonplace to contrast the academic world with the "real world," and I, as do all academics, have always protested the supposed contrast. Nevertheless, when I was forced to make such an all-engulfing decision between the two, I must admit to considerable trepidation about my staying power in that other world. Both worlds may be real, but there are differences. After all, courage is easy to come by in the classroom. How hard is it to take a stand and lead fearlessly when you not only give the lectures but mark the bluebooks? Still, I had been given the chance to live and bring theology into the life of a diocese and the church at large in a new way. I accepted the election.

Shortly after arriving in the diocese, I wrote a short summary of the faith entitled "The Capsule Good News," which was printed in pamphlet form and distributed to all of our congregations in copious quantity. Subtitled "An Affirmation of the Gospel to Guide the Lives of the People and the Work of the Diocese of West Missouri," this encapsulation was anchored with almost fifty New Testament references; different translations of the New Testament were referred to for specific points and emphases. The text of "The Capsule Good News, " minus its footnotes, follows:

> As Christians, we find peace and the meaning of our life in Jesus Christ, God's full presence in the world, the Word of the Father who calls us to new life in the strength of the Spirit. Because God's gift of himself to us overflows us, we cannot keep the Good News of God's love in Christ to ourselves; we must proclaim the gospel to all people so that *our* joy may be full. We are called by God's love not to "love in word or speech but in deed and in truth," for we are saved by power that works—not by talk.
>
> When it is said of the Incarnation that "God became man," the meaning is that God embraced and entered into the human condition in its entirety. God became truly human; so truly did God enter the human condition, that he tasted death for everyone. The message of the Christian revelation is that *God is love.* Jesus is God's love as a human person. But what does God love? To what do we owe the Father's revelation of himself in Jesus? Not to his love of a few people but to his love of the world! In what we have come to know as the "comfortable

words," we are told: "God so loved the world" that he "sent the Son into the world" so "that the world might be saved through him."

To be a member of Christ's body, the church, is to begin life in nothing less than a new world. In Christ we die to our old selves and the old world, for "all of us who have been baptized into Christ Jesus were baptized into his death . . . so that as Christ was raised from the dead . . . we too might walk in newness of life." If anyone is in Christ, he is a "new creation," or, as the New English Bible puts it: "When anyone is united to Christ, there is a new world." As living members of Christ's body, we participate in Christ's continuing act of recreation and reconciliation. Because it is in God's recreation that we participate in Christ, the goal of that recreation is nothing less than a "new heaven and a new earth," a completely new relation of people and things called the Kingdom. "Behold, I make all things new."

We have a guarantee and foretaste of the Kingdom in the gift of the Spirit and in the Holy Eucharist, where we eat and drink the first fruits of the Kingdom. In the strength of that heavenly food—the body of Christ, the bread of heaven—we proclaim the gospel of joy, earnest hope, and assured expectation. The gift of the Spirit is the Father's guarantee of the future and so the source of our freedom from anxiety and fear in the world.

Christians, people who dare to take Christ's name and who thereby claim to have died to themselves in him, must be Christ's presence in the world for the world. That is our comfort, as the comfortable words tell us, not escape from the world. The church as the body of Christ in the world today has the world, the whole human condition, as its object of concern. It cannot be Christ's body if it has anything less for its concern, for Christ has already died in his body for the world. That is the testimony of his love and our one hope! Only as we are in the world has the love of God been given to us; the purpose of our lives is to love what God loves by living in his love. In such living we know resurrection and victory.

Several years after the general distribution and discussion of "The Capsule Good News" in the diocese, I offered four "themes" to the diocese derived from the proclamation. Then, after processing by an ad hoc committee, the themes were adopted by Diocesan Council as our diocesan themes and then commended to the diocese in a brochure entitled, "On Being the Church Today in the Diocese of West Missouri." The brochure explained that, "We believe the Diocese of West Missouri should be identified by an attitude pervading all of its people, congregations, and work, an attitude of joyful thanksgiving for the freedom given us in the resurrection of Jesus from the dead. Living that freedom and empowered by the Spirit, God's love overflows us in a mission of proclamation, worship, and service."

The themes were held up as "one means of establishing the attitudes which determine our diocesan identity." I often referred to them as our theological compass. The four themes, as a compass, offered four interrelated points that gave both theological direction and proportion to the life and activity of the diocese.

Because the themes were meant to form attitudes, their repetition was not something to be avoided but desired. I asked the clergy to be as thematic and repetitive as possible in everything they did. In fact, when interviewing clergy who might take cures in the diocese, I specifically discussed the themes with them and asked whether or not such a thematic diocesan context would stimulate or hamper their pastoral creativity. More than once, I was told that such structuring was not a problem, that, instead, it was encouraging to be in a diocese that had a plan to do something.

Emphasizing a different theme each year—but, once all four were introduced, also stressing their interrelations—the diocese completed the repetitive four-year cycle of the themes four times during my active ministry. We printed posters of each theme and distributed multiple copies of them to each congregation for display. Banners depicting the themes were made and displayed at diocesan convention, and all of the departments and agencies of the diocese were asked to refer to the themes as frequently as possible in their work. I asked for the same repetition in the preaching of the clergy. In order to set an example, I preached on each theme in each one of my parish visitations—working the themes into the seasons of the church year—for sixteen years. I offered no apologies for carrying the same basic message to each congregation of our diocese in my preaching.

A woman once remarked to me at a visitation reception, "Whenever you come, we always know what you are going to preach about." I explained that I did not feel a desperate need to say something different at each congregation I visited, for, after all, I was only a witness to God's work. A good witness just emphasizes the truth and reports the facts for what they are. Our diocese was large and spread out, and, as bishop, I wanted the whole diocese to be exposed to and to be doing the same thing at the same time as much as possible.

Our first theme and compass point was that "God's Presence Changes the Status Quo." In developing the theme, I stressed that, in some mysterious way, God *is* personal presence. God is not an object or a thing somewhere out there in space—or even in heaven. The doctrine of the Trinity was an obvious reference. To recognize God's presence is to recognize him as *personally* present in the most intimate depths of our being. But when talking about God, the first thing that must be said about him is that God is absolutely different from us. It is God's difference from us that "makes" him God. The result of the two truths of God's personal presence and of God's infinite difference from us is that, when we recognize God's presence in our lives, we recognize that we must become different than we are. Change is neither dreadful nor difficult in God's presence. The uncomfortable thing—actually, the impossible thing—is to remain as we are. A change in ourselves is the inevitable result of recognizing God's presence in our lives and is the reason why, in this world and the next, the Christian life is described as a growth from glory to glory.

The second compass point proclaimed that "The Church is Community." In God's presence we are in each other's presence as agents of reconciliation. Sin is selfishness, pride, and separation, exactly the opposite of the *communion* of saints. A community concerned only with itself is not a community. It is collective selfishness! A true community, therefore, looks outward, not inward. It has concern for the wider community of all human beings. Community depends on communication and the recognition of interdependence. Communication is something we contribute as well as receive.

The third compass point always brought the easiest and most immediate positive response from people: "We Are Set Free in Christ." Everyone wants to be set free. But, while all people want to be free, Christian freedom is special because it is freedom *from* ourselves instead of *for* ourselves. Set free from ourselves, we are free for others; we are able to love others and be humble servants in Christ's name. The community which is the church is a community of liberated people. It is only because we are liberated from ourselves that we can be a community.

The fourth compass point was "Each His/Her Own Ministry in the Priesthood of Christ." As this theme informed the diocese, we taught that every act of a Christian is a priestly act, i.e., the means by which all things and events are meant to be united in Christ for the glory of God. Drawing from references to the royal priesthood of the people of God (Exodus 19:6, 1 Peter 2:9), we emphasized that every person has a special vocation within the royal priesthood of Christ. We stressed that the royal priesthood—the priesthood of baptism—is the basic priesthood of the church.

If the priesthood of the *laos*, of the people of God, is important, it ought to sound important. "Lay ministry" simply does not sound important to laymen and laywomen—or even to the clergy, no matter what such clergy say in their prepared remarks. The "royal priesthood," on the other hand, is at once basic, biblical, and arresting. Every Christian exercises the royal priesthood of Christ, and it is that basic priesthood of the church which it is the purpose of the ordained ministry to serve. Most significantly, the ministries of all Christians are found within community for community, for Christ's priesthood is one of reconciliation.

Once the themes had been adopted and put into place, we used them to structure not only the individual lives of our people but the programmatic life of the diocese.

A long-standing concern of the national church has been that the concept of "ministry" not be confined to the ordained ministry and that, accordingly, local Commissions on Ministry not narrowly confine themselves to the concerns of that special ministry. Our Commission on Ministry had a ready-made vehicle with which to promote the broader encouragement of ministry in our theme, "Each His/Her Own Ministry in the Priesthood of Christ."

So it was that the Commission sponsored short courses in the diocese on how to become an effective hospital visitor and how to be an intercessor. We were fortunate to have the Rev. Dr. William N. Beachy, a priest physician who was long a leader in the Order of St. Luke the Physician, head our spiritual healing and intercessory instruction. Special training courses were also offered on selected blocks of material in theology, Scripture, and history. Lay readers were especially encouraged to take these offerings. On one occasion, in an instructional unit on hospital visitations, a student reported, after his first solo visit to an intensive care unit, that he was so obviously affected by the sight of the tubes and machines attached to a member of his parish he was visiting, that the patient, sizing the situation up, ministered to him by suggesting that he come back another time when *he* was feeling better. What a testimony to the truth that we *all* have a ministry to others in Christ!

Not to overlook the ordained clergy, we began a continuing education program for them called, "Two for Two," For every two years of ministry served in the diocese, clergy were offered two weeks—in addition to vacation—for continuing education. The diocese and congregation contributed equally to the education costs.

To emphasize the communal nature of the church under our compass point, "The Church Is Community," we promoted a pulpit exchange among clergy. In such exchanges, members of bishop's committees and vestries were asked to accompany their clergy. We also compiled a "Mission Congregation Prayer List," which included a brief description of each congregation, and we featured mission profiles in our diocesan bulletin.

Because the diocese's fifty-two congregations are spread out over half a state, it is often difficult for some clergy to be with each other casually and spontaneously. As a means of better realizing the communal nature of the church among clergy, an informal "Winter Clergy and Spouse Conference" in the Lake Ozark vacation area was begun. The conference runs from Sunday afternoon through Tuesday lunch and is purely for recreation and relaxation. As instituted, there was communal permission for a person or persons to follow any schedule they wished and to participate in only the activities they desired. In the early days, we offered a "Classic Film Festival" the first evening, complete with boos, cheers, and popcorn. The second evening, we held "White Elephant Bingo"; attics were cleaned out for prizes, and the only way to lose was to win! The only other scheduled activities were meals, the eucharist, and a few hours of informal time for open discussion with the bishop. As time passed, by popular demand, Bible study was added—usually involving the next Sunday's propers to get a jump on sermon preparation.

The Department of Christian Education conducted a series of day-long workshops in each deanery on the theme, "God's Presence Changes the Status Quo." The purpose of the workshops was "to give local parishes and missions ideas of some possibilities and some materials which they may take back to their own parishes and incorporate, according to their particular needs and interests."

The Finance Committee used the same theme to emphasize that "God's presence makes a difference in our giving to the work of the church." Proclamation, worship, and service were criteria applied to all budget requests. Because "The Church Is Community," and to increase participation in decision-making, proposed budgets were presented and feedback offered at deanery meetings around the diocese instead of just at Convention, as had been done previously. To further emphasize the communal nature of the church, the convocational structure of the diocese was changed from one of canons who were appointed by the bishop to one of deaneries headed by deans who were elected by the people.

The themes also offered ready-made ideas for programming in the church schools of the diocese and in the summer programs of the diocesan camp. Realizing the all-too-prevalent tendency of the church to deny its true nature as a community by looking inwardly at itself instead of outwardly to the world, our diocese undertook a considerable period of study and joint exploration with the Diocese of Kansas. The two dioceses jointly sponsored Episcopal Social Services, which has begun to minister to the needs of the wider community on both sides of the state line that separates the Diocese of Kansas from the Diocese of West Missouri (and also divides the metropolitan area of Kansas City).

Such is a sampling of theological reflection influencing the lived experience of the church in the Diocese of West Missouri for eighteen years. The degree of explicit theological influence in the life of a diocese may have been unique in our church during that time. Whether the results of that influence produced better results than the "experiments" carried out in the small parish during my first years of teaching theology at the seminary, I do not know. It is not for me to judge, but I have tried to make my witness.

Bridge Building as a Metaphor for Parish Life

James C. Fenhagen

> All this is from God, who reconciled
> us to himself through Christ, and has given
> us the ministry of reconciliation.
> —*2 Corinthians 5:18*

Reconciliation is a powerful word in the English language. It is a word of tremendous hope, because it implies that those things in life that have become separated, and often destructive, can be reunited and healed. The greatest witness the church makes to the world is the way in which it lives out this profound theological truth. What we see in the Acts of the Apostles is not a collection of congregations that look alike, or even think alike, but rather, quite different communities of faith that had an amazing capacity to move beyond their conflicts in a way that bore witness to the fact that the reconciling power of the Spirit could transform difference into a source of new life and possibility.

In his second letter to the church in Corinth, the apostle Paul uses the word "reconciliation" to describe not only how God acts in the world but how we are called to participate in what God is doing. For Christians, it is God acting through the life, death, and resurrection of Jesus Christ that heals the brokenness of the world. God's concern for the reconciliation of the world is embodied in the life of Jesus of Nazareth. It is through our ministries of reconciliation that we continue to express the presence of Christ that lies within us all. Reconciliation is about building bridges. It involves more than convincing someone that your view of the world is more faithful to Scripture than his or her perspective. Bridge building involves more than winning or losing or whether or not to stay together or go our separate ways. Bridge building involves entering into the prayerful search for that point where all of us, with all our differences, meet in Christ. This is more than an institutional issue. It is a theological issue with profound consequences for the mission of the church in today's world.

The Bridge as a Metaphor of our Time

In his book, *The Magnificent Defeat*, Frederick Buechner tells a story that speaks eloquently to the situation we face today both in the church and in the world around us. Buechner asks us to imagine ourselves sitting in the corridor of a hospital after all the patients are asleep; we notice a stranger sitting close by in the silence. "The silence between you is very deep, so deep," Buechner writes, "that you can almost hear it," but the mystery of who you are and who the stranger is remains hidden. "Then maybe on impulse," Buechner continues, "you speak," and in the stranger's response, "a little bridge is built, and you can meet on the bridge."[1]

What Buechner is describing is an act of lived prayer, in which two people become so open to the Spirit that they unknowingly are drawn to that center, which is Christ himself. This is the gift that the church offers to the world, only to be seen, however, when—by the grace of God—we are able to be who we say we are.

Sunday Morning in the Local Church

I was very troubled on Sunday, December 20, 1998, when my wife and I entered the door of our parish church. I still carried with me the wrenching news of the day before—the day when the United States bombed Iraq, impeached the President, and the Congress exploded in partisan anger, leaving the nation deeply divided and very much "at sea." As the service progressed, my sense of sadness deepened, as if what I was experiencing in worship—the hymns, the reading of Scripture, the sermon—was pushing me to turn inward, to leave behind the events of the world as if they had no bearing on what I was there in church to do. I found myself struggling to make a connection.

And then, a remarkable thing happened. As we moved to the prayers of the people, with their familiar words, a special prayer was added. We prayed for those involved in our attack on Iraq—men and women of our armed services, those many persons killed and wounded by the bombings. We prayed for peace. We prayed for our country and the healing of our wounds as a nation. It did not take long, but what I experienced was like the building of a bridge that allowed me to connect those different parts of my life that were called out and touched by the Spirit. As the prayer ended, I found myself looking around the church and taking notice of people I knew. I saw a neighbor who had a son in serious trouble. I saw a woman—one of our few African American parishioners—who had just lost her job. I saw a man who, because of his long-held and very conservative theological position, has found himself more and more disconnected from his church. And I found myself, for a moment, becoming a part of each of their lives. I found myself not just praying *for* them, but praying *with* them, and I knew that, by the power of the Spirit working amongst us, bridges of immense importance were being built.

I have thought about this experience a lot since it happened. For me, it explains why I am drawn regularly to participate in the worship of my parish. Sometimes the experience is deeply meaningful, sometimes it is flat but familiar, sometimes it is disturbing. But I have come to know over the years that it is through the experience of worship shared with other Christians that bridges are built. These bridges help me overcome the deep separations that I experience so often within me and around me.

A World in Transition

As the millennium approaches, it seems almost meaningless to point out the speed with which we are all traveling. Because there is so little time to savor the "now," the gaps that separate us grow larger and larger. In an article in the *Sunday New York Times*, the novelist Richard Ford suggests that we are so overburdened with interruptions and unwanted information —calls from the telephone company at dinnertime, meaningless messages on our E-mail, requests for our opinions on this or that—that the "now" has become trivialized. We are quick to share opinions based, not on thoughtful reflection, but on half-truths or opinions posing as fact. Ford writes:

> Professing an opinion is not evidence of a deliberate choice bearing upon being right or wrong. . . . Rather it is merely a spasmodic way to intensify a passing moment—a *now*—by making an act one performs

seem to matter when it doesn't. . . . And instead of intensifying a moment, such hasty, feckless opinion-spouting trivializes it. In this case, a *now* has not been stolen, but wasted and devalued.[2]

When I think of the level of argument in which I often find myself, especially in areas related to politics and the church, I am myself convicted by Ford's words. In the name of achieving unity, I all too often am consumed by the passion of my own unreflective opinions, thereby contributing to the separations that wreck havoc on the world.

Two Great Gaps that Distort our Vision

As I look at the Episcopal Church in the United States in the closing days of the twentieth century, I see two deep separations within our common life; both are culturally shaped and both are the fruit of the sin that separates us from God. Although these "gaps" are deeply personal, they affect what we see and how we react to the larger world around us. These gaps are deeply rooted in and fueled by the overwhelming individualism that shapes our values and saps our motivation to build the bridges that we so desperately need. These spiritual gaps are familiar to all of us and can be simply stated as the deep separations that exist between *me and them* and *me and us*, separations that reflect our even deeper separation from God. Addressing these inner gaps, therefore, is not simply a matter of personal piety, but is an invitation to participate in the reconciling work of the Spirit that lies at the heart of the gospel.

It has often been said that, if you want to know what Anglican Christians really believe, don't look for carefully constructed articles of faith; look to the liturgies that shape our worship. I experienced the truth of this on that tumultuous Sunday in the parish church, when our eucharistic liturgy became a liturgy of bridge building. In our experience of worship, we can become bridge builders on behalf of the world.

Me and Them

The deepest separation we experience in the human family—and in the violence and brokenness it produces in every aspect of human life—goes beyond not caring; the deepest separation is not seeing. Nowhere in the Scriptures do we see this more vividly described than in Luke's account of Jesus' prophetic parable of the rich man and Lazarus, introduced in a way that allows us to stay protected until gradually we begin to realize that the parable is about us. "There was a rich man who was dressed in purple and fine linen who feasted sumptuously every day," we read. "And at his gate lay a poor man named Lazarus, covered with sores." And then we read that both men died and found themselves together at the heavenly banquet. When the rich man asks that Lazarus be assigned to wait on him, and relieve him of his agony, he discovers that between him and Lazarus, "a great gulf has been fixed, so those who might want to pass from here to you cannot do so, and no one can pass from there to us" (Luke 16:19–31).

It is only through the experience of death that the rich man discovers his isolation, allowing him to see Lazarus—whom he had passed by many, many times—for the first time. And the rich man, of course, is whoever is blinded by his own need to the degree that he cannot see beyond his limited world. We live in a world shaped by values that reinforce separation. When the accumulation of wealth becomes the bottom line by which we measure the quality of our lives, the expanding separation of rich and poor becomes a given, rather than a profound tragedy. When participation in the common life is seen through a racial lens, we continue to build and reinforce racial separation. Poverty and racism are not only cultural issues; they are deeply theological issues that reflect the world's pain at its deepest level.

The witness of the Christian church offers another vision, but at the same time must acknowledge that it is also a part of the problem. The gospel message is distorted by an uncritical piety that reinforces our individual relationship with Jesus at the expense of our communal responsibility. We seek out the words of comfort in the Scriptures without hearing also the words of the prophets that call us to account for our part in the brokenness that surrounds us. It has been a long time since I have heard a sermon in my parish on the message of the Old Testament prophets and, to my embarrassment, a long time since I have preached such a sermon. The person of Jesus is too easily reduced to the one "who walks with me and talks with me and tells me I am his own." But from the gospel perspective, such an affirmation does not stand alone without the recognition that we are seen by God in relation to others. In God's sight, we do not live apart from others. In God's world, there are no *thems*. We experience Christ in us as we respond to the Christ in all of us.

It is this reality that permeates the depth of Christian worship. In the liturgy of the eucharist we hear the words of Scripture, not as isolated individuals, but as participants in a community of faith. Our first response to what we hear is to affirm the truth that shapes our life story. "We believe," we say. And then we pray, first as individuals for our own concerns and the concerns of those in our immediate world, and then for concerns of those who live in worlds we do not know or rarely have experienced. And then, I believe, something happens that breaks our separateness. In some way known only to God, a bridge is built that gathers up all our separate needs and wounds and hopes, linking them to the cross on which Jesus himself makes eternal intercession for the world. How this happens, I don't know. At what metaphorical point in the eucharist this happens, I don't know. I believe, however, that there is some point at which the world we see and the world of the Spirit that lies just beyond our sight intersect. In that *now* moment we become part and parcel of the offering of Jesus Christ on behalf of the world. We become, in fact—if only for a moment—Christ's body in which the separation between *me* and *them* is bridged.

Me and Us

For years I have had a friend from whom recently I have become painfully estranged. He believes the Episcopal Church—in which he, too, is a priest—to be in deep trouble because of what he sees as a heretical disregard for the authority of Scripture. From my point of view, his obsession with sexuality and what he sees as the moral bankruptcy of the "national church" (not clearly defined) makes points of connection between us seemingly impossible.

I regret our inability to move beyond our differences, and I acknowledge the many times when I have contributed to our theological and personal impasse. What I have found most regrettable is our inability to talk in such a way that allows us into each other's worlds. I do not know how my estranged friend perceives me, but I suspect he sees me as one who rejects biblical authority, which, of course, I would deny. I have heard that he considers me naive about sexuality and inclusion and a much greater believer in the work of the Spirit in contemporary culture than he would consider traditionally orthodox. All these assumptions no doubt have some ring of truth, but of greater importance is the larger problem of the deep separation that we find in every aspect of our common life. Honesty demands that we accept the simple fact that committed Christians can see the same truth through different lenses.

To meet anyone at the level of connection that the Spirit makes possible requires more than good will or skilled communication. In Christ we meet one another at a point beyond our separateness. "Peace I leave with you; my peace I give to you," Jesus told his disciples (John 14:27). The peace of which he speaks is the fruit of abiding in the love of God which permeates the world. "As the Father has loved me, so have I loved you, abide in my love," we hear again (John 15:9). "You did not choose me, I chose you. And I appointed you to go and bear fruit, fruit that will last. . . . I am giving you these commands that so you might love one another" (John 15:16–17). This is not an institutional matter, a question of who is right and who is wrong. It is about the meaning of life in Christ, which lies at the heart of the gospel.

But as we all know, there are many, many times when—for whatever reason and despite the best efforts of committed people—the moment is not right and bridges cannot be built. The tentative peace that has just begun to be realized in Northern Ireland is the result of years and years of building a bridge of peace one stone at a time. There are times when the deepest connection that God makes possible means that some who have participated in the struggle find themselves forced, as a matter of conscience, to walk away. The ministry of reconciliation is a lifetime commitment. Sometimes the best we can do is to help create a climate within which a bridge can be built in the future.

In our common worship we have been given the way. After the prayers of the people have been offered and confession made, something quite remarkable occurs. We meet our neighbor or a stranger face to face with the words, "The Peace of the Lord be with you," and then the response, "And also with you." This simple ritual is more than a greeting or a time to hug a friend. It is an invitation to enter into the peace of Christ where all disconnections are bridged. As Doris Donnelly wrote, "Reconciliation is God's dream for the world. It involves restoring broken relationships, healing our deepest wounds, and transforming hearts in the peace of Christ."[3]

Every person with whom we share the peace of Christ is a reminder of someone else with whom there is disconnection. The passing of the peace is a form of covenant in which we accept the invitation of the Spirit to make connections with another. We then present the offering of our spiritual "bottom line" and receive in return the life of Christ in bread and wine, the sign of the promise of his peace to us. And then we depart with, "Go in Peace to love and serve the Lord," words that empower the ministry of reconciliation to which we have been called in baptism.

James C. Fenhagen

The Local Church as Bridge Builder

Whenever nations or races or groups or peoples of different faiths move through their separation to find a common ground, the peace of God is manifested in the world. Without having to negate our own deeply held truths, we can move beyond our self-imposed boundaries in order to embrace that deeper truth of the reality of the kingdom (dominion) of God in human history. When Jesus told his disciples that the kingdom of God was within them and amongst them, he was pointing to this reality. When the Berlin Wall came down, when a treaty of peace was signed in Northern Island, when Muslims and Christians find a way to live together on behalf of the common good, when a system of separation gives way to a vision of community that gives dignity to all people, the dominion of God is seen in all of its power. It is to this truth that the church as the body of Christ is called to witness in partnership with all others committed to the reality of God's peace, however understood. If this witness is to be made, it must begin first on the local level. It is the local congregation that bears the weight of the church's proclamation of the gospel. What then might constitute such an emphasis on the local level? I offer a few suggestions based on what I have experienced in the church and what I have come to believe is God's clear call to the church as we face a new world.

1. Begin with worship. This is the heart of it all. Plan carefully for every time in which a congregation gathers together to enter into the peace of God. Involve more people in the planning. Take time to help the congregation understand what we do when we "break bread together." Celebrate with breadth and with joy. Let worship be a time of connection where the "sacred" and the "secular" become one.

2. Teach about the practice of prayer. Honor differences. Learn to embrace silence. Be still and know that God *is.* Involve as many people as possible in praying for each other, for the church in its many separate parts, for the world in which we live. "Pray without ceasing," as the Scriptures tell us, which means making this a major emphasis of parish life.

3. Read, study, discuss, and pray the Scriptures. Note how different people with different temperaments respond. Enter in and discuss the tension you experience between the Word of God in Scripture and the Word of God who makes God known in the world through

the Holy Spirit. Develop the gift of discernment both as individuals and as groups. Be open to what St. Paul refers to as "transformation by the renewing of your minds" (Romans 12:2). Let it happen.

4. Let your church be an open forum where different points of view are honored. Take time to share personal stories. Be curious about where people come from and what it is that has shaped their lives. Reflect a minute about the last time someone expressed genuine interest in what you had to say, and vow never again to demonstrate a lack of interest in another child of God.
5. Tell the truth about our conflicts. Let nothing of communal importance be kept behind closed doors. Build on what Israel and the Palestinians have finally acknowledged, that there can be no connection until each side of a conflict is given the right to exist.
6. Spread out. Learn about what is happening in other places to strengthen our ministries of reconciliation. Don't keep the spirit of reconciliation locked in the church. Encourage bridge building in the workplace, in our communities, in our homes, in political gatherings. Bring people together who disagree and let them listen to one another. Get excited about the possibilities.
7. Work on building a community that freely shares the gift of encouragement with one another and seeks to live by the discipline of never making a point or getting control by the personal diminishment of someone else.
8. And remember what Jesus wanted us never to forget, "The hour is coming when you will be scattered, each one to his home, and you will leave me alone. Yet, I am not alone because the Father is with me. I have said this to you, so that in me, you may have peace. In the world there will be tribulation. But take courage: I have overcome the world" (John 16:32–33).

Notes

1. Frederick Buechner, *The Magnificent Defeat* (New York: Seabury Press, 1996), 124–125.

2. Richard Ford, *New York Times*, Sunday, Op-Ed Page, 3 January 1999.

3. Doris Donnelly, "Ambassadors of Reconciliation," *Weavings* 5 (January/February 1990): 18.

What It All Means: A Reflection on Deacons

Ormonde Plater

Some twenty years ago, the directors of the National Center for the Diaconate (descendant of the Central House for Deaconesses and ancestor of the North American Association for the Diaconate) were meeting in Chicago. One of the members was Bishop Wesley Frensdorff of Nevada. While the rest of us struggled to comprehend a presentation of our dreary financial condition, Wes quietly worked on a cross-stitch design, a pastime that he enjoyed during church meetings. There was a pause in the discussion. Without looking up from the frame, Wes said, "But what does it all mean?" We were stunned. This was the first time that anyone among us had suggested a theological dimension.

I had been a deacon for several years but was still trying to figure out what *it* meant. When I entered the canonical process in 1970, the order for which I became a postulant was commonly known as the "perpetual" diaconate (from a marginal notation in the published edition of the canons). The Episcopal Church had ordained perpetual deacons since 1952, and there were about five hundred of these men (no women yet). They functioned as curates in parishes, mainly by administering the wine in the eucharist and bringing the bread to sick and elderly parishioners in their homes. Having read for orders and serving without stipend, they were limited in function and, according to the 1928 Book of Common Prayer, inferior to the priests whose style and dress they closely imitated. Although, whatever Christian virtue they symbolized as ministers of lower rank was uncertain, they performed an unusual and valuable role in the congregation. Perpetual deacons represented diversity in ordained ministry and stability and continuity in the parish. Priests came and went; deacons stayed.

On the last day of 1970, unknown to me, the canon governing perpetual deacons went out of existence. (Also expiring was the canon setting forth the order of deaconesses, whose work among the poor and outcast had earned them praise but not permanence. Several dozen deaconesses were turned into deacons, whether they consented or not. One of those surviving, Gladys Hall, age 101, still calls herself "deaconess.")[1] In its place appeared a canon proposing a diaconate for men and women. It was based on the diaconate of the early church, but in many ways it was a new creation. This was the diaconate into which I was ordained in 1971. The trial rite we were using, later to be incorporated in the 1979 Book of Common Prayer, defined deacons as special ministers, clearly distinct from priests, serving directly under their bishop, who were to serve all people, especially the poor, the weak, the sick, and the lonely.[2] The actual ceremony tended to becloud this high ideal. For my ordination photo, the bishop had instructed me to dress in clerical clothing, a black suit with rabat and collar, and, in his sermon charge, he addressed me as "Father Plater, the new curate of St. Anna's." When a later bishop transferred me to another parish in 1996, the old-timers at St. Anna's were still calling me "Father." No amount of gentle persuasion and casual dressing could convince them otherwise.

I have recited this story partly because it illustrates the tenacity of a certain distorted emphasis, and hence confusion, in the ordering of the church. All the baptized have experienced it and are part of this syndrome of a church divided between the high and the low. (Several years ago a deacon reported to me with glee that in her first-floor office in the diocesan headquarters she was indeed serving "directly under the bishop.") Mainly in this essay, however, I intend to trace the effects of time and change on those of us who minister as deacons. My unwitting passage from old-style caterpillar to new-style butterfly symbolized a far larger pattern of metamorphosis.

Since 1970, the diaconate of the Episcopal Church has gone through several major changes or shifts in meaning and function. The picture that has emerged is not neat and orderly, with one change suddenly stopping as the next replaces it. All of the mutations continue to exist (simultaneously and often within the same diocese and even within the same deacons), although some changes have been more prominent than others.

The first of these new directions, replacing both the perpetual diaconate and the order of deaconesses, was a diaconate of social care. Deacons were commonly defined as ordained persons whose main job was to care for those in need. There was a temporary diversion from this purpose. After 1970, the order began to fill up with women who were waiting to become priests. Until the early 1980s, when these women finally found their way into their preferred calling, the diaconate reflected a huge bulge of transitional deacons. The remaining deacons, including a large number of women, found their ministerial model in the old deaconesses. According to a survey of deacons in the mid-1970s, the happiest deacons were those who served in soup kitchens, not at the altar. Their happiness reflected the high value of a service that located Christ among the helpless.

But there were problems. If, as we were discovering in the new Prayer Book, all the baptized are to "seek and serve Christ in all persons" and to "strive for justice and peace,"[3] why does the church need deacons to do what all are supposed to do? It did not help that many deacons had developed social ministries completely outside the church, sometimes as professionals, sometimes as volunteers. They showed up for an hour or two of minimal contact with parishioners on Sunday morning. How could we blame them for showing little skill or enjoyment in their role in the liturgy? In a common observation of the time, deacons are "outhouse" ministers, priests "inhouse" ministers, and the two orders represent two distinct and separate expressions of ministry. Like priests, deacons always run the danger of understanding ordination as a personal right, entitlement, or adornment, rather than as a communal disposition for the benefit of the church and its mission in the world. Ministry conducted largely outside the church, with minimal contact within the church, tends to distort one's view of the church as the body of Christ.

In reaction to this trend, by the mid-1980s the church had entered the second major shift in the modern diaconate. Deacons began to enlist, organize, lead, and encourage others in baptismal ministries of care. One advantage of this approach was that it placed deacons back in the church, and not just on Sunday morning. As the Prayer Book says, the threefold ministry is "a gift from God for the nurture of his people and the proclamation of his Gospel everywhere."[4] To fulfill this purpose, the diaconate must express a unified ministry, with both pastoral and social acts of charity, derived from and expressed in liturgy. Most deacons who represent this type of diaconate have retained a personal touch in the midst of administration. Their activity places them back in the church but does not take them away from the world outside. When Christian people experience these deacons in liturgy, they see an enactment of the kingdom breaking into the world.

The burdens of churchly ministry trouble some deacons. They are required to spend long hours in boring committee and board meetings and deal with people whom they do not normally identify as suffering or outcast. This is not the ministry for which they think God called them and for which they signed up. Even though the church uses organization and structure to proclaim the good news to the poor and to feed, clothe, and house them, many deacons want to be outside of what they perceive as a deadening bureaucracy. A healthier approach to institutional ministry is expressed by deacons who start charitable activities, get others to run them, and then move on to start another activity.

In the early 1980s, some deacons also began to develop ministries of peace and justice. Taking much of their inspiration from liberation theology, they regarded the goal of the church as building the kingdom of heaven on earth. In this schematic approach to ministry, deacons are agents of change. They enable transformation to take place. Instead of patching up the wounded, or in addition to such care, they attack the ills of society that cause injury and distress.

As baptized persons leading other Christians in ministries in the world, deacons in the 1980s began to pay more attention to the admonition in the ordination rite: "You are to interpret to the Church the needs, concerns, and hopes of the world."[5] It is not clear, however, that this statement is specific to the diaconate. All members of the body of Christ bear the world into the assembly and share in prayer and action for those in danger and need, both within and without. Even the main liturgical expression of this interpretation, leadership of the general intercessions, is granted also to lay persons. Nevertheless, deacons have developed several ways in which to speak to the church about the world. These include the prayers of the people but also presentations at diocesan conventions and similar forums, articles in diocesan and parish newspapers, and other attempts to raise awareness among parishioners.

As the 1980s drew to a close, it became evident that the diaconate in the Episcopal Church possessed an extraordinary vitality and richness. For my book, *Many Servants: An Introduction to Deacons*,[6] I conducted a modest survey of deacons in ministries in the world, observing that these were a "mirror image" of the ministries of all Christian peoples. Any attempt to define the diaconate by some narrow formula will do an injustice to the wide variety of what is actually going on. Fitting deacons into a conceptual straitjacket prevents them from carrying out the mission of Christ.

In the present decade, the Episcopal Church has experienced another shift in the meaning and functions of the diaconate. This is a recovery of the ancient concept that a deacon is ordained to the *diakonia* (ministry or agency) of the bishop. In a statement derived from *Apostolic Tradition*, the present ordination rite describes the deacon as called to "a special ministry of servanthood directly under your bishop."[7] The concept has received scholarly support from John F. Collins's *Diakonia: Reinterpreting the Ancient Sources.*[8] Although it is doubtful that many deacons have read this technical word study, deacons everywhere can benefit from Collins's conclusion that *diakonos* in the ancient Greek world meant an agent who acted for a superior in word, action, and personal attendance.

Both bishops and deacons have profited from closer and more frequent contact. Bishops have begun to make time in busy schedules to attend meetings of deacons. When deacons accompany bishops on their visitations to parishes and missions, the liturgical event takes on a new reality, and ministry acquires a different shape, less one-dimensional and more diverse and relational. By enacting their integral relationship, bishop and deacons show that the hierarchical ordering of the church is based, not on dominance, but on perfect harmony and unity. This is appropriate, since the Trinity is the model of all ministries joined in the body of Christ.

But what does it all mean? A theology of ministry finds its source in the Trinity and in Christ, as we receive him in Scripture and tradition. Our encounter with God takes place in history, especially in the unfolding experience of the church. The meaning of the diaconate is an example of this process. In the Episcopal Church (as in some other churches), the diaconate has evolved over the past three decades into an order with two natures, which I suggest we call "Classic" and "Romantic." These terms refer to the eras and cultural contexts in which the diaconate first flourished and eventually reappeared.

In the "Classic" diaconate of the early church, deacons served as the staff or household of the bishop, his ministers of state (including, in Rome and elsewhere, a prime minister or archdeacon). Ancient sources record the closeness of this relationship, in which deacons were the bishop's eyes, ears, and often mouth. Laurence of Rome is a prime example. As his bishop and fellow deacons were led away for beheading, Laurence begged not to be separated from the bishop with whom he had shared the blood of Christ. Three days later, Laurence shared death with them. The common ministry of bishop and deacons draws its strength from this ancient *koinonia* of love and blood. When we speak of deacons as servants of the church, working with the bishop, working with baptized persons in the local church to carry out Christian mission in the world, we are referring to the Classic nature of the diaconate. As Christ is to God, deacon is to bishop.

The "Romantic" nature of the modern diaconate draws much of its inspiration from the Romantic movement of the eighteenth and nineteenth centuries in philosophy, poetry and art, and social and political theory. Along with an emphasis on beauty, truth, and the harmony of nature, Romanticism glorified the common person and attacked the ills of society resulting from war and industrial expansion. By no coincidence, toward the end of the Romantic period, Christian leaders, especially among the Lutherans of continental Europe, began to restore the ancient order of deaconesses, as they conceived it. When we speak of deacons as servants of the poor, working among the poor and suffering, we are referring to the Romantic nature of the diaconate. As Christ is to the poor, deacon is to the poor.

The ordination rite expresses the Classic and Romantic natures in the examination of the ordinand. Called to serve directly under the bishop, a deacon is also "to serve all people, particularly the poor, the weak, the sick, and the lonely." The two natures are not an irreconcilable contradiction but interrelated aspects of a unified diaconate. Again, Laurence is instructive. The deacon who wanted to follow his bishop in death also identified the poor to the Roman magistrates as "treasures of the church." As deacon is to bishop, church is to poor.

Our encounter with God is timeless as well as historical. God reaches out from eternity and shapes us, and the central place where this happens is the liturgy. Created by the Holy Spirit, the community on earth reflects the community who is God. The liturgical roles of presider and deacon, in coordination with many others thus represent the divine truth that unity is best expressed by many. It is desirable to reflect on the meaning of all the roles, meditating on their functions to determine the special way in which each represents Christ and his church. In particular, the liturgical role of deacons concentrates on proclaiming the Good News to the poor, urging the people to pray for those in need, and overseeing practical arrangements to feed the hungry. This indispensable bundle of functions combines a divine and earthly purpose in which we can glimpse Christ, acting for God, in complete unity with God, as he brings good news of the kingdom, intercedes for all creation, and gives himself as bread and wine to the holy people.

Notes

1. On July 25, 1998, shortly after this essay was submitted for publication, Gladys Lucile Hall died at the age of 101. *Ed.*

2. The Book of Common Prayer (New York: The Church Hymnal Corporation, 1979), 543.

3. Ibid., 305.

4. Ibid., 510.

5. Ibid., 543.

6. Ormonde Plater, *Many Servants: An Introduction to Deacons* (Cambridge, Mass.: Cowley Publications, 1991).

7. The Book of Common Prayer, 543.

8. John F. Collins, *Diakonia: Reinterpreting the Ancient Sources* (Oxford University Press, 1990).

On the Future of Moral Theology

Stephen Holmgren

Most of us are all too familiar with the experience of attending a parish or diocesan meeting where issues of human sexuality or medical care lead to fractious debate and protracted parliamentary maneuvering. Leaving the meeting room for refuge elsewhere, we encounter a similar problem at book displays or in the coffee room. Persons who are curious about an author's exploration of particular moral questions turn to the index at the back of a book, looking for references to abortion, homosexuality, or capital punishment, in an effort to find out where the author stands on these questions. Likewise, discussions in the refreshment areas quickly turn to the positions that candidates for church office hold on various issues, and rarely seem to involve an effort to discern what process of reasoning might underlie his or her views. These are the kinds of situations that I frequently encounter when I visit my own and other dioceses and I fear that it is probably the same for you.

We live at a time when the future of Anglican moral theology seems most uncertain. Perhaps more than with any other aspect of our theology or church life, our efforts to discuss ethical issues are plagued by argument, frustration, and divisions between us. Too many of us have concluded from this that we are faced with a stark choice: we should either simply give up on trying to achieve a moral consensus through reasoned discussion with others; or, we should try to impose moral clarity upon the public life of the church through institutional means. If we can recognize that *both* of these choices involve the abandonment of a commitment to think hard together about important things, we have the opportunity to try to live out our baptismal covenant with Christ and his body through our moral reflection with fellow members of the church. I believe that we have real grounds for a hope that we can recover a more positive and confident view of the place of ethics in our community life. The grounds for this hope are the principles and resources for ethical thinking that we can recover from our rich heritage of Anglican moral reflection.

We can recover, for example, a far richer view of what ethics or moral theology is for the life of the church and the world. As someone who teaches and writes about ethics, I frequently encounter misconceptions about my field. Whether it is at the local Rotary Club, or at a diocesan convention, I find that many persons think they have a pretty good idea of what someone like me has to offer. Ethicists, or moral theologians, as we are also called in our tradition, are thought to be persons who tell others what to do. Alternatively, ethicists are thought to be persons who refuse to tell you what to do! The first assumption is based upon the notion that ethics basically involves rules for personal and community conduct, and that ethicists are those who compose and defend these rules as a professional activity. The second assumption, which is more typically encountered in settings such as hospital ethics committees, is based on the notion that ethicists are those who make matters more complicated than they really are. Ethicists, in this context, are seen as those who ask all sorts of difficult questions, and thereby evade responsibility for giving clear and direct guidelines which others might usefully employ. Another equally unattractive assumption about what ethicists have to offer is based on a perceived correlation between ethicists and practitioners of the law. In this case, ethicists, like lawyers, are sometimes seen as those who are able to twist ideas and meanings to personal advantage, thereby compromising the common good.

Lurking in and around these misconceptions about ethics or moral theology is what seems to me to be a basic confusion about the function of ethics in Christian community. The best illustration of this confusion can be found in the example that is so ready at hand, our church's effort to address the mystery of human sexuality. Resolution A-104s/a, adopted at the 1991 General Convention, marked a significant moment in our ongoing discussion of these issues. The resolution pledged "to work to reconcile the discontinuity between [the church's traditional] teaching and the experience of many members of this body." The convention also confessed its "failure to lead and resolve this discontinuity through legislative efforts based upon resolutions directed at singular and various aspects of these issues."

A common interpretation of the resolution's words about discontinuity finds in them a regretful acknowledgment of a situation that might be different with other issues. It is as if the appearance of a discontinuity between teaching and experience is something that should not be expected. Yet looked at in another way, I think we can recognize that, in a fallen world where the plan of redemption is sometimes all too slowly becoming manifest in our lives, there will always be discontinuity between the church's teaching and our experience, or between moral principle and everyday practice. As the apostle Paul confessed long ago, in words to which many of us can relate, "I delight in the law of God in my inmost self, but I see in my members another law at war with the law of my mind" (Romans 7:22–23). Whether it be moral principles to which I choose to hold myself accountable, or those conveyed through church teaching, it is characteristic of Christian human experience in this world that we are always involved in the effort to approximate our principles in our practice.

A second notable feature of this example is the possible implication that, at least with respect to some spheres of human life and ethical reflection, such a discontinuity between teaching and practice could be resolved "through legislative efforts based upon resolutions." This reading of the resolution tends to reinforce the impression that Christian ethics and church legislation are facets of the same enterprise. Here we may discern some confusion about the relationship between moral theology and community legislation. Clearly, we should always wish that our moral principles influence, and come to be reflected in, the resolutions and canons that our church conventions pass for the ordering of our common life. But I do not think that we should be comfortable with any assumption that would seem to equate the two related spheres of life. On the contrary, I believe that the future of Anglican moral theology will be stronger to the extent that we recover greater clarity about the different ways in which these two activities function. Given our historic Anglican reticence about surrendering the activity of conscience and moral discernment to external authority, we should be wary of accepting statements which seem to obscure the distinction between the guiding role of church legislation or discipline and the guiding role of conscience in individual experience and practice.

This possible confusion about the way that resolutions or canons function in communities, and the way that principles function in personal moral discernment, was further complicated by another aspect of our church's effort to address the mystery of human sexuality. The trial of Bishop Walter Righter, which received so much attention in the press, was problematic in a way that quite literally had nothing to do with the innocence or guilt of the man who was on trial. For the sake of contrast, consider the sorts of trials that we encounter in everyday life, such as the mundane traffic cases brought before our municipal courts or dramatic cases like the O. J. Simpson murder case. In these trials, the purpose is usually to determine whether or not the accused is really guilty of the specified infraction. However, for many persons, the Righter trial seemed to be convened as much for the purpose of determining whether ordaining non-celibate homosexual persons was inappropriate, as it was for the purpose of assessing whether or not an individual had violated the canons. I believe that this case, and others like it, will have the effect of further confusing the significant distinction that exists between related spheres of our ecclesial life. Personal and corporate moral reflection and discussion should not be confused with our desire to achieve clarity about these matters in the ordering of our community life. For such a confusion leads us to believe, falsely, that we can then substitute church conventions for the much more time-consuming and less efficient process of praying and talking together, and reading and considering each other's ideas.

Unlike a tendency that we often associate with the Roman Catholic Church and some communities in the "Free Church" tradition, the Anglican tradition has not generally provided its members with authoritative moral teachings that have binding disciplinary implications. The exceptions concern situations in which the church's moral view is reflected in structures for the ordering of its public life, as in the rites and canons regarding marriage and ordination. It is much more typical of our tradition, however, to articulate general moral principles—both through the work of individual theologians and through the medium of church assemblies such as the Lambeth Conferences—which then guide individuals and communities as they make decisions in daily life. For example, if I am asked—as a seminary professor or as a priest in the parish where I supply on Sundays—whether this or that action "is right," I cannot simply pull down an authoritative volume from my shelf and find "the answer." By contrast, as we recover the awareness that an Anglican moral response to issues and questions is one that is built and shaped, not simply found, the future of Anglican moral theology will be stronger.

Here we must be careful about what is meant by the choice of the words "built" and "shaped." Our approach to moral theology is strongest when we steer a discerning course between the hard rock of published and settled public answers to moral questions, and the whirlpool of arbitrary and private opinion. Our responses to moral questions and issues will have more authority when they cannot be dismissed as appearing to be the pronouncements of a particular individual or institution, at some particular point in time. On the contrary, our response will be more compelling when we demonstrate that the view we put forward reflects a consensus spanning particular communities and generations. Such a response will typically be built upon, and shaped by, a foundation composed of our Scriptures and the tradition of reasoned reflection that has been shaped by them, and by the contributions of those individuals and communities within our tradition who have addressed these or related matters before us.

The future of Anglican moral theology will be stronger as we recover a sense that the purpose of this theology is guidance, rather than regulation. Moral guidance will prove to be a resource both for the education and formation of conscience within individuals, as well as for the subsequent function of moral conscience in believers, in daily life. Similarly, moral guidance is equally important for the education and formation of Christian communities and will prove to be a resource for addressing moral questions and issues. We will be stronger as moral communities as we enable each other to think more effectively about moral principles, and not simply treat them as rules to be followed. We will move in this direction, as we perceive more clearly the parallel that exists between an individual's consideration of difficult ethical questions, and the similar process of a community's consideration of various issues. Each process of consideration involves the same need to build a case toward responding to the question in one way rather than in another.

I have used the term conscience as if the meaning of this concept is clear. In fact, it is not. It is not only in our church's recent wrestling with the mystery of human sexuality that an appeal to conscience has been highlighted. The same appeal is frequently made with respect to many issues in contemporary ethics. I believe that the future of Anglican moral theology will also be stronger as we recover a greater conceptual clarity about this important facet of our moral life. Particularly in North American and Western European contexts, reference to conscience in ethical discussions is frequently very individualistic. In modern Western social thought, we have worked to increase respect for the dignity of individual men and women and for the freedom we wish everyone to have as they think about moral questions and seek to act on them. As we have done this, we have tended to highlight individual choice without always placing a similar stress on the role of community and tradition. When the concept of conscience is invoked in connection with this positive regard for freedom and choice, conscience is often portrayed as having the role of a spiritual and intuitive guide in the affective or "feeling" aspects of consciousness. Despite contrary social directives presented to us by surrounding communities, despite the reasons presented by others for why we should respond in a certain way to moral questions, we wish to preserve the integrity of that guiding, internal voice, which "speaks" to us.

Yet, within the Anglican tradition, there has been a tendency to emphasize both the feeling aspect as well as the thinking aspect of conscience. Conscience should always be followed, we say, quoting a long-valued maxim. But conscience should also be educated, says our tradition. And if conscience can be educated, then there must be a thinking and reasoning aspect to conscience, which not only speaks to us from beyond our present commitments and point of view, but which also engages our circumstances through reasoning acts of discernment and evaluation. As we recognize this fact of everyday experience, and as we deliberately readjust our concept of conscience where needed to embrace both the affective and the cognitive aspects of consciousness, we will have a more adequate approach to ethics. We can continue to emphasize the freedom that is proper to the exercise of personal moral reflection. At the same time we can be more articulate about the way in which community and tradition might make claims upon the individual as he or she reasons with, and seeks to act in relation to, moral principles.

In these various ways I believe that the future of Anglican moral theology will be stronger as we recover some moral concepts and principles which will help us to be more effective in thinking and talking together about ethical issues. Though we certainly could learn from a study of the approaches which others in our tradition have taken concerning various ethical issues, what we can most profit from is, not so much their conclusions, but their assumptions and starting points. By paying more attention to how we do ethics and a little less attention to the conclusions at which others have arrived, our moral reflection and conversation will be both enriched and more civil. As we help restore a greater degree of confidence in our ability to address moral issues in our parishes and dioceses, we will be enabled to learn more from each other, and we will have more that we can learn from each other.

Is There Still a World Mission for the Episcopal Church?

Patrick Mauney

When Presiding Bishop Frank Griswold, in his first primatial visit abroad, traveled to Costa Rica in April, 1998, to inaugurate the Anglican Communion's newest province, he found an indigenous church with a rich history, much of it owing to the missionary activity of the Episcopal Church in the United States of America (ECUSA). Building on scattered British chaplaincies dating to the eighteenth century, as well as more modern migrations of English-speaking Afro-Caribbean peoples, ECUSA set out some forty years ago deliberately to form and nurture an ecclesial community that would, in time, become a self-governing, self-propagating, and self-sustaining church in Central America. In 1997, that goal was largely achieved when the General Convention granted the Central American dioceses' requests for autonomy.

It was not a trivial accomplishment. Surely there are few places on earth more complex and diverse than the tiny geographic area known as Central America. The new *Iglesia Anglicana de la Region Central de America* embraces five sovereign republics, each with its own laws, currencies, customs, and nationalistic passions (e.g., war between El Salvador and Honduras was once ignited by a soccer match!). On any given Sunday in the new province, services are offered in Spanish, English, Miskito and Mayan Quiché. European, African, and indigenous cultures coexist uneasily, with overt racism a daily reality. Savage civil wars of a decade ago still sow seeds of distrust.

Yet from this dauntingly complex and sometimes tragic reality, a new church has been born, a new focus of unity and mission has been forged.

At the 1998 Lambeth Conference, Central American bishops spoke in their own voices, no longer through the alien chords of the North American church. The missionary dream had become substance.

The substance is far from perfect, of course. The financial dependence of the new province on ECUSA is strong—far too strong—with self-support in any real sense a distant goal. Disquieting signs could be observed at the inaugural festivities: even though there was a large crowd, there was no visible ecumenical delegation and no local news media coverage of the event. Some observers might see the new church as little more than a collection of ethnic chaplaincies, maintenance-minded and largely marginalized from their civil societies. But this is a church determined to become more mission-minded. Whatever its faults—and the mother church in the north can hardly cast stones—the Anglican Church in Central America is a reality, an interdependent part of the global body of Christ.

This missionary "success story" can be recalled in other lands, in other times. China, Japan, Liberia, Brazil, and the Philippines were the earliest fields of foreign mission for the Episcopal Church. All are now autonomous churches, or parts of autonomous bodies. At the Indianapolis General Convention in 1994, the five dioceses of Mexico successfully petitioned for autonomy, and the *Iglesia Anglicana de Mexico* came into being early in 1995. Few overseas jurisdictions of ECUSA remain and most, if not all of them, expect to be parts of autonomous provinces of the Anglican Communion within the next decade. Encouraging autonomy for its overseas jurisdictions has been a stated world mission policy of the Episcopal Church for decades.[1] As a policy, it has rested on a theology of missionary expansion, taking as its implicit text the words of Jesus in the Great Commission of Matthew 28. It is clearly a policy that has borne fruit, at least on its own terms.

Some, however, would quarrel with those terms. Roland Allen, an English missionary of the last century whose long-neglected writings have become popular in recent years, criticized the missionary methods of his times as self-defeating. According to Allen, this was the very time in which the Episcopal Church was planting its overseas churches, instead of engendering truly indigenous, self-sustaining churches. The missionaries —generally with the purest of motives—transported wholesale the ecclesiastical, clerical, and social service structures of their homelands to the mission field. The result was a church alienated from the grassroots and thoroughly dependent on the mother church for its financial sustenance and the authority of its bishops and clergy. It was, in the words of a Brazilian, a "translated church" in everything from the Prayer Book and hymnal to the architecture of the local parish church and the method of its administration—a good American church, but, unfortunately, it was not in America.

The gloomy observation of Allen and his admirers has been borne out to some degree in the ECUSA experience. Unwieldy diocesan structures and, in some cases, near-princely bishoprics could not be supported, especially where the missionary activity had been focused on the poor and marginalized. This inevitably resulted in chronic financial dependence. However, few who visit ECUSA's present and former foreign dioceses would doubt that the gospel is preached and the sacraments celebrated, that people are being ministered to faithfully in body, mind, and soul. The world mission theology and policy of expansion that resulted in the creation of many new churches around the world can still be declared a success, even if a qualified one. Still, one is tempted to ask the question: what would the result have been if the missionary methods of Roland Allen (which Allen himself called the methods of St. Paul) had been employed by ECUSA? Why were they not? Did the Great Commission fit too snugly the glove of Manifest Destiny? What would have been the outcome if the Great Commission of Matthew 28 had been obeyed in ways echoing the words of Jesus in John 17:18—that is, in the simple, humble style of one who once enjoined his apostles to take nothing for their journey, neither staff, nor bag, nor bread, nor money.

The success of other world mission policies and goals of the Episcopal Church has been mixed. For example, our most recent complete statement of mission theology and policy—the 1982 report of the Standing Commission on World Mission—noted that it is the intent of the Episcopal Church "to recruit, train, send, receive, and sustain people to engage in a ministry of witness and service wherever there is mutually identified need." For many Episcopalians, missionaries are the heart of world mission. More than anything else (certainly more than impersonal grants of money, however generous), it is people who incarnate the mission mandate of the church in their willingness to forego the familiar comforts of home to cross boundaries of geography, culture, and language. Missionaries have powerful sign value. In order to affirm the value of missionaries, we do not have to accept a primitive understanding of them as the privileged elite who alone can bring the gospel to benighted heathen. Indeed, we commonly speak of "receiving" as well as "sending" missionaries, recognizing that we in the supposedly more advanced parts of the world have much to gain—perhaps our very souls—from the witness of those once seen as the objects of mission. In this sense, missionaries are bridge builders, nurturing the bonds of affection within the worldwide family of God. It is right that the Episcopal Church has a policy and program for the exchange of mission personnel throughout the globe. It is certainly sound theology. A church that does not send and receive missionaries, by whatever name they may be called, is a church that bears false witness to its origin.

Yet, in the sixteen years I have been on the national staff at the Episcopal Church Center, the number of longer-term appointed missionaries has fallen by more than two-thirds, continuing an earlier sharp, downward trend. Cuts to the national budget reduced the national church's ability to fully fund long-term missionaries. Furthermore, there are few funds for "receiving" overseas visitors, much less mission partners who can remain with us long enough to make an impact. When compared to other mainline churches, such as the Presbyterian, United Methodist, and Evangelical Lutheran, the Episcopal Church's missionary effort is minuscule.

The church's stated policy of assisting in the development and growth of indigenous leadership, both lay and ordained, in every part of the church, also has fallen afoul of the budgetary axe. In the same sixteen-year period that saw a huge decline in the number of missionaries, scholarship funds for advanced types of training that are unobtainable in partner churches have fallen by a similar large proportion. The overseas development office—established in the early 1980s to provide training for rural development in the Philippines, Haiti, Tanzania, and elsewhere (in my opinion, one of the most effective programs, ever, of the national church)—was terminated during the budget cuts of the 1990s. Since the 1985 General Convention, the world mission budget of the Episcopal Church has fallen steadily in real dollars, though not as a proportion of the total budget.

What, then, may we say about the world mission of the Episcopal Church in its current state? At a time when the Anglican Communion is being urged to move "from maintenance to mission," we in the Episcopal Church are hard pressed even to maintain the status quo. Have we run out of steam? Do we lack the will to accomplish that to which we have committed ourselves by policy and theology? Perhaps. More likely, I suggest, we have reached the end of one era and have yet to discern our world mission for the next one.

The era that has almost passed is the era of missionary expansion, in which churches were established where before there had been none. This era encompassed, to a greater or lesser degree, most of the history of Christianity, from the sending forth of the apostles "unto the uttermost part of the earth," through the great missionary expansion of the age of Western imperialism, until recent decades. Some assert that this missionary expansion mandate has not yet ceased. Those who make this argument will not only be found in conservative evangelical or fundamentalist churches outside the historic mainstream. Just a few years ago, an independent missionary organization was founded in the Episcopal Church precisely to plant churches among "the twenty-five least evangelized peoples of the world." While I have not seen a poll on the subject, I believe that relatively few Episcopalians give uncritical support to such an endeavor, since it raises profound questions about Christian relations with the other major world faiths. Specifically, it raises questions about targeting entire populations, with the questionable assumption that such peoples are somehow "unreached" by God.

We are in debt to Ian T. Douglas for his fine recent history of the foreign mission of the Episcopal Church.[2] Douglas takes us from the formation of the Domestic and Foreign Missionary Society in the early years of our history; through the institutional conceit of the "national church ideal" (good schools, good hospitals, and right-ordered worship) which dovetailed so neatly with the territorial expansion of the United States of America and resulted in the establishment of the overseas dioceses in Asia, Africa, and Latin America described above; to the traumatic dissolution of the national church ideal in the turbulent 1960s and 1970s. The recent history of our world mission, as we have seen, has been one of retrenchment and cutbacks. The Episcopal Church (and the Church of England, the Church of Canada, and the Church of Australia) is no longer the prime institutional mover of mission, but a "partner-in-mission" alongside the former colonial churches. Ecclesiastical "Manifest Destiny" is replaced by "Mutual Responsibility and Interdependence in the Body of Christ" (MRI). Douglas concludes that new ways have to be found to carry out the world mission of the church, within the spirit of MRI, beyond what he sees as the crumbling national structures.

I would add that new ways must be found quickly, or the Episcopal Church will have squandered its means. By far the largest percentage of the world mission budget of the national church (about seventy-seven percent) is designated as subsidies for present and former overseas jurisdictions. Since we have written covenants with most of these dioceses that call for a steady reduction in subsidy, and unless new uses are found for the money that thereby becomes available, I foresee the effective end of world mission funding within the next two decades—the end, certainly, of the level of funding to which our church has committed for the past century. The question must then be pressed: after the era of church expansion, is there still a world mission for the Episcopal Church?

Our theology commits us to mission, including world mission.[3] Where is this theology to be found? Theology in the Episcopal Church (and in Anglicanism in general) is a relaxed affair. Our genius seems to reside in a pastoral good sense, a tolerance for ambiguity, a valuing of experience, upon which one then reflects in the light of the Bible, innate reason, and the tradition of the church. As a rule, we do not find in Anglicanism the learned theological dissertations of the Lutheran, Roman Catholic, and Reformed traditions. What we find instead is the Book of Common Prayer. The maxim, *lex orandi, lex credendi* (the law of prayer, the law of faith), seems to describe us well. Notwithstanding the occasional monograph or pronouncement of General Convention, it is in the Book of Common Prayer that we find our theology, including our theology of mission.

In her fascinating article "Mission and Prayer,"[4] the late Marianne Micks analyzes the four American Prayer Books from 1789 through 1979. She finds that these books successively "show a growth, a deepening, and a broadening of understanding of the Church's mission."[5] Micks observes that from the earliest, the prayers indicate that "God's mission has as much to do with justice and peace among nations as with 'Christianity.'"[6] However, no one-sided theology of mission appears, in which good works is given priority over personal evangelism. The Anglican preference for "both/and" obtains. As the catechism puts it succinctly: "The Church pursues its mission as it prays and worships, proclaims the Gospel, and promotes justice, peace, and love."[7]

What caught Micks's eye was the veritable explosion of prayers for mission in the most recent Prayer Book, far exceeding the prayers for mission in the earlier editions. From the calendar, the daily offices, the orders for baptism and the eucharist to the catechism, it is clear from the prayers, versicles, and admonitions that all believers have a mission and that all are sent. We may conclude that the Episcopal Church possesses and professes a dynamic theology of mission. The church's theology of mission is incumbent upon all its members, and one against which all our ministries must be measured—whether in the United States or abroad.

At the same time, the Prayer Book divulges no strategies. It is silent on policies and programs. The church as a body must discern the ways in which the mission is implemented. As Douglas has pointed out, the mission consensus the Episcopal Church once enjoyed no longer exists. The consensus must be forged anew, through a renewed process of community discernment. It was for this purpose that the partners in mission (PIM) process was devised by the Anglican Consultative Council. In the PIM Consultation process, the church in a particular place would work with specially invited Anglican and ecumenical partners to analyze its context, discern its mission, assess its strengths and weaknesses for mission, and—while taking primary responsibility for its mission—invite the appropriate "partnership" of its sister churches.

ECUSA held two such PIM Consultations, in 1979 and 1993. These were, indeed, fruitful exercises. However, much of the focus was on the domestic mission and structure of the church. These consultations gave little guidance to world mission, other than the salutary admonition that, as a church of a political and economic superpower, the actions of ECUSA beyond its shores would always carry the potential for both great good and great mischief.

The recent efforts of the Episcopal Church in discerning its mission have been mixed. On the one hand, there was a decisive 1994 General Convention rejection of an Executive Council proposal to cease funding missionaries on a regular basis.[8] The constitutional notion that all baptized members of the church constitute the Domestic and Foreign Missionary Society remains a powerful one. The idea that ecclesiology determines missiology, that the whole church, and not just voluntary societies thereof, constitutes the missionary community, is a significant theological statement. It demands, for the sake of integrity, that the national church continue to sponsor and fund missionaries.

The decisive reaffirmation of the whole church as a missionary society has been undermined, on the other hand, by the inability of the Executive Council and the General Convention to make the hard choices entailed by a disciplined discernment of the mission of the church. Faced with the necessity for reductions in the national budget in recent triennia, the invariable, agonized response has been to make across-the-board cuts, refusing, in any significant way, to choose one program over another. The result has been fewer resources all around and an overtaxed national staff. We may contrast our approach with that of our neighbor, the Anglican Church of Canada, which recently chose to continue its national programs in world mission, ecumenical relations, and public policy advocacy, while relegating programs in education and congregational development to its dioceses.

However, the community of the Episcopal Church is larger than the official bodies of the Executive Council and the General Convention. Just as all politics are said to be local, mission, too, begins with the local church —the congregation and the diocese. Much has been happening at the grassroots level that contributes to the discernment activity demanded of the national church. From those convinced that the Episcopal Church does indeed still have a world mission has come a proposal for a broad-based Episcopal Partnership for Global Mission. Based on an existing world mission network, the partnership would bring together not only offices and programs of the Executive Council, but independent voluntary societies, dioceses, and congregations with a focused global ministry. The authors of the proposal, which now has the backing of General Convention, provide succinct theological affirmations that summarize the implicit theological statements of mission in the Book of Common Prayer. Precisely what functions the Episcopal Partnership for Global Mission might perform, and how they would be funded, remain to be negotiated with the Executive Council. The success of such a venture also remains to be seen, since a wide range of theological loyalties characterizes its proponents; furthermore, not a few of the voluntary societies operate on a shoestring. Whatever the outcome, the church has reason to celebrate a remarkable effort to bring together, in one institution, persons of diverse loyalties who are polarized over many issues. We can be united and energized in our belief that the Episcopal Church has a role to play in the larger world community.

If the grassroots is making its presence felt, so too is the global church. The 1998 Lambeth Conference was for many American bishops a sobering encounter with the reality of today's Anglican Communion. Meeting only every ten years, this Lambeth Conference was far different in makeup from its predecessors. Half the conference was from what we used to call the Third World; fully one-third of the gathering was African. The voices the Americans heard were not ones they were accustomed to hear. In the sexuality debate, for example, voices from Africa and Asia were forceful, occasionally strident, and judgmental, rooted in a biblicism that, to

Western ears, sounded simplistic, if not crude. Furthermore, these voices largely carried the day, leaving many Western bishops bewildered and hurting, wondering if the bonds of affection that have always characterized the Anglican Communion were strong enough to embrace them still.

As difficult as it sometimes was for many American bishops, perhaps the experience of the 1998 Lambeth Conference will come to be seen as an invitation to a deeper level of sharing. Heretofore, the Western church has been the generous banker whose financial resources have reflected the gross economic and power imbalances in the political order. Too often, money has been *the* defining element of our relationship with churches in the developing world. Although the concepts of MRI and PIM declare that we are all both donors and receivers in God's economy, churches in the West have struggled to imagine what they might possibly receive, as well as what they might share beyond their considerable financial resources.

With the recovery of emphasis on the baptismal covenant, which lies at the heart of the Prayer Book's affirmation of mission, the church is coming to think of itself less as an institution (e.g., as the benevolent banker) and more as a community, a *koinonia*, in which mutual ministry defines the work of the baptized. Mutual ministry implies a willingness to meet the other on level ground, as it were; a posture of vulnerability and openness; space wherein the Holy Spirit may move and the *missio Dei* find its ministers.

Might we as a church discern that the Holy Spirit is moving us from an expansionist to a dialogical mode of mission? To engage in dialogue means to share honestly and openly our deepest selves with another. Thus, in light of the experience of the 1998 Lambeth Conference, in which the gap between starkly different ways of interpreting Scripture (and understanding church order) became painfully evident, we are invited to find ways to share our experience of interpreting Scripture as Good News in the midst of a secular, postmodern society. How can fellow Christians in vastly different contexts—in Africa and Asia, for example—appropriate the resource of our experience as people of faith? How, conversely, may we come to appropriate the experience of the other in ways that do not alienate and tempt us to withdraw into self-defeating isolation? Such an exercise of mutual ministry—done in humility as we root out the arrogance imbedded subtly in us as Christians living in an economic and political superpower—is essential as we discern the world mission of the Episcopal Church in our day.

Finally, our discernment may lead us to reflect on what we are learning of biodiversity: that the intricate web of life is highly interdependent and, therefore, fragile. The community of faith is not exempt from this reality. In my work as a national church executive, representing ECUSA in a variety of ecumenical and interfaith settings, I am frequently disheartened by our refusal to combine our resources and energy for ministry with the whole people of God. How many Episcopalians today know of the "Lund Principle" and our church's official endorsement of its declaration that we will not do alone as a church what we can do with other Christians? And may not this same principle apply also in our encounters with those of other faiths? Instead of Christians targeting the "least evangelized," for example, what if Christians and Muslims worked together to target the least loved?

In summary, the Episcopal Church has, from its beginnings, embraced both a domestic and a world mission. Its theology of mission has been copious, clear, and inescapable, visible and audible whenever and wherever the Book of Common Prayer is opened. For most of its history, a consensus about the world mission of the Episcopal Church ensured the planting and nurture of churches in the far reaches of the globe. In the contingencies of history, both the era of missionary expansion and the consensus that informed it have largely come to an end. Discernment of the new era is required, but urgently, before resources now devoted to world mission disappear. The Prayer Book theology of mutual ministry offers a way forward, as we engage issues demanding a dialogical rather than an expansionist model of mission. Is there still a world mission for the Episcopal Church? Emphatically, yes; but in a far different spirit and form from the present and past.

Notes

1. Overseas Review Committee, "Interim Report to the House of Bishops," *Journal of the General Convention of the Protestant Episcopal Church* (1970): 561–585. See also the final report in the 1973 *Journal.*

2. Ian T. Douglas, *Fling Out the Banner: The National Church Ideal and the Foreign Mission of the Episcopal Church* (New York: The Church Hymnal Corporation, 1996).

3. By world mission, I simply mean mission beyond the geographical boundaries of the United States of America. The mission of the church is the

same, whether domestic or foreign. See The Book of Common Prayer (New York: The Church Hymnal Corporation, 1979), 855.

4. Marianne H. Micks, "Mission and Prayer," in Philip Turner and Frank Sugeno, eds., *Crossroads Are For Meeting: Essays on the Mission and Common Life of the Church in a Global Society* (Sewanee, Tenn.: SPCK/USA, 1996), 5–23.

5. Ibid., 5.

6. Ibid., 9.

7. The Book of Common Prayer, 855.

8. Faced with the necessity of steep budget cuts, the Executive Council proposed, among many other measures, cutting national funding for salaries and benefits of appointed missionaries, while providing staff assistance to congregations and dioceses who would fund these same missionaries.

In the Shadow of Death: A Theology for the Church's Military Chaplaincy

William C. Noble

Theology must be living and real. Our beliefs come alive in the context of the people and the situations we encounter. As Christians, we believe that there is no place and no enterprise, no matter how remote or terrible, into which Jesus would not have gone to carry the love of God. There is indeed today no place and no enterprise too remote or too terrible for him to be present. Insofar as the Christian church is concerned, this is the most basic reason for the military chaplaincy. If the ministers of the gospel are called to be Jesus' hands and feet, his voice and arms, and if they are to carry his strengthening word and healing embrace into all the world—even into such dreadful contexts as armed conflict and war—then, from the Christian perspective, this taking of Jesus Christ into the hell of combat and into the face of death is the most fundamental reason for the military chaplaincy.

The first defining context for the military chaplaincy is war. Reflecting on the terrible battle of Atlanta in the War Between the States, General William T. Sherman is quoted as having said, "War is hell." Jesus, as the creeds express it, descended into hell and goes there again and again with those who participate in armed conflict. The Rev. Donald Gum, a hospital chaplain and veteran of the Vietnam War, offers a unique and dramatic exposition of this idea. Chaplain Gum says that, when Jesus appeared to his disciples after his resurrection, the doubting disciple Thomas would only believe if he were able to touch Jesus' wounded hands and side. Don asserts —taking some liberty with the scriptural record—that Jesus spoke directly to Thomas and said, "Here, Thomas, take a look at this. I can take it! I have already taken it, and I will take it again and again with you and for you."

Because there is to be no context too terrible or frightening for Jesus' presence and his touch, military chaplains have carried his word and his touch into the hell of armed conflict again and again. They have done this for centuries, and, so long as human nature remains unchanged, they will again. Although other justifications for the military chaplaincy are made, (e.g., chaplains have a Constitutional justification in that they guarantee religious freedom within the military context), the taking of Jesus Christ into the hell of combat and into the face of death by the chaplain is the defining and justifying reason for the military chaplaincy from the Christian perspective.

The Christian military chaplain prays for peace and prepares for war. Beneath the chaplain's ministry of preaching, teaching, counseling, and the offering of the sacraments of the church, there must be a profound concern for the faith of each individual soldier, sailor, marine, or airman within the chaplain's care. Faith, loyalty, and love for friends motivate the individual in combat. Although the chaplain is a non-combatant and does not bear arms, the chaplain must be concerned with the faith of the individual who does bear arms because it is faith, at least in part, which moves the combatant to stand in the face of death on the day of battle.

The presence of the chaplain on the battlefield before battle is no luxury. Regardless of liturgical or sacramental practice, the chaplain is expected to break bread and to share a blessed cup of wine with those who call themselves Christian as well as with some who do not. For the Episcopal chaplain, this loaf is the bread of life and this wine is the blood of Christ. As a servant of God and a sign of the holy in this dreadful context, the chaplain is there to encourage, to bless, to listen, and to forgive.

The chaplain is not in the military to make a more efficient military, but to provide good pastoral care for men and women engaged in a very dangerous occupation. The chaplain is not a unit talisman to be trotted out to the field like a mascot before a football game, but is always located as far forward as possible on the battlefield where he or she is sometimes coach and sometimes cheerleader. If the provision of good pastoral care makes for better combatants and a better military, then to use the jargon of the Army, the chaplain is indeed a "combat multiplier."

Today few Americans would object to our nation's having an adequate and strong military force for defense, and some of those who earlier questioned even a defensive role for our armed forces have come to appreciate the military because of the successful humanitarian, peacemaking and peacekeeping missions in Africa, Haiti, and Bosnia. Nevertheless, when the military applies deadly force in a focused, organized, and measured way in the fulfillment of its mission to our country, it breaks things and kills people—sometimes from a distance and sometimes close up. Although very few are called upon to kill, the chaplain is there to hear their confessions. Such a confession is not likely to be spoken in a confessional or even at an altar rail. It may simply be heard when the soldier, sailor, airman, or marine, says, "Chaplain, I am sorry that I did that, and I can't forget it." The military chaplain is called and sent by the church to forgive, to encourage, and to bless those who are engaged in a terrible and unique occupation, the profession of arms.

The military, as with other institutions, fulfills its mission with the help of very powerful myths. There is the well-known demonizing myth of the enemy who is pictured as less than human. There are also the not-so-well-recognized myths about ourselves: the myth of glory and the myth of invincibility. The work of the chaplain is most valuable when the myths of glory and invincibility no longer work, when the reality of death can no longer be denied.

Consider these two very powerful but very different reactions of parents whose sons have been killed in war: one parent proclaims, "He was my son, and his service to our country was glorious"; the other parent says, "He was my son, and he is dead." How can these two views ever be harmonized? Should we first celebrate the patriotic sacrifice, or salute the pain at the center of the heart? From a later time and another genre, the tragic beauty of the Vietnam Memorial in Washington, D.C., lies in its ability to honor the dead without forced or faked glory. The chaplain is called to a similar mission: to honor the individual offering of the dead, to speak to the living of resurrection hope, and to make no suggestion of trumped-up glory.

When the soldier puts on the combat boots, the web gear, and flak jacket, and snaps the strap of the Kevlar helmet, the soldier feels invincible. It is a myth; it is a lie. Just days before the end of the Gulf War, the only female helicopter pilot was interviewed for television. The reporter asked her, "You seem to enjoy doing your work so much; aren't you sometimes afraid?" "No, I love my work, and I am simply doing my job." One day after President Bush declared the cease-fire with Saddam Hussein, her helicopter crashed into the desert sand, and she died. People die in the military, and when people die, the first question from every set of lips is, "Where is the chaplain? Where is the one who will make sense out of this senseless occurrence?"

During the Vietnam War, one officer whose best friend was killed in combat said this after a memorial service conducted by a chaplain for his fallen friend:

> I was afraid and thought that I could not face the fire and threat of combat again. Then the chaplain held the memorial service for Jim. Somehow my pain and my fear went away at the same time. I knew that Jim was important and that the offering of his life had been honored. For some strange reason, after the memorial service I was no longer afraid for my life.

Although the encouraging role of the chaplain finds its focus and final meaning on the battlefield, it is a well-known role for the chaplain in a variety of less threatening circumstances. The second defining context for the military chaplaincy is training. The chaplain encourages from the top of the rappel tower; before the soldier-of-the-month board; at award ceremonies; in adventure training; from a podium on graduation day; in counseling sessions (marriage, personal, religious); before deployments and during deployments. Whenever the chaplain applauds achievement, urges other service members to try something new to better themselves, exhorts them to study, to risk failure, to attain a goal, to try again, or to do what they think is too hard for them, the chaplain is doing the work of the church. In this context, it is the work of cheerleader and coach.

The armed forces, as an institution, constitute the third defining context for this chaplaincy. The chaplain serves in the military to bring a measure of civilization and civility to what is sometimes brutish business. The military, like many other institutions, is sometimes mean. I actually have seen written acknowledgment of this in the printed materials for the military chaplaincy as it is being re-envisioned for the Russian armed forces, but I do not think you will find this idea articulated by the American military. However, what is true of the Russians is true, in my opinion, of Americans. The reality has to do with human nature.

The armed forces are built on the idea of the promotion of the most able. It is a system of promotion that almost always works, but there are situations in which it does not work because of ignorance, the lack of professional integrity, or meanness. In these cases it would seem to be the promotion of the luckiest, the meanest, and the cleverest. In any case, whether or not the promotion system is working as it should, everyone in this system of social Darwinism is expected to be without flaw. The promotion system—up or out—makes for a zero-defect environment with no room for failure or forgiveness. In this context the Christian chaplain must speak of the worth of those who make mistakes, recognize the value of imperfect persons, and celebrate—as foolish as it may seem—the invaluable contributions of the stupid and slow.

The military is largely composed of people in whom our society has invested very little. The military enlists much of its membership from the young, the poor, the least educated, and the minorities. Despite the fact that, today, most recruits are high school graduates—with many coming from American middle-class society—the military is still disproportionately composed of persons who, according to the values of our society, do not matter very much.

In 1988, when I was serving as chaplain to the Division Support Command of the First Armored Division, then arrayed along the East-West German border, the first sergeant of the headquarters company telephoned and asked me to see a young soldier who was about to be kicked out of the Army. Although it was the end of the work day, I said, as chaplains are always expected to say, "Send him over." The young man came to my office and for fifty minutes told me how he had come into the Army in desperation, having dropped out of school, alienated his parents, and lost several jobs in a row. In the Army for less than six months and at his first duty station, he was already threatened with a discharge. He was, in a word, a loser. After listening and after saying there was not much that I could do for him, I directed him to the door. As he stood for a second in the doorway, I said (and I really don't know why I said it), "Don't forget; I'm for you!" He stopped in the doorway, slowly turned around, and I saw that he was crying. Impatiently I said, "What's the matter now?" He said, "That's the first time in my life anyone has ever said they were for me."

The ministry of the military chaplain is the work of the parish priest: preaching, teaching, counseling, preparing persons to receive the sacraments of the church, speaking, caring, listening, and touching. The work of the military chaplaincy is exactly like the work of parochial ministry, yet the military chaplaincy is different. The contextual characteristics and demands of the military environment and institutions shape the ministry of the military chaplain into a ministry that is the parochial ministry and more. These demands of the military on Christian ministry not only give definition to the military chaplaincy but also show why the church must always have a strong military chaplaincy, so long as the possibility for armed conflict remains. In this way, our theology of the presence and availability of Christ's love can be realized in some of the worst of times and situations.

A Place of Integration and Synthesis: The Challenge of Seminary Education

Martha J. Horne

The seminaries of the church have a unique and critical role to play in forging the ongoing connections between theology and the church. The goal of a seminary curriculum is the formation of men and women who will be deeply rooted in the theological traditions of the Christian faith, spiritually centered, and trained to help others recognize God's presence and work in the world. Essential to the mission of any seminary are certain basic tasks. They include the spiritual formation of its students, the academic grounding of its students in the traditional theological disciplines of the Christian faith, and the development of certain professional skills for the practice of ministry. These three foci of a seminary curriculum are closely interwoven so that each reinforces the other, if the curriculum is working properly.

Seminaries exist in a peculiar tension. They are, on the one hand, graduate schools with classically academic goals, standards, and values. They are also professional schools, charged by the church with the preparation of leaders who possess the necessary skills for the practice of ministry. Like parish churches or monastic communities, they are properly concerned with their students' lives of prayer and relationship with God. As places of spiritual, academic, and professional formation, seminaries teach students to think theologically and to make connections between the Christian gospel and the life of the world.

The different components of a seminary curriculum can present competing, and sometimes conflicting, demands on the time of students and faculties. Students often complain that academic demands inhibit their spiritual development; faculties sometimes chafe under the expectations and demands of ecclesial authorities, which they fear will undercut the academic enterprise; bishops and other clergy lament the lack of specific skills or leadership abilities among recent seminary graduates. Effective theological education requires that these three strands be maintained and held in the proper tension to facilitate the intersection of theological reflection with worship and pastoral care. Achieving the right balance is difficult and has always posed a special challenge for seminaries. Several factors, including the changing nature of the students, the faculty, and the church, have made the challenge more difficult in recent years.

Those of us who work in seminaries know that many in our church are critical of our work. Some allege that seminaries have not kept pace with the rapidly changing nature of the church and newly emerging patterns of ministry. Others fear that graduates are not equipped for ministry in a post-Christian society marked by greater religious plurality and growing racial and ethnic diversity. At the heart of those concerns is the question of whether seminary graduates can adequately relate the content of the faith to the daily lives of men and women and, especially, to the growing numbers of unchurched people in our country.

The purpose of this essay is to identify some of the factors that have made it more difficult, in recent years, for seminaries to foster the necessary synthesis of theological reflection and pastoral practice, which is central to the mission of a seminary and vital to the life of the church. Because the seminaries exist for the church and its ministry, these are not simply "problems" for seminary faculties and boards of trustees to resolve internally; they are, in fact, matters of concern for the whole church, and their successful resolution will require cooperation among all the interested parties.

Much has been written in recent years about the changing demographics of student enrollment in theological schools, but there has been little acknowledgment of the profound ways in which these changes affect the work of theological education and, consequently, the work of integrating theological reflection with pastoral practice. Long gone are the days when Episcopal seminarians were young single men, mostly white, reared in Christian homes, recent graduates of liberal arts colleges and universities, living on campus and attending seminary full-time. The average age of students in many seminaries is now over forty. Unlike previous generations, many students now come with spouses and dependent children;

some need to maintain outside employment or care for aging parents; and some can only study on a part-time basis. Few are lifelong Episcopalians, and some are not only new Anglicans, but also new Christians. As a result, many are unfamiliar with the content of the Bible, have limited knowledge of the Book of Common Prayer, and only minimal awareness of the theological traditions of our church.[1]

Not only has the profile of students changed in recent years; so also have the routes they take to seminary. A recent stint in a four-year liberal arts college, once taken for granted, is now more the exception than the rule. Students frequently enter seminary from backgrounds in engineering, computer science, or business administration, with little exposure to the arts or humanities. Almost all have earned a baccalaureate degree, but many arrive at seminary with no formal training in philosophy, foreign languages, literature, or other courses that have traditionally provided the foundation for theological education. Writing skills are often so weak that most seminaries now offer basic tutoring in English composition.

These problems are not unique to theological education, nor are they limited to graduate schools. Officials of colleges and universities bemoan the fact that increasing numbers of entering college students need remedial work.[2] Whether in seminaries or other institutions of higher learning, the effect is the same: basic courses in the school's curriculum cannot be taught until remedial work is done. The alternative is for faculty to recalibrate their teaching to a lower level to provide information and knowledge once assumed upon admission. Writing skills must be learned before a student can frame a theological argument. A survey course on the Bible introduces many students, for the first time, to the texts, the characters, and the literary devices of Scripture. A theology lecture on Aquinas can begin only after an introduction to Aristotle, while a church history course must chronicle not only the spread of the Christian church, but also the history of Western civilization. Each course must adjust its starting point to compensate for a lack of previous exposure.

The integration of the different theological disciplines and the synthesis of theology with pastoral practice cannot occur unless a suitable foundation has been laid. Seminary faculties are now doing more of that foundational work, with no additional time allotted for the task. The national church, dioceses, and accrediting bodies push for more additions to the seminary curriculum. Concerns about ecumenism, globalization, multiculturalism, and evangelism lead to new requirements, while different groups within the church call for new required courses to encompass a wide spectrum of specialized areas such as church planting, ministry to teenagers and young adults, ministry to senior citizens, etc. Some have suggested the addition of another year to seminary, but current pressures are all moving in the opposite direction. Many older students are eager to begin their ministries, and most seminaries and dioceses are financially unable to support a longer period of education and formation.

The situation is further complicated by the non-academic demands facing many seminarians. Students in their thirties, forties, and fifties, many with spouses, children, aging parents, and long commutes, rush from class to job to family responsibilities. There are few blocks of time for sustained reading and thinking, and limited opportunities for discussions and out-of-class give and take with fellow students and faculty. Lacking adequate time to mull over readings or class presentations, students doggedly move from one deadline to another, eyes firmly fixed on due dates, oblivious, sometimes, to the connections that might be made among their assignments—or simply too busy or too tired to make those connections. Integration of theory and practice is hard to achieve under such conditions.

Older students, many newly arrived from professional careers in other fields, tend to receive and process information differently, constantly checking it against their own perceptions and the experiences they bring from their previous vocation. Many of these students, conscious of advancing age and zealous in their sense of call, are impatient with traditional methods of teaching and learning. They may prefer a more inductive style of learning or be impatient with material they feel is too abstract or too theoretical, always asking, "Will I be able to use this in my ministry?"

Seminaries, and the bishops and the dioceses that send these students, need to give more thought to the pedagogical challenges (and opportunities!) posed by these seminarians and the new issues they raise. There are, no doubt, creative solutions to be found. One possibility, for instance, might be some new and creative thinking about the transitional diaconate. Might it be used as a time to think intentionally about making connections between the deacon's academic preparation and the new ministry he or she is exercising? Medical internships have long been conceived as times of transition between study and practice for physicians. Perhaps a similar model would help address the current situation in the church.

The changing nature of faculties in seminaries provides a second challenge to the critical work of integration and synthesis. Throughout the nineteenth century and well into the twentieth, most faculties entered seminary teaching directly from parish ministry. That trend has changed, with seminary faculties now including more laity and fewer ordained Episcopalians with significant parish or pastoral ministry experience. Episcopal seminaries are small communities, with little turnover among most faculties. Although some still begin their seminary teaching with parish or pastoral experience, it quickly recedes into the past as the years go by. It may be important for seminaries to develop incentives for faculty members to spend some time in parish or other institutional settings at regular intervals to keep them engaged with pastoral concerns. Those opportunities would not replace traditional sabbatical periods for academic research and writing, but would supplement them with a different type of research.

Since the middle of this century, most seminaries have required that faculty who teach in the "classical theological disciplines" of Scripture, church history, theology, and moral theology, hold doctoral degrees in their area of specialty. In a recent study of seminary faculty, the Association of Theological Schools in the United States and Canada found that more than half of the faculty members teaching in seminaries today received their training in one of twenty-five Ph.D. programs.[3] Furthermore, the majority of these schools have been greatly influenced and shaped by a model of theological education described by David Kelsey as the "Berlin" model.[4] Characterized by rigorous and critical academic research and study, this model has been the formative educational influence on the majority of faculty members now teaching in our seminaries. There are obvious advantages to that model: the acceptance of scholars in the theological disciplines by scholars in other academic disciplines, for example, and the establishment of professional standards for certification, evaluation, and quality control. With those advantages, however, have come some forces that can inadvertently impede the process of integration and synthesis.

Graduates of university doctoral programs often bring to seminary teaching a set of assumptions, practices, and values about education that are more closely allied to the Academy than to the church. As specialists needing to focus their research and writing on a narrow topic for their dissertation, they may lose their connections, at least temporarily, with the other theological disciplines. Remembering how hard they labored to become proficient within their own disciplines, they are highly reluctant to offer opinions outside those disciplines. As a result, both seminary faculties and curricula become highly compartmentalized, while the theological discourse of the community becomes more and more fragmented.

Seminary faculties, following the practice of most colleges and universities, typically arrange themselves into departments corresponding to their academic discipline and area of specialization. The seminary curriculum, in turn, is divided into similar discrete areas, with courses developed and taught within those divisions. The work of integrating the theological disciplines is often left to the student, as is the task of integrating the student's academic learning with the practical skills of ministry he or she is learning in field education or in practical or pastoral theology.

There are several ways in which seminaries can help facilitate the necessary integration of the theological disciplines, and the accompanying synthesis between theological reflection and pastoral practice. One is to introduce more opportunities for interdisciplinary courses, with faculty members working together across traditional disciplinary boundaries. A liturgics course, for example, might draw on the resources of many faculty members: a historian to trace the historical evolution of the church's liturgy; a theologian to reflect on the aesthetic dimensions of liturgy, and to make connections between the liturgy and the classic doctrines of the church; a biblical scholar to uncover and explore images and language from Scripture within the liturgy; a church musician to incorporate the musical treasures of the liturgy; and a pastoral theologian (or local cleric) to connect the worship of the church with the pastoral needs of the people of God. Seminars might be formed, not within a particular discipline, but across disciplinary lines. Biblical scholars might join with historians, pastoral theologians, ethicists, and moral theologians to explore the ways in which the Christian tradition speaks of money, the exploitation of the weak by the powerful, and the growing disparity in our world between those who have money and the goods it can procure, and those who do not.

Interdisciplinary teaching requires a considerable investment of faculty time, but the ultimate rewards can be significant, both for the faculty involved and for the students. In order for these ventures to succeed, a climate of conversation and trust must be created among seminary faculty, as well as opportunities for faculty to work together in a variety of ways across departmental lines. Incentives can be developed to encourage faculty to collaborate more in interdisciplinary courses. It may be important to think of new ways to order a faculty within a seminary. New ways of shaping the formal academic curricula of seminaries are certainly needed. When those have been developed, new faculty can be hired who have the experience, the interest, and the motivation to work in creative ways to enhance the work of integration and synthesis.

A second way to foster the synthesis is to invite local clergy or lay leaders to work with faculty, either within classroom settings or in class preparations, to help make the connections between the academic content of the class and the pastoral practice of ministry. New partnerships and alliances need to be created and nurtured between seminary faculties and diocesan bishops, local clergy, and lay leaders, as well as with other educational or social service institutions. In addition to enhancing the seminary curriculum, such alliances and partnerships will also help the participants to understand the particular challenges faced by one another, and to recognize the different gifts each brings to the ongoing life and work of the church.

One of the charges most often leveled at seminary faculties is that they are too far removed from the daily life of the church. Respected as accomplished scholars within their chosen academic disciplines, faculty members are sometimes perceived as having little real understanding of the changing nature of the church and its ministries. To make matters worse, they are sometimes suspected of having a stronger allegiance to the academic and professional guilds that formed them as scholars than to the church.

Faculty members, on the other hand, often feel that they are underused resources for the church's ongoing theological reflection. They may receive more recognition and affirmation from the academic guilds or professional societies, such as the American Academy of Religion or the Society of Biblical Literature. They are perplexed by the perception that they are somehow distant from the life of the church. They cite their personal affiliation with a local congregation and note the number of Sundays spent teaching or preaching or the days spent leading retreats, "quiet days," and workshops for congregations and dioceses throughout the country. Most seminary faculties understand their scholarship to be in the service of the church. It is not surprising, then, if they feel confused and resentful when they are described as being partly responsible for the gap between the pastoral life of the church and its ongoing theological reflection. The establishment of working partnerships between seminary faculties and other church constituencies can help to overcome the misunderstandings that currently threaten to undermine the collaborative work that is essential between the seminaries and the church they mean to serve.

The seminaries of the Episcopal Church are an important resource for the life and health of the church. Collectively they hold in trust a long tradition of intellectual inquiry that takes seriously the life of the mind, one of the distinctive characteristics of Anglicanism. Seminaries can be powerful agents in the church's ongoing work of relating the great truths of the Christian faith to the daily lives of men and women. They cannot and should not work in isolation, however. The success of their mission depends on their relationship to the church that called them into being, the church they seek to serve. Properly understood and lived out, the relationship between church and seminary is one of reciprocity, a mutual exchange of the insights each has from its own particular vantage point. Seminaries need to hear the voices of the faithful, bearing witness to the God who has tested and tried their faith amidst the struggles of human existence. Similarly, the church needs to hear the voices of those who teach in seminaries, offering to the church the accumulated wisdom of nearly two thousand years of theological reflection, as well as the excitement of new discoveries. Both are important for the continued vitality and vibrancy of the Episcopal Church—a church that exists not for itself, but for the proclamation of the gospel and the kingdom of God.

Notes

1. Education for Ministry (EFM), developed by the School of Theology of the University of the South, has helped considerably with this problem. Students who enter seminary after completing the four-year EFM curriculum are better equipped for the seminary experience.

2. Higher education officials in Virginia, alarmed by the $40 million spent on remedial courses in colleges, have proposed a plan to require that local school systems issue a "warranty" on their high school graduates and promise to pay the cost of any remedial courses they require in college. (An interesting idea for conversation between seminaries and the dioceses who send them students!) Virginia Benning, in *The Washington Post,* 23 November 1998, A01.

3. Philip S. Keane and Melanie A. May, "What is the Character of Teaching, Learning, and the Scholarly Task in the Good Theological School?" *Theological Education* 30 (Spring 1994): 36.

4. See David Kelsey, *Between Athens and Berlin: The Theological Education Debate* (Grand Rapids: Wm. B. Eerdmans Publishing Co., 1993).

Teaching Liturgy: A Subversive Activity

Louis Weil

The title of this article is drawn from a comment which I have often made to students in the course of almost four decades of seminary teaching. One student (during my years at Nashotah House) referred to this as my "special vocation to push the piety button." He was referring to the fact that my approach to the teaching of liturgy has never been merely to communicate historical or theological information, but to help students preparing for ordination to see how the history and theology of the liturgy actually touch the lives of the people who participate in the church's rites. This approach to the teaching of liturgy certainly was not in evidence during my own years in seminary, when, as I have realized in retrospect, there was no evident intention of bringing our historical or theological insight to bear upon what was actually going on in our parishes and missions in the celebration of the rites of the Book of Common Prayer. It is for this reason that I have often seen my own vocation as a teacher to have been stimulated in reaction to what I did *not* receive at seminary in this very important area of pastoral ministry.

In fulfilling this pedagogical purpose, I have often "pushed the piety button" for students by obliging them, to the best of my ability, to bring our knowledge of the liturgy and the implications of a well-grounded sacramental theology to bear upon the liturgical norms of their future roles as liturgical leaders. Sometimes this purpose led to painful transformations of their personal piety, which was no surprise to me. I had gone through exactly the same experience, not in my seminary years, but later during the course of my doctoral study, after having had three years in pastoral ministry which had already forced me into serious reflection on the nature of sacramental ministry. I found that my own personal prayer and ritual practices, whether in private or at the altar, required scrutiny in the light of increasing knowledge of the origins and use of ritual gestures. In this process, I realized that piety operates at a deeply visceral level. We may think that we have reasons for what we do (for example, when we make the sign of the cross or some other ritual gesture), but in reality these gestures become part of our body language for prayer in the process of our coming to committed faith. In that context, they do not require *reasons* for their legitimacy. We may have seen them done by a priest whom we respect, or we may have become a member of a parish community in which such gestures were part of its ritual language. These gestures, then, become integral to a deeply interior experience, and in themselves, apart from any *reasons,* are, thus, justified in practice. Later, to find ourselves in a community where they are not done or to find ourselves listening to a professor who suggests that they may not be appropriate forces us to reflect on such practices in a self-critical way for which we are not prepared.

This is what my former student meant by "pushing the piety button." In spite of its being painful, however, I have believed for a long time that it is necessary for future liturgical leaders to reflect on what they do in the celebration of the liturgy, and why they do it. They are modeling a body language of prayer which affects the members of the congregation and influences the way each member understands how those who are not ordained relate to the liturgical act: "Should I be doing what the priest is doing? Or is that something which pertains only to the priest, which means that I am an observer?" Once while assisting a bishop with an ordination, I observed gestures during the eucharistic prayer which even I, a professional liturgist, never had seen elsewhere and which were intensely distracting from the central action. The bishop's response to me —when I commented (very politely!) that his liturgical style was quite complex— was, "I've done it that way for years." That is simply not justification enough for an idiosyncratic ritual pattern which draws attention away from what God's people are gathered to do.

Thus, the teaching of liturgy has been for me an act of subversion—the subversion of a non-reflective piety which fails to come to grips with the church's authentic tradition of bold and uncluttered signs which manifest the reality which they signify. As we reclaim the fact that the celebration of the liturgy is not a private act of the clergy which the laity are permitted to watch, but rather a common action of the whole gathered community, the presider may be best understood within a shared ritual context. In this shared context, the participation of the people is as fundamental to the action as is the role of the ordained. In spite of the liturgical renewal of recent decades, and in spite of the tentative emergence of a baptismal ecclesiology, the implications for the reshaping of liturgical practice have not been generally realized. So the task remains in the formation of candidates for ordination to see themselves, yes, as designated pastoral leaders of particular communities, but not as the primary agents in the liturgy. When the baptized members of the church assemble to celebrate the liturgy, *all* of the participants may quite appropriately be understood as "celebrants," each fulfilling the diverse and complementary roles which shape the liturgy as authentically the work of the people of God.

This vision has remained at the heart of my ministry as a teacher of candidates for ordination and in the liturgical renewal of the ordained. What I bring to this work is a lifetime of experience and reflection on the meaning of the liturgy in the life of the church, and the awareness that my own journey of faith has been grounded in an unfolding awareness of the integral place of corporate worship in the lives of Christians. My own life experience has been a major aspect of what I am able to give to students in the classroom: not merely the dry facts *about* the history of the liturgy or assertions *about* the theology of the sacraments, but a personal story about how the church's worship has shaped the life of one believer. This vision was communicated to me through my own pastors and teachers. It is a profound and yet subtle form of evangelization in which Christians who seek to live the signs of the faith they profess are at the same time witnesses to others of the power of that faith in our lives. This is the mysterious truth at the center of Anglican identity: if you want to know the God in whom we believe, join with us as we pray.

The Beauty of Holiness, the Holiness of Beauty

The initial fact of my experience of the liturgy was that it was awesomely beautiful. This first experience occurred when I was fifteen. I was a member of a group of students who traveled from our high school in New Orleans with one of our teachers to spend several days in Washington, D.C., to observe, as they told us, "the workings of our government in action." Most of our group were Jewish, but the teacher was herself a

Quaker. The Sunday during our trip happened to be Easter Day, and the teacher said that anyone who wanted could join her to go to the National Cathedral for the service. I have absolutely no idea why I decided to join the small group who accompanied her, but I still remember the impact of the experience. It was the first time in my life that I experienced the relation between beauty and worship. I can still remember the impact upon me of the beauty of the then-incomplete cathedral, and the beauty of the music which was sung. I remember nothing else from this first experience.

I learned many years later that the beauty of the liturgy had taken a significant place in the apologetical literature produced by Anglican writers in defense of the worship of the Book of Common Prayer against the Puritans, who attacked the Prayer Book as a fabric of the "inventions of men," and as not offering a pattern of worship faithful to Scripture. This debate took place not only in England, but also in the American colonies.[1] Another recurring theme in this literature is the usefulness of the Prayer Book as a basis for both corporate and private piety.[2] Such writings formed a powerful resource for Anglicans against the detractors of the Book of Common Prayer. They also contributed to, I believe, a tendency to glory in the Prayer Book as well as to use it. This created a mentality of complacency with which Anglicans confronted the pastoral imperatives for significant change that emerged in this century: the liturgical and ecumenical movements, and the realities of radically different social situations in our world. The traditional rites began to seem inadequate.[3]

My own experience in seminary was indicative, I feel, of the negative impact of a common attitude among laity and clergy alike regarding "our incomparable liturgy." My one course in liturgics at seminary was nothing more than a series of lectures on the minutiae of the evolution of the Book of Common Prayer (e.g., detailed information on the most minor adjustments to the text from 1549 to 1928). In spite of my strong love for the liturgy which had been nourished in my home parish in Texas, I found this course at odds with my own liturgical experience. The course seemed to have nothing to do with the lived reality of the church's worship. The liturgy is not a static aspect of the church's life: it is a manifestation of its identity. As each generation of the church is incarnated in differing times and places and cultures, the fleshing out of that identity in its patterns of corporate prayer will continue to find new forms. If I may adapt the words of Jesus, "the liturgy was made for mankind, not mankind for the liturgy."

I believe that this approach to the teaching of liturgics in seminary courses created a mindset of extreme conservatism with regard to proposed revisions of the Prayer Book and the presumption—which operated into the 1950s—that revision entailed no more than adjustments to what Archbishop Thomas Cranmer had written in the sixteenth century. Pastoral realities, of course, create imperatives, and certainly the pastoral leadership in parishes and missions often made common sense adjustments and deletions. There existed, however, clergy who interpreted the authority of the Prayer Book in the strictest terms, and, in general, a kind of fundamentalism about the authority of the Prayer Book which restrained such adaptations almost to a standstill. I remember one incident at evensong during my years at the General Seminary. The Director of Music, Raymond Brown, had adjusted the four-verse setting of the *Nunc dimittis* so that it would be sung in three verses, thus permitting the sense of each line to come through without an awkward pause at the asterisk.[4] After evensong was completed, an alumnus who was visiting found Dr. Brown in the sacristy and quite angrily asked him by what right was he changing the Prayer Book. The bewildered musician responded, "All I have done is to remove one asterisk." The alumnus responded, "If you change one asterisk, it is all up for grabs." Although this point of view was extreme, it did exist, and it does reflect the enormous reserve in the Episcopal Church with regard to the Prayer Book, a reserve which remains as a natural conservatism regarding familiar texts.

Yet we can find such reserve even regarding texts which are new to the Prayer Book. When the 1979 Prayer Book was authorized, I found that the version of the *Exsultet* which was published in the rite for the Easter Vigil omitted certain phrases which I felt were important for the theological integrity of the text.[5] Knowing that in the Middle Ages this text had been used in a wide variety of versions of greatly varying lengths, I felt that it was legitimate to see if I could restore these phrases to the new Prayer Book version without disturbing the integrity of its shape. My version was intended for our own use at Nashotah House, but it was received with such a wide acceptance that we decided to publish it. A short time later, a priest commented to me that he was quite disturbed by my editing of this text. He said, "Now that we have restored the Easter Vigil, why can't we just all do it the same way?" This attitude—that unity is maintained by uniformity—must be taken seriously; it has dominated some traditions since the Reformation.

Prior to the invention of printing, the liturgy never served in such a literal way as the basis of unity. The idea of an "Act of Conformity" imposed by a monarch to require adherence to an authorized liturgical form is much more a political document than a religious one, a document which reflects the painful polarizations of the Reformation and beyond. We are living now in a very different time. Rather than defining our identities by the differences in our patterns of worship, the ecumenical movement has enabled us to see how much in the common liturgical inheritance belongs to all of us. Further, in the face of the cultural and social diversity of our worshiping communities, it is impossible for a single authorized text to be appropriate "at all times and in all places," even for the members of one religious tradition. In our world, the imperative is to work for the recovery of an understanding of the liturgy as giving expression to the particular gifts, culture, and circumstances of a worshiping community, drawing into synthesis both local and universal elements.

The Fundamental Connection

For me, then, the imperative in preparing candidates for their liturgical ministries after ordination is to help them to make the fundamental connection between liturgy and life, and to recognize that our corporate prayer is not an archaic museum piece for which we are the curators, but rather the place where the whole fabric of human life is brought into the focus of the transforming work of God in Christ. In the classroom, I often remind students of the need to "make the connections," to see how the liturgy is absolutely fundamental to the life of faith, that it is the point in our lives, Sunday after Sunday, week after week, when the ordinary people of God are reminded of the depth of God's love and are invited once again to offer their lives in thankful response. In this perspective, of course, the liturgy is not an action dominated by the clergy, but it is seen as the action of the whole community of faith.

This pedagogical approach is closely linked to my own reasons for doing advanced study in liturgy in the first place. My goal is always to link theological reflection with pastoral practice, thereby linking the seminary classroom to the parish community. My own hunger to make this link confronted me early in my teaching ministry with the shocking realization that many parish clergy viewed our seminary faculties with suspicion, that professors were often seen as living in "an ivory tower" which incapacitated them to deal with the practical realities of parish life, including the weekly routine of liturgical celebrations. I have had to recognize that in some instances seminary faculty members have earned that reputation. My consistent purpose, however, has been to help to shape a new model in which there is constant exchange between the resources which our seminaries offer and the day-to-day realities of parish life. The ministries of pastors and teachers are complementary, and, in fact, ideally they should overlap. In my own academic work, it has never occurred to me that I am not involved in pastoral ministry. If this were the case, then I would not want to be involved in the academic aspect of the church's life.

It was a providential gift to me that my own ordained ministry began as a missionary priest in Puerto Rico—and not only in Puerto Rico, but in the very rural, southwest mountain range of the island. Nothing could have been more foreign to my own experience of the church up to that time. I was to minister to coffee and fruit farmers, many of whom were illiterate. Both life and ministry were very basic. I arrived in Puerto Rico to undertake this ministry shortly after my ordination to the diaconate, and immediately I found myself dealing with a completely new way of living: there was the change that I was now in holy orders, of course, but I was also in a culture with a different language and with a pattern of life quite different from my urban and rather elitist background. The learning curve was steep, and, in one experience after another, I saw that the models of pastoral ministry which I had heard about in the classroom, or seen among parish priests I knew, would not work in this Latin American context. What I took for granted was not taken for granted here, and vice versa. As I undertook pastoral care for the sick or dying, as I confronted the almost superstitious attitudes about baptism, and as I learned to discern between genuine eucharistic piety and bargaining with God, I realized that an integral part of my ministry would be to explore in depth the fundamental meaning of sacramental living in this very different cultural setting. This was no longer textbook theory about the sacraments: it was dealing with bedrock experience. I had to learn how to teach and preach and model the meaning of the gospel in a culture which was not my own. To my mind, there were more failures than successes, and I cannot know what fruit my ministry in Puerto Rico yielded. But for me, the gifts were enormous in the impact of this pastoral experience upon my future work as a teacher. I had to learn how theology is lived, and that is an imperative which I have continued to place before seminary students ever since that time.

It is in this connection that I have come to see the teaching of liturgy as a subversive activity. My having lived in a third-world situation for a few years and, later, having lectured in Central and South America (sometimes in situations of extreme poverty), I have been relieved of the myopia of looking at the Episcopal Church and the Anglican tradition only through the eyes of an Anglo-American experience. This has permitted me to encourage my students to have a larger vision of the potential of Anglicanism to fulfill an authentically catholic vocation (that is, "according to the whole") and to see the great principles of its tradition taking flesh in the whole range of human cultures and conditions. For this, there can be no idolization of any one model of its liturgical tradition.

With regard to the future, there are two important areas concerning the liturgy in which academic reflection and pastoral practice must intersect. First, there is the impact of cultural pluralism upon the Prayer Book tradition as we have known it. The publication of *A New Zealand Prayer Book* in 1989 heralded a new era for official books of worship in the Anglican tradition. Here was a Prayer Book which took very seriously the culture in which its communities worship. This imperative is equally applicable to us in the Anglo-American world, and certainly true for Anglican presence in other cultures around the world. It has serious implications for the future evolution of the Prayer Book tradition.[6] At a meeting of the Standing Committee on Liturgy and Music (SCLM) in Baltimore in October, 1998, Frank Hemlin, the Publisher of Church Publishing Incorporated, spoke of the coming impact of computer technology upon the American church's public worship. This will permit parishes "to custom-design their own liturgies, week after week. What this signifies is that the era of the bound Prayer Book and of the bound hymnal is over."[7] There can be little doubt that such a prospect would be gravely disturbing to many Anglicans in provinces around the world, but it is important to place this new technology in historical perspective. We must remember that the first editions of the Book of Common Prayer in the sixteenth century were possible through a revolution in technology that had occurred only a century earlier, the invention of printing. Although the enormous impact of computer technology upon our culture may seem to menace much that we see as humane in our liturgical tradition, the technology itself is neither good nor ill. The question before us is how this technology will be used by the church in the face of its important role within our culture. It will inevitably shape many of our expectations about public worship as more and more parish communities take advantage of the possibility to "custom-design their own liturgies, week after week." At the very least, this new situation will demand of liturgical leaders, both lay and ordained, a greater insight into the nature of liturgical actions than was required when all that clergy thought necessary was to open the Prayer Book and begin the service. That never really was adequate preparation, but before long it will be an impossibility. This shift will, of course, create new demands upon the character of seminary education regarding the liturgy and new imperatives for continuing education for clergy. This is not a death knell to the liturgical tradition of Anglicanism, but it will certainly mean the transformation of how that tradition is "realized" within our parish communities.

The second area in which academic reflection and pastoral practice must intersect is related to the emergence in recent decades of what is called "a baptismal ecclesiology." We may now see this as an inevitable development of the recovery in recent decades of a sense of the important role of baptism in the lives of Christians, not merely as a ritual of infancy, but as a sacrament which defines the orientation of one's life within the community of faith. In the centuries immediately behind us, a hierarchical ecclesiology has dominated in the church's self-understanding. In this framework, the primary actions of the church's life were identified with the work of the ordained clergy. A baptismal ecclesiology opens up the horizon of the Christian life to see all members of the body of Christ as being called to service, each according to the particular gifts given by God and discerned by the church. This ecclesiology places all the particular gifts of the laity in an equal and complementary relation to the particular gifts which the church looks for in its ordained leaders. There is no question of superior or inferior. This understanding, of course, has important implications for our understanding of the liturgy, not as something which clergy celebrate for passive observers, but as the common action of the whole assembly of God's people.

These changes will have significant impact upon the life of the church, and it will require the "subversion" of many inherited views still strongly held by committed Christians. It will be only through cooperative reflection that we shall be able to move forward confidently into what is for us uncharted territory, but such movement is an imperative for us as we seek to serve God faithfully in a constantly changing world.

Notes

1. The series of sermons preached by Thomas Bisse on "The Beauty of Holiness in the Common Prayer" (1716) is a characteristic example of this literature (London: William & John Innys, 1728.) In the American colonies, the same theme was echoed by the famous "Yale apostate" (for his conversion to the Church of England), Samuel Johnson of Connecticut, in his sermon "On the Beauty of Holiness in the Worship of the Church of England," preached at Stratford in 1749. In Herbert and Carol Schneider, eds., *Samuel Johnson: His Career and Writings*, vol. 3 (New York: Columbia University Press, 1929), 515–547.

2. The literature in this regard is quite rich. We may note, for example, a sermon preached in 1681 by William Beveridge, the Bishop of St. Asaph, on "The Excellency and Usefulness of the Common Prayer," *Works*, vol. 6, J. Bliss, ed. (Oxford: *LACT*, 1842–1846), 370ff.

3. Paul Gibson, the former Liturgical Officer of the Anglican Church of Canada, has discussed these factors with insight in a recent article, "What is the future role of liturgy in Anglican unity?" in David R. Holeton, ed., *Liturgical Inculturation in the Anglican Communion*, Alcuin/GROW Liturgical Study 15 (Bramcote, Nottingham, U.K.: Grove Books, 1990), 17–22.

4. One can see immediately how this was done by comparing this text in the 1928 and 1979 versions of the Prayer Book. The Book of Common Prayer (New York: The Church Hymnal Corporation, 1928), 28; The Book of Common Prayer (New York: The Church Hymnal Corporation, 1979), 66.

5. The Book of Common Prayer (1979), 286–287.

6. See the recent article by Marion J. Hatchett, "Unfinished Business in Prayer Book Revision," Paul V. Marshall and Lesley A. Northup, eds., *Leaps and Boundaries: The Prayer Book in the 21st Century* (Harrisburg, Pa.: Morehouse Publishing, 1997), 3–41.

7. Reported in an internet message on the SCLM meeting, October 28, 1998.

College Chaplaincy and the Future of Theology

Jacqueline Schmitt

Behind the football games and band concerts, Sunday night suppers and Episco-discos, lurks the ulterior motive of campus ministry. Part of the pastoral care of students moving from adolescence to young adulthood is to encourage thoughtful reflection on the experiences of life. As a corollary to their academic education, the church's ministry to young adults is to nurture theological thinking, a way to put together all they learn and yearn for with the purposes God may have for their lives and for the world.

In this process, the historical and traditional resources of the church play a part, but necessarily only as a foundation or starting point. "New occasions teach new duties / Time makes ancient good uncouth,"[1] in the words of the old hymn. Each generation is called to re-envision the tradition that shaped them and to rethink that theology for the challenges of a new day. To reflect, as we are called to in this volume, on the future of theology and the Episcopal Church, then it seems we must concern ourselves with how to encourage theological thinking among the younger generations.

I have lately found two resources helpful as I work toward this goal. One is the life of a theologian from the late nineteenth and early twentieth century, Vida Dutton Scudder. The other is a recent book, *Common Fire: Lives of Commitment in a Complex World*,[2] in which the authors seek to understand what nurtured a hundred or so ordinary people committed to the common good. The authors saw a need, in this increasingly complex and interrelated global society, to ask why and how ordinary people rose above self-interest and demonstrated a life-long commitment to making "the new commons" a better place. They sought out

> people who, while working in very concrete settings, saw their commitments to particular people, groups, and concerns as finally a part of the survival and prosperity of the whole earth community . . . people who could hold together the "micro" and the "macro," who were able to connect their everyday work with the larger concerns of the new global commons.[3]

The authors discovered several patterns in the experiences of these people, especially in the teenage and young adult years, that seemed to form their characters toward commitment to the common good: an upbringing "good enough" to foster a sense of trustworthy belonging; some constructive engagement with persons other than their own "tribe"; and significant mentors who inspired these people to think they could make a difference. Although the persons who are the subjects of *Common Fire* may or may not be consciously religious (most are, however), it struck me that the patterns of life discovered by the authors are the patterns which lead people to think theologically about their experience.

I came upon Vida Scudder when doing some research into Episcopalians active during the "social gospel" years and found her story a useful case study in theological reflection from lived experience. Living at the turn of the twentieth century among the first generation of college-educated women, wrestling with the profound social changes of the industrial era, a devout Episcopalian and a committed socialist, Scudder grasped the challenges of her day and continued to change and grow with the times. The hallmarks of the committed life, as spelled out by the authors of *Common Fire*, provide benchmarks to look at Scudder's life and to suggest ways we can encourage the kind of reflection on lived experience that leads to theological thinking.

Vida Dutton Scudder was born in 1861 in India where her parents—who were comfortable although not extremely wealthy New Englanders—had moved as young, promising, energetic Congregational missionaries. David Scudder was drowned in a swimming accident in India when Vida was less than a year old. The young widow and her infant returned to Boston, and then lived extensively on the "Grand Tour" of the artistic and cultural capitals of Europe.

Other than the exotic locale of her birth, there is nothing particularly remarkable about Vida Scudder's early life. Missionary life, while unusual, was a respectable and unsurprising pursuit, especially for someone like David Scudder and his devout and thoroughly mainstream Congregational family. Without going into what constitutes—by late-twentieth-century standards—a "good-enough" upbringing in mid-Victorian New England, we can say safely that Scudder's childhood, however marked by the tragic death of her young father, was loving, secure, and trustworthy enough to enable her to face the world with confidence.

Several of the patterns mentioned by the authors of *Common Fire* can be found in this brief description of Scudder's family and what about it may have contributed to her later theological thinking:

> They were independent people who possessed a strong strain of humanitarian idealism. In the days when the timid and the time-serving persecuted the abolitionists and defended slavery, these high-minded Brahmins sympathized with the unpopular cause because it was righteous. Sometimes, though, family loyalties were strained when a relative's independent spirit seemed to pass beyond the limits established by sound common sense. For example, consider "Aunt" Eliza Scudder, a fiery, outspoken opponent of slavery, who rejected her Congregational heritage at first for Unitarianism, but finally for Anglo-Catholicism. . . .
>
> Another relative who strained family loyalties was the black sheep, Uncle Horace Dutton. This young brother of the famous publisher [E. P. Dutton] became a Christian social reformer devoted to the service of the poor. He worked in city missions, brought criminals and vagrants home to supper, and followed Christ's injunction to the rich young ruler by giving away every cent that he possessed. Eliza Scudder and Horace Dutton may have upset their more cautious and conventional relatives, but they were accepted because they were good people and, for all their eccentricities, they were members of the family. They must have been warm and genial souls because they captured the affection of shy, young Vida; she cherished them almost as much as the memory of her missionary father who had gone halfway around the world to save his fellow man by preaching the gospel. The family's characteristic independence and humanitarian idealism were passed on to Vida, and when she reached maturity she never hesitated to defy convention in the service of humanity.[4]

This combination of the "good enough" parenting with what the *Common Fire* authors call "a home with open doors," was seen in the lives of the people they studied. Their childhood homes

> ranged widely from cramped to spacious, barren to opulent. But common to most was a core of love surrounded by a kind of porous boundary allowing interchange with the wider world, planting seeds for participation in an enlarged sphere.[5]

Such homes provided hospitality to people and ideas from a wide variety of places and points of view, and tended to be places of conversation about what was going on in society. These homes were part of neighborhoods, in many senses of that term. Some benefited from the ethnic or cultural diversity at their doorsteps. The homes, like Scudder's, in a more homogenous setting, consciously embraced the larger city and even the world. This was literally true in Scudder's case, where she and her mother traveled for years, largely in pursuit of the arts and high culture.

Upon returning to Boston, Vida Scudder entered the Latin School for her high school education, and the Trinity Church of Phillips Brooks for religious formation. The Broad Church theology of Brooks, America's leading exponent of Frederic Denison Maurice, was Mrs. Scudder's choice, and at first Vida resisted leaving the traditions of Congregationalism, but then she embraced and was deeply influenced by what she saw and heard at Trinity. Vida's intellectual life was awakened at newly-established Smith College, where she was graduated in 1881. She and her mother spent the next year in Europe, where Vida studied at Oxford. It was during this sojourn that she laid the foundations of the life as a devout Anglo-Catholic and committed socialist. Hearing John Ruskin lecture was the turning point:

> The point of my desire was an intolerable stabbing pain, as Ruskin and the rich delights of [Oxford], forced me to realize for the first time the plethora of privilege in which my lot had been cast. That pain has continued at intervals to stab my spirit broad awake ever since.[6]

When she returned to the U.S., several forces converged on Vida in increasingly painful ways. She was one of the first generation of college-educated women, bright, full of expectation, but with no social outlet for those skills or interests. She had traveled widely throughout Europe, had lived in England, and brought a perspective to American society different than that of her peers whose experience was limited to this culture. She had made a theological journey from Congregationalism, a mild and liberal Calvinism, to Anglicanism, even to High Church Anglicanism, with its appreciation for the ancient and medieval past and for order and hierarchy. And she had this "intolerable, stabbing pain" of realization about the injustices of society and a longing for solidarity with the workers and the poor of that society.[7]

> She felt that her life had no purpose and she became bored and disillusioned once again. Marriage was the conventional solution to her problem, but she was not conventional. What could an unmarried, financially secure woman with a "nebulous sense of social radicalism" do? Of course there was always the family and the Church, Boston's women's clubs claimed some time, but none of these resources satisfied her longing for reality. A line from a dialogue she wrote in collaboration with her friend Sophia Kirk a few years later sums up her disappointment with her life. "We lead sham lives in our youth, and the sham knowledge deadens for us the reality."[8]

Vida Scudder's struggles during her young adult years are the most interesting to me—as a college chaplain—for it is during these years that we find the closest parallels with young adult experiences today. Common to young adults at any time and of any social class is learning to find one's place in the world. Questions of love and work, of authority and trust, loom large. I see this among the students I work with at Northwestern University, who plunge into the "big questions" of life with fervor. They are reevaluating old commitments and figuring out their own place in the world. At lunch one day a student fresh from her first week in a philosophy class announced that Existentialism was *her* philosophy; it was the best fit with how she looked at the world. Across the table another young woman remarked that she was a Stoic. Learning about Stoicism in high school had convinced her of that, and then the two of them discussed the points of each with the fervor of a convert. Another student told me that she was taking a break from the Episcopal Church right now. She had read some feminist theology over the summer and could not find a way to reconcile the tradition with her experience. She was interested in Buddhism now.

The undercurrent of these lunch table (and very late night) conversations about philosophy is a passion and an energy that shows me that young adults are engaged in more than word games. Just as their bodies are energized and sexually charged, their minds are working overtime, evaluating, pondering, developing the faculties of critical thinking. Young adults are figuring out who they are, who to trust, and what role they will play in the world. Theology, perhaps unformed or immature but certainly recognizable as "talk about God," is popular among this age group. As the authors of *Common Fire* state:

> By "work" we do not mean simply a job or career but rather a sense of one's calling—born from some reflection on life's purpose. Whether or

> not one is college bound, the task of young adulthood is to find and be found by a viable life "dream"—and to go to work on it.[9]

One of the most important ministries of the church is to provide safe, trustworthy "mentoring environments"[10] where young adults can go about this work. To provide these places seems to me essential if we are to nurture these young people into mature faith and commitments, and if we are to encourage them to be theological thinkers.

One of the most popular movements on campus these days is volunteer service, projects like Habitat for Humanity or the Crop Walk or various charitable fundraisers. More significant lately, though, is the rise in interest in service learning, during which serious reflection is built into the process of doing good. The most sought after opportunity for volunteer service at Northwestern is Alternative Spring Break, a completely student-led program. The purpose for the week of service is as much changing the heart and mind of the participant as it is building the house or working in the soup kitchen or attending to the needs of people with AIDS. I have more than a hunch that this program is sought after by students because it gives them the opportunity to connect their feelings and their thoughts. They do something good, yes, but in the context of planning and organizing a trip with their peers to another city or state, of meeting and learning to care for people different from themselves, and of engaging in personal and group reflection on what they are doing and learning.

Vida Scudder would have found common cause with young adults of today. Like the students who developed the Alternative Spring Break program because they had a fire to do something but no arena in which to do it, Scudder was part of a mentoring community, a group of friends and colleagues who shared the dream and supported each other in commitment to the challenges and hopes they faced.

In longing for something useful to do, she turned back to scholarship and wrote a paper on modern poetry, which led to an M.A. from Smith College, and eventually to a position teaching modern literature at Wellesley College, beginning in 1887. By then her thoughts about the possibilities for college women struck a more optimistic note:

> Into this world . . . [of] life with bewildering and contradictory theories, yet bent, as no other age has ever been, in the analysis of social evil and the right of social wrong—into this world we are born—we, the first generation of college women. In a sense, we may represent a new

> factor in the social order. . . . Surely, I may at least say, that we make ourselves significant if we will.[11]

Scudder brought enthusiasm into the teaching of young women, and became a prolific scholar and writer in many fields of literature, as well as social thought. Her important interests included the Italian saints, especially Francis, Clare, and Catherine of Siena. For many years she taught the popular course at Wellesley, "Social Ideals in English Letters," which became her best known book.

But as a young woman, her most significant work was done in her volunteer time. In Boston, she knew and attended the churches of pioneering Anglo-Catholic social activists—W. D. P. Bliss's Church of the Carpenter and Charles Henry Brent's St. Stephen's Church. Both were in poor neighborhoods, both committed to socialism. With other college women friends, she began to think about beginning a settlement house, based on Toynbee Hall in London but, in this case, staffed by women. They formed the College Settlements Association and opened the Rivington Street Settlement in New York in 1889, two weeks before Jane Addams and Ellen Gates Starr opened Hull House in Chicago. Early in the next decade, settlement houses opened in Philadelphia and in Boston (Denison House, where Scudder came to spend most of her non-teaching hours).

In her autobiography, *On Journey*, in a chapter entitled "The Terrible Choice," Scudder described her difficult embrace of three worlds: the academic, the social activist, and her family:

> By this time—I speak now of the early 20th century—St. Francis had touched the springs of my life. The call of Lady Poverty rang clear, I longed to make an ultimate surrender. The comfort and security of my life, the beauty of the Wellesley campus, the charm of my pleasant home, filled me intermittently with loathing. I suppose the blood of my missionary father was running hot in my veins.
>
> When in New York, usually on settlement business, I would often stay in the home of my uncle, E. P. Dutton, the publisher, a stately house where the foot sank deep into rugs, where good pictures graced the walls, where all was ordered softly to suit the two dear elderly people. . . . From there I would go down to the push carts, the crowds, the grim excitement of Rivington Street. I found the contrast excruciating.[12]

Scudder often mentioned the deep pain of her awareness of the difference between her circumstances and those of the people she met through her socialist awakening. Something along that order is common to the experience of students on Alternative Spring Break trips. The authors of *Common Fire* named this "constructive engagement with otherness" and found it to be the most important factor which contributed to the lifelong commitments of the people they studied.

> At some point in their formative years virtually everyone in our sample had come to know someone who was significantly different from themselves. This was not simply an encounter but rather a *constructive engagement* by means of which they could empathetically recognize a shared humanity with the other that undercut the old tribal boundaries and created a new "we" from a former "they."[13]

For Scudder, this experience of her young adult years provided the fodder for a long life of reflection and theological thinking. Her mature theological synthesis blended Christian faith and socialism, specifically an Anglo-Catholic faith inspired by the Italian saints Catherine of Siena and Francis of Assisi and a thoroughgoing, unapologetic Marxism. In all her long life and her many published works, social allegiances, and church affiliations, she wavered from neither.[14]

The authors of *Common Fire* are concerned with the large, humanistic goal of nurturing environments that support the development of persons committed to the "new commons," as they call it. The factors which contribute to the moral development of young adults seem to me, however, to be the essential ones the church must nurture if we are to develop the next generation of theological thinkers. Theology which carries truth about the human encounter with God should resonate not only in and for the generation in which it is written but for future generations as well, and for such theology to resonate it must be connected to authentic and reflected-upon human experience.

During the young adult years, we are at our most receptive to deep ideas and deep feelings, and built into our psychological development—paralleling our faith development—is the desire to connect the two. The authors of *Common Fire* are concerned about nurturing young adults into people committed to the common good, able to make the kinds of decisions and actions to keep us going into the twenty-first century.

Throughout our lives, our capacity to reflect theologically on our experience continues. Ideally, that capacity should deepen and broaden as we mature. Many Christian educators now term their concerns as "Christian formation," emphasizing that the process of our formation in the faith, our ability to use theology or words about God, to understand our life experiences, continues throughout a lifetime. To reflect on our experiences in our young adults years provides one wellspring of theology. We can use those reflections as a foundation, as did Vida Dutton Scudder, for a lifelong encounter between our actions in the world and our thoughts about God.

Notes

1. James Russell Lowell, "Once to ev'ry man and nation," Hymn 519, *The Hymnal 1940* (New York: The Church Pension Fund, 1940), part of his longer poem, "The Present Crisis," 1845.

2. Laurent A. Parks Daloz, et al., *Common Fire: Lives of Commitment in a Complex World* (Boston: Beacon Press, 1997).

3. Ibid., 15–16.

4. Bernard Kent Markwell, *The Anglican Left: Radical Social Reformers in the Church of England and the Protestant Episcopal Church, 1846–1954* (Brooklyn: Carlson Publishing, Inc., 1991), 140–141.

5. Daloz et al., *Common Fire*, 28.

6. Vida Dutton Scudder, *On Journey* (New York: E. P. Dutton and Co., 1937), 84.

7. Markwell, *The Anglican Left*. I am grateful to Markwell for his observations in his chapters on Vida Scudder, the only significant historical treatment of her life.

8. Ibid., 146.

9. Daloz et al., *Common Fire*, 44.

10. The concept of the "mentoring community" comes from the work of Sharon Daloz Parks and Laurent A. Parks Daloz in particular.

11. Quoted by Arthur Mann in *Yankee Reformers in the Urban Age* (Cambridge: Harvard University Press, 1954), 201.

12. Scudder, *On Journey*, 176.

13. Daloz et al., "Lives of Commitment: Higher Education in the Life of the New Commons," *Change* (May/June 1996): 15.

14. Secular as well as church historians note Scudder's contributions to society as well as to theology. See William O'Neill, *Everyone Was Brave: A History of Feminism in America* (New York: Quadrangle Books, 1971), 137, in which Vida Scudder is profiled in the chapter, "Ten Who Led the Woman Movement." O'Neill, writes, "For the largest part of her long life she was both a socialist and an energetic Episcopalian. Although she was a pioneer settlement resident and a supporter of many good causes, it was as a writer that she made her chief contribution to the movement for social justice."

Theology in Song: The Hymnody of the Episcopal Church

Raymond F. Glover

"The Hymnal is the layperson's book of theology," is a statement often made about the songbook of the people of God.

The psalms, the primary source of song for the earliest Christians, certainly convey a profound understanding of the nature of God as creator, defender, and judge, and of God's saving actions in history. The hymnody of the New Testament (the gospel songs of Mary, *Magnificat*; of Zechariah, *Benedictus Dominus Deus*; and of Simeon, *Nunc dimittis*; with the song derived from the Epistles to the Corinthians and the Romans, *Pascha nostrum*; and from the Book of Revelation, *Dignus es*, and *Magna et mirabilia*) expands these understandings and enriches them with strong Christological images.

Although the early church fathers, including Augustine, had "mixed feelings" about the use of music in worship, Ambrose testified to the power and place of hymnody through the hymn texts he wrote for his persecuted flock in Milan. Those texts in turn established the pattern and structure of the monastic office hymns with their rich biblical and liturgical references, poetic metaphors for theological tenets, and clear statements of faith. In those first centuries, the great hymns, *Gloria in excelsis* and *Te Deum laudamus*, appeared, the latter with its legendary connections with the baptism of Augustine by Ambrose.

It is not the purpose of this essay to trace the historic development of Christian hymnody, but, in a presentation on the theology of Christian song, mention must be made of the vernacular hymns of Martin Luther, the great reformer and "Father of Congregational Song," as profound statements of theological truth; and of the texts of Isaac Watts in his concern that the exclusive use in England of metrical settings of the psalms limited the singer to an Old Testament understanding of God. It was Watts who first, as he said, "made David sing like a Christian." He thus expanded the biblical and theological vocabulary and understanding of seventeenth-century English Protestants. The texts of Charles Wesley—the other truly great English hymn writer—are rich with theological, biblical, and liturgical references, as well as personal statements of his own experiences of God's actions in his life, which, when we sing them today, become our expression and understanding of God's actions in our own lives.

The Church's Process for Determining Theological Appropriateness

The theological soundness of congregational song has been a high priority in the deliberations of the Episcopal Church, especially when hymnal revision is authorized. Therefore, the hymnody of Episcopalians is authorized for use only after study, serious deliberation, and approval of both houses of General Convention.

The precedent and procedures for the approval of hymn texts by General Convention was established with the approval of the first hymnal of the Episcopal Church in 1789. Over the decades a particularly comprehensive process has developed. The Joint Commission that prepared *The Hymnal 1940*, for example, provided the model for evaluation of texts in the most recent revision, *The Hymnal 1982.*

Early in its work, the Standing Commission on Church Music (SCCM), empowered by General Convention to prepare for hymnal revision, appointed a theological committee under the leadership of the Rev. Dr. Charles Price of Virginia Theological Seminary. The committee also included members of the theological committee of the Standing Liturgical Commission, which recently had prepared the revision of the Book of Common Prayer. They evaluated all the texts in *The Hymnal 1940* and its supplements for possible inclusion in the revised hymnal and made suggestions for textual revision. Their thoroughness assured the church that the theology of its song not only embraced the historic teachings of the church, but also reflected the theological principles of the liturgies of the 1979 Book of Common Prayer.

In 1979 the General Convention gave its approval for the revision of *The Hymnal* and empowered the SCCM to prepare a book of proposed texts for the 1982 Convention. Shortly after the 1979 convention, the SCCM restructured itself into three distinct subcommittees, one of which was a text committee under the joint leadership of Price and the Rev. Dr. Marion J. Hatchett, Professor of Liturgics and Music at the School of Theology, University of the South, Sewanee, Tennessee.

In the summer of 1980 the SCCM, under the direct mandate of General Convention to present to the 1982 Convention a collection of texts for a revised hymnal, formally organized the structure for their work in "A Philosophy for Hymnal Revision." In it were articulated standards for the evaluation of hymn texts, clearly implicit in the preliminary work of the theological committee. Its third article states, "Hymn texts serve as a practical book of theology for the people of God and should present the Church's teaching authentically and fully." The body of the article further states, "Only texts which have been judged theologically sound are being recommended for inclusion."

As a result, the texts of *The Hymnal 1982* present and illuminate in poetic form theological tenets of the church. Among them are statements on the nature of God, of the Holy Trinity, of Christ—his incarnation, the nature and meaning of his death, his resurrection and ascension—of the Holy Spirit; of baptism and eucharist; of the doctrine of the church and the nature of its mission; and of Holy Scripture.

To expand the theological review of texts proposed for a revised hymnal, reader consultants selected by the bishops of every diocese in the church reviewed and evaluated everything being considered for inclusion. As a result, many texts were emended. In early 1982 the SCCM's completed report to General Convention contained 595 texts for possible inclusion in a revised hymnal.

Prior to Convention every bishop and deputy to the Convention received copies of the report for study. In late August, the hymnal revision committees of both houses of the convention, meeting in joint session in New Orleans, held open hearings on the report. As a result, alterations were made in the proposed texts, many of them reflecting the need for expanded use of inclusive language. Ten proposed texts were deleted, and five deleted from *The Hymnal 1940* were restored. Among the restored texts was the children's hymn, "I sing a song of the saints of God,"[1] omitted because of the very poor quality of its poetry and the questionable theology of the statement in the final stanza of the text, "for the saints of God are just folk like me, / and I mean to be one too."

Changes in the report included additional alterations in texts, the restoration of a few texts deleted from *The Hymnal 1940*, and the deletion of one proposed text. These changes were approved by action of the House of Deputies. The report, thus emended, was sent to the House of Bishops where it was approved, thereby establishing the authorized texts of the hymnal of the Episcopal Church.

In reality, the lack of general use throughout the church was the reason most often cited for the deletion of texts from *The Hymnal 1940*. However, two very popular texts were deleted on theological grounds: the James Russell Lowell text, "Once to every man and nation," and the Clifford Bax text, "Turn back, O man." Although the use of the word "man" in the first line of each text gives them an exclusively masculine focus, that was not the prime reason for their being dropped. In the very first line of the Lowell text, the singer is confronted with the statement that only "Once to every man and nation / Comes the moment to decide." Lowell was writing about the ethical and moral questions facing the United States in 1845 with protests over the aggression of the war with Mexico and the possible annexation of land that would permit the expanded use of slavery. Although a statement of historical fact, the line does not express theological truth. It is, therefore, unacceptable. Further, Lowell's use of a metaphor which seems to equate "some great cause" ("the strife of truth with falsehood, / For the good or evil side") with "God's new Messiah" is bad theology. There is only one Messiah, Jesus Christ, our Lord!

The next theological problem in this text arises in stanza three with Lowell's poetic use of "toiling up new Calvaries ever" as a metaphor for the event described at the beginning of the stanza, "By the light of burning martyrs / Jesus' bleeding feet I track."[2] Again this may be good poetic imagery, but it is not good theology. There was only one Calvary, the hill upon which Jesus, the Christ, was crucified!

The problem in the Bax text is its rampant humanism, the philosophical concept that humankind will save itself by its own actions, by "pulling itself up by its own bootstraps." This is unfortunate, for there is otherwise much truth in the text. For example, although there is ambiguity about the nature and meaning of "thine inner God," there is truth in the fact that humankind still does recognize the need to "Turn back, . . . foreswear thy foolish ways." Then there are the unfortunate realities in stanza two:

Age after age their tragic empires rise,
Built while they dream, and in that dreaming weep:
Would man but wake from out his haunted sleep,
Earth might be fair, and all men glad and wise. [3]

Omitted is the centrality of faith in our work for change in the world. The post-communion prayer in the Rite One eucharist expresses this clearly:

> And we humbly beseech thee, O heavenly Father, *so to assist us with thy grace*, that we may continue in that holy fellowship, *and do all such good works* as thou hast prepared for us to walk in. . . ."[4]

The Theological Riches of Texts in The Hymnal 1982 *and Its Supplements*

The breadth and quality of new texts in *The Hymnal 1982* have greatly expanded Episcopalians' understanding of the important theological tenets of the church.

A text by the seventeenth-century divine, Samuel Crossman, opens with a beautiful, poetic statement of the nature of God's love inherent in the full dimensions of God's gift of God's Incarnate Son, Jesus Christ, who took on "frail flesh and died."[5]

My song is love unknown, my Savior's love to me,
Love to the loveless shown that they might lovely be.
O who am I that for my sake
my Lord should take frail flesh and die?

Succeeding stanzas retell in stunning verse the course of our Lord's life. In the final one we respond to his act of selfless love:

Here might I stay and sing, no story so divine:
never was love, dear King, never was grief like thine.
This is my friend, in whose sweet praise,
I all my days could gladly spend.

The true and paradoxical nature of love, as evidenced in the life of our Lord, is no more clearly nor beautifully expressed than in the text "Morning glory, starlit sky,"[6] by the contemporary English theologian, W. H. Vanstone. Its inner stanzas fully define the nature of God's love for us:

Open are the gifts of God, . . . hidden is love's agony

. . . .

Drained is love in making full, bound in setting others free,
poor in making many rich, weak in giving power to be.

In the penultimate stanza, this paradox is revealed in the life-giving act of Christ upon the cross:

Therefore he who shows us God
helpless hangs upon the tree;
and the nails and crown of thorns
tell of what God's love must be.

The hymn's final stanza brings to a climax the paradox of the cross:

Here is God: no monarch he,
throned in easy state to reign;
here is God, whose arms of love
aching, spent, the world sustain.

What more wonderful ways do we have to "mark, learn, and inwardly digest" these spiritual truths than when we sing and pray them?

Another text in which theological realities of the faith are stunningly presented is the Christmas poem, "A stable lamp is lighted,"[7] by Richard Wilbur, one of the finest American poets of the last quarter of the twentieth century. In his text we are confronted with the mystery of the incarnation, the fact that God would offer us, his sinful creatures, the gift of his only begotten and sinless son, who would come among us, suffer human pain, be crucified, die, and be raised on the third day that we might be saved from sin and death.

The poetic centerpiece of the poem is the word "stone" which, in the hands of this fine poet, conveys rich and varied images and meanings. Stones take on life and become witnesses of crucial moments in the life of our Lord. In stanza one, Wilbur refers to the stone foundation of the stable in which Christ was born. The stone used in the roadway upon which Christ rode on the first Sunday of the Passion is the focus of stanza two. In stanza three, "stone" is used forcefully to describe the hearts of humankind who brought Christ to his cruel and painful death. Stanza four sums up these aspects and the meaning of Christ's incarnation and life among us. It opens with paradox: "But now, as at the ending, / The low is lifted high" and moves on with the freedom of poetic imagery in which "The stars shall bend their voices, / And every stone shall cry." In its final line we have our response, a song of praise to God for God's ultimate gift of love to us in Jesus Christ,

And every stone shall cry,
In praises of the Child
By whose descent among us
The worlds are reconciled.

Brian Wren, in a text[8] written quite early in his career as a hymn writer, expresses the transforming nature and meaning of eucharist. In stanza one, we come to the Lord's table as individuals:

I come with joy to meet my Lord,
forgiven, loved, and free,
in awe and wonder to recall
his life laid down for me.

In the following stanza, Wren conveys the reality that in eucharist we are part of a worldwide body of people who come and in the experience find "the new community of love / in Christ's communion bread." The transforming nature of Christ's presence in the eucharist is described in stanza three where, "As Christ breaks bread and bids us share, . . . That love that made us makes us one, / and strangers now are friends." Stanzas four and five complete the cycle of transformation, "And thus with joy we meet our Lord" and,

Together met, together bound,
we'll go our different ways,
and as his people in the world
we'll love and speak his praise.

Since the publication of *The Hymnal 1982*, the resources for the church's congregational song have been greatly enriched and expanded with the publication of hymnal supplements. Through use of these collections, we benefit from more recent works that enrich and expand our understanding of theological truths. The most recent supplement, *Wonder, Love, and Praise* is the source of the following theologically rich texts.

In 1993, for the consecration of the Rev. Mary Adelia McLeod as Bishop of Vermont, Charles Price wrote, "God beyond all human praises,"[9] an eight-stanza text full of fresh images and descriptive phrases that expand our understanding of the nature of God. In the first three stanzas we discover God as: "God, beyond all human praises;" "God of harmony and beauty, God of floods, by tempest blown, / God of Nature's jealous order;" "God of history's plan unfolding . . . ; God of freedom, God of mystery;" and in the penultimate stanza: "God of all our new beginnings." How wonderful it is when creative minds and spirits like Price's enrich our congregational song and challenge our stereotypes about the nature of God!

John Thornburg, Pastor of Northaven United Methodist Church, Dallas, in his 1994 text, "God the sculptor of the mountains,"[10] continues to expand our vision of the nature of God. In it he has penned such biblically rooted images as: "sculptor of mountains, . . . miller of the sand, . . . potter of the land, . . . womb of all creation." In stanza two the images are rooted in the Old Testament story of the Exodus: "nuisance to the Pharaoh, . . . cleaver of the sea, . . . pillar of the darkness, . . . beacon of the free, . . . gate of all deliv'rance." Thornburg, in stanza three, focuses the images on Christ, the second person of the Trinity; "unexpected infant, . . . calm, determined youth, . . . table turning prophet, . . . resurrected Truth." And in the final stanza he returns to images of God as creator: "dresser of the vineyard, . . . planter of the wheat, . . . reaper of the harvest, . . . source of all we eat, . . . host at every table."

A deeply moving sense of the Christian meaning of death is the theological thrust of the text "Give thanks for life"[11] by the New Zealand hymn writer Shirley Erena Murray. In his descriptive notes on this text in the *Leader's Guide, Wonder, Love, and Praise*,[12] the Rev. Dr. John L. Hooker calls our particular attention to the text's relationship with the Easter and resurrection themes of the Prayer Book liturgy for the dead. In each stanza we are called to give thanks. First, "thanks for life the measure of our days"; then, "thanks for those who have made their life a light / caught from the Christ flame bursting through the night" and "thanks for the love by which our life is fed, / a love not changed by time or death or dread" are the foci of stanzas two and three. The familiar image of wheat, as found in John's gospel, is recalled in stanza four. Here it is likened to hope which, like seed planted in the ground, "does its life retain, / in resurrection to grow green again."

In the few texts presented here, we have but a small picture of the theological truths available to us in our congregational song. They are truths found in the works of poets past and present that offer us opportunity to expand our understanding of God; of the meaning of God's love for us in the gift of his Son, our Lord; of the meaning of Christ's life, death and resurrection; of the meaning of eucharist; of the Christian meaning of death; and countless other important theological tenets. Through their use, we encounter the living Lord, and our lives can be changed. Here is a testament of God's presence in the church throughout the ages and a source of hope for its renewed and ongoing life!

Notes

1. *The Hymnal 1982* (New York: The Church Pension Fund, 1985), Hymn 293.

2. *The Hymnal 1940* (New York: The Church Pension Fund, 1940), Hymn 519.

3. Ibid., Hymn 536.

4. The Book of Common Prayer (New York: The Church Hymnal Corporation, 1979), 339 (emphasis added).

5. *The Hymnal 1982*, Hymn 458.

6. Ibid., Hymn 585.

7. Ibid., Hymn 104.

8. Ibid., Hymn 304.

9. *Wonder, Love, and Praise: A Supplement to The Hymnal 1982* (New York: The Church Pension Fund, 1997), Hymn 745.

10. Ibid., Hymns 746, 747.

11. Ibid., Hymn 775.

12. John L. Hooker, *Leader's Guide, Wonder, Love, and Praise: A Supplement to The Hymnal 1982* (New York: The Church Pension Fund, 1997).

That God May Be All in All: A View from the Margins

Travis Du Priest

The Thin Places

Future Christianity is generating itself from those who have fled to the margins.—*Sr. Wendy Beckett*

On my desk are: some notes from a young M.F.A. graduate on post-modernism and the need to deconstruct Christianity for future believers; a letter from a seventy-year-old New Englander who wants to live as a religious solitary; an E-mail from a fifty-year-old widow seeking to form a religious community; a fax from a friend in the South recommending that believers stop praying in order to draw nearer to God; and finally, a letter from a once-frequent visitor to the Shrine of Blessed James DeKoven recounting certain spiritual "conversations" that occurred there.

Each of these correspondents is searching, as I suspect we all are—Episcopalians and those unable to connect with organized religion alike—to unravel "the surplus of meaning"[1] we experience in the cosmos. The usual explanations and answers don't seem to help us in this search. What we need and look for are metaphors. Metaphor, as psychologist Marion Woodman accurately puts it, is the language of the soul, bridging the physical world and the spiritual world.[2] Metaphor is also the language of healing as it "speaks" and acts upon the whole person—body, mind, and spirit—providing the key that unlocks simultaneously conscious understanding as well as the "surplus" and mystery of the universe.

The Episcopal Church has a rich heritage of liturgical and meditative arts and a special attachment to symbolic and artistic expression of God's charity and compassion, and yet how well does the church and those who speak and write theologically within the church's fold really help people to live in places of paradox and to find the necessary metaphors of meaning? Do we not first need to reflect on the nature and structure of our pedagogy? To develop a pedagogy of experience and practice?

I think sometimes we get things a bit backwards in our instruction, in our church schools and confirmation classes: we teach the meaning of the creeds and doctrines first, instead of allowing time and space to listen carefully to questions; instead of hearing the deep yearnings connected to the hidden mysteries of the universe; instead of validating people's spiritual experiences. I wonder if we should not do more practicing and modeling before our teaching and preaching? First should come the practice of prayer (which is quite natural to youngsters), the stories, the reflective and meditative skills, the questions, and the experiences of relationships whereby God is being formed in what novelist Annie Dillard calls "the gaps and crannies" of our lives. Later can come the meaning behind the doctrines.

By teaching the reflective arts as early on as possible, by practicing prayer and silent reflection and meditation with our communities of faith, we can in time speak carefully of the meaning of the creeds and the church's doctrines, thereby undergirding our public, liturgical arts. As British philosopher and theologian Don Cupitt reminds us in his books,[3] Scripture itself presents a metaphor of what can happen; scriptural language "conjures up" the possible, creates a freedom and liberty at odds with those who would box God into rules or package and control prayer with routine. We can then begin to help our people understand and experience Scripture and the Prayer Book first as love language rather than as a book of advice or a book of set worship patterns and creeds.

A deacon-philosopher of the church puts the matter this way: "It all begins with spirituality; that is how and where we can come to know God. . . . Theology studies God, but God is available for study because of the spiritual depth to which we must find our way."[4]

My thesis is quite simple: the church has distanced herself, in liturgy, symbol, and teaching from the spiritual experiences of her people, thereby widening the gap between her theology and the spirituality, or lived theology, of her people. For there to be a meaningful future to theology in the Episcopal Church, her people and those who rise up as her theologians must recover the primacy of spirituality.

This fissure between received theology and spiritual experience is very real in the Episcopal Church. A few years ago, when Professor John Booty was publishing his landmark series of essays in *The Episcopalian* entitled "What Makes Us Episcopalians?" he included a piece on experience.[5] I was a Fellow at the College of Preachers in Washington, D.C., at the time, working on a project called "Preaching the Hidden Life," and I remember one lunch on campus at which all of the deans of the Episcopal seminaries were present. One seminary dean went on and on at great length about the inanity of introducing "experience," of all things, into the so-called classical three-legged stool of Anglicanism: Scripture, reason, and tradition. Nothing was more anathema to this theologian than Booty's explanation of the historic role spiritual experience has played in the theological history of the Episcopal Church.

Where exactly do I sit? From what perspective do I see the church and her theology and her people's religious experiences? I sit in one of the church's "thin places." I use the phrase, borrowed from the Celtic, in two senses: first, to describe a place where earth and heaven intermingle naturally and closely—a holy shrine; second, to describe a place where people feel comfortable slipping in and out of organized religion—a threshold.

In my ministries within the Episcopal Church (as Director of The DeKoven Foundation for Church Work in Racine, Wisconsin—a venerable institution of religious education, recreation, and spiritual reflection—and also as Chaplain at Mary's Margin, a small house of prayer west of Milwaukee, operated by the Sisters of St. Mary) I live in a "thin place" in both senses. At the heart of the DeKoven Foundation is a shrine: The DeKoven Center, a place of hallowed prayers for 150 years and the resting place of Blessed James DeKoven. Both DeKoven and Mary's Margin attract a wide spectrum of people from all walks of life and experience, many of them non-Episcopalians. Consequently, I frequently encounter people on the threshold: people who are just now finding faith and edging toward the church, and others, disillusioned for whatever reason, who are easing slowly out of the church. I have found, though, that both sets of people have an equally keen awareness of the spiritual dimensions of life, the world, of their own inner selves and God.

I have listened to many life narratives such as this one, elicited from a young journalist of whom I asked the question, "So, what is your background?" This is his (paraphrased) answer:

> I grew up Presbyterian, did the Sunday school thing, didn't really think much about church, but remembered the Bible stories—they really stuck, went deep inside me. I became increasingly interested in "the

mystery of creation," and when I was a junior in high school I was attracted to an esoteric community in San Francisco which was essentially Christian but which drew from all sorts of religious perspectives and vocabularies. As I listened, reflected, and waited, I slowly realized that Jesus was in all this mystery and indeed was at the center of it; he was the vocabulary of Western religious experience. Later I discovered C. S. Lewis's *Surprised By Joy*, and then I began to discover meaning behind the doctrines of the church. I now describe myself as an esoteric Episcopalian.

Many I listen to and talk with speak of themselves as being "on the margins" of the church and of our culture: one of them wonders if her ordination discernment committee will accept the poems she wants to write instead of the expected essay; another has recently started attending The Mindfulness Center of Milwaukee and has shared with me the gift of her "Gatha Book"; another recounts her interesting, experimental attempts to quantify the physical effects of prayer; yet another recounts in great detail her visions of her stillborn child and of the Virgin Mary who appears holding the stillborn child.

I have come to think of myself as something of a "reservist": on call for special maneuvers; on call to be with people from a perspective "outside" of the parish; to give a view from the margin; to be with them in the liminal place of life. My real work—as a bi-vocational and, sometimes, tri-vocational priest—has always taken place on what a Lutheran pastor friend calls "the outposts of the church": classrooms, industrial plants, hospitals, retreat centers, military sites, camps, religious communities, and the "thin places" of spiritual direction. All of the places where I find myself are places of retreat, meditation, liturgical experimentation, spiritual direction, learning—but, above all, places of nonjudgmental healing for the soul; places where people's experiences of God and the world are honored; places where biblical imagery and story and theology are the handmaidens of spirituality; places where we are prepared to be attentive, so that, when a prayer rises up, we notice.

Turning Inward

The first disciples . . . model in stark reality the ways we see to avoid being drawn by God out to the margins of our life and beyond.
—*M. Robert Mulholland, Jr.*

As I go about my ministries, listening to people, many if not most of whom live in the margin, I hear a yearning for deep inner work; a desire to be "awake," as Anthony de Mello[6] expresses it; a desire to be "mindful" of the smallest details of the daily round, as Thich Nhat Hahn[7] teaches; a desire to peel away divisions between people—divisions often fostered, according to Toni Packer,[8] by strict religious adherence. I hear a longing to spend more time in "thin places" such as Mary's Margin or DeKoven Center, or a monastery, or an art museum on a quiet Monday morning; to be in places of acceptance and receptiveness.

As I listen, as I speak, I learn that openness and acceptance bring their own clarity of awareness, that is, bring their own transforming grace: precise, clean, unencumbered with "echoes arising from [an] inherited past."[9] In these sacred places and, increasingly, in more and more "places apart," the mystery of the cosmos and of human interconnectedness is allowed to be simply what it is—not "muzzled" by a rush to doctrine, by a claim of ecclesiastical authority, by the press of orthodoxy, by the cry of *sola scriptura*, or the latest rage of contemporary American Protestantism, waving "the Jesus flag."[10]

More and more people are becoming aware that the kingdom is something we are in; that prayer is something we are a part of; that Christianity is first and foremost Oriental in nature and, therefore, mystical.[11] Archbishop Michael Ramsey never lost sight of this and insisted that theology cannot be separated from prayer. Likewise, the Orthodox Church consistently affirms that mysticism is at the heart of theology. Many young people I meet and talk with do not—at least, not at first—ask what I believe, but what my practice is.

I also hear a sincere wish for more direction in things spiritual, not just classes or adult forums, but genuine direction, modeling, and practicing in prayer and what I like to call the meditative arts. I do not sense a desire to separate life into secular and spiritual, but an increased desire to explore the inner life and connect more fully and more deeply with the created world. To enable its people to be fully alive, aware of their inner lives, and awake to the world: this is the work of our future church and of her theologians!

I hear as well a heartfelt longing to be able to talk openly and maturely about the sense of God's absence in our lives—aridity and feelings of abandonment. A friend with whom I have an active spiritual correspondence asked last spring why the church did not celebrate Ascensiontide more fully, rather than immediately focus on Pentecost and the coming of the Holy Spirit? Here is a wonderful opportunity, she thought, to celebrate, if briefly, the absence of Christ before the bestowing of the Holy Spirit. She understood, as do I, the liturgical and theological reasoning behind the lections; and yet, this spiritual concept so pressing in people's own lived experience is all but neglected by our public liturgies which so beautifully celebrate triumph and presence.

In all my years of active ordained ministry I have heard but one Good Friday meditation preached on the actual abandonment of God experienced in Our Lord's cry, "My God, my God, why hast thou forsaken me?" It was by a Lutheran pastor at a college chapel, and was possibly the most moving and poignant preaching I have heard.[12] The passion of the meditation lay in its stark acceptance of the theological necessity of abandonment. The overemphasis of presence, as Henri Nouwen points out in his essay on absence in *The Wounded Healer*,[13] only perpetuates a sentimental Christianity that has no understanding of celebrating simultaneously and paradoxically Christ's presence and absence "until He come again."

A correspondent from the West Coast asked me not long ago to write something that might help people find that inner place amidst their active lives. He spoke of the need people have "to form in their invisible lives—their inner lives—ways of devotion comparable to that of physically going on retreat."[14] Benedict Reid, the former Abbot of St. Gregory's Abbey in Michigan, calls such a place an "inner cell"; Bishop William Swing has called it a "chapel of the mind and soul." The building of an "inner cell" and assimilating a theology of absence is life work for us all. Here is the pressing need of our churches and church entities and a clear task for our theologians who see their work related to the lived spirituality of people.

My experience with retreats, both attending and conducting them, has taught me that to turn inward is not to escape the world but to become more complete and more alert to the relation of the individual and the community. I have learned that the inner retreat is ongoing and that, eventually, the individual becomes his own or her own innkeeper;

the purpose of the retreat house run by this innkeeper is hospitality—hospitality to ourselves and our experiences. A poem I was given on retreat puts it this way:

> This being human is a guest house.
> Every morning a new arrival.
> A joy, a depression, a meanness,
> some momentary awareness comes
> as an unexpected visitor.
> Welcome and entertain them all!
> Even if they're a crowd of sorrows,
> who violently sweep your house
> empty of its furniture,
> still, treat each guest honorably.
> He may be clearing you out
> for some new delight.
> The dark thought, the shame, the malice,
> meet them at the door laughing.
> and invite them in.
> Be grateful for whoever comes,
> because each has been sent
> as a guide from beyond.[15]

My ministry as "innkeeper" for DeKoven's active retreat ministry has helped me to understand this poem's inner inn and inner innkeeper more clearly. Just as I could not and should not choose the guests I welcome as retreatants at DeKoven, neither should I exclude any aspect of life from the inner inn. All emotions and experiences should be welcomed to the inner inn. Creating the inner inn (or "cell" or "chapel of the mind and soul") and establishing a life lived inwardly revivifies the life lived outwardly. One provocative writer expresses the inward/outward dynamic even more dramatically:

> The servant church is energized and shaped by the spirit and emboldened to break old boundaries. The effect of these two attributes provides a powerful balance—one is an empowering innerness and the second an explosive outerness. The first concentrates on the richness of our commitment, the depth of faith, and a focus on basics. The second moves beyond our boundaries to a kind of lavish inclusiveness in ways that shatter old patterns.[16]

It is that "empowering innerness" that the world outside of the church is discerning but which the Episcopal Church has sometimes neglected to its detriment. For decades we have kept Scripture historical rather than personal and interior; theology, an academic study rather than the handmaid of spirituality; and the practiced examples of prayer, verbal and ritualized rather than meditative.

St. Paul writes: "After that will come the end, when he [Christ] hands over the kingdom to God the Father. . . . And when everything is subjected to him, then the Son himself will be subject in his turn to the One who subjected all things to him, so that God may be all in all" (1 Corinthians 15:24, 28). It is precisely this handing over of the kingdom and God's becoming all in all that people are experiencing through "intuitive connection"[17] in our world today. The power of "innerness" and its accompanying "explosive outerness" already is a worldwide reality, but largely outside the institutional church. Its extent is enormous if subtle, spreading among groups of Christians who care not at all for traditional denominational boundaries, who worship and study and share bread and wine and silence together in small gatherings, spiritual communities, and conferences.

The spiritual reality that has become immensely clear to me during my priesthood on the margin is that the Spirit is unifying all those seeking Wisdom and Spirit. Creating not a bland uniformity; but rather a community of communities—people seeking to understand and learn from one another. As Fr. Benedict Reid, OSB, puts it in the title of his book, there is *A Spirit Loose In The World*.[18] God is, in fact, right before our eyes, becoming all in all.

The future is, of course, imbedded in the now, in the present moment; and what we are doing now is charting the course for that future. What we say and how we act in this given moment plants the seed that will flourish or die in what we call the future. Those who speak from the margins of their own inner lives and from the margins of the outer world are often likely to be unheard or overlooked:

> Those who follow God to the margins and beyond will always experience criticism if not ostracism at the hands of those who believe God is centered within their comfortable status quo.[19]

For both an individual or a group,

> Genuine experience with God is always a decentering experience. The God whom we thought we knew and understood . . . this idol we called "God" is suddenly eclipsed by the troubling, disturbing, uncontrolled

> God who decenters our life by coming to us from the margins and beyond to call us to an often unimagined center where we experience new dimensions of Life.[20]

God is no more in stillness than in motion; nor in silence any more than noise. Nor is God in balance but perhaps rather in tension—the bowing of a cello, back and forth, as each of us calls out to the opposite.

Spirit whirls through the world as Spirit will, uprooting here, planting here, seemingly making distinctions here, clarifying underlying unities there. A friend who leads a solitary life devoted to prayer under vows of obedience to her bishop just received a prayer cap from a devout Amish couple in Montana. Upon receipt of the cap, my friend wrote:

> I was in tears as I read [about the gift]. Now I am connected with a wonderfully generous Amish family in Montana. Will wonders never cease? The news was a holy moment—a moment when time seemed to stop and I became aware of the intense connection between all God's people—a connection that bridges even ultra-traditional customs and beliefs. It all comes together in God. Rejoice with me in God's gift of unity to us all.[21]

This Spirit is moving people everywhere to seek clarity, focus, and perspective in their lives. In other words, the Spirit moves us toward the "things of the Spirit," toward recognizing created life as a vessel of soul. This same Spirit unifies people as fellow seekers and manifests itself in a great variety of spiritualities: Celtic, Native American, African American, Feminist, New Age. None totally new, of course. Even New Age theology has its roots in the nineteenth-century American transcendentalism of Whitman, Emerson, and Thoreau. But all of these spiritualities are present for public view and inspection, inviting new adherents in ways and numbers unknown to former generations. And along with these now-traditional spiritualities, add what many are calling "Cosmic Spirituality," an attempt to identify all those throughout the world who sense an intuitive, unifying response to the transcendent numinosity of life.

As a result of these emerging and often merging spiritualities, there is a harmony of spirit with spirit, crossing nationalities and race and religions. Teachers such as Thich Nhat Hahn and the Dalai Lama from Eastern traditions speak lovingly and poignantly about Christ and his teachings. These intuitive connections[22] are spreading—sometimes hidden, sometimes manifest—throughout our cultural consciousness. And there are many encouraging trends, especially among parishes that have shifted from an instruction mode to a formation mode with the youth of the parish.

A young woman in discernment for seminary and ordination, currently youth director of a suburban parish near where I live, told me about her youth group and their conversations about the great religions of the world. She said that at first the young people had a tendency to giggle about other customs and traditions, but slowly they realized they were in a safe place, a place of formation rather than strict instruction. When they saw that it was safe *not* to make judgmental statements but, rather, to react genuinely to what they heard and saw in the spirituality of others, their comments gained in depth and perception.

One teen, now a Russian major and religious studies minor in college, had decided at age sixteen that she did not want to be confirmed. Her family, friends, and rector did not pressure her but gave her the space she needed to look at other religions and make up her own mind. She declared that she was a Buddhist but continued to attend her "Journey to Adulthood" class. The following year, she chose to be confirmed, exclaiming "It's all one; it's all one!" The oneness of the spiritual quest had "confirmed" itself in her life and liberated her to sing her song in Christian words and notes.

Several months ago, a young priest under thirty and a woman in a religious order—both friends of mine—led a youth retreat in Missouri. They decided to introduce the young people to a new reality—that of the contemplative life and meditation. No balloons, no pep rally. They decided to remain adults and not play at being children, creating an artificial environment of hype and excitement. The results were overwhelmingly affirmative: the teenagers were lifted into another realm of reality, a new place "to be" in their Christian lives, and my two friends were invited back for next year.

Likewise, my friend Georgi Boyle of St. Christopher's, River Hills, Wisconsin, E-mailed me that her work with junior high school children has taught her that "pat morality and biblical shoulds and shouldn'ts snap them shut like Venus flytraps. What they need and, I think, want is a chance to express themselves safely and a place to reflect on their own innerness." She further observed that this safety and openness is "what we've been deterring in the church. We have not allowed children to be the natural mystics that they are."

Are there Episcopal theologians who will articulate the necessary inner work for our church, so that, on the parish level, theology will become the handmaiden of spirituality in all its rich variety of forms and expressions, helping us all to be the "natural mystics" that we are?

Facing Outward

> This is one of the most exciting times to be on a spiritual quest. This next generation may be sent by God to rebuild religion.
>
> —*The Rev. Martin Smith, SSJE*

We need to recapture an understanding of the primacy of spirituality as it is shared by all human beings, all religious traditions and faiths throughout the world. Anthropologists of religion such as Mircea Eliade point out time and again that there is no culture unearthed so far in human history that has not borne witness to belief in an afterlife or a transcendent God. Contemporary writer Ellen Gilchrist expresses it beautifully:

> Two of the old Neanderthal people found in the caves at Shandar in Iraq were so severely crippled that they must have been completely dependent on the members of their group for a long time. Also, these people buried their dead in graves lined with flowers. Clearly, we have been human for a long time. Clearly, the first thing we did was probe the mystery and the last thing we will ever do is probe that same mystery.[24]

Surely Christianity is properly understood as a part of this great tradition of worldwide spirituality, and this recognition strengthens, rather than undercuts, our Christian faith.

Many mainline churches seem at times hopelessly locked in a cerebral understanding of Christianity. Statements are still issued affirming the correctness of one religion over against another. The Roman Catholic Church, for example, has in 1998 reaffirmed its position that Anglican orders are "null and void."[25] Intriguingly, I was invited several years ago to preach and receive communion during the Week of Christian Unity at a Roman Catholic mass in Toronto, Canada, at which the male celebrant stood and approached the altar for the prayer of consecration only. All other liturgical acts were performed by the community of Roman Catholic sisters who had invited me to preach and stand with them around the altar for communion.

Along with statements of condemnation and separation, attempts are made to foster reconciliation, but often have little effect on the churches themselves. Years of unitive efforts on the part of Archbishop Michael

Ramsey—between the English Methodists and Anglicans, for example—ended in vain, failing for a lack of votes, as did the 1997 attempt to deepen relations between American Lutherans and Episcopalians. This "now" is likely to be the mainline church's future.

Some religious writers warn strongly that the church and religion can even be a barrier between the believer and God. An anonymous Episcopal priest-poet writes in a poem he sent me: "how religion becomes at times a bed of gravel into which you crash, headlong, four times a day, your life a handful of rocks (as Spinoza had it) shaken in a cardboard box by Someone or No one whose face you'll never see." A friend E-mailed me during Lent that she was giving up prayer in order to firm up a growing and close relation with God. Thomas Merton and other contemplatives have written emphatically about giving up prayer and going directly to God.

At a recent retreat at DeKoven Center, Dean Alan Jones of Grace Cathedral in San Francisco said that, if people really knew why they were in church, they would wear seat belts and crash helmets, but because religion has become so pallid in some quarters the church can actually be one of the best places to avoid contact with the living God. Are there theologians who can lovingly articulate the barriers religion can construct between people and God?

A recent correspondent to *The Living Church* wrote,

> It might be the situation that the traditional explications of the faith . . . are simply gobbledygook to the very people with whom we wish to share our faith, leaving them unattracted to the Church, let alone to the ranks of its clergy (fewer than 300 priests under the age of 35). If the Church was smart enough to think and teach in new terms in the first century, why can't we be just as savvy 2,000 years later?

And another correspondent wrote,

> If indeed we are approaching a postmodern and even a post-Christian future, it behooves those of us who are Christ lovers living out our "spirituality" within the Church to learn to discuss our faith with those modernists rather than entrench ourselves behind narrowly defined Church walls.

Yet another wrote, "Americans are deeply interested in spirituality. The tragedy is they are not finding it in the mainline churches, and so they feel compelled to seek elsewhere."[26]

Couple these observations with the new "global cosmogenesis,"[27] that is, the understanding of the universe as a single enfolding creative event, that Ihab Hasan speaks and writes about, and we see that more and more people "feel at one" with others and the universe while watching faith traditions and denominations perpetuate a divisiveness—Roman Catholics, Anglicans, Orthodox, Lutherans—and these are the mildest examples among liturgical Christians who have a great deal in common and try to be civil to each other, excluding mainstream Protestantism.

Each group fosters its own spirituality, but it seems to me that people are increasingly able and inclined to sniff out weakness and falseness if that spirituality claims a triumphalism in the midst of a pluralistic world where people, especially those on spiritual quests, "feel as one." A deacon from Oregon recently wrote in *The Living Church*,

> The ministry of my wife . . . and me is deeply involved in dialogue with those outside the Church, and we find a good many are baptized Christians who departed the Church for its failure to provide them with a meaningful spirituality . . . I spent a number of years in the "New Age" movement and eight years studying Eastern spirituality . . . I can say that most of those modernists . . . are deeply searching for a meaningful relationship with God."[28]

People intuitively sense the hidden unity among all who bend the mind and heart toward Spirit. How can perpetual divisiveness increase a legitimate and lasting spirituality, one that supercedes boundaries put up on earth between religious groups, among Christians, much less among those of differing religions?

A Grounded Openness

Now is the time for "yes, and" rather than "no, but."—*Ihab Hasan*

Let me note one irony here. As I myself have encountered more and more people of the "cosmic spirituality" bent, I have found my own personal prayer life, religious vocabulary, and spiritual practices and worship greatly enhanced. But not at the expense of my own convictions and customs. At the same time, I have become more "who I am," that is, a Christian humanist, Anglo-Catholic Episcopalian: one who holds, in the words of the Principal of St. Chad's, University of Durham, England, where I did a year of theology, "a generous catholicism" as the heart of his own spirituality.

As I have reached out to the widest possible spiritual community—not to convert but to accept and embrace—I have been drawn into a much deeper reverence for the Communion of Saints, the Blessed Sacrament, and devotion to the Blessed Virgin Mary. Whenever possible, I have tried at DeKoven to bring out of the storehouse as many older customs and practices as possible: eucharistic adoration, processions to the Shrine of Blessed James DeKoven, silent retreats, saints' days kept with solemnity, and a Candlemas festival which rounds off the Christmas season in the tradition of the annual Candlemas Festival and Ball at St. Chad's College, Durham.

I have watched this phenomenon with interest myself and now see no contradiction in holding openness and faithful affirmation in tow at the same time. The phrase I have adopted along with "generous catholicism" is one I read in a book by a Canadian priest: "grounded openness."[29] I see no need to subtract from another's position of faith to make my own greater or more valid. With the assistance and wisdom of Krister Stendhal, Mircea Eliade, and others, I have attempted, with varying degrees of success, to overcome the Christian fear of being too accepting of others. As St. Paul sees clearly, the end result of all this is up to God, not up to me. To embrace, love, learn from, even worship with "others," does not "deduct" from my Christianity. In fact, it has deepened it and in many ways brought me to newer understandings of my own priesthood and catholicism.

I have come to see that, as there is one humanity, there is also one faith, one love, one prayer—all from the heart of one God—so also there is only one esteem: esteem for one's own tradition only furthers esteem for the tradition of others. Are there theologians among us who can help the Episcopal Church listen and carefully pay attention to what comes to us through the faith of others, not diminishing but strengthening our own faith? Are there theologians among us who can help us learn from our own meditations, from our deepest, interior, image-producing self? And from our own experience of Spirit?

Throughout the world, among people of faith, a deep connection binds us together. The exacting commitment one has to his or her own tradition becomes, as it were, the beacon that we let shine before humanity; not a beacon to blind, but a beacon of authenticity to which others are inevitably attracted, thereby affirming one's own faith amongst a variety of faiths while also honoring the hidden unity of Spirit which binds humanity together.

Are there Episcopal theologians who can assist us in seeing that this Spirit is not alien to the Episcopal Church?

Spirit's power is kindled on the margins of the church and the world, in "thin" places where diverse souls dwell, fueled by a longing for Spirit. In fact, Spirit's power moves toward multiplication of minorities rather than ecumenical blending into sameness. More and more people profess interest in God. And eventually the insightful seeker learns that faith is the only tribute humanity can return to God.[30] People are drawn to and by Spirit, not necessarily to and by the church of a given religious tradition. They want to "give," "to express something somehow," but often can't find the appropriate setting which allows for openness and clarity.

Life Among the Weeds

If we accept paradox, we can hold together intolerable contradiction.
—*Marion Woodman*

There is one God. There is one faith, shared by all children throughout the world and by all conscious men and women. There is always unity, hidden from the mainline eyes by human barriers erected in theology, piety, and doctrine. The peculiarity of any one religion is in its externals, its liturgies, and cultic rites that define who a person or culture is—not in the hidden and mystical world of Spirit. As Ihab Hasan put it, "universal mystical experience underlies all mystic traditions of humanity. And the mysteries of faith mandate heterodoxy, not orthodoxy."[31] Grounded openness means a refusal to be bullied by choices of ideologies and theologies.

Those of us who are Episcopal Christians have received a glorious heritage which each year is being broadened by the rapid expansion of Anglicanism throughout the globe, especially in Southern Hemisphere nations. Our love of liturgy—and our insistence that our worship according to the Book of Common Prayer is our theology—equips us to stand firm in our own tradition yet embrace those of other traditions. Our tradition of artistic beauty, goodness, and tolerance frees us from arrogance, or can do so. A sense of "grounded openness" allows us to love our tradition, our church, and Christ our God more without having to denigrate others in order do so.

Unity is a mystery; it is hidden. It exists "underneath" the ground of national churches and differing world religions. To acknowledge this mystery in art, silent prayer, the meditative arts, and even on occasion in triumphalistic liturgy, saves us from the coldness of condescension.

This is where I live. On that margin, in that liminal landscape between the church and the rather prudishly-termed unchurched. Out of my experience I extrapolate one final metaphor which speaks to me of the experience of an Anglican theology which seeks, or is allowed to be, the handmaiden of spirituality: the English garden.

Several years ago I served as host for Lord and Lady Runcie when the former Archbishop of Canterbury was awarded an honorary degree and was commencement speaker at Carthage College, Kenosha, Wisconsin, where I am on the faculty. During his visit, Lord Runcie shared with me a paper he had written using the English garden as a metaphor for doing theology (the Archbishop's choice of metaphor no doubt was influenced by the fact that Lady Runcie is herself an avid gardener who led in the restoration of the Lambeth Palace gardens). In the paper, he spoke of the necessity of working, pruning, cutting, and tending the flowers in their proper borders. But he also spoke of the necessity of allowing some flowers to wander outside their borders and become part of the walkways or even part of the untended fields with their neighboring weeds.[32]

Both are needed in the church—the well-trimmed borders and the risky adventurers among the weeds. It is that margin between flower and weed, the place in between, the place that treasures both the tradition and the unknown and tries to mediate between them, as flowers are surrounded by weeds and as weeds are surrounded by flowers. Here is the place many of us are, a place quite inviting to seekers and a place quite comfortable for conversation with "others."

Are there Episcopal theologians who can prune the flowers and allow for life among the weeds at the same time? Theologians gifted in language arts, myth, and literature who can track down and articulate metaphors of collective faith and collective doubt? Theologians who grasp the compelling and deep necessity of metaphor, "the language of the soul," the language that bridges doubt and faith, body and soul?

Two distinctly different Episcopal voices—one a young man just out of graduate school; the other, an English professor near retirement—have told me how "boxed in" they feel on Sunday morning by having to recite the Nicene Creed immediately after a homily which has just opened them to think and to expand their horizons. Are there theologians whose commitment is to change with continuity, bridging the past and the present?

It has been my observation that suspicion arises when the garden flowers mix with the wildflowers, natural grasses, and weeds. The theology of many clergy and laity rejects the spiritualities of the lived, direct relation with God, particularly if that direct relation smacks of mysticism. Likewise, spirituality can often shun theology, claiming that reason and tradition are too "heady."

Are there theologians who can bridge these gaps? Theologians who are comfortable within the precious place of the mandorla—the almond-shaped space formed by two overlapping circles—that place of paradox in which many Episcopalians live but struggle to articulate as their "witness" and profession of faith? And theologians eager to assist others to articulate the places of faith-paradox of their lives? Are there theologians awake to the new "cosmic" movements abroad in our culture, and open to the stirrings and sometimes wildness of the Spirit so vividly manifest on the margins of the church? I hope so, because the dynamism is already here and is shaping the future of Western faith.

Are there seminary theologians who will articulate and model the needed space and rationale for interior mission work prior to and along with proclaiming the Word of God? It is heartening to learn that at least one of our Episcopal seminaries—Bexley Hall in Rochester, New York—begins its school year with a retreat and is committed to a program of ongoing spiritual formation for faculty and students alike.

Are there liturgical theologians who have experienced contemplative liturgies, as well as the triumphalistic ones for which we are so well known? And who will articulate such needs to the church before inner work and outer expression in liturgy is dissolved and forgotten in the sea of church growth movements and renewal currents?

Are there theologians themselves on the margins of the faith geography who are engaged with "people seeking deeper meaning in life but for whom traditional religion isn't always an obvious choice"?[33] Lisa Miller in a *Wall Street Journal* piece points out that often such people "turn first to secular alternatives—college courses, psychotherapy, self-help books . . . ."[34]

Are there Episcopal theologians well acquainted and comfortable in these various arenas? One of my theology professors in divinity school was fond of saying, "You want to read the greatest American theologian? Read William Faulkner."[35] Are there Episcopal theologians immersed themselves in literature and the arts who can assimilate the experience of the believer, the humanism of culture, and the tradition of the church, and give voice to that place of "both-and," inviting us to live more fully and completely with the "surplus of meaning" in that place of invitation itself, the threshold?

Appendix

The Episcopal Church of the twenty-first century will be a church that:

1. lives out of the paradox, out of the mandorla, where sacred and profane overlap, where Christianity overlaps with other faiths, where doubt and belief produce a sense of grounded openness
2. bridges the past and the present in a spirit of "generous catholicism"
3. teaches and forms not so much religion as a living spirituality
4. practices prayer in a variety of forms and functions
5. derives its strength from those who have fled to the margins
6. teaches and practices the meditative arts of contemplation and sitting still
7. balances explosive outward dynamism with greater interior stillness and power
8. guides children from the earliest ages to awaken to their inner lives
9. points in liturgy and community to the links between the exterior and interior of our lives
10. forms teachers and spiritual leaders who practice and teach awareness and attention as basic tenets of the spiritual life
11. places spiritual formation on equal footing with history and theology in its seminaries
12. encourages its seminaries to teach and practice the praying and reflective arts
13. produces theologians and spiritual leaders open to the centrality of literature and the arts
14. fosters not only "remembrances of things past," but also the "spirit-to-spirit connectedness" of the present moment
15. presents candidates for holy orders who are enrolled in three seminaries: the classroom; the dynamic, contemporary world; and a holy place of stillness and retreat
16. fosters candidates for holy orders well acquainted with the tenets, practices, and practitioners of other Christian faiths and other world religions
17. fosters spiritual direction among its members, seminarians, and spiritual leaders
18. encourages its deacons, priests, bishops, and laity to balance activity with withdrawn intentional solitude

19. equips more and more people to speak honestly and lovingly out of their own lives' experiences, of times lived with—and times lived without—faith
20. has taught its people that faith is "doubt negotiated" rather than "intellect checked at the door"
21. plants more and more communal experiments which seek to express the life of God's kingdom on earth
22. holds up, funds, and encourages more and more special ministries as ways of exercising active and contemplative lay and ordained ministries
23. encourages more young people to try a vocation in the religious life, even as a routine part of becoming an adult Christian
24. creates more and more religious life options, especially for young people to explore, if only for a few months or a year, before entering the vocation of marriage or single life or the world of commerce
25. encourages religious orders, retreat houses, and other institutions to accept older people into the fullness of their life
26. takes its confirmands on retreat with their bishop and visits the cathedral of the diocese with the cathedral's dean
27. balances its worship life more consciously between "cathedral style" and "monastic style," each diocese encouraging regular meditative celebrations of the eucharist
28. blesses its church calendars in Advent or New Year's and invites its members to celebrate birthdays, anniversaries, and special occasions with prayer and meditation amidst the communion of saints
29. makes available to every member a good translation of the Bible, the Book of Common Prayer, *Lesser Feasts & Fasts*, and *They Still Speak* or *The Brightest and the Best*
30. holds up for honor and respect the Mother of Our Lord, the Blessed Virgin Mary
31. teaches and preaches the hidden life and fosters and explores the mysteries of our lives hidden in Christ in God
32. fully appreciates spiritual dryness and assists peoples' incorporation of barrenness into their personal spiritual journeys
33. balances victory and triumphalism with the inevitable times of aridity and sense of absence in her liturgies, sermons, and counseling
34. celebrates the sense of the absence of God as well as the sense of God's presence

35. lives by a more authentic lectionary, fully following the way of Mark, the way of Matthew, the way of Luke, and the way of John in given years, without merging the gospels for special times or events
36. makes sure its seminarians spend at least one year in a seminary of another religious tradition or in a non-sectarian divinity school, or at least in another Episcopal seminary of differing churchmanship or heritage.
37. assists each member in finding personal metaphors which articulate "the surplus of meaning" in the universe
38. trains its members to witness to the "we" of the catholic faith and not the "I" of personal salvation
39. produces fewer and fewer bulletins and lectionary inserts, and more and more well-trained listeners and inwardly equipped liturgical worshipers
40. preaches gratitude for life and God's generative Spirit as its primary theological tenet

Notes

1. Dairmuid O'Murchu, *Reclaiming Spirituality* (New York: Crossroad Publishing Co., 1998), 14. See also his previous work, *Quantum Theology* (New York: Crossroad Publishing Co., 1997).

2. Marion Woodman, *Addiction to Perfection* (Toronto: Inner City Books, 1982). See also "Addiction to Perfection" (Boston, Mass.: Shambhala Lion Audio Tapes).

3. See Don Cupitt, *The World to Come* (London: SCM, 1982); *The Leap of Reason* (London: SCM, 1985); and *Christ and the Hiddenness of God* (London: SCM, 1985).

4. Paul Holbrook, Jr. "Marginal Notes: A Letter" (August 1998), 1.

5. John Booty, "Active Charity Bolsters Faith: . . . Episcopalians Struggle to Live Creatively in Present Experience," *The Episcopalian* 147 (January 1982): 12–13. See also idem, "Roots in England; Testing in America," *The Episcopalian* 146 (September 1981): 6–7, 16; "Scripture Unfolds God's Sacred Drama," Ibid. (October 1981); "Tradition Illuminates the Church's Mind," Ibid. (November 1981): 18–19; "Faith Needs Reason and Reason Needs Grace," Ibid. (December 1981); and "Scripture, Tradition, Experience, Reason," *The Episcopalian* 147 (February 1982): 12–13. See also *What Makes Us Episcopalians?* (Wilton, Conn.: Morehouse-Barlow, 1982).

6. Anthony de Mello, *Awareness* (New York: Doubleday, 1992). See also idem, *One Minute Wisdom* (Garden City, N.Y.: Doubleday, 1988); *Sadhana:*

A Way to God (Garden City: Doubleday, 1984); *Wellspring: A Book of Spiritual Exercises* (Garden City: Doubleday, 1986); and *Praying Body and Soul* (New York: Crossroad Publishing Co., 1997).

7. See Thich Nhat Hahn, *Present Moment, Wonderful Moment* (Berkeley: Parallax Press, 1990). See also idem, "Being Peace" audiotape (Parallax Press, 1993).

8. Toni Packer, *The Work of This Moment.* (Boston: Shambhala, 1990). See also idem, *The Light of Discovery* (Boston: Tuttle, 1995).

9. O'Murchu, *Reclaiming Spirituality*, 23.

10. Krister Stendhal, "The Lure of Oneness and the Grace of Pluralism," 25th Trinity Institute (New York: 1994), videocassette. See also Stendhal's "From God's Perspective We Are All Minorities," in *Explorations* (1998).

11. See Cupitt, *The World to Come.*

12. Harold Kruger, Good Friday Meditation, Seibert Chapel, Carthage College, Kenosha, Wisc. (1978).

13. Henri Nouwen, *The Wounded Healer: Ministry in Contemporary Society* (New York: Doubleday, 1979).

14. Ward McCabe, letter to author, 5 February 1998. See also my article "Turning Inward, Facing Outward," *Reflections* (1987); and "Ministry on the Margin," *The Living Church* (June 1998): 2.

15. Anonymous poem given by Sister Dorcas, CSM, to author on retreat at Mary's Margin House of Prayer, July 1998.

16. Bennett Sims, Retired Bishop of Atlanta in Ward McCabe, "Prophetic Witness: The Christian Community and the Future of the World," *Kairos* 92 (December 1997): 1.

17. O'Murchu, *Reclaiming Spirituality*, 59.

18. Benedict Reid, *A Spirit Loose in the World* (Summerland, Calif.: Harbor House (West), 1994).

19. Robert Mulholland, Jr., "Life at the Center—Life at the Edge," *Weavings* 13 (July/August 1998): 28.

20. Ibid., 29–30.

21. Anonymous letter to author, 21 July 1998.

22. O'Murchu, *Reclaiming Spirituality*, 59.

23. Ellen Gilchrist, *Falling Through Space* (New York: Little, Brown, 1987), 69.

24. "Vatican Brings Anglican Orders to Question," *The Living Church* 217 (26 July 1998): 6. See also Michael J. Tan Creti, "Habitually Null and Void," *The Living Church* 217 (16 August 1998): 3.

25. John E. Lamb, "Providential?," Ibid., 5. See also Jack Roddy, "Spiritual Matters," *The Living Church* 217 (13 September 1998): 21–22; Michael Gemignani, Ibid.: 21.

26. Ihab Hasan, "Between Nihilism and Belief: Spirit in the Post-Modern World," (lecture given at the Center for Twentieth-Century Studies, University of Wisconsin, Milwaukee, February 14, 1997).

27. Roddy, "Spiritual Matters," 22.

28. See also M. Thomas Thangaraj, *Relating to People of Other Religions: What Every Christian Needs to Know* (Nashville: Abingdon, 1997).

29. Ihab Hasan, lecture.

30. Ibid.

31. Lord Robert Runcie, lecture transcript, presented to me at The DeKoven Center, May 1991.

32. Lisa Miller, "Can You Go Back?" *Wall Street Journal*, 10 April 1998, 2–3.

33. Ibid.

34. Dieter Georgi, Former Professor of New Testament, Harvard Divinity School, Harvard University, Cambridge, Mass.

Contributors

Robert M. Cooper has served as a parish priest, a college and university chaplain and teacher, a university and seminary professor, and a pastoral psychotherapist. He taught at Nashotah House and the Episcopal Theological Seminary of the Southwest. He has also been a Visiting Scholar at the Church Divinity School of the Pacific, and an Affiliate Scholar at the Boston Psychoanalytical Society and Institute. He is a Fellow of the American Association of Pastoral Counselors. He was a member of the Coalition for the Ordination of Women to the Priesthood and Episcopate. He served as a member of the National Board of Examining Chaplains; and as a member and vice-chair of the Standing Commission on Human Affairs and Health. He served as poetry editor of the *Anglican Theological Review*.

Ian T. Douglas is Associate Professor of World Mission and Global Christianity at the Episcopal Divinity School in Cambridge, Massachusetts, where he also serves as Director of Anglican, Global, and Ecumenical Studies. He is a priest associated with St. James' Church in Cambridge. He held positions as a Volunteer for Mission in the *L'Eglise Episcopale d'Haiti* (the Episcopal Church of Haiti), and as Associate for Overseas Leadership Development at the Episcopal Church Center. He is past Secretary and Chair of the Standing Commission on World Mission for the General Convention of the Episcopal Church, and current Convener of the Episcopal Seminary Consultation on Mission. He is the author of *Fling Out the Banner! The National Church Ideal and the Foreign Mission of the Episcopal Church.*

Travis Du Priest is Director of the DeKoven Center and Warden of the Shrine of Blessed James DeKoven in Racine, Wisconsin. He also teaches literature and non-fiction writing classes as a member of the faculty of Carthage College in Kenosha, Wisconsin, and serves as Book Editor of *The Living Church* magazine. He is Chaplain for the Community of St. Mary (Western Province). He was named Distinguished Teacher at Carthage College.

Tilden Edwards was the founder—and has served for the past twenty-five years as Executive Director of—the Shalem Institute for Spiritual Formation. He was Associate Rector of St. Stephen and the Incarnation Church in Washington, D.C., for five years. He is the author or editor of six books on the spiritual life, including *Living in the Presence*, *Sabbath Time*, *Spiritual Friend*, *Living Simply Through the Day*, *All God's Children*, and *Living with Apocalypse*.

James C. Fenhagen is a priest of the Episcopal Church, ordained in 1954. He has served as a parish priest, a diocesan Director of Christian Education, a teacher, and a writer. For fourteen years he was the Dean and President of the General Theological Seminary in New York City. Just prior to his retirement in 1994, he served as the Director of the Cornerstone Project of the Episcopal Church Foundation, a program in its initial stage aimed at developing stronger support systems for clergy. He was Rector of St. Mark's Parish in Frederick County, Maryland; St. Michael and All Angels Parish in Columbia, South Carolina; and St. John's Georgetown Parish in Washington, D.C. He was Director of Christian Education for the Diocese of Washington, and a teacher and administrator at the Hartford Seminary in Hartford, Connecticut. He is the author of five books dealing with spirituality and ministry, including *Ministry for a New Time* and *Invitation to Holiness*.

Reginald H. Fuller was Molly Laird Downs Professor of New Testament at Virginia Seminary, 1972–1985. He also served as Baldwin Professor of Sacred Literature at Union Theological Seminary, New York, 1966–1972; Professor of New Testament Languages and Literature, Seabury-Western Theological Seminary, 1955–1966; and Professor of Theology, St. David's College, Lampeter, Wales, 1950–1955. He was President of the Society of New Testament Study, 1983–1984. He participated in the national Lutheran-Episcopal dialogues (I–II), and the international Anglican-Lutheran dialogue. He is the author of *Foundations of New Testament Christology* and *Preaching the Lectionary*.

John M. Gessell served on the faculty of the School of Theology at the University of the South, 1961–1984. He was Professor of Christian Education, assistant to the Dean, and Professor of Christian Ethics. He was Editor of *St. Luke's Journal of Theology*, 1972–1990. He received the John Nevin Sayre Peacemaker's Award from the Episcopal Peace Fellowship in 1994.

Raymond F. Glover is Professor of Music and Chapel Organist at Virginia Theological Seminary. He was General Editor of *The Hymnal 1982*, and Editor of *The Hymnal 1982 Companion*. He was also one of the editors of the Second Supplement to *The Hymnal 1940*, and *Hymns III*. He was President of the Association of Diocesan Liturgical and Music Commissions. He was a consultant and member of the Standing Commission on Church Music of the Episcopal Church, 1970–1980; and a member and past member-at-large of the Executive Committee of the Hymn Society in the United States and Canada. He was also a founder and past President of the Association of Anglican Musicians. He served as Organist and Choirmaster of the Episcopal Cathedrals in Buffalo, New York, and Hartford, Connecticut; and of St. Paul's Church, Richmond, Virginia. He taught at the Berkeley Divinity School at Yale, 1964–1970, and was Head of the Music Department, St. Catherine's School, Richmond, Virginia, 1976–1980. He is the author of *A Commentary on New Hymns*. He currently serves as a member of the Bishop's Commission on Liturgy and Music of the Diocese of Virginia.

James E. Griffiss is Editor of the *Anglican Theological Review*, and theological consultant to the Presiding Bishop. He has served as visiting professor of theology at Seabury-Western Theological Seminary since 1995. He was William Adams Professor of Philosophical and Systematic Theology at Nashotah House, 1971–1990. He also taught at the Seminary of the Caribbean, 1961–1971, and the Church Divinity School of the Pacific, 1990–1991. He has participated in various ecumenical conversations. His publications include *The Anglican Vision* and *Naming the Mystery*. He is General Editor of *The New Church's Teaching Series*.

Frank Tracy Griswold is the twenty-fifth Presiding Bishop and Primate of the Episcopal Church. Bishop Griswold is a liturgist, and served as cochair of the Standing Liturgical Commission of the Episcopal Church. In his ecumenical role, he cochairs the Anglican-Roman Catholic international consultation. Over the years, Bishop Griswold has led numerous retreats and clergy conferences.

Charles Hefling is a Professor of Systematics in the Theology Department at Boston College, and an adjunct faculty member at Andover Newton Theological School. He recently served as Priest Associate at the Church of Saint John the Evangelist in Boston, and he has been a presbyter of the Episcopal Diocese of Massachusetts since 1974. He is the author of *Why Doctrines?*; and editor of two volumes in the *Collected Works of Bernard Lonergan* and of *Our Selves, Our Souls and Bodies: Sexuality and the Household of God*. His current project is *The Meaning of God Incarnate: Christology for the Time Being*.

Stephen Holmgren is Associate Professor of Ethics and Moral Theology at Nashotah House, where he has taught since 1992. He has served parishes in the Diocese of West Tennessee. He is working on the *New Church's Teaching Series* volume, *Ethics After Easter*.

Martha J. Horne is Dean and President of the Protestant Episcopal Theological Seminary in Virginia, a position she has held since 1994. She was Associate Dean for Administration at Virginia Seminary 1988–1994, and also taught Greek. She was recently elected Vice President of the Association of Theological Schools in the United States and Canada. She is a priest canonically resident in the Diocese of Virginia, where she is Priest Associate at St. Paul's, Alexandria. She has also served at St. Andrew's, Burke, Virginia, and Christ Church, Alexandria, Virginia. She served on the Board of the Cornerstone Project, 1987–1994.

Alan Jones is Dean of Grace Cathedral in San Francisco. He was the Stephen F. Bayne Professor of Ascetical Theology at General Theological Seminary, 1972–1982. He also served at General as the Director and Founder of the Center for Christian Spirituality. He is the author of *The Soul's Journey: Exploring the Three Passages of Spiritual Life with Dante as a Guide*; *Sacrifice & Delight*; and *Passion for Pilgrimage*.

Harold T. Lewis is Rector of Calvary Episcopal Church, Pittsburgh, Pennsylvania. He is also adjunct professor of preaching at Pittsburgh Theological Seminary. He has been an overseas missionary in Honduras and Zaire, and has served parishes in England and the United States. He was Executive Director of the Office of Black Ministries at the Episcopal Church Center, 1983–1984. He is the author of *Yet With a Steady Beat: The African American Struggle for Recognition in the Episcopal Church*, and the forthcoming *Christian Social Witness*. He wrote the introduction and several hymn texts for *Lift Every Voice and Sing II: An African American Hymnal*. He is a member of the board of the Anglican Theological Review; the Advisory Committee to the Anglican Observer to the United Nations; the General Board of Examining Chaplains; and the Fund for the Advancement of Minorities Through Education (FAME).

Patrick Mauney is Director of Anglican and Global Relations at the Episcopal Church Center, where he has held a variety of positions since 1982. He has served parishes in the dioceses of Rhode Island and São Paulo, Brazil. He is a representative of the Episcopal Church on MISSIO: The Mission Commission of the Anglican Communion. He also serves as vice-chair of Church World Service and Witness, the mission, relief, and development arm of the National Council of Churches.

Mark A. McIntosh is Professor of Systematic Theology and Spirituality at Loyola University of Chicago. He is a priest of the Diocese of Chicago, and served as assistant to the Dean at St. James Cathedral in Chicago. He now serves as a Sunday assistant priest at the Church of the Redeemer in Elgin, Illinois. He is the author of *Christology From Within* and *Mystical Theology: The Integrity of Spirituality and Theology.*

Leonel L. Mitchell has served parishes in New York and Indiana. He was Professor of Liturgics, Seabury-Western Theological Seminary, 1978–1995. He also served as Assistant Professor, Department of Theology, University of Notre Dame, 1971–1978; also at Notre Dame, he was Director of the M.A. Program, 1974–1978, and Summer Session Chairman, 1975–1980. He was a Lecturer in Church History and Liturgics, Berkeley Divinity School, 1969–1971. He has served on the Standing Commission on Liturgy and Music of the Episcopal Church. He is the author of *Lent Holy Week Easter, and the Great Fifty Days*, and *Pastoral and Occasional Liturgies.*

William C. Morris, Jr., served as Episcopal Chaplain to Davidson College, the University of Mississippi, and Louisiana State University. He is the Interim Episcopal Chaplain at Tulane University. He was Vicar, and then Rector of All Saints' Church in River Ridge, Louisiana, where he served for twenty-seven years. He was Chair of the Department of Communications in the Diocese of Louisiana. He edits the *LECA Letter* for the Louisiana Episcopal Clergy Association, and serves on the Editorial Committee for *LEAVEN*, published by the National Network of Episcopal Clergy Associations.

William C. Noble is Executive Assistant to the Bishop for the Armed Forces of the Episcopal Church. He retired from the United States Army in 1995 after serving as an Army chaplain for some twenty years. He edited *The Military Chaplains' Review*, a professional journal for chaplains, and also edited and published the current Army field manual on the chaplaincy, "The Unit Ministry Team." He was Division Support Command Chaplain in the 1st Armored Division, Nuremberg, Germany; and pastor to the American Community at Supreme Headquarters Allied Powers Europe, in Belgium. He now serves as part-time priest-in-charge at St. James' Church, Eatontown, New Jersey.

Ormonde Plater serves as a deacon at Grace Episcopal Church in New Orleans, Louisiana. He has been active for many years in the renewal of the diaconate. He is a member of the Council of Associated Parishes, an Anglican group advocating liturgical renewal. In 1997 he was appointed to the Standing Commission on Ministry Development, serving on a task group charged with drafting a theology of ministry for the Episcopal Church. He is the author of several books on ministry and worship, including *Many Servants: An Introduction to the Diaconate* and *Intercession: A Theological and Practical Guide.*

Jacqueline Schmitt has been the Episcopal Chaplain at Northwestern University since 1994. She served a variety of parishes in the Diocese of Central New York. She worked with the Episcopal Chaplain at Columbia University while attending seminary. She later served as Chaplain at Syracuse University and North Carolina State University. Since 1987, she has served as Editor of *Plumbline*, a journal of ministry in higher education. She recently coauthored a chapter in *Disorganized Religion: The Evangelization of Youth and Young Adults.*

Gardiner H. Shattuck, Jr., has served parishes in Massachusetts and Rhode Island, and he was Rector of the Church of the Ascension, Cranston, Rhode Island, 1986–1990. He has taught church history courses in the School for Deacons and in the School for Ministries of the Diocese of Rhode Island, and he has served on the governing board of both schools. He also works as the Book Reviews Editor at Cowley Publications. He is author of *A Shield and Hiding Place: The Religious Life of the Civil War Armies* and coauthor of *The Encyclopedia of American Religious History.* He is currently completing a book entitled *Dwelling Together in Unity; Episcopalians and the Dilemmas of Race.*

Robert Boak Slocum is Rector (part-time) of the Church of the Holy Communion, Lake Geneva, Wisconsin, and a Lecturer in Theology at Marquette University. He has also served parishes in Louisiana. He is coeditor of *Documents of Witness, A History of the Episcopal Church, 1782–1985*, and editor of *Prophet of Justice, Prophet of Life, Essays on William Stringfellow*. He is coeditor of *An Episcopal Dictionary of the Church*, and author of the forthcoming *Life, Movement and Being, An Introduction to the Theology of William Porcher DuBose.*

Philip Turner was Dean of the Berkeley Divinity School at Yale, 1991–1998. He was Professor of Christian Ethics at General Theological Seminary, 1980–1991, and Professor of Christian Ethics at the Episcopal Theological Seminary of the Southwest, 1974–1979. He was editor of and a contributor to *The Crisis of Moral Teaching in the Episcopal Church*, and *Men and Women: Sexual Ethics in Turbulent Times*; and author of *Sex, Money, and Power: An Essay in Christian Social Ethics.*

Arthur A. Vogel was Bishop of the Diocese of West Missouri, 1973–1989, and Bishop Coadjutor of the Diocese of West Missouri, 1971–1972. He taught at Nashotah House, 1952–1971, where he was Sub-Dean and William Adams Professor of Philosophical and Systematic Theology, 1965–1971. He served on the first International Anglican-Roman Catholic Commission, 1969–1982, and the second International Anglican-Roman Catholic Commission, 1983–1990. He also served on the national Anglican-Roman Catholic Commission, 1964–1984, of which he was cochair, 1973–1983. He is the author of *God, Prayer, and Healing: Living with God in a World Like Ours*, and *Radical Christianity and the Flesh of Jesus.*

Louis Weil is the James F. Hodges Professor of Liturgics at the Church Divinity School of the Pacific. He has been a member of the faculties of three seminaries of the Episcopal Church: The Episcopal Seminary of the Caribbean, Nashotah House, and, since 1988, Church Divinity School of the Pacific in Berkeley, California. His work as a teacher extends over almost four decades, and during that time he has lectured on four continents. He is the author of *Gathered to Pray* and *Sacraments and Liturgy: the Outward Signs*; and coauthor of *Liturgy for Living*. He has also written numerous articles on various aspects of the church's worship. His other interests have led him to work in the areas of aesthetic theology and ecumenical studies.

J. Robert Wright is the St. Mark's-Church-in-the-Bowerie Professor of Ecclesiastical History at General Theological Seminary, where he has taught since 1968. He was also an instructor in church history at the Episcopal Divinity School from 1966 to 1968. He has served Episcopal/Anglican parishes in America and in England. He has been a member of, or consultant to, the Anglican-Roman Catholic Consultation in the U.S.A., and he serves as theological consultant to the Ecumenical Office of the Episcopal Church. He has been a visiting professor at Nashotah House, Philadelphia Divinity School, Claremont School of Theology in California, Union Theological Seminary in New York City, Trinity College in Toronto, and St. George's College in Jerusalem. He is editor of *On Being a Bishop: Papers on Episcopacy from the Moscow Consultation 1992* and *They Still Speak: Readings for the Lesser Feasts.*

Paul F. M. Zahl is Dean of the Cathedral Church of the Advent, Birmingham, Alabama. He has also served as Rector of Episcopal churches in Scarborough, New York, and Charleston, South Carolina; and he was Curate of Grace Church in New York City. His publications include *Who Will Deliver Us?* and *The Protestant Face of Anglicanism.*